RUDOLPH, FROSTY, AND CAPTAIN KANGAROO

· · · · · · ·

The Musical Life of Hecky Krasnow— Producer of the World's Most Beloved Children's Songs

· · · · · · ·

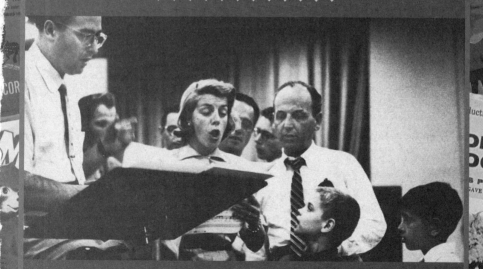

A Memoir by Judy Gail Krasnow

· · · · · · · · · · · ·

SANTA
MONICA
PRESS

Published by: Santa Monica Press LLC
P.O. Box 1076
Santa Monica, CA 90406-1076
1-800-784-9553
www.santamonicapress.com
books@santamonicapress.com

Printed in the United States

Santa Monica Press books are available at special quantity discounts when purchased in bulk by corporations, organizations, or groups. Please call our Special Sales department at 1-800-784-9553.

ISBN-13 978-1-59580-026-8
ISBN-10 1-59580-026-3

Library of Congress Cataloging-in-Publication Data

Krasnow, Judy Gail, 1942-
  Rudolph, Frosty, and Captain Kangaroo : the musical life of Hecky Krasnow, producer of the world's most beloved children's songs / by Judy Gail Krasnow.
    p. cm.
  ISBN-13: 978-1-59580-026-8
  ISBN-10: 1-59580-026-3
  1. Krasnow, Hecky. 2. Sound recording executives and producers—United States—Biography. 3. Children's songs—United States—20th century—History and criticism. I. Title.

ML429.K88K73 2007
781.64092—dc22
[B]
                                                            2007033595

Cover and interior design and production by cooldogdesign

· · · · · · · · · · · ·

Contents

. . . .

. . . .

IN MEMORY OF

My father, Hecky Krasnow
They're still singing your songs, Dad

My mother, Lillian Drucker Krasnow
The chapters continue, Mom

My uncle, Bob Krasnow
I kept my promise and wrote this book

DEDICATED TO

Hecky's grandchildren and great-grandchildren

. . . .

· · · · · · · · · · · ·

ACKNOWLEDGMENTS

· · · · · · · · · · ·

I wish to thank my parents for their love and a life filled with stories; my Uncle Bob for eliciting my promise to write this book; Barbara Dudash for insisting I save my father's scrapbooks; Terry Ryan, author of *The Prize Winner of Defiance, Ohio*, for her role in my acquiring Amy Rennert as my literary agent; Amy Rennert for her sage advice and constant faith in this project; Pamela Feinsilber for her editorial wisdom in creating the proposal and for her guidance in expanding one's own stories through research; storyteller and writer Susan Klein for her guidance and assistance with the timeline and focus on just whose story I would tell; Jon Guyot Smith for his invaluable information; Sherry Walsh, at age 103, for her vivid memories and insights; storyteller Carrie Sue Ayvar and her mother, Alice Silverblatt, for their never-ending encouragement and hours spent reading and editing the initial chapters of this book while bearing with my fluctuating moods as I sought an agent; Bill Roorbach for his book *Writing Life Stories*; David Bonner, author of *Revolutionizing Children's Records: The Young People's Records and Children's Record Guild Series, 1946–1977*, for sharing information and contacts; Peter Muldavin, the Kiddie Rekord King and author of *The Complete Guide to Vintage Children's Records*, for his superb website, wonderful tour of his collection of 78-rpm children's records, and for photos of album covers; Mitch Miller for his reminiscences about my father and Columbia Records; Milt Okun for his long and informative conversation regarding Hecky, The Chad Mitchell Trio, and the record and publishing business; Chad Mitchell, who filled me in on the whole story of the trio and their work with Hecky; Helen Darion for her reminiscences about Hecky and Joe; Arthur Shimkin for his insights and leads to Sony BMG; Tom Doerr for his help at Sony BMG; Thomas Tierney, Director of Archives at Sony BMG, for his assistance and access to the archives; my son Josh Markewich and my grandsons Tim and Andy for their hospitality when I did research at Sony BMG; my son Sam for his initial input and constant enthusiasm; my son Noah for playing the devil's advocate; my daughter Sarah and son-in-law Tom Christiaens for their love, support, and for allowing me to take over their living room in Belgium in order to write while caring for Sarah after her back operation; my granddaughter Ayla, who asked me daily to tell her stories about her great-grandfather and my childhood which helped me to write these stories; my sister Stephanie Schamess, who was always there for me when I asked questions whether she had the answers or not; cousin Jean Eisenberg Back, who responded promptly to my inquiries and sent needed photos; cousin Dede Krasnow for her detailed research regarding Hartford and National Iron and Steel; cousin Jerry Krasnow for his memories and marketing input; aunt Pauline Krasnow Mirkin, Hecky's last living sibling, for her 88 years of memories; cousin Simmy Mindell and Angela Chalellia for their hours of laughter and stories about my grandparents; cousin Karen Eisenberg Sheingold for the wonderfully creative years we shared as children; Susan Aberman for reading chapters and offering comments; Josh Aberman for information about the history of the music business; the South Florida Writers' Association for their support and insights; Rosa Douglass and Don Hyink, who were there for my every up and down, who listened to each story 10 times over, who translated my malaprops and mixed metaphors, who never stopped believing, and who supplied champagne whenever a step along the way called for celebration; and, of course, Jeffrey Goldman, publisher of Santa Monica Press, and my editor whose enthusiasm for this project and accessibility has made the book a pleasure to complete and a dream come true.

—Judy Gail Krasnow

**FOREWORD BY BILL HARLEY,
GRAMMY AWARD-WINNING STORYTELLER,
SINGER, AND AUTHOR**

Music That Lasts

· · · · · · · · · · ·

t is a dumb trick, but one that works so well, every year I can't help myself from using it. Sometime in December I will say to an audience, "Here's a song I just learned" and start to sing:

"Rudolph the Red-Nosed Reindeer, had some very shiny toes."

That is as far as I get before the catcalls begin. Four-year-olds scream "Nooooo!" Eight-year-olds stand up in protest. Twelve-year-olds laugh and shout. Adults groan and shake their heads. I stop, bewildered, the audience corrects me, and I start again, only to butcher the next line. For the next six or seven minutes, I wander through the song, mangling every line, being corrected again and again by a more and more outraged audience, until finally, they gleefully sing the song without my help. I have done this in daycare centers and with symphony orchestras—toddlers and cellists alike shouting out in horror, protest, and joy. It is frightening how well it works.

My guess is there is no other song I could destroy with such wonderful results. A song that elicits a response like that is a magical thing—a rare little bit of genius, so simple one can only shake one's head in wonder, mystified by its grandeur. We owe this all to Hecky Krasnow, who found the song and championed it until it became what it is today. It was only one of his many accomplishments.

Krasnow was a gifted musician who could see into the heart of a good song, and the heart of a child as well. He knew that good music for children made a difference, and for a short, beautiful time in the history of recorded music, he made a difference himself. A large difference. In the late 1940s and early '50s, Krasnow was given enough leeway and power to create a body of work that has survived half a century, setting a standard for what is possible in music for children and families.

Much of what passes for "children's music" is condescending and poor in quality. It shows a remarkable lack of understanding for the emotional lives of children and families. Either overly didactic or particularly juvenile (in the pejorative sense of that word), much recorded music for children neither challenges nor honors the people it professes to entertain. It is a commodity—something to be consumed and discarded. By contrast, in Krasnow's work, you can find what distinguishes many gifted artists from others—he assumes the intelligence of the audience.

I suspect Krasnow's first measure of the worth of a piece of music, regardless of an audience was: Does it appeal to me as a musician? And what makes a good piece of music for children? Pretty much the same thing that makes a good one for an adult. A strong melody, easily remembered. A strong rhythmic sense. A healthy dose of repetition in melody, rhythm, and language. Relevance of lyrical content. All these elements are present in the work Krasnow produced. In addition, he insisted on finding the finest artists available to record the material. They brought their own genius to the work.

. . . .

It makes sense that Krasnow brought this sensibility to the world of recorded music for children. The son of Jewish immigrants, trained to be a concert violinist by maestro Leopold Auer and at Juilliard, and living in New York, he was part of a broad generation of Jewish songwriters and entertainers, from Irving Berlin to the Gershwins to Lieber and Stoller and Carole King, who produced the great American songbook. The irony of Krasnow producing timeless Christmas songs is inescapable. If only we all were so ecumenical.

Krasnow's tenure at Columbia occurred at a special time in the history of recorded music. Radio was still central to the lives of Americans, with a noted absence of the niche marketing and Arbitron ratings it suffers from today—everyone listened to everything, whether it was the radio dramas or the Metropolitan opera, the variety hours or the novelty numbers that popped up now and again. The World War II generation was home and producing children in numbers never before seen in this country. A good song was a good song, and a good singer was a good singer. That would all change very shortly—a young man from Tupelo, Mississippi, was absorbing white country and black blues, singing for his mother. The record companies would discover that the baby boom generation would buy music in a way never before dreamed of, and the technology of delivering that music was changing rapidly—from 78s to LPs to that handiest of commodities, the two and a half-minute 45-rpm record. But radio was destined to become the handmaiden of television. Soon, the music business would become more of an industry, and less of a vocation.

. . . .

Things changed, and will change again. Since Krasnow's tenure, children's music has gone through several rebirths—once in the late 1970s and early '80s, when independent labels began to release recordings by grassroots folk artists. Many of them (myself included), were deeply influenced by the work done for children by folk artists Pete Seeger and Ella Mae Jenkins, recorded by Moe Asch on Folkways in the '50s and '60s. Some of these artists (the Canadians Sharon, Lois & Bram; Fred Penner; and Raffi) and a handful of American artists (including Cathy Fink and Marcy Marxer; Rosenshontz; Tom Chapin; and Peter Alsop, to name a few), have produced innovative, vibrant work. Today, there is a new generation of people working for younger children— fueled in part by television and video. But still, presently, the notion of a song that entertains a broad demographic—six-year-olds, 13-year-olds, and 40-year-olds—is beyond the ken of the music industry. Those songs are out there, but marketing has balkanized the population—12-year-olds are seen as too sophisticated for liking something that actually speaks to their lives and adults are sold something else.

But music will survive the business of it. People will find a tune and hum it if it is memorable, and learn words that are clever and relevant. While it might seem like it now, music and money are neither inevitably nor inextricably linked (although one hopes it is possible to make a living at it!). Yip Harburg, who wrote the words to "Over the Rainbow" and "Brother Can You Spare a Dime," said that words make you think thoughts, and music makes you feel a feeling, so a song makes you feel a thought. Songs are part of being human, longer and stronger than business or technology. For now, we still have what Hecky Krasnow produced. I, for one, am very grateful for that—even if audiences threaten my life when I sing them wrong.

CHAPTER 1

A Gut Instinct Produces a Classic

ecky Krasnow's new life began in the spring of 1949. He was three days into his job as head of Columbia's children's records department, or kid-disks as they were called. As the artists and repertoire (A&R) man, he was to select what was and wasn't to be recorded, who would sing, act, narrate, and play musical instruments on these records while also producing, directing, and engineering the recording sessions.

The sheet music and acetate demo for a new song, "Rudolph, the Red-Nosed Reindeer," sat on his desk. Every A&R man, and hence every major record company in the country, had already rejected it. But my father liked it. It had a simple and sweet melody, and a message that appealed to his years of fighting for the underdog. His instinct told him that many people all across America would like it, too.

"Are you crazy, Hecky?" Columbia Records vice president Goddard Lieberson asked. "Doesn't the fact that it was rejected by Decca, Mercury, RCA, Capital—every damned record company in the country—tell you something?"

"Yes. It does. It tells me that they are wrong," my father dared to answer. "You are fully aware, I am sure, that Montgomery Ward, an absolutely huge department store chain, asked one of its copywriters, Robert L. May, to write a storybook for

Ward to give to customers as a gift from the store. His little book is the story of a red-nosed reindeer, teased because of his red nose. He ultimately helps Santa and is accepted and loved by all."

"Yes, I know, I know. Six million copies of this illustrated story are already in the hands of Ward's customers, and there would be more copies, except for the paper shortage that WWII caused when the little book was printed." Lieberson sounded impatient. He wanted to get on with the point he wished to make: that the song didn't merit recording.

Hecky realized he had to argue this one like a lawyer, "Doesn't six million copies tell you something? Namely that people *like* this red-nosed reindeer?"

"Hecky, if we handed out records as a free gift, whether people liked them or not would be inconsequential. People always like to get something for nothing."

"But there is already an inbuilt audience for the song," my father continued his case.

Lieberson interrupted, "Look, Hecky. Montgomery Ward gave the copyright to Robert May in Christmas of 1947, an extraordinarily magnanimous gesture for a corporation: that is to give the copyright to an employee. But that has to tell you something too. If Ward thought money was to be made from it, do you think May would now be the sole owner of the copyright? Then, May asks his brother-in-law, this Johnny Marks, to write a song. He thinks he can make some money off of his idea."

"Well, wouldn't you?" my father asked. "He likes his little story and knows that out of those six million customers, lots of them must like it too."

"People want holidays like Christmas to remain the same each year—the same Santa with the same Mrs. Santa, the same eight—not *nine*—reindeer, the same elves for heaven's sake! Maybe the book with its pictures is cute—and remember free—but the song is far too simple, I mean plain—no spice—nothing catchy, no hook that would make people want to sing or hear it."

My father refused to give up. "Goddard, I just have a feeling, a gut instinct, that this song will take off in spite of—or maybe because of—its simplicity. People like stories about some unlikely critter or person unexpectedly becoming a hero.

"Hecky, you know how much I want you here at Columbia. I am convinced that you and no one else are the one for this job. But if this is the kind of song you think we should invest in—I don't know, I just don't know. Recording is too expensive for us to make mistakes, and I believe pursuing this piece of maudlin nonsense is a great mistake. Christmas songs have short shelf lives. They have to make it big on the radio and in the record stores in six weeks or they represent losses to the company."

"You told me when you hired me that I would be on trial this first year," my father looked Goddard in the eye. "You said I would rise or fall on my own good or bad decisions. How will you know what my capabilities are if you tie my hands behind my back before I've even begun?"

Lieberson, along with one other record mogul, Walter Legge of EMI in England, was considered the most influential executive in the recording field from the 1940s into the 1960s. Lieberson's innovative style had made Columbia the leader in the production and sales of classical music, which was highly popular from the '30s through the mid-'60s. After Hitler rose to power in Europe, Lieberson had wooed many talented performers, such as conductor Bruno Walter and pianist Rudolph Serkin, to Columbia and built an impressive catalogue of the classics. He was also instrumental in recording decades of important musicals and original-cast albums.

He spurred profound technological changes as well. Until the '40s, the existing technology had created great frustration in the recording studio. Recording their music on each side of rather quickly revolving 78-rpm records, orchestras had to interrupt their playing every three minutes, four under optimum circumstances. Long classical pieces often came in sets of 20 to 30 records, which meant the listening experience was disrupted every time the heavy, cumbersome records had to be changed. RCA Victor had developed the smaller and lighter 45-rpm, but its speed still called for many interruptions and numerous records. Under Lieberson, Columbia had recently begun marketing a 33-rpm long-playing record, or LP, which could hold up to 15 minutes per side on a 10-inch disk and 22 minutes per side on a 12-inch disk. This revolutionized classical listening and ultimately that of jazz, pop, and rock.

Perhaps Lieberson's willingness to try new and uncharted paths made him feel, in spite of his skepticism, that my father might be onto something. Lieberson's reputation among those who worked for him was that of a boss who hired those whom he thought were the best in their fields, to trust them, and to give them the necessary leeway to make their own decisions.

"Okay, Hecky," Lieberson conceded eventually. "You have a point. Go ahead with the song. I just hope," he added as he left Hecky's office, "that I don't have to say, 'I told you so.'"

My father then decided which artist he wanted to sing the song: Gene Autry. Autry was already a Columbia Records artist, with many hits in the country-western field—songs like "Back in the Saddle Again" and "Tumbling Tumbleweeds." Hecky liked the warmth and naturalness of Autry's voice and thought it would appeal to all ages, from Junior on up to Grandma and Grandpa. Other well-known cowboy singers recorded albums and starred in the musical westerns of the '30s and '40s, among them Roy Rogers, Rex Allen, and Tex Ritter. Cowboys, it seemed, competed for fans like baseball teams. It was this cowboy my father was rooting for.

When Lieberson learned my father's choice to sing what he believed was a doomed song, the debate started all over again. "Hecky, how could you even consider a cowboy? This is children's music, not country and western, not pop!" Fed up, he stormed out of the office, the sound of the closing door reverberating loud and long behind him. Lieberson felt conflicted. If he allowed Hecky to record the song and it failed, it would reflect poorly upon him as well as upon Hecky. Edward Wallerstein, the current president of Columbia was due to retire in the next year or two, and Lieberson was the number one candidate to replace him.

. . . .

Hecky, too, had some momentary misgivings. Up until now, his father Harry had virtually controlled the path his life would take and the work he would do. The road had been a rocky one with dubious success. Now, for the first time, he had won this job based upon his independent actions, talent, and a book he managed to write and get published. Here he was, three days into the job and taking a stand against his boss, whose experience in the record business far exceeded his own. He sat down at his desk, his head in his hands. His heart raced and his stomach cramped as he considered all that he'd left in Hartford, Connecticut, to move to New York. He thought of the roomy two-story house with its beautiful garden that he and Lillian had sold, of his helpful and loving parents who lived nearby, of his brothers and sisters, the friendly neighbors, all the congenial musical and political activities, of Lillian's reluctance to purchase the three-family house in Yonkers whose roof she'd have to share with Hecky's sister Helen—and most of all, of Steffi, the daughter he'd left with his parents so that she could finish junior high school in Hartford. Then he picked up the sheet music. He took the demo, and put it on the phonograph in his office. As he listened, the anxious thoughts disappeared, replaced with a certainty that he was right. Hecky's first decision in this new job was to record a song he believed in when others did not.

. . . .

A couple of months later, in June 1949, my mother Lillian and I accompanied my father to Los Angeles, where he was to meet the West Coast executives of Columbia Records and, under the guidance of already experienced recording engineers, learn how to engineer sessions he'd also produce. On his agenda was the recording of an album called *The Glooby Game* with The Modernaires, a popular quintet heard on the radio daily all over the country.

More important in my eyes was that he would also be meeting with Hollywood movie star and singer Dinah Shore to discuss the possibility of her recording songs and stories for children. Dinah and my father would have lunch with some other executives, and my mother and I would join them towards the end of the meeting and have dessert. I could barely contain my excitement about meeting Dinah Shore. I loved her song "Buttons and Bows." She was the star of the movie *The Belle of the Yukon,* and I was going to sit at the same table with her. Best of all, she narrated the animated film *Bongo*, which told the story of a performing bear who escapes from the circus and tries to live in the wild. Wow! I was going to meet Dinah Shore!

The first night we were in Los Angeles, my mother, father, and I walked along famous Hollywood Boulevard. I imagined all the stars walking upon the same sidewalk my feet now touched. When we entered the lobby of the posh Roosevelt Hotel, where we were staying, I was sure it was a palace. A red carpet led the way to the check-in desk, where a man in formal uniform greeted us cordially. Gold-colored brocade couches, high-backed chairs with ornate designs in red, purple, and green, shining gold and silver ashtrays, and glittering crystal chandeliers met my eyes as I gazed around while my father took care of checking us in. The floors looked like the marble ones upon which Cinderella danced with the prince while wearing her glass slippers. I felt that I'd walked into a fairy tale or fallen down a hole like Alice to begin a most amazing adventure. I sensed that my father's job had opened the door to Wonderland and to an enchanted life for me, his Juddie.

． ． ． ． ． ． ． ． ． ．

While I reveled in my excitement, my father braced himself for his most important task: delivering to singing cowboy Gene Autry the sheet music for Rudolph. My father sent a courier to Autry at his Hollywood home. This special delivery served to emphasize the importance of the song and was a faster way of delivery than regular mail, which, from New York to California, would have taken weeks. Autry delayed in contacting my father, and every time Hecky called, he got a different excuse as to why Autry was unavailable to talk. The days soon turned into a week, then another week. In two more weeks, we'd return to New York. Finally the phone rang. But it wasn't Autry. "Well, Hecky?" said Lieberson. "Is it a go, or has your cowboy the same opinion of the song that I have?"

Meanwhile, back at the ranch—and the cowboy did have a ranch, in Berwyn, Oklahoma—the singing cowboy was still reluctant to give Hecky an answer. Autry described his hesitation a few years later: "Up to then, strangely enough, I'd never recorded what the trade calls a kid-disk—all my numbers had been pop, western, or country. Frankly, I wasn't too enthusiastic about my possibilities. . . . It seemed a pretty drastic departure [but] I didn't want to offend him. . . ."

As Lieberson called and called, Autry stalled and stalled. One night, knowing he had to reply one way or another, Gene Autry showed the song to his wife, Ina. She was a country-western singer and rodeo star herself. She went to the piano and played and sang it. Then she said, "Why, how sweet, how interesting—a song that tells the story of an underdog who finally manages to become a big shot!"

"I didn't see that," Autry told his wife. "All I was seeing was me recording a song for a kid-disk. . . . I mean, recording for kids? I don't think so, though I like the message of the song, now that you've made it clear."

"Go ahead and do it," she encouraged. "You'll never know about it until you try."

Early the next morning, the phone in our hotel room rang. "Hecky Krasnow here," said my father, clearing his smoker's throat, his voice sounding three octaves lower than it would later in the day.

"I have a call for you from Mr. Gene Autry," he heard. "Go ahead."

"Hello, Gene. I thought I'd never hear from you."

"Hecky, I must confess I've been procrastinating. I'm still not sure about the song."

My father looked as if someone had just stuck a knife in his back. "Well," his voice cracked as he reached for his cigarettes.

"But sure or not, Ina says I should do it, so I will record 'Rudolph, the Red-Nosed Reindeer.' June 27 is good for me. Can you clear the studio for ten o'clock in the morning?"

My father's expression of relief let my mother and I know the knife was now out of his back. "Let's call it a deal. June 27 at ten in the morning it is!"

"Just for your information, Hecky," Gene added before they hung up, "it's the message of the song that won Ina's heart and made me decide to record it."

Elated, my father said goodbye and turned to my mother. "Honey, Mr. Autry just confirmed why this song has something special. I am so thrilled the Autrys understand its appeal!" My father saw in Rudolph all the hard-working immigrant laborers who continued to build this nation without due recognition; he also saw the plight of the Jews, still stereotyped as having noticeable noses. His gut response was that the song would give all outsiders and little guys, all the common folks around the country, someone to identify with; he saw Rudolph as an underdog, offering a story of hope and courage. And the song was certainly entertaining.

. . . .

June 27 arrived. "Rudolph" was the first recording session for Columbia that Hecky not only produced but also engineered. We got to the studio well before 10:00 A.M. My mother and I sat with my father in the control booth on a couple of chairs pushed against the wall, watching through a soundproof glass panel as the studio filled with musicians and singers. The tall, rectangular microphones of the era, with CBS in large letters at the top, were positioned so that the singers could stand or sit on a stool, as they preferred. Hecky was busy flicking a switch on and off so that he could talk to those setting up in the studio.

I watched with curiosity and great admiration as my father's long, graceful fingers adjusted one switch and then another on the large and intricate board controlling volume, sound, and effects. Everything had to be perfect, since there were only two recording tracks: one that would record the vocalists and one that would record the orchestra. On each track, the volume could be raised or lowered and the base, middle, treble, and reverb set for the best sound possible. The process recorded a live performance: a singer could not overdub his or her voice (that would be made possible in the late '50s by guitarist-singers Les Paul and Mary Ford). If someone made a mistake, the piece had to be rerecorded from the beginning. There was no mixing and mastering afterward. That couldn't be done with two tracks and a final monaural product. What was recorded live in the studio is what listeners would hear on the record.

In the right corner of the control booth, in a closet-sized, glassed-in room stood a narrow, rectangular, table-high sandbox. For me, this little room was definitely an ear-opening experience. Several hooks hung on the wall. On each hook were gadgets from which an array of sounds could be made: lions roaring, bulls bellowing, cats meowing, ducks quacking, birds calling, horses neighing, boats whistling, cars crashing, horns tooting, trains chugging or whistling, and crowds applauding. While the musicians were setting up, the sound effects man, a short, round, balding, jolly fellow bouncing with energy whom everyone called "Baldy," gave my mother and me a private demonstration. He pounded hollow melon rinds and coconut shells in the sand to create the sounds of a horse walking, trotting, cantering, or galloping. He handed the rinds and shells to me, and put his hands over mine, guiding me while I made the sounds. Then he let go, and I did it myself. I could make the horses go faster or slower, and my imagination went back to those covered wagons, Indians, and herds of buffalo. If this wasn't exciting enough, Baldy, using his mouth, cheeks, tongue, and voice, emitted the sounds of a wolf howling, a faucet dripping, a saw cutting, and all kinds of sirens so real that, closing my eyes, I could imagine being back in noisy New York City. Later that night, in the hotel, I attempted to make the sounds I'd heard Baldy emit as he inspired a new profession in my dreams: to be a sound effects man.

My father talked with Baldy about adding winter sounds, sleigh bells and the like, to the recording of "Rudolph." Not many were necessary, however, since they decided Gene Autry, the Carl Cotner Orchestra, and the Pinafores, the trio of backup singers, were all the simple song needed.

My father knew the old adage time is money and money is time. He understood that the bottom line does not make an exception for artistry in the recording studio. Lieberson had emphasized this before sending him off to California, once again expressing his feelings about "Rudolph."

"I still don't understand how you think a cowboy is going to appeal to anyone but those who watch cowboys, even if he has a nice voice. His movies aren't for kids, his songs aren't for kids, and we don't all live in the Wild West fighting bad guys and Indians. This had better work, Hecky. It is costing this company a fortune."

By 10:30 A.M., the band had arrived, the backup singers were there, but the singing cowboy was nowhere to be seen. You could always tell when my father was stressed: his shoulders started hunching up and he began emitting loud, deep, involuntary breaths. His shoulders were inching toward his ears now, and those involuntary breaths were becoming more frequent. My mother worried that tension would aggravate his stomach condition, Crohn's disease. She tapped Hecky's shoulder. My parents always addressed each other with the word "Honey." The intonations they used varied with their mood, message, or feelings of affection, anger, or concern. *HUHney* was the emphasis my mother gave the endearment now. This cadence indicated that she was attempting to nip a tantrum in the bud. "*HUHney*," she said again, tapping his shoulder. "Relax. Nothing is worth getting sick over."

"Life has its tense moments," he barked, defensive and worried. "Where the hell is Gene Autry?"

The Carl Cotner Orchestra, which accompanied Gene on most of his recordings, had tuned up and now sat twiddling violin bows, cleaning woodwind mouthpieces, polishing finger smudges off wooden instruments, sipping endless cups of coffee. The Pinafores had warmed up their voices and practiced their harmonies, then shown one another wallet photos and put on lipstick. All the microphones were in position. The singing cowboy had yet to arrive. The telephone rang.

"Hecky, has the session begun?" It was Lieberson.

"Goddard, we're all set to go."

"I want this one done quickly."

"It won't take long. From what I understand, Gene Autry is not one to do several takes. We're set to go."

To pass the time and try to cut the increasing tension, Hecky told the orchestra to do a run-through. The musicians sight-read their music without delay. He rehearsed the Pinafores. They knew their harmonies well. More than 30 minutes passed. Each minute cost a fortune. The telephone rang again.

"How many takes have you done thus far, Hecky?"

"We've been rehearsing."

"Rehearsing? I assume you've hired professionals. How much rehearsing do they need?"

At that moment, Hecky looked up and saw Gene and Ina Autry, at last.

"Goddard, Gene Autry has just arrived. Now we can get going."

"Just arrived? You didn't tell me he was late. That's over 30 minutes of our money wasted!"

"We'll do a quick run-through, and then, I am certain, we'll have it on the first take."

"I have it in mind to call this off if you aren't finished within an hour!"

My father hung up the phone and walked out of the control booth to Gene and Ina. He didn't have to be told that Gene had imbibed too much Christmas cheer well before the holiday season.

Ina preempted any questions. "Just get me some milk and orange juice, and we'll have him singing in no time. Gene's not an alcoholic, but whenever he belts down a few scotch-and-sodas, he doesn't tolerate them very well, not even the day after."

My father left Ina, who seemed experienced in these matters, to tend to her husband. "Gene," my father called through the booth a few minutes later, "while we're waiting, let's do a run-through."

Gene slowly walked to the mike. His pitch, words, tempo, and rhythm were sluggish. He sounded tired, not mellow. Hecky sat in the booth tapping his fingers all over the board making geometric designs, first circles, then squares, and then circles again. His extreme nervousness and, more important, extreme anger permeated the studio. Since the Crohn's restricted my father's intake of alcohol, and one of his brothers was an alcoholic, he found the reason for the delay doubly distressing. "So this is the singer I thought would be good for a homey, warm family sound," he muttered.

"Honey." (This time it was *huhKNEE*.) My mother put a hand on each of his shoulders. "Worse than tension is anger. Calm down. It's not your fault."

"I know it, for God's sakes." His voice became a shout. "I know it already!" When my father raised his voice this way, it indicated that he knew my mother was right, but his anger had reached a point where it was almost impossible for him to calm down, as though his blood was simmering, reaching boiling point as he felt there was no way out of a bad situation. He lit another unfiltered Chesterfield. We heard a few more of those involuntary breaths. Then he said, "I still think it will be a popular song—a hit, in fact—if he sobers up. But the clock is ticking!"

He flicked the switch to be heard in the studio. "Ina, how long do you think it will take for him to sober up? Goddard Lieberson is on my back and saying he'll call this session off in one hour!"

My mother sat down in her chair again. She had a leak in her aorta due to a bout with rheumatic fever when she was 16. Her neck harbored a vein that worked hard to pump blood when she was nervous or upset. This vein now made a dart that tried to escape from under her skin and hit a target with the force of a bullet. The vein pumped out, then in, out, then in. Some lines from a folk song I'd heard many times popped into my head. "Sometimes I feel like a motherless child/I'm a long way from home."

I thought that my sister and I would end up motherless children if this recording session continued. Our mother's words of worry rang in my head, too; for sure, my father would have a bout with Crohn's. Maybe he would die. Maybe we'd not only be motherless but father-less—orphans to be placed in a horrid home like Oliver Twist! At this moment, my father's new job did not seem like a journey into an enchanted life at all.

The phone rang. "What is going on, Hecky? You have 40 minutes left, and then I am calling this off, and it goes, pardon the pun, on your record as a failure of judgment."

Ina Autry gave Gene milk and then orange juice to drink. The passing time could be seen in the cigarette butts piling up in the ashtrays, the stained and discarded coffee cups, the emptying box of peanut brittle (a snack supplied by one of the Pinafores), till finally a lone peanut sat amid the white ruffled cups that had held the sweet, sticky candy.

Twenty minutes later, with 20 left to go if Lieberson ended the session as he'd threatened, Gene miraculously sobered up, or at least could act and sing as if he had. The band and the Pinafores took their places at the microphones. Except for the sound of breathing and a swallow here and there heard through the microphones, quiet filled the studio. "Stand by for take one," Hecky's voice cut through the silence. He counted to five and signaled the orchestra to begin. Then he cut the musicians off. "I want to adjust the equalization a little more. Carl, have the band play a few measures." Hecky listened through his earphones and fidgeted with the knobs on the board. "That's it. Okay, stand by for take two."

After the introduction, accompanied by the sound of chimes, Gene's warm and pleasant voice sang out: "You know Dasher and Dancer and Prancer and Vixen . . ."

But Hecky, not one to function well under a ticking clock, had forgotten to silence the ringer on the telephone. This had been a good take so far, with promise of being the final one. Should he pick up the phone? Distracted by the ringing, he finally stopped the recording.

"Wrap it up, Hecky. Time's up," came Lieberson's voice.

"It sounds good, Goddard, really good. One more take. Trust me on this one. One more take will do it."

"Thirty more minutes. That's it."

My father took a deep breath. His shoulders inched their way down. What he'd heard before the phone rang made him happy. The words and melody were already stuck in his head—a hook, it's called in the trade: that combination of words and melody that goes through your mind over and over again, even when you haven't been listening.

Hecky flicked the on switch. "Take three," he announced through the glass. Then he sat down at the control board and donned the leather earphones inscribed with the letters CBS. He lifted the pointer finger of his left hand and flicked it in the direction of the band, gesturing to Carl Cotner and the musicians to begin. He waved his right hand, his fingers playing an arpeggio in the air, signaling Autry and the Pinafores to sing. His dark, unruly eyebrows went up and down, his characteristic way of saying, "Okay, let's go."

As he listened, his fingers touched one lever and then another, bringing up the volume of the band or lowering it, adding reverb to the voices, sliding the levers on the big master soundboard up and down for more middle, treble, or bass. The sound enveloped us as it poured through the control room speakers. My mother sat back and smiled. I felt the fairy tale return. My life was enchanted, for sure. Gene's mellow voice sang:

You know Dasher and Dancer and Prancer and Vixen,
Comet and Cupid and Donner and Blitzen,
But do you recall
The most famous reindeer of all?

Rudolph the red-nosed reindeer
Had a very shiny nose
And if you ever saw it
You would even say it glows

All of the other reindeer
Used to laugh and call him names
They never let poor Rudolph
Join in any reindeer games

Then one foggy Christmas Eve
Santa came to say
Rudolph with your nose so bright
Won't you guide my sleigh tonight?

Then all the reindeer loved him
As they shouted out with glee
Rudolph the red-nosed reindeer
You'll go down in history!

Autry finished singing. The band played the final few notes. "That's the take! Thank you everyone," Hecky said as he lifted the receiver of the telephone again. This time he asked the operator to dial a number: Columbia Records and, once it was reached, the office of Goddard Lieberson. Only 15 minutes had passed since Lieberson's last call. "Goddard," my father said, "we're done early. 'Rudolph, the Red-Nosed Reindeer' has been recorded. We're calling it a day."

· · · · · · · · · · ·

The song was transferred by electricity from sound waves onto a new recording device, magnetic tape, and then imbedded through grooves onto vinyl. It made history as the first record ever to go platinum, selling over one million records. As Columbia's biggest hit, "Rudolph" would bring in huge sums of money for the company and make millions for

Gene Autry and for its composer, Johnny Marks, who would continue to be a prolific writer of popular Christmas tunes. "Rudolph" spawned dolls, picture books, party costumes, toys, an annual television special, and the sale of millions of videos each and every year.

As an employee of Columbia Records, my father received his biweekly paycheck and a $500 bonus. But he'd earned the respect of Goddard Lieberson and the industry's other moguls, and as Columbia's president, Edward Wallerstein, told him in a thank-you letter, "In spite of the tribulations the industry has gone through, you have helped to put Columbia today in the strongest position it has ever held."

Hecky was at the start of a brilliant career.

· · · · · · · · · · ·

CHAPTER 2

The Violin and the Fiddler

· · · · · · · · · · ·

After the success of "Rudolph," Hecky Krasnow was a name known by every mogul in every record company. Singer Gene Autry became a household name, and it wasn't difficult for my father to persuade other celebrities to record for children. They were now willing to put aside their reservations about recording kid-disks and hope for at least a modicum of Autry's huge success. Soon the name Hecky Krasnow was recognized by many of Hollywood's most famous stars. Aspiring songwriters clamored to have Hecky Krasnow hear their compositions. Artists were delighted when he produced their sessions, for he gained a reputation as an outstanding director and recording engineer. Hecky Krasnow was well-known in New York, Hollywood, England; and in our hometown of Yonkers, he and the mayor ran neck and neck as to who was the most important man in the city. Yet, a ghost lurked in the corners of my father's being: a ghost that periodically reared its haunting head and admonished him that his successes were never quite good enough.

I knew little about the life my father had led prior to my entering it, but my father's past touched my present every time he played his violin, with my mother accompanying him on the piano. My lullabies, as I lay in bed hearing the sounds coming from the living room, consisted of melodic pizzicatos, allegros, and andantes. My father's past became my present when we'd visit others with whom he played chamber music, or when our family would go to Town Hall and hear an evening of classical music with names on the program like Yitzhak Pearlman. The strains of a Mozart sonata inevitably filled my father's eyes with tears.

His own father, my grandpa Harry Krasnow, wept while listening to operas, literally sobbing each time *Madame Butterfly* poured out her tragic story on the radio or his RCA Victor phonograph. He'd make the long train trip into New York City from Hartford, Connecticut, to the Metropolitan Opera House to hear the likes of *Petrushka*, and wept openly in public at its tragic beauty. Perhaps Harry's love of music found its roots in listening to his own father who, as a cantor, wailed Jewish chants in ancient melodic modes.

Photos piled high in boxes, and scrapbooks filled with frayed, yellowed newspaper articles I'd kept after my parents' deaths offered clues to my father's past and, conceivably, to the ghost that mocked his achievements. Headlines in these old articles read, "Hartford's sixteen year old virtuoso to give violin debut," and "Hartford's own prodigy called 'genius' by Auer." Others showed photos of an austere, bearded old man captioned, "Master Leopold Auer, resident violinist of czars, kings, and queens." I learned in these articles that Leopold Auer only took on young students whom he believed could follow in his footsteps and delight the ears of royalty and cultured audiences around the world, students like Mischa Elman, Jascha Heifitz, and Ephraim Zimbalist. Leopold Auer had accepted a twelve-year-old student named Hermann Krasnow. Hermann's grueling audition with Mr. Auer was described in detail on the pages of these old, crumpling newspapers.

The articles following the audition indicated that the talented youth's career lay ahead of him, unquestioned and non-negotiable. Like young Mozart with his father, young Hermann and Papa Harry (so Harry dreamed, planned, and told many journalists in the interviews) would traverse the world together as Hermann thrilled eager audiences playing his violin. This dream never materialized. The answers could not be found by asking family members. A shroud of ignorance, real or purported, surrounded the topic, and it was a subject never mentioned by my father.

Men of Harry's generation most often had sons who followed in their fathers' footsteps. Not Hecky. As I read through the vast number of articles in the crumpling scrapbooks, clues to his past and the ghost shadowing his life began to unravel. They began in Kiev, Russia.

. . . .

In 1903, the Cossack soldiers, with their orders and sanctions from Czar Nicholas II, rampaged daily throughout the large province of Kiev, raping, pillaging, and plundering in the villages and homes of Jews. Jews had lived for 10 centuries in Russia and continued to be feared because they refused to participate in the Christian religion dominating the land. The education Jews gave to their sons and the resultant intellectual thinking posed a threat to the czars' absolute power. Ignorant peasants were easy to control; people who thought for themselves were not.

In Kiev, the Krasnow family had been out working. They returned home to find their house in shambles. Harry Krasnow, the eldest son, had just turned 16. He would now be conscripted into the czar's army, as were all male Russian youths. There, Harry would serve for 25 years or until death, whichever came first. Worse, he'd be forced to participate in the horrific atrocities engaged in by the Cossacks against the Jews. To Harry's parents, the thought of never seeing their son again was more comforting than the nightmare of his having to serve the czar and perpetrate anti-Semitism. Thus, Harry was put on a boat and sent to America. As a young boy, he'd been a blacksmith's apprentice. With this background, officials at Ellis Island assigned him to continue this work with a blacksmith in the city of Hartford, Connecticut. Harry would become Hecky's father and my grandfather.

In another town in Kiev, three sons in the Wohlenscheppen house lay dead. The parents and two of their daughters, Sarah and Helen, and Helen's newborn son, Harold, heard the sounds of the stomping boots and bloodthirsty curses of the approaching Cossacks. They hid, terrified but unnoticed, in some bushes, stifling the cries of the baby. Three other daughters, Sascha, Anna, and Blumma, had already left for America. Max Mindell, husband of Helen, had also immigrated to America and planned to send money to bring Helen and the baby. Max and Helen didn't know it would take eight long years for this to happen. Counting on Max to pay Helen's way, Sarah's two grieving parents took the last of their savings and sent her, at age 16, to the land of freedom, hope, and promise. At Ellis Island, Sarah's last name was shortened to Wohl. Immigration officials sent her to the city where her sisters lived, the same city as Harry: Hartford, Connecticut. Sarah would become mother to my father and my grandmother.

The Hartford that Harry and Sarah lived in was a city rich in literary and manufacturing history, long thoroughfares lined with prosperous farms, and the beautifully designed Keney and Elizabeth Parks, where all could wander along ponds filled with ducks, sweetly scented flowers, and shady trees. Literary residents had included Mark Twain, whose grand house shared a lawn with Harriet Beecher Stowe. Another neighbor of these famed authors was actor William Gillette, best known for his role as Sherlock Holmes and as the benefactor who created the famous medieval Gillette Castle in Haddam. Hartford's founding father, Samuel Colt, built the historic edifice Colt Firearms Factory, where in Twain's *A Connecticut Yankee in King Arthur's Court*, the hero, Hank Morgan, is hit on the head and dreams that he is in sixth-century England. Twain said of Hartford, "Of all the beautiful towns it has been my fortune to see, this is the chief. . . . You do not know what beauty is if you have not been here."

. . . .

Harry and Sarah both lived in the less glamorous sector near the factories and railroads. Harry showed great talent and a promising future. Fathers had their eyes on him as a prospective husband for their daughters. He had his eyes on Sarah, a woman ahead of her time with a far more fiery temper than Harry. She refused his proposals until he threatened suicide. As an immigrant and woman with no rights, she and her sisters feared she'd be blamed, arrested or deported should Harry carry out his threat. Sarah insisted that no *schadchen* or matchmaker would ever consider Harry and Sarah for a couple. She stood her ground until fear of deportation prevailed.

Sarah Wohl and Harry Krasnow, each aged 20, were married in 1907 and moved to an apartment on Earle Street in the center of the Jewish neighborhood. Sarah gave birth to Hecky in the apartment on Earle Street on February 15, 1910. She and Harry named him Hermann and, in true Jewish tradition, were delighted to have a firstborn son. The name Krasnow would continue, the traditional bris, or circumcision, could be held, and later a bar mitzvah; and Harry would have a son to work with him and take over his business.

Shortly after my father's birth, Harry's dream of establishing his own business became reality with the founding of National Iron Works. He purchased a rundown building on Talcott Street, near the Connecticut River and the railroad, and, with the help of hired workers, repaired the structure. My father's political activism sprouted from seeds planted by his father. Harry opened a union shop in a day and age when most workers were fired for even considering joining a union. His workers were well paid, treated with respect, and most worked for him their entire employed life, retiring with union pensions. Harry felt great satisfaction with his new and growing business.

Sarah soon gave birth to Albert. The family moved to a small house on Westbourne Parkway in the Blue Hills area of West Hartford, an area where Jews, along with other upwardly mobile immigrants, were settling. There, my grandmother gave birth to Abraham, who, in his teens in order to get decent employment, would change his obviously Jewish name to Robert or Bob for short. At the time of Bob's birth, my father had just turned four.

One day, Aunt Sascha came to visit. She never came without some gift for the boys, and they couldn't wait to see what lay in the bag she now carried. For the two older ones, out of the bag Sascha pulled two toy violins and bows to play them. Al, at two and a half, already showed signs of great mechanical curiosity and aptitude. He immediately looked at the object in hand, turning it upside down, right side up, and banged upon its strings with the bow. Then he loosened the strings, tightened them, and loosened them, all the while noticing the difference in the sounds they made. When his toddler mind was satisfied with what it wanted to know, he put the toy down and searched for something else to occupy him.

Hermann, however, not knowing quite what to do with the toy, asked Aunt Sascha to show him. She obliged. "Put this part under your chin. Hold this part up with your left hand, up a little higher, a little more. Perfect. Now, hold the bow in the right hand, here like this. Now move it back and forth as though you are tickling the strings."

Hermann "tickled" his new toy, discovering an array of sounds. He played it all day. Thus, my father began to play the violin. It took some adjustment, for he was left-handed. However, as his school teachers, following the practice of the time, hit his left hand with rulers and forced him to write with his right hand, he became ambidextrous.

Every day, he played that toy violin. After doing his chores, and in between helping his mother with the baby and tending to Al, he would find a room where he could close the door and, without interruption, practice on his beloved toy. Two years later, Sarah was cleaning his room. She noticed the scratched, dented, broken-stringed violin, and, thinking it was now unusable, she threw it out. My father was inconsolable for weeks.

Perhaps the loss of the toy instrument proved a temporary blessing. To distract him from his sorrow, Harry bought him a bicycle. In the next few years, he learned to ride a bike and play baseball, a game that would always pose as jealous mistress to his love of music. Baseball had swept the nation's interest in 1911, when the adaptation of a ball with a cork center ultimately enabled players like Babe Ruth and Lou Gehrig to thrill fans with their numerous and amazing home runs. My father was seldom without a bat and ball in hand, organizing the neighborhood boys into teams. Upon occasion, five brothers and a teenager who came to visit relatives living in the neighborhood joined these teams. The five brothers grew up to be known as the Marx Brothers. The older boy, Chaim Arluk, changed his name to Harold Arlen when he composed songs like "Over the Rainbow."

It was in these years outdoors, batting balls in the empty lots between houses and in Keney Park (which lay only a couple of blocks away), that my father's name evolved into "Hecky." "Hell" was a forbidden curse word at the time, but my father apparently raised a lot of it. Instead of using this forbidden word, family, neighbors, and friends said that Hermann raised a lot of "heck," and all began to affectionately call him Hecky. "Hermann" sat on the back burner for formal occasions.

. . . .

By the time my father was nine years old, he was the eldest of six children. His sister Helen was born some 18 months after Abe, and the twins, Sylvia and Pauline, just under two years after Helen. When Sarah saw two babies at once, she pleaded with the doctor to give her a hysterectomy. She knew nothing about the hormonal effects of such an operation. The doctor knew almost as little and agreed to the operation. Overnight, my grandmother went through, in effect, menopause. She was 31. She moved into her own bedroom soon after.

Harry and Sarah's mismatched relationship didn't change radically after the hysterectomy. Matters simply escalated a few steps further. Harry, now knowing he was the father of six children and would have no more, turned his energy toward the lives of these offspring. He would decide what each child would do with his or her life. His children would do well and make him an exemplary father. He began with Hecky.

The memory of my father's reaction to the toy violin had not escaped Harry. His son's obsession with the instrument, weeks of grief over its loss, and obvious love of music caused Harry to wonder whether his beloved eldest son truly had a gift to play the real violin. In planning his children's lives and his own posterity, Harry knew that one of his sons must take over his hard-earned and ever-growing business. Albert showed great interest in how things worked. He was a more aggressive child than Hecky, and that would make him better suited to business. Al could be the son that worked with his father and took over the business when he retired. Harry was thrilled that this would free Hecky to become a musician. Yes! A musician for a son: hopefully, the proverbial fiddler representing the heart and soul of the Jewish spirit.

. . . .

One night, when my father refused to eat the chicken soup placed before him for the third night in a row as a cure for the colds traveling through the house, Harry promised him that if he'd stop his fussing and just finish his dinner, he would receive a surprise. A surprise when it wasn't even his birthday or a holiday was enough incentive for Hecky to lick the bowl clean. Harry then left the room. When he returned, in his hands he held a violin made of lustrous wood glowing with a warm brownish-blond hue with genuine, high quality strings. The horsehair bow came with a container of rosin to keep it in good shape and slide across the strings with ease.

Hecky darted from his chair and put the instrument under his chin. He ran the bow across the strings and tickled the fretless neck with his fingers. It certainly was not the sound of a Mozart sonata, but the tones were actual musical ones—a scale that, with practice, would sound perfect.

As Harry smiled with joy, Sarah held her head in her hands and said, "*Fun dayn fiddle tzu Got's a lidle.*" (From your fiddle to God's ears.)

"Great promise," were the words spoken by the three teachers Harry found for Hecky in Hartford, as they described his playing and rapid progress. "Extremely talented young boy," they all agreed.

Harry encouraged Hecky and set strict rules regarding the number of hours he was to practice daily. My father's love of the instrument was evidenced by his willingness to practice, how he cared for the violin, polishing it, frequently changing the strings, rosining the bow, and in the ever-more-beautiful sounds he played upon it.

After my father had studied for three years, Harry announced to Sarah, "It's time that we find out if our son is truly destined to be a virtuoso. I've arranged an audition in New York with Rudolph Larsen, Leopold Auer's assistant. If Larsen thinks he is sufficiently talented, he will arrange an audition for him with Leopold Auer himself."

"Leopold Auer?" Sarah gasped. "Harry, Auer is known around the world as the violin master. Harry, he has played in the courts of czars and kings. Harry, Auer has taught Mischa Elman, Ephraim Zimbalist, and Jascha Heifitz! Our son is talented, but you are going too far with this, too far and too fast. Our Hecky is just a boy, Harry, and you know what tension and pressure do to his stomach."

"Talent cannot be hindered by fear. His stomachaches can be overcome. We have to find out if our son is truly destined to be a world-famous fiddler. His love of the instrument and the music he plays on it must be tested."

"Harry, please, give him a few more years of lessons. Think of how the poor child will feel if he doesn't pass such an audition. He may never want to play again."

"Sarah, can't you believe that a child of yours may also be a Heifitz?"

. . . .

The audition would take place in May of 1923. Hecky had just turned twelve. Harry made sure that his son diligently practiced every piece suggested by Mr. Larsen and that he practiced for hours each day. May arrived, and my father passed the Larsen audition. The audition with Auer followed shortly afterward. Herr Auer, calling him Hermann, greeted my father, impressing him with his tall presence, stern look, and air of authority. They talked briefly about the studies Hermann had engaged in so far, the extent of his repertoire, and his ability to sight-read.

"Now, Hermann, I'd like you to meet Miss Giles, Vera Giles, my accompanist. You will have the honor of playing with Miss Giles." Herr Auer opened the door and called to her. She entered looking only slightly less stern than Auer because of some color on her face in the form of rouge and lipstick.

"You must be Hermann," she said as she extended her hand to shake his. "And this must be your father." She faced Harry and shook his hand. "I suppose we should get started. Let us make sure the violin and piano are in perfect tune."

Hecky stood, trying to hold himself still as he felt a pain dart through his stomach, his heart race, and his mouth go dry. He looked at Harry, who knew what he was asking with his eyes. Hecky had never played with an accompanist. Should he confess this to Mr. Auer? Harry signaled his son in favor of honesty.

"Herr Auer, Miss Giles," he spoke in a voice cracking from both anxiety and puberty. "I have never played with an accompanist before."

"Well, then," Mr. Auer looked at Vera and raised his eyebrows as though asking her if they should continue with the audition. Deciding to do so, he stated, "Well, then, this will certainly be the best test of all. If you can play the highly difficult Concerto in D Major by Mozart and play along with Miss Giles, you shall surely be worthy of my tutelage, truly facile on the violin. Let's begin. Tune your instrument."

Letting the music soothe and guide him, as it always did, riding upon each phrase and allowing it to carry him to the next and yet the next, Hecky played the Mozart concerto skillfully, and kept pace with Miss Giles.

"Good. Good," Auer commented at its finish.

Vera nodded her head in agreement. "I will leave you to the master now," and left the room.

"Mr. Krasnow," Herr Auer addressed Harry," Hermann has passed the audition. You have a very talented child. With his genius, he should become one of the greatest. You do understand, however, that maturity, too, plays its part." Looking at Hecky, he said, "Hermann, you are without doubt, a prodigy. But it is the years that follow that determine—more work, more study, more life." To Harry he said, "That is what they all must have to reach the heights."

My father felt proud of himself, and rightfully so. He had done what very few were able to do: passed the grueling test of an audition with Leopold Auer. "We will meet every two weeks," Herr Auer told him. "I expect you to practice each and every day. When you come for your lesson, the practice must show. You must be far beyond where you were two weeks previously and ready to reach even greater heights in the two weeks following," he emphasized. "And dedicate at least one hour nonstop to practicing scales. They are the rudiments. Without them and the facility they develop, you cannot play anything else well." They shook hands, gave all necessary thanks, congratulations, and Harry and Hecky left to board the train back to Hartford.

At the train station, Harry bought Hecky a glass of milk and a jelly donut. Thrilled, exhausted, and hungry, the jelly donut tasted like manna from heaven. For the rest of his life, my father could not pass a donut shop without buying jelly donuts and eating them with enjoyment bordering on worship.

Riding home on the train, Harry thought about his business. It gave him great satisfaction to think of his ever-growing success. Now, ecstatic about his son Hecky, he couldn't wait to share the news with Sarah, his brother Harold, his brother-in-law Max, and a host of others who would share his joy. Yet, he knew with every click and clack of the train wheels that he was going home to a wife who did not love him. Harry found sustenance in music. It was the one thing that filled his life with beauty. Now, he could count on Hecky and his violin to keep this feeling of beauty beating in his heart. Hecky sensed this and knew that as Leopold Auer's pupil and Harry's son, he would have to live up to the expectations of two men, like two fathers, each an authority figure in his own right.

Harry and Hecky returned home from New York and told Sarah of the success. "*Oy, mayn Bubeleh,*" she gave Hecky a huge hug as happy tears ran down her cheeks. "I am so, so proud of you. A prodigy! Herr Auer's student! *Mayn Got!* Whoever thought of such a thing?" She was extremely proud, but she worried even more. As a student of Auer, her beloved son Hecky could not waiver in the number of hours he had to practice each day. When he was not in school, he'd have time for nothing but his violin. Harry forbade him from lifting a hammer and nail. He could not do anything that might harm his slender, long fingers, now coddled for his violin and the life of a prodigy. Secretly, he still played baseball. Whether warm or cool weather, his brothers brought their coats with them. "Hit the ground, Hecky," they'd yell if they saw anyone passing by who might tell Harry, and they'd cover him with their coats.

. . . .

For several days before my father traveled into New York City for his lessons with Auer, he often suffered severe stomachaches. Chills, sometimes fever and diarrhea, accompanied these along with debilitating pain.

The several doctors Harry and Sarah took him to could not diagnose these stomach upsets. The doctors simply said, "They are caused by tension."

Sarah worried. If the pressure of being a child prodigy caused her son to be chronically ill, then perhaps this pressure and tension should be removed from his routine. "Harry, there are children who study instruments and play as a hobby. Maybe this is what our Hecky should be doing." One of Sarah's favorite sayings was *"Abi gezunt!"* (As long as you're healthy!) She believed a person's health and well-being essential, for without it, proper achievement could not occur. If attaining one's goals fostered good health and happiness, the person was on the right road for his or her life. If such pursuits made one sick, a different road should be sought. She loved Hecky dearly and attempted to protect him, viewing his situation through the eyes and heart of a nurturing, concerned mother.

Harry continued to see the situation through his perspective: the strong father encouraging and supporting his son to pursue what the father truly believed to be the son's destined success. "Sarah, Hecky will just have to get used to tension. One day he will have to overcome stage fright too. Young Mozart obviously found ways to keep his nervousness at bay while appearing before nobility. So can our son."

For the four years my father studied with Leopold Auer, Mr. Auer expressed the fact that Hecky was making progress. He never uttered the word "excellent" regarding his students. The grandest word of praise ever heard when a student played well was "good." He told Harry that Hecky's progress was "good, quite good. The boy is truly talented. He will ripen with maturity."

My father had just turned 16 when Harry heard these words from Auer. Of these words, Harry ruminated on only those of Hecky's progress, not those stating that maturity would assist this progress. Harry concluded that it was time for his son, the prodigy, to have his debut. He announced to Sarah that he was going to arrange this most important event.

"Harry," my grandmother tried once again to be heard regarding her concerns over her son, "he is so young. Four years is not enough time to perfect his playing. Even Mr. Auer has spoken of more life, work, and study."

Harry would hear nothing of it. "Sarah, child prodigies must be just that, children. There is a difference between an 18-year-old and a 16-year-old virtuoso."

"Harry, a virtuoso is a virtuoso. It is what the audience and the critics *hear*, not whether the musician is one age or another!"

Harry continued with his plans and proceeded to make arrangements for what would become one of the most talked about, publicized, gala cultural evenings the city of Hartford hosted. He engaged Parsons Hall, the elite of Hartford's concert halls for the event. This was reflected in its admission prices, the highest in the city. Names that appeared on the marquee included Austrian-born Fritz Kreisler, who, like Auer, entertained the royalty of Europe. Word spread rapidly throughout the town once the night of April 12 was booked. Young Hermann was viewed as a potential city celebrity to be added to the list of the famous and venerable residents whose names were forever to be in history books. There wasn't a newspaper in the city that didn't have something to say promoting the debut.

"Hartford will have great cause for pride if this boy with his inborn talent and technical perfection fulfills his early promise and follows in the footsteps of the other students of his master, Auer."

Leopold Auer, though in his 80s, intended to travel from New York City all the way to Hartford for the event, and this aroused even more hoopla. He, too, had been interviewed by the papers and made front-page news. Hecky's violin could be heard through open windows up and down the street as he practiced hours each day in preparation in between his trips to New York to practice with Vera Giles under Auer's scrutiny.

At home, Hecky was relieved of any and all chores in the house. Abe and Al took over, even babysitting the girls. Abe dared to ask Harry, "Pa, what are you doing to Hecky? He's still just a kid like Al and me." Frightened whenever Hecky had bouts of stomachaches, and knowing how much Hecky loved playing ball with the gang, Abe had the chutzpah to say to Harry, *"Pa, Hecky has never even given a concert!"*

In a ferociously loud voice, seldom heard from this strict but somewhat gentle father, he yelled at Abe, "Children must respect their parents' decisions, obey their rules, and not question them. Did you hear that? Not question them—ever! I know what I am doing! Your brother is a genius, and the world deserves to hear him." Harry stormed out of the room.

. . . .

The night of the debut neared. Hecky's stomachaches grew more severe. Harry took him to additional doctors. Still the doctors could find no cause; and still, Harry encouraged Hecky saying he had nothing to fear, nothing to worry or be so nervous about. "You are a genius, son. You must live up to this gift of yours. I will be the proudest father in Hartford, in the whole world."

April 12 arrived. Leopold Auer sent a telegram that he would be unable to attend due to illness. "Regret not being present at your debut. Best wishes for success." Hecky was relieved that Auer would not be there judging every glissando, pluck, and arpeggio, but disappointed that he would not be at such an important milestone in his life. He respected Auer for his unquestioned mastery of the violin. He revered him for his immeasurable ability to impart knowledge of the violin, the instrument Hecky truly loved. He feared Leopold Auer because his demands and expectations mirrored the consummate father figure whose expectations must be fulfilled or the child deemed a failure.

The audience filled the hall, coming from Hartford, New Haven, and New York. Auer's quote greeted them on the front of the playbill; "A genius," it read. Harry passed out cigars in the lobby. After all, the prodigy he'd created would, in essence, be born before the audience tonight. Cantors Harry knew from Hartford and neighboring towns came to hear the music of a young man who, in just a few hours, would become the city's musical son and another proud name in the ever-growing list of brilliant and talented Jews sharing their gifts with the world.

Hecky stood behind the curtains attempting to keep his hands warm amid the cold sweat of nerves. The doctor had given him medicine to hopefully calm his stomach. He felt he was about to embark on the dangerous journey of climbing the highest mountain peak in the world. Only when he reached the top could he rest.

He tuned his violin one more time and waited for the signal from the stage manager that the curtain was to be raised. He could hear the audience as their excited talk filled the air like a swarm of buzzing bees around the honeycomb. The lights went out. The buzz turned into the silence of anticipation. Sounds of rising curtains filled the air. Spotlights lit the path to the piano. The stage manager gave the signal. Sixteen-year-old Hermann Krasnow walked out onto the stage in his tuxedo and bow tie, his dark hair slicked back in the fashion of the day, his blue eyes sparkling in the intense light. In his hands he held the vintage violin Harry had bought him for the occasion, a violin made in the 1770s by a master violin maker in Italy. Even the violin had been praised in the articles preceding the debut as "an instrument that could only enhance the great talent of its musician."

Rousing applause filled Parsons Hall. Hermann took several bows and finally gestured for the audience to please be quiet. He introduced Miss Vera Giles, and after the two positioned themselves, the program commenced. The first piece was Handel's Sonata in F Major. The audience applauded for several minutes when the piece ended. A representative of the Hartford City Council approached the stage with a huge floral horseshoe. On it, the name Hermann Krasnow was inscribed in large letters upon a purple ribbon.

The concert continued with the intricate Concerto no. 2 in D Minor by Bruch. The first part of the program was dedicated to the more difficult pieces, and finished with the *Louis XIV Gavotte*. After a brief intermission, some lighter fare was offered. This included *Hebrew Melody* by Achron and Lillian Boulanger's well-known *Cortege*.

The audience responded with a standing ovation and long, enthusiastic cheers demanding several encores. One critic wrote, "Had the audience written the critiques, Hermann Krasnow would be known around the world along with the Heifitzes of the violin world."

Other critics, however, suggested that the use of Parsons Hall for a debut had done the "talented youth a serious injustice," setting him up as an already successful violinist "on the level of Kreisler." They unanimously felt that a smaller, more intimate, less pricey hall would have allowed his "genius to shine." They praised his "technical facility, admirable tone, varied program and beautiful instrument." They noted some "roughness of execution and youthful lack of differentiation in style."

Leopold Auer's words about practice and maturity echoed in Harry's head for a long time after that night of April 12, 1916, as his dream of traveling throughout the world with his genius son came to an abrupt end. Prodigies must be lauded full scale from the moment of their debuts. There is no room for words like "roughness of execution," or "youthful lack of differentiation in style." My father was lauded as a "very talented musician with great promise," but his debut failed to launch him upon the world. As the light of a candle quickly flickers out when snuffed, the dreams of eight years of Hecky's boyhood ended in one debut. Worse, he hadn't reached the peak of the highest mountain. He couldn't rest. Throughout his life he'd strive to reach that peak, receive the accolades, and know that his father, Harry, was satisfied.

Once it was evident that a student of his was not to become a world-renowned fiddler, Auer would no longer teach him. In the weeks following the debut, Leopold Auer informed my father that he had done all he could for him. He suggested that, with his talent, he was sure to find a place playing with a fine symphony orchestra, giving solo concerts, and teaching others. However, to establish the necessary credentials to do these things and to learn the details of theory required to teach violin, he must go to the Juilliard School of Music or another such institution dedicated to training serious artists.

All those years of dedication and practice could not be cast away simply because of a failed debut. My father loved music, and his talent went unquestioned, though the degree of just how high that talent could now take him had dropped by several points. The decision was made to go to Juilliard where he was, of course, accepted. However, the specter of the failed debut had entered Hecky's life. The mountain peak still loomed before him.

CHAPTER 3

Hard Times and New Beginnings

illian Drucker, a talented pianist, entered Juilliard at the same time as Hecky. Her father, now deceased, had been a business acquaintance and friend of Harry's. Like Sarah and Harry, Lillian's parents, Samuel Drucker and Rachel Leah Turetsky, had escaped the pogroms of Russia. Both had lived on farms in a little town at the foot of the White Mountains, or the Caucasus, in Ukraine named Ekitrinislav after Czarina Katherine the Great.

In 1896, Czar Nicholas II reigned. Samuel Drucker, 15 years old, returned to his family's farmhouse to find that the Cossacks had ransacked it. Sprawled throughout the blood in each room, were the corpses of his entire family. Terrified, and not knowing if the soldiers would return, he dug up the rubles hidden under a floorboard, saved for just such a catastrophe, and booked his passage to America.

In a nearby farm, Rachel Leah was spared, as her mother, in a desperate attempt to save her daughter, cried out under the filthy, panting body of a Cossack raping her as his prelude to murdering her, "Don't kill *Rose*. She's not a Jew. She's the maid."

The Cossacks threw Rachel Leah into the pigpen on the farm as punishment for working for Jews. As she lay unconscious, the hungry animals gnawed at her legs until a Russian

Orthodox priest heard her cries, rescued her, nursed her back to health, and raised sufficient funds to send her to America. Wearing several pairs of thick cotton stockings (as she would for the rest of her life) to cover the gashes made by the pigs' sharp teeth, she boarded the same boat as Samuel Drucker. Frightened and alone, the two married on the boat. They were as unsuited to each other as Sarah and Harry. Later, it became a family joke riddled with truth that Sarah Krasnow and Sam Drucker would have been a good match, while Rachel Leah, who called herself Rose, the name uttered as her mother died, would have been the perfect wife for Harry.

Because they had both lived on farms, immigration officials sent Sam and Rose to a small town in Iowa to farm. Sam had enough money with him to purchase a decent plot of land with a quaint farmhouse. Rachel was soon pregnant with the first of their eight children, only two of whom would live to reach the age of 30, most of them dying from scarlet fever, measles, and diphtheria. On this farm, Sam and Rose's eighth child and only girl, my mother Lillian, showed great talent for playing the piano. She earned free lessons from the one piano teacher in the area in exchange for playing the pedal organ in the local Presbyterian church on Sundays and holidays.

When Lillian was 10, Sam wanted his talented daughter to have more access to culture than a small Iowa farm town offered. He sold the farm and moved the family from quietude and rusticity to Bruckner Boulevard in the bustling Bronx. Here he established a dry goods store. It was an immediate success, and within two years, he opened another store in the Blue Hills area of Hartford. He traveled with his family back and forth between the Bronx and Hartford. The Krasnows and Druckers became friends. Hecky and Lillian shared their love of music. Sarah liked Lillian. Young as she was, Sarah instinctively felt that she'd make the perfect wife for Hecky when the time came.

But tragedy befell the lives of the Druckers. With only four of their children still living, diphtheria took the life of yet another son. Sam Drucker, a strappingly healthy man, suffered from a burst appendix and developed peritonitis. Without penicillin to fight the growing infection, he died. Rose was left widowed with no money, a 15-year-old daughter, one son, Freddy, living in Chicago, and another, Harry, living in the Bronx with her and Lillian. Harry hadn't done particularly well in school, preferring sports, particularly wrestling. He had no business experience except for helping Sam in the store. Rose had none. Lillian played the piano. The most they could hope for was to sell the store and get enough money from it to live on while they reordered their lives. The Hartford store had burned down not long before Sam's death in a fire that destroyed several shops on the street where it stood.

. . . .

Soon after her father's death, my mother contracted rheumatic fever, which left a hole in her aorta. Doctors warned that it was unlikely she would live beyond age 40 and that she should put aside any thoughts of motherhood, for she would risk death should she become pregnant. Her brother Harry, now 25, felt responsible for supporting his mother and sister.

Harry Drucker went to the gym daily to wrestle. Scouts came there looking for promising athletes to coach and train, supporting them all the while. Then they'd sign them up, book them in the ring, and hopefully make hefty profits from their fights. Some of these scouts made their big bucks in shadier endeavors. Word of Sam Drucker's death and the financial struggle that lay ahead for Mrs. Drucker and her young daughter had spread rapidly in the neighborhood. Some new scouts came to the gym where Harry Drucker worked out daily. They observed Harry carefully and sized up his talent—and his personality. Harry, like his mother and sister, had a trusting nature and took what people said and their promises at face value. His resulting innocence became fodder for any con man who smelled the scent of it.

"You know, son," the scouts told him, "you could be a champion wrestler if you'd let us train you. We'll pay you well during training. How does $10,000 over the next twelve months sound? Mrs. Drucker and your sister Lillian will live like a queen and a princess."

Harry began his training. My mother and Bubbe Rose (as I'd later call her) lived well. Harry bought my mother a beautiful Chickering baby grand piano that would eventually grace each house my parents lived in and on which my father would compose and arrange so many of the songs he'd write and produce.

At the end of the first year, Harry's trainers approached him. "Harry, you're a born wrestler, and in our opinion, you're ready for your first fight. This one's for practice before you start the big time. You gotta move into that ring step by step."

"Who's my opponent?" Harry asked thrilled.

"Your first arena is this city. You toughen up in a tough city. Here's your first assignment. It'll build up courage; the kind of ruthless indifference a wrestler has to feel toward his opponent if he's gonna win."

They gave him the address of the place he was to go. Then they handed him a long iron bar and said, "Take this with you, Harry. It's a dangerous part of town. People can get unruly there. Don't be afraid to use it on someone's back or head if circumstances call for it. You're on the right side, Harry, on the right side."

When Harry arrived at the address, the truth hit him hard. He'd been sent to a factory where union workers were out on strike. Now he understood the reason for the iron bar. To acquire that "ruthless indifference," his trainers wanted him to practice union busting, plain and simply—to work as a thug!

Harry would wrestle. He loved the physicality of it. He liked the challenge of thinking quickly on his feet. Wrestling was a legitimate sport with a set of fair fight rules. But to injure workers because they were fighting for their rights? No Drucker did that, no decent wrestler either.

Harry returned to his trainers and gave them the iron bar. "When you have a wrestling match for me, I'm ready. But don't ever expect me to be a union thug."

"Harry, you better think twice," they threatened. "Otherwise, we'll call it a deal. You pay us back the $10,000 we've already invested in you. You have until next Friday—you know what we mean."

"I can lend you maybe $300," Harry's uncle Abe Drucker said when he sought his advice. "Maybe that will hold them off while we think of something. I think we should go to the police." The police claimed they could only get involved if the men actually harmed Harry physically. It was obvious that they were also in cahoots with the factory manager.

Friday arrived all too fast. Harry offered the men the $300. They threw it back at him. "I'll sell the piano," he said, feeling a pang of pain in his heart for Lillian at the very thought. "I need time though."

"Sorry, nothing doing. Now get outta here."

On Fridays, Harry came home early to cut the challah bread and light the Sabbath candles. It was a hot summer night. My mother and Bubbe Rose stood at the window of their fourth-floor apartment and looked out onto the vestibule below, a red brick circular driveway where horses and carriages stopped in front of the entrance doors, and now, more than not, automobiles. They saw Harry walking up the sidewalk. As he neared the vestibule, a black limousine kept pace with him. Harry had his hands in his pockets and his head bent low. Usually, he looked up towards the window and waved hello. The limousine followed him onto the vestibule. Suddenly, loud explosive pops rang through the air, one after another. Blood ran like a river on those bricks. The limousine sped away.

Rose, realizing her son had been shot, instinctively began to run toward him. The course she took for her run led right out the window. Rose wasn't tall, but she had the characteristic Ukrainian big-boned build and had put on some weight over her years of childbearing. As she leaned out the window, Lillian, slight of build and barely five feet tall, grabbed her feet. Rose was thrusting her arms all about and screaming.

Lillian was attempting the impossible trying to hold onto her mother and pull her back inside. "Don't let go! Don't let go!" Her head screamed to her. She nearly fell out the window as Rose flailed and screeched in anguish. "I'm coming to you, Harry. I'll save you, Harry. Wait for me," she called to her son as he lay in a growing pool of blood.

Suddenly, Lillian felt like she wasn't in her body and only her head was pulling Rose's body into the room. Her head said, "Mamma, you can't die. Mamma, I will pull you in . . . in . . . in . . ."

Rose fell onto the floor inside. In that moment, Lillian knew that her mind could control impossible things. She knew her mind could give commands to her body, and, if these commands were felt deeply enough, if they were urgent enough, important enough, her mind could accomplish what her body could not. Harry was so good, so kind. He had always been there for her, a solid rock in her life, and she had loved him as both a friend and older brother. Through his death, Lillian found the secret to her life: *mind over matter.* My mother didn't just recite these words: she practiced them.

Freddy Drucker sent his mother money from Chicago. Uncle Abe helped out when he could. But Rose knew she'd have to find a husband, and she did. He was referred to as Old Man Levy in family stories. Eventually, Old Man Levy gave Rose $5,000 and left her for a younger woman, but not before Lillian graduated from Juilliard.

At Juilliard, Lillian accompanied Hecky on the piano. Hecky fell in love with Lillian Drucker, four-feet 10-inches short, kind, energetic, with sparkling green eyes that danced to her warm smile. Hecky captured Lillian's heart. On July 5, 1929, both aged 19, Hecky and Lillian married in the new house Harry had purchased in 1927, at 60 Canterbury Street, a few blocks away from their house on Westbourne Parkway. Here, guests gazed at the mural of Venice that ran up the entire winding stairway delimited by an ornate brass railing built by Harry. An orchestra played in the corner of the large living room, where guests alternately waltzed, jitterbugged, and kazatzkied. Sarah's homemade food adorned tables in the cool basement, which, lacking electricity, was lit by hanging Japanese lanterns filled with candles. Wed under a chuppah in the backyard, also lit by candles flickering under the moonlight, my father and mother were accurately dubbed "the lovebirds of the family."

. . . .

After the wedding, they moved to Washington Heights, New York, and opened a music school located at 567 West 170th Street. The Krasnow Studio of Musical Art offered violin, harmony, piano, ear training, music history, appreciation, and private instruction by competent graduate teachers. Many students came, and it looked like Hecky and Lillian had found a successful future in this music school. They also gave concerts in small halls throughout the city and for fund-raising events. Here, they handed out their cards and acquired further students for the school.

A few months after their wedding and the opening of their quickly thriving school, Black Tuesday swept across the nation on October 29, as the stock market crashed and the Great Depression rolled over the country like a river breaking the confines of a dam. Hecky and Lillian attempted to keep the school open by catering to the wealthy, but those who could afford the luxury of lessons were few in number. Times grew harder, and my parents had to close their school.

Their talent and resourcefulness enabled them to survive by accepting invitations from the still rich and famous to play at their grand parties. Pay included leftover food. As I grew up, and heard their descriptions of these parties, I gained insight into their near lifetime affiliation with the Socialist Party and its more equitable distribution of property, ownership, and food.

Hecky played his violin in the tuxedo and bow tie he'd worn for his debut. Lillian wore the classic long black skirt and white blouse that characterized the apparel of female musicians in orchestras. On the plush East Side of Manhattan, where most of the parties were held, a doorman dressed like a British butler ushered them to the service elevator. Musicians had talent, but not money, and the front elevator was barred to their economic class. The elevator was usually operated by a black person dressed in a uniform resembling that of a bellhop in a hotel.

Leaving the elevator, they were ushered by house servants through the service entrance to the kitchen, then into a hallway that led to the parlor where they were to play. As they walked through the hallway, whose walls most often bore paintings with the signatures of world-renowned artists, Hecky and Lillian looked into the rooms they passed. They viewed tables festooned with fountains, from which imported champagnes splashed into crystal glasses as servants pushed upon spigots. Gold tableware, ornate china, and silver goblets that soon would be filled with an array of aged wines added to the sumptuous scenery en route to the parlor. Glitter abounded as diamonds and other jewels of varying hues sparkled around the necks, arms, and fingers of the female guests. Tables stood laden with enormous platters of caviar, tartar, pheasant, roasts of beef, lamb, and whole pigs with apples in their mouths. Gourmet cheeses, fruits, pastries, and sorbets of orange, green, yellow, and pink sat like colorful paintings on tablecloth canvases. Expensive flower arrangements added more color and heavenly scents to the array.

Once in the parlor, Lillian usually found a shining black Steinway concert grand piano. Sometimes, but rarely, it would be the piano of a different maker, such as a Knabe. She warmed her fingers on its keys as Hecky tuned his violin. Chairs with velvet covers of green, gold, and maroon stood waiting for their audience to sit upon them. Perhaps it wasn't The Hermitage or Versailles, but it well could have been.

Hecky and Lillian were hungry. They dreamed of the leftovers they would be lucky enough to eat later because they were graced with the talent to play music that pleased the rich. They could not understand how all the food that would not be given to them and the servants would simply be discarded without pangs of conscience. The gluttonous amount of food was far too abundant to be finished by the guests, and, in such wealthy circles, it was considered poor breeding not to leave food on one's plate. Where was charity? On the streets all over America, people were starving because of economic reasons beyond their control.

In spite of his access to food, my father continued to suffer from horrific stomachaches. He assumed it was because much of what he was given to eat had been cooked in rich sauces and that these were the cause of his almost uncontrollable diarrhea. He could not afford to see a doctor. "I just tried to watch what I ate," he later told me. "But when hunger is everywhere you turn and you know this is all you may have to eat for many days, you eat it."

One day, carrying his violin when returning home from another engagement, a man with a few apples and the classic sign, "Apples 5¢," approached my father. "Sir," he said, "I can see you are not rich, but I also know you have a roof over your head, shoes without holes, and every now and then, you buy an apple from me. How are you managing? Where did you get your job?"

"I'm a musician," my father told him. "Usually, we musicians struggle when times are good. Oddly enough it seems, when times are hard, we can at least get by. People seem to crave entertainment in difficult times. It offers an escape."

"Music," the man replied. "I assume that's a violin. You are fortunate."

"Sir," my father said, "I think music is God's way of reminding us that there is still beauty in life. Music gives us hope."

My father also earned money playing as a gypsy fiddler for those rich enough to still afford dining over candlelight at the finest New York restaurants. He'd don a black bandana, a white shirt with sleeves that widened at the cuffs, a sash around the waist to hold up the bloomer-style pants, and patent leather boots. He'd quip, "If I'd have wore a patch over one eye, I'd have looked like a pirate." Demeaning as he found it, he got used to entering through back doors and service elevators. The kitchen entrance he was required to use assaulted his nose with the stench of accumulated garbage. As he carried his magnificent 1770s violin and the memory of years of study with Mr. Auer, each entry through that door reminded him that Heifitz, Elman, Zimbalist, and Kreisler were walking through palace doors and grand concert halls. He resigned himself to the fact that, as he said, "Musicians were often viewed no differently than waiters, especially those musicians who needed money badly enough to work in restaurants. Both were considered lower class workers, except that waiters carried trays and musicians carried instruments."

My father put away his pride and frustration, as nearly every night, both the waiters and musicians reaped the benefit of a plate of scrambled eggs, more protein than most could even dream of at the time. Some nights, they were given salad, not well tolerated by my father's stomach. He could not refuse the offering, however, for the chef would frown upon anyone rejecting his handouts, and such an ingrate risked getting no further meals. Sometimes, Hecky would say he had another gig and was allowed to take the food with him. My mother would be well fed by the contents of the "doggie bag." She'd eat the leftovers with relish after returning from playing the piano in a local silent film theater, where, as her fingers created the emotional background music, she swooned over Rudolf Valentino and concentrated hard in order to keep in tempo with Charlie Chaplin's screen antics. As for Hecky, the cramping in his gut grew more severe. It seemed that whatever ailed him was aggravated more from not eating than from eating food that disagreed with him. He assumed that his intestinal problem would go away when he could again eat at regular intervals. However, doubt and fear overcame him when he could not leave the house due to extreme nausea, diarrhea, and severe pain.

．．．．．．．．．．．

In 1935, Franklin Delano Roosevelt established the Works Progress Administration. Life and its financial concerns improved for my parents and millions of others across America. Hecky and Lillian became active in the Federal Music Program. The FMP gave employment to thousands of unemployed musicians, providing venues for symphonies to play, opera companies to sing, choruses to be heard, dancers to dance, music teachers to teach, and students to learn. Hecky played with a variety of FMP orchestras while giving theory and violin lessons to eager students who'd been deprived of any instruction since Black Tuesday. Both my parents were performers in many WPA concerts.

Numerous dance schools were in operation under the auspices of the WPA, and Lillian was hired as the accompanist for several of these. It was here that she met a dancer named Marjorie Mazia, daughter of a famous Yiddish poet and Zionist, Aliza Greenblatt. Marjorie Mazia would soon dance with the Martha Graham Company. Modern Dance was opening new vistas as pioneers in the art, such as Isadora Duncan, Ruth St. Denis, Doris Humphrey, and Martha Graham, changed the course of dance history forever. Not only would Marjorie Mazia make her own inroads in this new form of dance, but in 1945 she would marry songwriter and folk singer Woody Guthrie. Woody's songs were already making waves across the nation as they reflected the struggles of America's workers, Okies, the homeless, union organizers, and FDR's beneficial projects, like the building of the Grand Coulee Dam. Lillian accompanied Marjorie Mazia's dance classes.

．．．．．．．．．．．

In November of 1935, Lillian realized that she was pregnant. The doctor had a serious talk with her. "Mrs. Krasnow, with your heart condition, this pregnancy could kill you."

"Well, what am I supposed to do about that?" she asked.

"There are some things that can be done." The doctor didn't elaborate. Lillian knew that, with sufficient money (as with the rich), a doctor would often perform a safe abortion, illegal or not. She didn't respond to the doctor's statement. She and Hecky didn't have the kind of money required, and they both wanted children.

The doctor continued, "I cannot impress upon you strongly enough the severity of your heart ailment. A leaking aorta is not to be taken lightly. I don't mean to frighten you, but simply to let you know that it is touch and go for your heart withstanding pregnancy, but the actual trauma of birth could cause your death. You will have to spend the next months in bed."

"If I don't move around," my mother told him, "I feel terrible. I think movement is what keeps my blood pumping through the hole in my heart." If she was frightened, she refused to give in to the doctor's dire prediction. "Mind over matter," she told herself.

On July 9, 1936, she gave birth to my sister, Stephanie. It was necessary in the difficult financial times for both Hecky and Lillian to continue their work. Though Lillian had curtailed her work to a degree during the pregnancy, she now would have to resume it full-time. My parents left New York City and returned to Hartford to live with Harry and Sarah. The grand house on Canterbury Street had been sold shortly after the stock market crash. Harry had bought another house right around the corner at 36 Plainfield Street. This house may not have been as big, but was large enough to accommodate the entire family.

The house was a haven of intrigue for a child with its beautiful wooden floors, which framed colorful Persian rugs. Dark mahogany side tables hosted candy dishes filled with hard candies of all textures and flavors and scrumptious dark chocolates filled with cherries. An austere Victorian-framed couch warmed the room with its maroon color and velvet fabric. The dining room table seemed to open endlessly to seat the whole family for Seders and was roomy enough for us children to slip under when the Seders seemed interminably long. There we could gaze at legs and shoes with endless fascination. The irresistible, yet frightening, attic housed chests filled with old wedding gowns, flapper dresses, high-heeled shoes, and letters written in unfamiliar alphabets. Sweet scents filled Grandma Sarah's room, emanating from the mirrored perfume tray upon which stood an array of bottles and atomizers of different sizes and shapes. In corners and on tabletops stood mysterious looking lamps crafted in iron by Grandpa Harry and lit with red, green, or yellow light bulbs.

. . . .

It wasn't difficult for Hecky and Lillian to become part of Hartford life. Here, too, they gave concerts under the WPA programs, taught violin and piano, and Hecky played with the Bushnell Theater Symphony Orchestra. He had been away from the city long enough for his failed debut to be essentially forgotten in the more immediate concerns of the Depression, and he felt he could start life anew. Their friends, many met through WPA projects and political meetings, included several doctors dedicated to the medical movement and clinics of Drs. William J. and Charles H. Mayo. Drs. Will and Charles initiated group practice as the demands of their surgical practice became too busy for them to handle alone. This new group developed medicine as a cooperative science, utilizing doctors of various specializations under one roof: pediatricians, clinicians, specialists, and laboratory workers. All united for the good of the patient. The doctors believed that "individualism in medicine could no longer exist." Hecky and Lillian agreed with this philosophy and supported this trend in medicine along with their friends, Dr. Herb Schwartz, his psychologist wife Rosalind, psychiatrist Dr. Jack Little, and Dr. Sophie Kliegman, a pioneer woman gynecologist and promoter of family planning and birth control. All of them attended meetings with the Mayo doctors.

Lillian spent many hours at the famous Randall School of Drama accompanying dance and drama improvisation classes. One of the students in these classes was a handsome, talented young man named Ernest Borgnine, who later became known for his many roles in films, especially as Fatso Sergeant Judson in *From Here to Eternity*. Sarah took care of Steffi, as the family came to call her. Harry's company was doing well, in part because so many WPA projects involved construction and necessitated iron and steel, including the building of approximately 650,000 miles of roads, 78,000 bridges, 125,000 buildings, and 700 miles of airport runways.

Food was always on the table at Sarah and Harry's. With his mother's good home cooking, my father seemed to be doing well. But any divergence from a normal eating schedule, too much dairy, or acidic foods and roughage, could provoke days of unstoppable diarrhea or gastritis.

"I can't find anything wrong," commented the doctor Harry took Hecky to, just as all the other doctors Harry had taken him to in the past had said. "He just seems to have a sensitive stomach and must stick to a bland diet, no diversions."

Hecky grew thinner and thinner. What he ate and the amount he ate seemed to make no difference. Not quite one year later, just a few weeks after Hecky's twenty-sixth birthday, the family sat down for dinner. As he lifted a bite of food to his mouth, a stabbing pain jabbed his stomach, and Hecky fell off his chair onto the floor. He looked white as a sheet, and his hands turned cold as ice. An ambulance rushed him to the New Haven General Hospital, part of Yale University. Lillian waited hours, frightened as emergency surgery was performed to find out the cause of Hecky's collapse.

The surgeon discovered a duodenal ulcer. During the delicate operation, the main artery in Hecky's stomach burst. His heartbeat indicated near failure as his blood pressure dropped drastically. The surgeon spoke with urgency to those in the operating room. "I suspect Mr. Krasnow is suffering from a deficiency Vitamin K, necessary for clotting. If we can stop the bleeding you will clearly see why. His intestines are blocked in numerous places, and the flesh has decayed. The patient is dying."

An attendant went out to prepare Lillian for what seemed the inevitable. Inside the operating arena, the surgeon resorted to the only remedy that might hold hope: an untried drug for clotting. Hecky was given an injection of the experimental drug. Several minutes later, to the surgeon's great relief, the bleeding slowed, and the clotting process began. The attending doctors observed the amount of diseased flesh in the small intestine and concluded that the decay must have occurred over several years. The condition looked similar to intestinal tuberculosis.

"I think this is a case for Dr. Burrill Crohn," the head surgeon commented. "We have to work fast now and remove the blockage. It's far beyond repair. We'll send it to Crohn for his study, whether or not the patient survives. I have to remove a good portion of the stomach muscle in order to remove the intestine and then resection it." Sixteen of the thirty-two feet of small intestine were surgically removed and the rest resectioned. Most of Hecky's stomach muscle came out too.

"I am truly amazed that your husband survived," the surgeon told Lillian. "Understand he is dreadfully weakened and will be confined to bed for weeks. He will have to learn how to move without the support of his stomach muscle. We will fit him with a corset, and this will help. We intend to summon Dr. Crohn, a leader in gastrology research, to examine Mr. Krasnow and the diseased intestine we removed."

To everyone's surprise and relief, Hecky pulled through. Weak as he was, his body fought off infection and the effects of the surgery four years before penicillin would be patented and mass-produced. Three months after surgery, he left the hospital to begin a long, difficult recovery at home.

Dr. Burrill B. Crohn examined the removed, diseased intestine. He was noted for his research of inflammatory bowel disease, often mistaken for intestinal tuberculosis. Eleven patients were under his study at the time of my father's operation. Hecky became the twelfth. All had suffered symptoms similar to Hecky's, and all had begun to feel the discomforts sometime in their youth or no later than their mid-30s. The symptoms included frequent attacks of diarrhea, severe abdominal pain, nausea, fever, chills, weakness, involuntary anorexia and its accompanying weight loss caused by the cilia not being able to absorb nutrients for long stretches of time. The disease left all of its victims with totally debilitating pain, blocked, decaying intestine that necessitated removal, and periodic bouts of depression.

"Mr. Krasnow," he informed my father, "the danger of further intestine ceasing to work, including the colon, is a very real possibility. I don't yet know what this disease is, what causes it, and, as of now, it has no cure. I do know that the other 11 of my case studies to date show that stress, as well as certain foods, aggravate the condition. With only 16 feet of small intestine left, you can't afford to lose much more, if any, and you certainly don't want to irritate the colon. Living without one is not pleasant. Hot spices, too much dairy, alcohol, roughage must be ingested with moderation, if at all. Eat more bananas than apples, though cooked apples are okay. Stay away from fried foods. Be careful and sensible about what you eat."

"Dr. Crohn, you mentioned stress. Life can't be totally stress-free." Hecky wondered what work he could do that did not carry with it some stress.

"Whatever you do in your life, how much *constant* stress it places upon you is something you will have to take into consideration. Stress, as I have observed in my patients, is the biggest enemy. It can cause the intestinal tract to constipate or cause diarrhea. It can cause ulcers. It can cause gastritis, even in those who are healthy. Avoid stress."

Dr. Crohn continued with his study of the ailment from which his 12 patients suffered. The numbers grew as the ailment could be separated from intestinal tuberculosis. Years later, this illness was characterized as an actual disease and named Crohn's disease. It is now known to be an autoimmune disease in which the body rejects its own intestines. Careful diet and a stress-free life are still prescribed as necessities for those with this disease and, to date, though treatments have advanced, no cure has been found.

After several weeks in the hospital, my father returned home. My mother worked full-time giving piano lessons and accompanying classes at the Randall School. Sarah cared for my father and Steffi. Sarah, in essence, became Steffi's mother, and Pauline and Sylvia, older sisters. The house at 36 Plainfield Street was home to Steffi, even though after one year, my parents, with the help of Harry, purchased a house that had become available at the foot of Plainfield Street on the corner of Blue Hills Avenue. Keney Park lay only two blocks away. There, without much effort, my father could take Steffi out to play. However, when not otherwise occupied, Steffi spent her days and many nights at Granny and Grandpa's up the hill.

My father was too weak to hold his violin and practice for long periods, and for the first time since he had received the gift of his first real violin at age nine, his present one sat in its case more than under his chin. Over a period of three years, as his strength slowly returned, Steffi would spend time with him while Lillian worked. Steffi was a sprite-like, blond, hazel-eyed little girl who loved to dance around the house making up rhymes and melodies. Hecky delighted in her and her already apparent love of words and music. In an article for the trade papers after the success of "Rudolph," my father spoke about these years with Steffi.

> It all began in 1939 when I rediscovered the wonderfully exciting and uninhibited world of childhood. My three-year-old daughter, Steffi, developed a flair for making up little jingles about all the subjects and objects that seem to fascinate youngsters. With all my musical training I had not as yet composed my first symphony or even a divertimento for three woodwinds and double bass. Here was my chance to put this training to use. I would copy down these jingles, and I would now be a composer. Ten years of advanced composition would at last be put to use. Within a few months, Steffi and I had composed over seventy-five little tunes and we had the time of our lives doing it.

Steffi's inspiration grew beyond just a father-daughter pastime. Hecky gathered all the songs into a folio titled *Happy Time Tunes* and sent these to music publishers. He said in the same article, "It appeared that *Happy Time Tunes* were turning into 'Sad Time Tunes' as the rejection slips came in the mail."

Finally, the director of a growing and popular children's record company called Musicraft called. "I'd like to meet with you, Mr. Krasnow. The songs you sent show a studied and caring understanding of children, what they think about, what they like to hear, and how they like to move around or dance to what they hear."

The meeting resulted in total success. The tunes inspired by Steffi were released on four records produced and directed by Hecky. Musicraft commissioned him to write and produce five more kiddie albums.

Writing and composing occupied his time, lifted his spirits, and decreased the growing boredom of being homebound. The stress and inadequacy he felt as he saw Lillian leave for work every day while no paychecks came to him lessened as each new work he wrote brought in money and, most importantly, a sense of purpose, an outlet for his musical gifts, and much pleasure. The numbers of albums he was hired to create grew. They included Hecky's story adaptations and original music for *Aladdin and His Wonderful Lamp*, *Chicken Licken and The Little Red Hen*, *Peer Gynt and the Trolls*, *Songs and Singing Games*, *The Ugly Duckling*, *The Sorcerer's Apprentice*, *The Story of the Three Bears*, *Songs of America*, *The Nutcracker Suite for Children*, *Hansel and Gretel*, and *Mother Goose*. Columbia and Victor Records also commissioned him to write and produce albums for them including *Rhumpy the Rhino*, which became a long-standing classic of children's fare.

As my father said in the article quoted above, "Though I wasn't aware of it at the time, I was launched on a new career."

CHAPTER 4

A Profession for the Fiddler

. . . .

I n 1939, my father's sister Helen and her husband Phil Eisenberg visited Hartford. Phil was a professor of psychology at
Brooklyn College. Helen, propelled by a combustible combination of ambition and anger at Harry, who firmly believed
a woman's place was in the home, worked and put herself
through college, much to Harry's chagrin. Like Sarah, Helen
was a woman ahead of her times. With three older brothers as
mentors, she followed the masculine example set by Hecky,
Al, and Bob, who were encouraged by Harry to develop their
brains as well as their brawn. With Hecky as her eldest brother
and often caretaker, she experienced manliness with a gentle
refinement. His musical studies instilled a cultural sensitivity
and knowledge that Helen respected and admired. The two were
extremely close siblings from the time of Helen's birth, when
Hecky, often in charge of the younger children, established a
protective relationship with her, especially since she was the
first girl born to Sarah. Later, opposing Harry, he stood up for
her right to attend college. Harry certainly had enough money
to pay for Helen's education. He simply refused and would
not budge from his position. Though always close to them,
Helen was also jealous of her twin sisters, and could not compete with their role as the adorable babies to be doted upon.

At Brooklyn College, Helen met an intelligent, cultured, tender, and kind man in Phil. Phil and Hecky found much in common and quickly became close friends. Helen was pleased, for this only deepened her ongoing, close relationship with Hecky. Lillian adored Phil and felt she had gained a brother in him. For Lillian, Phil became a link that brought her closer to Helen, whom she respected, but the two women had few traits in common. Helen smoked, drank, cursed, and knew how to drive a car well—the antithesis of the image of the perfect housewife of the era. Lillian was a lady, well-mannered, gentle, and nurturing. With all of the losses and close calls she had experienced in her life, she was still the optimist. Even the hole in her heart was always half full, not half empty. Helen harbored a bitter side.

Sarah adored Lillian, and this fueled simmering coals of envy in Helen who, to be one-up with her, let Lillian know that she, Helen, had a college education. The word "intellectual" slammed back and forth between the two women like a ping-pong ball between two paddles. Helen always served the shots. Helen made very clear that the Juilliard degree Lillian had earned could not compare to a college degree. Helen set a pattern for competition in their relationship, including her demands upon Hecky, which were often akin to a mother competing for attention with her son's wife. Fortunately, Phil's presence kept these differences, jealousies, and demands at bay. The four grew extremely close to one another. Peace and friendship, rather than rancor, dominated.

. . . .

During the visit to Hartford, Phil and my father took Steffi to Keney Park. Steffi had just turned three. The two brothers-in-law began a discussion that so absorbed them, they totally forgot about Steffi. This absorption characterized their friendship for years to come, and we would all experience situations resulting from what we called "an acute case of the absent-minded professor syndrome." In Keney Park, Steffi ran off by herself, following a duck behind a cluster of bushes. Her father and uncle were oblivious to her disappearance. Their charge and duty to watch her had evaporated entirely from their minds as they shared views and opinions on a variety of topics from politics to human behavior. Suddenly, Hecky remembered that Steffi was with them. He looked around, realized how far they had walked along the path and cried out, "My god, Phil! Where is Steffi?"

The two reversed their direction and headed back the distance from which they had come. "Steffi, Steffi," each called out frantically.

Several minutes later, they heard a little voice singing, "A little birdie said to me, 'How are you, Stephanie?'"

They ran in the direction of the sound and found Steffi, undaunted, happily sitting behind a bush watching some waddling ducks while singing. Hecky picked her up horrified at the thought that he might have lost her. "Oh, my darling, I'm so sorry. Daddy loves you. Are you okay?"

Steffi, having no idea that anything was wrong, pushed away from his hug and clearly signaled that she wanted to watch the ducks again. Hecky put her down. Steffi continued singing. Her singing triggered a new topic to transport Hecky and Phil into another fascinating world: the song Steffi had been singing and continued to sing.

"It's a simple little song," Phil noted, the psychologist in him taking over. "She created it unaware of the pangs of composition, oblivious of anyone's critical evaluation."

"Children love to sing, Phil," Hecky responded. "Steffi sings all the time, and when her little friends come to visit, they always sing while they play. But, outside of the rhymes children create for themselves, outside of Mother Goose verses and a few modern tunes thrown in, what songs are there for children?"

"Hecky, I don't know. I haven't a clue, but I have an idea. Let's go to the library and see what song collections for kids are available."

The next day, the two went to the library, this time leaving Steffi with less distractible, more reliable caretakers: Sarah and her aunts. Hecky and Phil checked out several anthologies and then went to the music store, where they bought further collections. Some of the titles were misleading, either sounding as they called it, "cutie putie," definitely not like something they'd want a child of theirs to hear. Other titles made the contents sound too stuffy for children. They looked inside each book, and this served to educate them on poorly titled books as well as acquaint them with what music was actually available for young children.

Hecky and Phil brought these books home and called in the neighbors' children. Hecky played and sang while Phil observed and wrote notes. They noticed that many of the songs in the collections did not capture the youngsters' attention and concluded that most writers of children's songs weren't even aware that the songs they wrote did not and would not engage those for whom they were created. Both Hecky and Phil agreed that the songs were written with adult standards, which assumed that if the words appealed to children and the themes were childish enough, kids would like the songs. What my father and Phil's observations showed them is that, if songs were to appeal to children, the children's needs and interests had to be taken into consideration when writing them. Hecky and Phil had a new project: discovering what the needs and interests of children were and writing appropriate material for them.

Phil had to return to New York, but promised to come back to Hartford soon. Hecky, now fully recovered from his medical ordeal, could travel to Brooklyn to visit Phil. In the interim, each would read what other investigators of children's fare had to say. Each committed to forming groups of children in schools, neighborhoods, and community centers to test songs on them, finding out which ones they liked and which they didn't and why. Determined to find the answers, Hecky said, "We'll compare them, analyze them, and find out what makes a good song for children just that—a good song, one they take to."

"Hecky," Phil suggested, "the psychologist in me says that we should set up principles, a hypothesis, and see if it works. The hypothesis will be: if the needs of children are taken into account when writing music for them, they will respond, participate, and, of their own volition, sing the songs."

"Phil," Hecky enthusiastically announced, the composer in him ignited, "I intend to write many new songs and compose music to familiar verses that we know children love."

Hecky did just that. He gained the cooperation of mothers from the synagogue Harry had built, the first Orthodox synagogue in West Hartford. They remained after Sunday school one day and allowed their children to dance and sing as Hecky played songs for them. Hecky worked with

Steffi's pre-kindergarten class. The teacher made his songs part of the Show and Tell session. Hecky began by singing a song called "Hippety-Hop to School," the poem by Elizabeth Daniel and music by Hecky.

> We're off to school now, Hippety-hop,
> At corners we will surely stop;
> To look each way, both near and far,
> And make real sure there isn't a car.
>
> Across the street we'll Hippety-hop,
> But in the schoolyard safe we'll stop;
> "Hello!" to friends and teacher we'll say,
> And then we'll Hippety-hop out to play.

The first time the children heard the song and the words "Hippety-hop," they immediately turned into a room full of bunnies. On the words "Hello, to friends and teacher we'll say," they started waving hello. One child grabbed the hand of another standing nearby, and started shaking his hand. On the third singing of these two simple verses, some in the classroom turned into cars, steering imaginary wheels and making engine sounds when they heard the word "car." There was less constant hopping and more gesturing, such as putting hands on the forehead and bending to look left and right after the lines, "At corners we'll stop to look each way." When the song was repeated at the end of the session, a few children sang the "hippety-hop" at the end of the fist line of each verse.

They squealed with giggles at this song, poem by Edward Lear, and music by Hecky.

> I was once an apple pie
> Pidy,
> Widy,
> Tidy,
> Pidy,
> Nice insidey,
> Apple pie.

Steffi's teacher sent a note home that for the rest of the morning the children laughed each time they repeated (with great frequency) the words "pidy, widy, tidy apple pie."

One song based upon a poem by Rose Fyleman brought tears to one little child, who, through his sniffles, cried, "I don't want to hear it. I'm afraid of mice."

I think mice are nice—
Their tails are long,
Their faces small,
They haven't any chins at all.

Their ears are pink,
Their teeth are white,
They run about the house at night.

They nibble things they shouldn't touch,
And no one seems to like them much.
I think mice are nice.

But in spite of some tears, this song brought eager responses from several children, who all called out at once telling personal mouse tales until told by the teacher to raise their hands and they would be called upon in turn.

"I saw a mouse running across the floor in our kitchen. I screamed real loud. He scared me, but mommy said he wouldn't hurt me."

"I have a pet mouse. His name is Squeaky and he really, really squeaks."

"My daddy put out something called a trap to catch a mouse 'cause there's so many mouses in our basement."

"I can sing three blind mice, three blind mice, see how they run. See how they run. . . ."

Hecky and Lillian organized a "Sing a Song" party for Steffi's neighborhood friends. Hecky repeated the songs sung at the synagogue and school at the party. Again, the responses to the songs were participatory and enthusiastic. At the party, a theme prevailed prompted by the song "The Train Engine." With the author unknown, Hecky took poetic license and adapted the words as well as writing the melody.

> Chooker, chooker, chooker, chooker,
> Chooker, chooker, chooker, chooker,
> Hear the engine puff, engine, puff, engine, puff,
> Hear the engine puff, engine puff chooker choo.

Other verses included, "Toot, toot, hear the whistle blow, ding-dong, hear the bell ring, all aboard, hear the trainman shout." The house turned into a veritable train as the children puffed, rang, and chooker-chooed for the duration of the party. Hecky and Phil's tests were proving their point. Some songs obviously didn't have the right ingredients for success. In response, the children's noise had nothing to do with the words and melodies they were hearing, and their attention definitely strayed as Johnny kicked Jimmy and Susie got up to go play in the dollhouse. These were crossed off the list of appropriate and engaging songs.

The groups of children upon which the material was tested clearly indicated that when the songs spoke to their interests—rhythmical, repetitive sounds and/or topics of interest and concern for them, the children responded by moving to the sounds with joy and abandon. They listened intently and soon repeated what they'd heard, even told about related incidents they'd experienced, as with the song about mice. Hecky and Phil's observations demonstrated that young children learn and remember through movement, not just through listening. They noted that when a young child moves around while hearing a song, this is not a rebellious act of poor behavior. Instead, the child is actually learning through this physical response. In this manner, the child both internalizes what he or she hears and simultaneously develops coordination skills.

. . . .

Over a couple of years, Phil and Hecky compiled their own collection of songs into a book called *Little Folks Book of Song and Verse.* Phil wrote the introduction and notes. Hecky credited his biggest inspiration—Steffi.

"If Stephanie and the other children loved the songs, then many more children should also love them. For that reason, we made this book, hoping that other children would sing them, and through this experience learn to love the greater works of music as they grew older."

The very first song in the book was a song my father had written for Steffi during his recuperation.

Pigga Wigga, Pigga Wigga,
Let us dance the Jigga Migga.
Clap your hands—run, run, run;
Clap your hands—run, run, run.
Pigga Wigga, Pigga Wigga
Let us dance the Jigga Migga.

The book drew the attention of newspaper reporters, and Steffi was photographed at the piano with Hecky. The songs from the book were recorded for Musicraft Records. Teachers used the book for classroom teaching. At this time, books and records were sold separately, not as packages together.

Children's records were increasing in popularity and growing in number. They proved to be an enriching source of entertainment for youngsters. Simple toys, books, radio, live performance, and occasional films were the only source of media entertainment available to children. The audio experience prevailed as technology was pushing records into the forefront.

In the '40s and into the mid-'50s, children were considered those from ages three through sixteen. The vast differences in the ages of children were, of course, taken into account in the entertainment provided for them. At each level, material, always with an educational element, was gleaned from folk and fairy tales, classic picture books, and series published for each age group. Children's record companies with names like Young People's Records and Golden Records were sprouting up across the nation. Major record companies including RCA Victor, Mercury,

Capital, and Columbia were growing interested in producing children's fare. Hecky and Phil, now done with their collection of songs, began researching records available for children. As they had studied what appealed to the very young child, they now investigated what interested children at each new stage of development on up into their teens. Their research continued for several years with another book brewing in the back of their minds: one that would educate parents and guide them in purchasing records for their children.

．　．　．　．　．　．　．　．　．　．　．

Hecky was experiencing relatively good health, give and take a bout of pain and diarrhea. Harry felt it was time for his son to get back to full-time work, that Lillian could not forever be the stable source of income. Hecky agreed, but still wished to pursue the path of music. "Pa, I need a little more time. I believe the things I am doing—writing, performing with some orchestras, recording for Musicraft, teaching violin—all of this will come together and provide the necessary income."

"Hecky, a man earns the family's basic bread. The life of a musician can't be trusted to put bread on the table consistently, or at least not the same amount of bread." Look at Steffi. She needs her mother," Harry advised.

If Steffi could have expressed her views at her young age, she would have been perfectly happy to stay under Sarah's wings and the additional ones of her aunts and their many doting friends. Thirty-six Plainfield Street was her home. Lillian, forced by circumstances to be the family's breadwinner since Steffi's birth, had grown used to her independence and bringing in the paychecks. It gave her a sense of accomplishment known to few women of her era.

Harry continued to see things his way: for Hecky to play with a symphony orchestra periodically and write songs for children was not a profession. Harry had money. He insisted that he open a hardware store with Hecky as manager. But Hecky had never been allowed to handle tools, and HK Hardware Store soon closed for lack of customers. It was then transformed into HK Haberdashery. Hecky's retail skills proved equally lacking. Sarah was fed up with Harry's well-intentioned plans for Hecky, and she had no idea what her son would do to make a living for the rest of his life.

"*Genug iz genug!*" My grandmother announced emphatically as she entered the house of her Italian friends, the Chalellias, just around the corner on Canterbury Street. When distressed, my grandmother reverted to expressing her distress in Yiddish. "*Genug iz Genug!* Enough is enough!" my grandmother's tongue was in full swing. "*Ikh darf es vi a lung un leber ahfen noz!*" (I need it like a lung and liver on my nose!)

"Sarah, Sarah," Mrs. Chalellia said, while indicating that my grandmother should sit down in a chair and she'd get her a cup of tea. Sarah's sister Helen, also visiting with her daughter Simmy, beckoned Sarah to sit next to her, which she did.

"Pa says, 'Hecky, you come be the bookkeeper at National Iron Works, your Pa's own business.' What does Hecky know from iron and steel? He knows violins! If the company books could be written with a bow and the numbers kept in musical notes, Hecky could do the books!

"Pa sets him up in the hardware business. What does Hecky know from hardware? From the time he picked up the violin, his precious fingers could not be hurt. He never cut his own bread for Pa feared he'd cut his finger with the knife. Tools? Hecky should know tools? A fiddler selling hardware?

"Clothes? *Mayn* Hecky learned early to dress for his concerts like a *Choshever mentsh*, a man with worth and dignity. So, Harry says, 'Sarah, forget the hardware. Forget the books. We'll put Hecky up in a haberdashery. Our Hecky, he'll do well at it.'

"'Hecky will do well,' my eye! If he could fit customers with violin strings and rosin their bow ties like he rosins his bow, he would do well. But no. *Mayn Hecky iz ein mensch mit asakh zmires, un veynik kneydlekh*, a good man of many songs, but few dumplings."

"Don't worry, Sarah." Helen said. "*Der gleichster veg iz ful mit shtainer*. The smoothest way is sometimes full of stones. Your Hecky will find his way."

"Hecky doesn't have to find his way," she looked at Mrs. Chalellia, Helen, and Simmy, this time with an impish look in her eyes and the ends of her lips turning upward as though breaking into a laugh. "The father takes care of his son. That's okay. Harry and me?" she said. "We know just what we should do. As a matter of fact, we will do a *mitzvah*, a good deed, a *very* good deed. We'll put Hecky up in the funeral business. You'll see! People will stop dying!"

. . . .

If my grandparents had put my father into the funeral business and people had stopped dying, the world would have been a much happier place. Millions died as World War II broke out. Harry's National Iron Works went into full round-the-clock production as the war necessitated the manufacture of ammunitions. Al and Bob were both working for their father, and now, Hecky, wanting to make his contribution to the war effort and unable, due to his physical condition, to join the services, went to work alongside his brothers and father.

During the war, Hecky served as Harry's driver and his assistant, answering phones, taking orders, and delivering supplies. Much of the ammunition was produced in New London, Connecticut, and Harry was given gas rations to travel there and anywhere else the business called for.

In New London and surrounding areas, large two- and three-story homes had been built prior to the war and now stood unsold as people didn't want to live in them with no way to get around. The rustic looking houses were sided with large, brown, rough wooden shingles and topped with gray slate shingles on the roofs. Many had waterfront footage facing the Long Island Sound. Harry wanted a home where his family could gather, particularly during the spring and summer months. It was then, the house in Old Saybrook, Connecticut, along with 100 yards (including beachfront and extending into the water itself), was purchased for a mere $7,000: the house at which the entire family would gather each summer; the house that we all felt was home, the core and essence of the Krasnows, the umbilical cord to which we were all irrevocably attached.

Not long after the bombing of Pearl Harbor, Lillian became pregnant. Again, the doctor warned her of the danger, particularly because another pregnancy would add to the strain that the first had caused upon her heart. "Mrs. Krasnow," he admonished, "you must remember that it is not only your living daughter that you bore, but another child you lost to a stillbirth after six months. We can take measures. Your life is in danger."

My mother was incorrigible. "Mind over matter," she told herself. "I fooled them twice, and I'll fool them again!" During this pregnancy, she did remain at home. Hecky was earning a steady salary working for his father.

I was born on December 8, 1942, at 7:30 A.M. wartime, which was actually daylight savings time. My father was so agitated when my mother went into labor, hoping the strain of the birth would not leave him without his beloved wife, that he threw his pajamas into the toilet, rather than the hamper. This would not have been so horrible, except that he flushed the toilet, left the bathroom, took my mother to the hospital, and later, returned to a flood running down the stairs to the first floor. My birth necessitated a forceps delivery, which pulled my head into the shape of a dunce cap. Grandma Sarah feared I would be a *meeskite*, so ugly that I'd spend my life scaring people. Fortunately, my head resumed a human shape, and my grandmother's anxiety subsided.

Helen had given birth to a baby girl, my cousin Karen Eisenberg, only six weeks earlier. Our near mutual births brought Helen and my mother closer as visits increased, and Karen and I were virtually raised as twins, sharing the same carriage, playpen, clothes, and spending much time together. We grew up from birth not knowing life without each other, like conjoined twins attached at the soul. My father and Phil's relationship was cemented by the sharing of their baby daughters' lives. Though the war effort occupied more time than their creative efforts during the first few years of Karen's and my lives, their collaboration continued. As the war ended, Phil and Hecky were engaged in their research with full vigor again. The beach house in Saybrook gave them the opportunity during summers to spend weekends together, as the uncles and fathers came to spend their Saturdays and Sundays off from work.

The two were once again lost in their own world of ever-blossoming creativity.

They continued investigating which songs, music, and stories appealed to children of varying ages. They studied the development of children's ability to create mental pictures as their test groups listened to music and stories. They observed how this increasing ability leads to the understanding of more abstract tales and complex songs. Phil offered his psychological expertise while my father researched the responses of different age groups to classic fairy tales, books, and a variety of songs and musical compositions. They gathered records, studied their effects upon children, and kept a log of the sales of records and which records were purchased by which age groups. They listened to all of these records and reviewed them, categorizing which level of child development they were appropriate for, or if they were appropriate at all. They intended to put all of their findings together in their book, which they titled *A Guide to Children's Records*.

By this point, Phil and Helen had a second daughter, Jean. My mother now remained at home tending to our house and to Steffi and me. With the war over in 1945, Harry once again was concerned about finding a stable future for Hecky. Working with Phil on a potentially publishable book would not put food on the table. Harry opened the haberdashery store again. My father had shown *some* ability in this field, certainly more than in the hardware business, and Harry believed that with Lillian now at home full-time, Hecky would put his nose to the grindstone and make a go of it. The store hours would still allow him sufficient time to practice his violin, to give an occasional concert, and to continue his periodic engagements with the Bushnell Theatre Orchestra when a musical, ballet, or opera was presented.

During this time, Bubbe Rose had a stroke. I moved into Steffi's room so my mother could take care of Bubbe in my room. She died there. The stain on the sheets in the shape of my Bubbe and the horror of the undertakers carrying her out of my room and our house in a body bag gave me nightmares for a long time to come. A few weeks earlier, my dog, Dropsy, named for his big, drooping ears, died of edema and had been carried out by the Humane Society in a bag. Bubbe's death was my first real intimation that we humans, like our pet dogs, are mortal. A new bed did not make my sleep at night any more peaceful. I was glad when my father told me we were moving to New York.

. . . .

Crown Publishers published *A Guide to Children's Records* in 1948. A few months after its release, my father received a call from Columbia Records. The executives at Columbia had read the book and were duly impressed. They offered Hecky the position of artists and repertoire man, who was in charge of selecting what material would be recorded for children and which artists would record it. They wanted him to establish a children's record and education department and build a large catalogue of records for children of all ages. They made it clear that the big record companies saw a huge future for kid-disks with the ever-growing technology in vinyl and plastic, and hence in record manufacturing.

"Hecky," Vice President Goddard Lieberson said, "*A Guide to Children's Records* proves to us that you are definitely the most knowledgeable person in the field. Your musical training both with Leopold Auer and at Juilliard, and your impressive catalogue with Musicraft Records can only enhance your ability to produce the quality products that we wish to sell."

The family, including Helen and Phil, who had traveled to Hartford from Brooklyn, gathered around the table at Harry and Sarah's house. The mood was celebratory. Harry let Hecky know how very happy and proud he was about this job offer. The mountain peak Hecky had failed to reach in his violin debut still challenged him. He hoped in his new position that he could prove to Harry—and to himself—that he could succeed on his own, and through music, that all those years of training were not for naught.

The family discussed how the move to New York would be made. Phil and Hecky intended to continue their successful collaboration, focusing on creating songs and albums that Hecky could record at Columbia. Why live apart? Financially it would make sense for the two families to live in the same apartment or dwelling. The search began. A three-family house was located for sale on Douglas Avenue and

Trausneck Place in North Yonkers. It was close enough to the Yonkers railway station for Hecky and Phil to take the train into New York City each day. Our family could live on the first floor, Helen and Phil on the second and twin Sylvia, now married and pregnant, on the third floor with her husband, Bernie Passel. When the Passels moved in a few years, as they knew Bernie's job would demand, the third floor could be rented as a further source of income.

One major problem remained: what to do with Steffi. Steffi was 12. She had known nothing but Hartford all her life. Her friends were there, and she had another year of junior high until she would enter high school. She didn't want to leave everything she knew behind, and, after much discussion, my parents felt that she shouldn't be forced to leave so abruptly. The compromise was made that she would remain living with Harry and Sarah, finish junior high, and make a wholly new start, coming to Yonkers when she began high school. This decision was the hardest part for my father in accepting his new job.

The irony of leaving Steffi behind did not give his thoughts rest in these decisive moments. Were it not for his illness and his years of recuperation with Steffi, her inspiration, and the catalyst she proved to be in Hecky's and Phil's collaboration, Hecky would not be venturing into this new job in the world of children's records. He would never forget the sound of the song he'd heard Steffi sing in Keney Park in the spring of 1939: *A little birdie said to me, "How are you, Stephanie?"*

CHAPTER 5

Ballads and Baseball

he hills of North Yonkers are very steep, and our tall,
three-story white house with its green shutters stood
on a near-vertical incline. The back and front entrances
to the house were positioned on a hill called Trausneck Place,
the back door at the top of the hill, the front door towards
the bottom. The houses in our neighborhood were carved into
the New York side of the Palisades. The neighbors across from
our garage had to maneuver their car up and down a gravel
and dirt driveway, a piece of a cliff that descended into wild
brush, trees, and jagged rocks. Stick shifts and no power steering developed very skillful drivers.

Our driveway lay at the bottom of our house with the
garage and a large basement situated under our living room,
which faced the intersecting street called Douglas Avenue. The
road ran westward for approximately one mile downhill from
our driveway. At its foot, Douglas met Broadway, where one
had to go right or left. Broadway ran southward from our little
town uphill all the way into downtown Yonkers. At Broadway
and Douglas, we could board the Number 2 bus to ride to
the Yonkers library, the train station, a clothing and jewelry
store, and Woolworth's five-and-dime. Here we bought everything
from toys to bathroom curtains, yarn, school supplies, Keds
sneakers, and shirts and shorts for the summer, all well-made
items stamped with the "Made in America" and "Union" labels.
My weekly dollar allowance enabled me to purchase yo-yos,

candy, Cracker Jacks, pens, pencils, and marbles, even jewelry to play dress-up.

Broadway flattened where it met Douglas Avenue and where our cozy local neighborhood mom-and-pop stores stood: Robbins Pharmacy, where Joe Robbin's son Michael delivered prescriptions when anyone in the neighborhood was ill; Dugan's News Store, where we bought candy bars, *Superman, Archie,* and *Classic* comics; the shoemaker, to whom we brought saddle shoes that he transformed into orthopedic shoes for me; the barber, with his red-and-white candy-striped pole; and one small but adequate supermarket, Gristedes, which housed a fresh butcher and seafood shop.

One block north of Douglas, another hill began, Roberts Avenue, which rose steeply eastward and proved a strain for any transmission, automatic or shift. Going westward, Roberts Avenue remained flat, and around the corner in this direction lay our elementary school, P.S. 16, a small red brick building that stood on a sunny, grassy hill and was reachable by climbing about 50 white concrete stairs. Across from P.S. 16 stood a brown wooden Catholic church, which the majority of P.S. 16 students hurried to for catechism every Wednesday when the church bells began ringing as soon as school let out. Daily Karen and I, and later Jean, walked to and from school, building our muscle strength walking up Roberts Avenue to be with our school chums, then cut across where Bellevue Avenue intersected and veered to the south, leading to Trausneck Place after a series of S-like curves.

The Trausneck Place hill proved an excellent training ground for Karen and me. Here, we learned the art of expert roller-skating on our steel skates, which we strapped onto our shoes and adjusted with metal keys as our shoe sizes grew. The speedy, ball-bearing wheels on these skates allowed us to roll fast and as smoothly as though we were sliding on ice. We perfected our skills as trick bike-riders, even riding these two-wheeled-Schwinn, no-gears "horses" sidesaddle. We learned the ins and outs of the alert life of traffic cops as one or the other of us, or a friend, would of necessity stand at the bottom of the hill and warn of oncoming traffic or signal that the coast was clear.

The first thing we had to learn, however, was that this was not the melting pot that Hartford was, made up of our grandparents and other immigrants of varying ethnicities. Ethnicity now took second place to the pervading religious identification of Christianity. We children were second generation from our immigrant grandparents. North Yonkers housed children of Polish, Irish, Lithuanian, Italian, and other descents. The unifying factor among the people was twofold: they were born and raised Americans, and they were Christian. Holocaust or not, anti-Semitism still prevailed, along with very definite stereotypical images of who and what Jews were.

World War II had ended a short four years prior to our move. Though the Catholics and Protestants surrounding us had their own disagreements among one another, they unanimously viewed us as heathens bound for hell unless, of course, we converted. We children heard whispers we had not heard before. "They're Jews. They don't believe that Christ is our Lord." The Engles, the brave Jewish family first to move to North Yonkers, resided in their home diagonally across from ours on Trausneck Place. They advised, "Like our son Richard, if your children do well in school, which I'm sure they will, they'll be respected. The teachers will see to that. They favor intelligent students." From an early age, we learned that intelligence was a characteristic most often attributed to the Jews, one which caused respect accompanied by resentment. Since neither the Engles nor we were the stereotypical rich bankers, moneylenders, landlords, pickle vendors, or Zionists—nor did we attend synagogue each Saturday or wear long black coats and hats—we were somewhat of an enigma to our neighbors.

"Be proud of who and what you are," our parents told us when Karen and I first set off to attend kindergarten at P.S. 16. We would hear this many times in various incantations, as we heard the word "kike" and were called "Christ killers" by our peers, who told us frequently and with vivid imagery of how *we* nailed the Son of God to the cross, that *we* had killed Jesus. We had no idea why we were accused of killing Jesus. Frankly, we knew little about Jesus at our young age. We learned early to stand up for ourselves, for others, and to respect the beliefs and differences among the people of our neighborhood and the world. Imbued by my parents with FDR's message, "You have nothing to fear but fear itself," I'd set off to school each day unafraid to speak out about the rights and wrongs of whatever incidents came my way.

．．．．．．．．．．．

While we were acclimating to our new home and life, my father and Goddard Lieberson were engaged in their battle over the controversial "Rudolph." These two also disagreed about who should and should not sing on recordings for kids. Perhaps it was my father's classical music training that inspired his belief that children, while listening to lyrics that related to their needs and interests, should hear songs sung by artists whose voices and phrasing would elevate their listening skills and whose manner would not be that of singing "down" to them. Lieberson felt that parents would buy records with artists who performed solely for kids: clowns, puppeteers, and magicians. "Hecky, why would a parent buy a record for a child by someone they associate with music for grown-ups?"

"Precisely, Goddard, because the parents enjoy the singers they hear and know. They like to share with their children and would much rather listen to a familiar, good voice. It will entice them to listen too, and, of course, to buy the records. What you know is what you get and it is comfortable because you know what you are getting."

Goddard Lieberson could not refute my father's thinking. He was also fully aware, to quote Ted Wallerstein, Columbia's president, that the company was "about as bad in the children's field as it is possible to be." He knew that kid-disks represented a considerable percentage of the total record business of the country and were growing rapidly in popularity as the main source of entertainment for youth. Columbia had to get its share of this business. He remembered Wallerstein's words, "Mr. Krasnow is highly capable of putting us where we want to be. To do this, if he has the ability described, he must have a free hand and he must first spend our money, in these very tough times, only on the items which he thinks can very quickly get us a big market."

Though everyone at Columbia knew that Wallerstein was nearing retirement, he was still very much in command. Again, Lieberson found himself having to let go of his own opinions about who should or should not record for children and give way to this newcomer, Hecky Krasnow. As he saw it, Hecky would either bring the company to victory or even greater loss. "'Rudolph,' Gene Autry, and now Burl Ives?" Lieberson found himself saying one more time, "Okay, Hecky, do what you think is best, but I just don't see it your way."

. . . .

Hecky could hear the gentle, rich tenor voice of Burl Ives appealing to a child's fantasy while reassuring the child at the same time. The folk songs he sang were often filled with tales of animals that enchanted children: quacking ducks, sly foxes, trickster monkeys, helpful whales, and innocent frogs. *Animal Fair*, he thought, what a great title for an album by Ives. And the man looked like a gentle giant. "Rudolph" wouldn't be recorded until summer or released until just before Christmas. Animals were a year-round topic.

As for the parents, how could they resist buying a record with the name Burl Ives on the record jacket? Ives had appeared in the 1938 musical *The Boys from Syracuse*. The whole nation had heard the folk songs he popularized on his CBS radio program, *The Wayfaring Stranger*. His songs were sung around campfires and in schools, songs with titles like "Big Rock Candy Mountain," "Blue-Tailed Fly," and "I Know an Old Lady Who Swallowed a Fly." He'd performed at the Village Vanguard, in concerts with famed folk singers Pete Seeger and Josh White. His songs appealed to all ages.

Burl agreed to make the album. He had been recording for other record companies, including Decca. He liked the idea of recording for children and accepted the contract my father offered him with Columbia. My father produced and recorded the *Animal Fair* session. My mother attended. That evening, we sat around the dinner table sharing, as we always did, what happened to each of us during the course of the day.

"Juddie," my father said, "You will love the songs I recorded today, and one of these days you will meet Mr. Ives. Burl is a huge man with a pointed beard and pleasant voice. If his hair and beard were white, you would think he is Santa Claus. He is sweet and jolly."

"I liked his wife," my mother volunteered. "She's his business manager and she's an accomplished musician too. She sang along in one of the songs. What's it called, honey—'Preacher Caught a Goose'?"

"Close, honey." My mother was the second original Mrs. Malaprop, but always on track with her mix-ups. "It starts with 'Preacher went a-hunting . . . He went hunting for a gray goose.' The title is 'The Gray Goose.' Juddie, you've heard it sung by Huddie Ledbetter, you know, the folk singer called Leadbelly, the one I told you had been in prison for a long, long time and was later released and recognized for his amazing 12-string guitar playing and the work songs he sang, like "Pick a Bale of Cotton." He wrote "Goodnight, Irene.""

"I love that song. Does Burl Ives sing songs by Leadbelly?"

"Burl sings all kinds of folk songs."

"I feel like we've known Burl and Helen Ives forever," my mother said with a happy sigh. She loved people and was always thrilled to make new friends. "It seems that the Iveses and we like the same music, plays, share much the same political views and, what can I say—we just got along so well in those short few hours. I really had a good talk with Helen Ives. I like her. And what a cultured gentleman Burl is."

"So, you are now friends," I commented.

"Instant ones," my mother replied. "I miss Steffi, and Ma and Pa, and Hartford, but I'm beginning to like it here. I like your job at Columbia, honey."

"So do I, Dad. It's exciting. Can I be excused to go upstairs and play with Karen?"

. . . .

About a week after the recording of *Animal Fair*, my father brought home a test pressing of the album, a shiny black vinyl disk that he could listen to and make sure the recording was as he wished it to be and, as always, to share with my mom and me. I heard Burl Ives's melodic tenor voice, well-played, simple guitar accompaniment, and words and melodies that painted vivid pictures in my mind and prompted me to express them by dancing.

"It works," my father said. With a tone of glee he turned to my mother, "Honey, look how our Juddie is inspired to dance!"

He was right. I couldn't stop moving. Each song prompted me to act it out. I hunted the gray goose, played dead like the mouse in "The Tailor and the Mouse," displayed my pitifully long ears in "The Rabbit," rocked an imaginary baby to the sweet, whimsical sound of "Buckeye Jim." I listened to that test pressing over and over, and within a week, I was singing the songs, "The sow took the measles, and she died in the spring. . . ." Karen joined me, and the two of us danced and sang the entirety of *Animal Fair*, Karen, with her naturally lyrical soprano voice, singing sweet harmony over my alto, expressive, husky renditions.

When the album was released, other children across the country—and their parents—responded with the same enthusiasm. The album made the top of the charts in *Billboard* and *Variety*. Columbia had a big seller with Burl Ives. As for me—and who knows for how many other children—*Animal Fair* made me yearn to play the guitar. I held an imaginary instrument and plucked its strings of air as I sang,

Mr. Rabbit, Mr. Rabbit, your ears are mighty long.
Yes, kind sir, they're put on wrong.
Every little soul must shine, shine.
Every little soul must shine, shine, shine.

I brought the album to school. My teacher, Miss McKenna played it for the class. Like a tongue-twister contest, the class tried to sing as fast as Burl,

There was a tailor had a mouse. Hi diddle um come feedle.
They lived together in one house. Hi diddle um come feedle.
Hi diddle um come tarum tantrum through the town of Ramsey,
Hi diddle um come fiddle dee dee, Hi diddle um come feedle.

My father's imagination had further been captured by a quintet of one female singer and four males, a quintet of great fame and appeal: the Modernaires. Why not have them record an album? They, like Burl Ives, would certainly entice the purchase of a children's record. The Modernaires had helped bandleader Glenn Miller become a success with their hit renditions, sung with superbly blended, non-vibrato-style, tight-sounding five-part harmony. Songs like "Chattanooga Choo Choo," "Don't Sit Under the Apple Tree," and "Moonlight Cocktail" were just a few of the songs ingrained in the listening minds and hearts of the American public and in Europe, too, as they had entertained troops during World War II. They sang with many of the popular big bands of the era and were heard on the leading radio shows of the day. The Modernaires would certainly bring attention to the Columbia children's catalog.

A potential project sat upon Hecky's desk. Its title was *The Glooby Game*, script and lyrics written by Peggy Aylsworth and music composed and arranged by Glenn Osser. It called for a girl and four male voices. The script's content included all the criteria Hecky and Phil had proposed in their book: listening, action, entertaining dialogue and songs with good lessons to be learned, mental images to be formed, and the imagination to be stretched. The title alone caught Hecky's fancy. What child wouldn't love to say the word "glooby," or be intrigued by a game in which grown-ups in your neighborhood entertain you by pretending to be someone you ask them to be? This would be perfect material for the Modernaires, who agreed to record it.

On the album, Paula Kelly, female vocalist of the Modernaires, takes a walk through the neighborhood meeting the postman, the milkman, the local cop, and the grocer. She asks the mailman to become a clown. He consents and makes her laugh while singing a song about making people happy and what fun it is to be silly sometimes. The milkman agrees to be a cowboy and, in a cowboy drawl, he invites the curious girl to ride out to the open prairie with him on imaginary horses. He sings about herding all the cows that give us milk, which the milkman delivers to each home in quart bottles that jingle like a song. The neighborhood cop walks the girl across the street as the two sing of crossing when the light is green and waiting when it's red. Turning into a magician, the cop spins a musical yarn of fairy folk, gloomies, goobies, and bobolinks, a song which he reminds the girl she can sing whenever she wants to travel to the world of make-believe. The grocer sees her eyeing the licorice sticks and offers her one. He becomes Santa Claus and sings, "If I have two, and you have none, there's always one to spare: so share, share, share."

Listening to this album today, one hears the future sounds of *Mr. Rogers' Neighborhood*: the welcoming ambience and the kind respectful tone that Fred Rogers and all the characters on his program used in speaking to children. Through its content and the development of listening skills, the album encouraged what, 20 years later, *Sesame Street* with its staff of educators and psychologists would attempt to do through the medium of television. Children watching *Sesame Street* absorb already-made images dancing across the screen. In contrast, the audio experience of listening to records developed mental skills through which the child created his or her own images, a skill that goes hand in hand with learning to read. As Hecky emphasized in *A Guide to Children's Records*, children from infancy through the teen years gradually develop the ability to form ever-more-complex mental images. It is a growth process that ultimately results in creating one's own pictures of characters and scenes, making reading an individual imaginative visual experience. Listening is essential to this development. When it was released at the end of August 1949, *The Glooby Game* was recommended as outstanding fare for children and reached the top of the charts.

. . . .

I had heard my parents talk about Jackie Robinson since I was three years old. Robinson was discussed with such import that I sensed this was a famous person who was changing things that needed changing. By the time I was six and a half, I knew who Jackie Robinson was and that he had risked his life so that blacks could play in baseball's major leagues. I had been to Ebbetts Field and listened to innumerable baseball games on the radio. I heard my parents cheering for the Brooklyn Dodgers and with great enthusiasm for Jackie Robinson and another player named Pee Wee Reese. When I asked questions about these two, I was told how black baseball players could only play in the Negro League until a man named Branch Ricky, general manager of the Brooklyn Dodgers, hired Robinson. First, he was sent to Canada to play with the International League. There, spectators were thrilled with his amazing baseball talent. The frequently used saying "quicker than Jack Robinson," my parents informed me, had been an old English saying that now was associated with Jackie Robinson because of his speed and ability to steal bases. Branch Ricky, realizing that Robinson was a baseball gold mine, defied all racial odds and signed him up to play with the National League right here in the U.S. However, Robinson had to sign a contract that for two years required him to remain silent in the face of the racial taunts, which he was sure to receive. One of his favorite quotes after this two-year moratorium was, "I'm not concerned with your liking or disliking me. . . . All I ask is that you respect me as a human being."

My parents explained to me how this courageous man had to withstand death threats and bear the indignity of segregation when he traveled with his team. They told me that Jackie Robinson was an educated man and a patriotic one who had fought with the army in WWII. I learned about court-martials when my parents told me the story about Jackie Robinson defying illegal segregation on an army bus and how he faced a court-martial as a result. My mother and father pointed out how resistance to Robinson slowly dwindled as he showed his incredible prowess on the ball field and how his success encouraged integration in pro football, basketball, and tennis. His nonviolent response to the taunts, jeers, and threats gave others the courage to respond similarly and to fight for the rights of blacks in this manner throughout the country. I felt great admiration for Dodgers teammate Pee Wee Reese (who had been raised in segregated Louisville, Kentucky) when I heard how he put his arm around his black friend when fans hurled insults at Robinson nonstop from the stands for three hours. Reese, unwavering, withstood insults for befriending and defending Robinson. Such behavior unified the Dodgers, who ultimately rallied around their black teammate.

My father loved baseball. He knew the entire nation delighted in the sport and how youngsters everywhere dreamed of growing up to make a name for themselves as master batters, pitchers, catchers, and fielders.

Tapping into the nation's preferred pastime of baseball, he initiated a series of recordings to add to the Columbia catalog, *Baseball Tips from the Stars*. Players, including Yogi Berra and Phil Rizzuto, through situations in a story, give tips to youths about playing the game. The series would begin with the two controversial, respected, and beloved players, Jackie Robinson and Pee Wee Reese. They would record the story of *Slugger at the Bat*. The date of the recording was set for July 19, 1949.

Like my parents, I was a baseball fan. I viewed these two players as being in the same category as Abraham Lincoln. Earl Robinson's *Ballad for Americans* was frequently played upon the phonograph in our house. From it, the opening lines of the Gettysburg Address were already implanted in my mind: "Fourscore and seven years ago our fathers brought forth on this continent a new nation, conceived in liberty and dedicated to the proposition that all men are created equal." I insisted that I be allowed to attend the recording of *Slugger at the Bat*, even if it meant coming home for a few days from Grandma and Grandpa's beach house. I'd leave Karen, collecting crabs, and floating in the big tubes made from inner tires, in order to meet history. That's the way I viewed Jackie Robinson and Pee Wee Reese. They were living history.

My father didn't object. In fact, he said, "Juddie, I'm pleased and proud that you feel so strongly about this. There's a lot of work to do in this world to make it what it should be. You and Mother can take the train into New York, and we will take it back to Ma and Pa's for the weekend with Uncle Phil, just like Phil and I do each weekend."

. . . .

Grandpa Harry drove my mother and me to the train. After a few hours, we arrived in New York. My father met us, and we all boarded the train to Yonkers to get a good night's sleep before the recording session the next day.

Going to New York the next morning, we sat enveloped in smoke from the pipes, cigars, and cigarettes in the mouths of men absorbed in newspapers or documents pulled out of leather briefcases. So this was how my father began each working day. While an unfiltered

Chesterfield hung from his mouth, he pulled the script out of his brown briefcase and made marks on it as my mother and I talked. I was beside myself with excitement and repeated this fact to my mother innumerable times as the train chugged along. I could feel my parents' excitement too. Today was more than just a recording. We were meeting our two favorite Dodgers.

Taking a taxi from the station, we arrived at the studio on 30th Street and Third Avenue, one block from the historic Little Church on the Corner located at 29th and Third. This church, formed in the year 1848, was called the Church of the Transfiguration. Informally, it became known by its other name. It was one of the first Anglo-Catholic parishes of the Episcopal Church in New York and had been a station for the Underground Railroad and a refuge for runaway slaves during the Civil War. Recording this session so close to a historic site of significant refuge for blacks seemed most appropriate.

The custodian had already opened the studio when we arrived. My father set up the board and instructed the attendant as to where to place the microphones and music stands. The sound effects man, an energetic, jolly man (sound effects men, I noticed, seemed to be energetic and jolly) tested various gadgets for appropriate sounds.

I kept looking at the studio clock in eager anticipation of the entrance of the two ball players. My heart pounded wildly each time I thought of them walking through the door. The band arrived and set up. The narrator, Carl Frank, came in. Frank had appeared in the film *The Lady from Shanghai* with Rita Hayworth and Orson Welles in 1947 and would continue to have major roles in films and series such as *Mandrake the Magician, Kraft Television Theatre, Naked City,* and *The Edge of the Night.* He was an added treat, for my parents and I thoroughly enjoyed *I Remember Mamma,* the Friday night television series that began in 1948, starring Peggy Wood as Mama Larson, Judson Lair as Papa Larson, Robin Morgan as Dagmar, and Irene Dunne as the grandmother. Carl Frank played "Uncle" Gunnar Gunnerson. Though we didn't have a television yet, we had seen episodes at the homes of friends. Carl Frank's presence added further excitement to the day, and I felt like I would explode with joy.

Finally, the studio doors opened, and in walked a tall, handsome Jackie Robinson followed by a short shortstop, Pee Wee Reese. I, the *pisc* of the family, the one who always had words ready to pour out of my mouth, was speechless. I stared in utter awe. I watched my father walk to the two Dodgers and heartily shake hands with them. My father's smile could have lit a whole street in New York City with its glow. I knew, looking at him then, that this recording was a dream come true for him as well as for my mother and me. After saying his hello and introducing Robinson and Reese to Carl Frank and the other actors who were there— a few men and some young boys hired from the choir from The Little Church Around the Corner—finally, my father brought Jackie Robinson and Pee Wee Reese into the control room to meet my mother and me. Suddenly, as Jackie extended his hand to shake mine, I realized that I was holding the hand of the black man whose courage emboldened others to stand up for equality. My hand was holding the hand that held bats and made home runs for a baseball team that, though it didn't have the winning streak of the Yankees, represented the American Dream of working one's way up and never giving up hope. The Brooklyn Dodgers were the Rudolph of baseball. Then, Pee Wee Reese turned to me having said hello to my mother. He, too, took my hand, and I nearly burst out of my skin to think I was shaking the hand of the man who caught and fielded so many baseballs, the hand of the man who'd dared to publicly put his arm around Jackie Robinson and, by so doing, made a statement to the world about acceptance. Finally, amidst the awe and admiration, my tongue returned, and my words spewed forth. "You are my very favorite players in the whole wide world. I love you. I love the Dodgers. I am so, so, so happy to meet you today. So happy."

"Well, for a young girl you certainly know how to express yourself, Judy." These words uttered from the mouth of Jackie Robinson to me. Wow!

"I like your pigtails. I bet you can throw a good ball," Pee Wee Reese said.

"I sure can. I am the captain of our neighborhood softball team. I can bat pretty well too."

"Maybe by the time you grow up, there will be women baseball players playing in the big leagues," Jackie said. I believed him. Maybe women would play one day. Maybe I could be on the Brooklyn Dodgers someday.

"Time to start recording," my father announced from the booth over the microphone. "Take your places, and we'll do a sound check and run-through. I'll record it in case we want to listen."

The story was slated to be a two-record, 10-inch rpm album. My father gave the signal to start. Music and hoopla open the story. Over this come the voices of boys on the local neighborhood team in the story, the Badgers. They argue about the game they would play the next day against the West Side Orioles: which moves should be made, how to pitch, how to bat. The bully of the team insists he should not bunt, that bunting is for chickens. "I'm a good batter," he cries, "and bunting won't go on my batting average record." The boys continue the vocal antics of playing in a sandlot a couple of blocks from Ebbetts Field, when Jackie Robinson and Pee Wee Reese walk by. They hear what is going on and stop to talk to the boys, giving pointers on pitching and fielding. They remind the bully that there are times when bunting can get more people onto more bases than a home run, depending on how many are on base. The bully disagrees and is slightly embarrassed when another teammate realizes that the two men look exactly like Jackie Robinson and Pee Wee Reese. When the two pros introduce themselves, the team can't quite believe that these two men are really who they claim to be.

Jackie and Pee Wee invite them to the game that night. The boys are thrilled. At the game, the youths point out to their bully teammate how various players used bunts rather than trying to hit big, and how this appeared to be the right move for the moment. The next day, the boys' game is in session as Jackie and Pee Wee walk by. Since they have some time before the evening game, they decide to watch. The Badgers notice them in the bleachers, and are inspired to give the game their all, except for the bully who still insists he wants his batting average to go down in local history and refuses to bunt, even when bunting would be preferable. Looking at the two Dodgers sitting there, the bully has a change of heart, does bunt, and the team brings in all the players on bases and wins the game. "See, boys," Jackie and Pee Wee tell them. "Baseball is about a player doing what is best for the team. That's what makes the real hero."

. . . .

The recording went smoothly. After the first side was recorded, a lunch break was called. We ordered hero sandwiches from a genuine Italian deli a few blocks away. The meatball hero I ate on freshly baked bread with homemade mozzarella cheese, abundant garlic, and the taste of olive oil, with its scent like that of a grove of olive trees on a breezy day, became viscerally implanted in my memory, for I ate this particular sandwich alongside Jackie Robinson and Pee Wee Reese. I felt very important as they asked me about my softball team and gave full attention to my answers.

"We play on the top of a huge and steep hill," I explained. "There's a flat area on the top, but across the street, another hill begins. One time I hit the ball so hard that it crossed Bellevue and disappeared all the way down the other hill. We never could find it."

"It sounds like you could be a slugger at the bat," Pee Wee commented.

"Just don't forget to bunt when it is appropriate," Jackie reminded me.

I got further personal tips on playing as I told them about my other team members and the moves they often made. I felt my hairs stand on end as I thought of the school year beginning and all of us back playing ball and me telling my teammates that Jackie Robinson and Pee Wee Reese suggested that Billy Reid stand with his feet a little further apart, Dorkas Murray make sure her mitt was the right size, Billy Whelman reach forward for the ball rather than back away from it, and Douglas Morton warm his arm up well before pitching.

At the end of the recording session, a photographer arrived and took a publicity photo of Hecky with the two baseball players—my father in a picture with Jackie Robinson and Pee Wee Reese! This was surely heaven. Afterwards, I went over to Jackie and said, "You and Pee Wee are my heroes. I think you are the best ball players and the most coura-geous people I know."

"Come here," he said. Jackie sat down on a stool and signaled me to sit on his knee. I eagerly obeyed. With his arm around me, Jackie Robinson said, "Never stop loving—and playing—baseball—for you softball, but you'll graduate to a hardball. And always remember to stand up and fight for what you know and feel in your heart is right. Judging from what I've heard you say today, that is just what you will do." Then he gave me a big kiss on my forehead. "Now run along," he said.

I floated away on the magical wings of my father's job.

CHAPTER 6

Pink and Blue

. . . .

inah Shore ranked number one on my father's persuade-to-record-for-kids list. When my father first met her at lunch in Hollywood in June of 1949, the summer of the "Rudolph" recording, all appeared amicable between them. Dinah Shore was what my parents called "a true lady." She was elegant while also appearing down-to-earth. Her smile radiated warmth, sincerity, and friendliness. Her manners were impeccable without one feeling Emily Post, Queen of Proper Etiquette, sat upon her shoulders. There was nothing coarse, crude, or rude about her. Great businesswoman that she had already proved to be, she had no hard edges, and her femininity remained unscathed by her success. She didn't flaunt a blatantly sexy image like so many female celebrities of her day. She appeared pretty, elegant, kind, sweet, and openly sentimental. Quite frankly, though Dinah was a blond and my mother a brunette, Dinah was incredibly much like my mother Lillian—a warm, sweet, sentimental lady in her own right.

This did not go unnoticed by my father and mother. I even commented to my parents after that Hollywood lunch, "I can't believe such a famous person is so much like you, Mamma." That lunch launched the seeds for a dialogue that would continue for years in our family. It escalated each time Dinah Shore came to New York or my father went to Hollywood. A spark of special energy permeated when they were together, and their eyes held a particularly bright light as they spoke and laughed with each other. My father was not the type of man who would be unfaithful. He was far too loyal and moral. Yet, if he would have had an affair, I firmly believe it would have been with Dinah Shore, provided, of course, that she was willing. The dialogue between my parents, inspired by my father and Dinah's singular rapport, ran as follows:

"Honey, if I die," my mother would say, "you should marry Dinah Shore."

"But she's already married and has a daughter," my father would answer.

"But other than me," my mother would continue, "she's the only one suitable for you."

"She is married. Don't die," my father would reply.

"Come on. Admit it. You have a soft spot for her," my mother wouldn't relent.

"HUHkneeee, you know I only have a soft spot in my heart for you."

"But if I die, you need someone like me, and she is the closest to me."

"I told you, don't die. End of conversation!"

One school holiday, my mother took me to my favorite place in New York, the Museum of Natural History. After we'd seen every dinosaur and mammoth bone in the vast institution, we met my father at his office and were to go out to dinner, then drive home with him. My mother and I arrived at Columbia on the heels of Dinah Shore, who swept into the lounge and secretaries' area outside of my father's office. We heard her warm voice. "Hi everyone. How've you all been? So nice to see you."

My father's face lit up, his eyebrows lifting practically to his hairline as they always did when he smiled a big smile. As Dinah was about to knock on the doorframe to announce her arrival, my father walked out of his office. The two hugged hello and talked animatedly, seemingly oblivious to all around them.

"So good to see you, Hecky. You're looking good and handsome as ever."

"Dinah, you are radiant as always. All set for your engagement at the Wedgwood Room?"

"I hear it's a sellout. But tell me about you. What projects are you up to these days? Oh, it's just so nice to see you again."

My mother said to me, albeit in her usual lighthearted manner when teasing, "If I didn't know your father, I might be a very jealous woman. But I am flattered that the *other woman* is so much like me. I think it's time to go out and say hello ourselves."

I was too young to answer, just approaching 10. Those were the days before Britney Spears and the establishment of tweenies advertising made precocious sexual beings out of girls as young as six years old. I was naive like other girls my age, but I remembered this moment all of my life. It was a small awakening for me in matters between males and females, a slight glitch I felt in my parents' otherwise seemingly total lovebird relationship.

My mother took me by the elbow, and strutted into the area outside of my father's office. Extending her hand toward Dinah, she smiled her equally-as-charming-as-Dinah smile, shook hands and said, "So good to see you again, Dinah. How are George and Missy?"

"Lillian, how nice that you're here, and Judy, my how you've grown taller." Dinah and my father returned to the world of all present.

. . . .

The friendship that ultimately developed between my father and Dinah Shore began far more coldly. It actually held all the rancor of a genuine romance novel where the heroine and the man she meets appear to be enemies at first, disagreeing about most things, and at total odds over one particular issue or course of action. They bicker, seem worlds apart, and it appears that never shall the twain meet.

Dinah Shore had a dream to record sweet, melodic lullabies. She was certain that her pleasant voice would lull little babies all over the country to sleep at night, making their parents' lives so much easier. Her dream had an accompanying business plan. For infant girls, the album would be pink and the songs filled with images of sugar, spice, and everything nice. For boy babies, the album would be blue, and the lullabies selected, while soothing, would contain words that painted more boyish images of action. These albums would not only be sold in record stores. They would be merchandised largely in the layette departments of major department stores and be suggested as gifts to be purchased for expectant or new mothers. Baby showers were rivaled in popularity only by showers for brides, and the usual gift of a blanket or a silver cup, ad infinitum, could be varied by a suggestion from the salesgirl for a lullaby album.

Hecky was not enthusiastic about Dinah's proposed plan. Two lullaby albums produced prior to his arrival at Columbia had not done well at all, and even with some recent new promotion and album cover changes, were still not doing well in sales. Dinah insisted her lullabies would prove to be exceedingly successful sellers if they were sold as gifts in those cherished baby departments. She insisted she was right and did not wish to even consider recording any other material until this lullaby dream of hers came true.

"Mr. Krasnow," she said, "These albums are a unique gift. What buyer wouldn't look for something new and unusual to give? It all depends on where one looks. No one would walk into a record department in a store and ask for an album for a newborn infant. But in the layette department, if the salesgirl is on her toes, she can point out this special gift to the customers. It's an irresistible gift."

"I wish I could agree with you, Dinah, but in the past lullaby albums have not done well at all," Hecky wished he didn't have to burst her bubble.

Dinah refused to have that bubble burst. "Mr. Krasnow, you are talking about Dinah Shore singing lullabies. I am sure no one of my popularity has sung them. And I assure you they have never been sold in layette departments before." Having spoken her mind to Hecky, Dinah began a correspondence with President Ted Wallerstein whom, as a top Columbia artist, she knew well. "I know what I am talking about, Ted. You have seen the results of my decisions in the past. They have been successful. Mr. Krasnow is simply being belligerent about this idea."

When Hecky sent the matter to the company's marketing research department for them to investigate, Dinah sent another letter to Ted Wallerstein expressing her thoughts. "I am not sure this Mr. Krasnow is enthusiastic enough about my idea to present it as favorably to the researchers as I can to you."

Wallerstein wrote to Dinah as diplomatically as possible. "Had this been a year ago," he made clear, "I might have responded differently. But things have changed. We hired Mr. Krasnow based on a thorough search of capable people. We must compete in the children's market or the whole company will suffer a financial blow. We put the matter of all children's records in his hands, trusting him to very quickly get us a big market. Mr. Krasnow is now in charge and must make the necessary decisions. Please be patient. See what research comes up with. If they and Mr. Krasnow don't agree, we will discuss the matter again."

Bob Kirsten in the research department got to work on the topic right away. In a memo on August 25, 1949, he had this answer for Hecky: "By the time a child would be old enough to appreciate the lullabies on his record the child would rather have a good rousing story. Also, it was felt that such a record would provoke animosity on the part of mothers, because of the fact that the record would ostensibly be taking the mother's place."

Kirsten went on to say that research also showed that "children do not care too much for women's voices on records." In the era when stay-at-home mothers were numerous, the voice of a woman was associated with mother. Kirsten wrote, "When father comes home at night, it's a special treat for the child. Similarly, a male voice on a record livens things up, making a change from that associated with the daily routine and constancy of being with mother." Regarding the sale of lullabies, Bob Kirsten noted, "It is not conceivable that people would buy records for a newborn child nor is it conceivable that a record set would be the kind of gift that would be saved until such time as the child is ready to use it."

Hecky, with his answers in hand, informed Dinah that the research had suggested the lullabies were not a feasible project. He wanted Dinah Shore to record. She was known and loved throughout the nation, and he was certain that her popularity would spill over into the sale of a children's album sung and narrated by her—woman's voice or not.

Several scripts for albums sat upon Hecky's desk. Reading through them, he came across one called *The First Day at School*, with music by Gerald Marks. Marks, a self-taught pianist, began composing songs in the 1920s. His career led him to write for Broadway musicals and

Hollywood films. His titles included hits like "All of Me" (1931), "Mount'n Gal" (1936), and "That's What I Want for Christmas," written for Shirley Temple's film, *Stowaway* (1936). Milton Pascal, lyricist and composer for several Broadway revues and comedies, including *Along Fifth Avenue, Follow the Girls,* and *Artists and Models,* wrote the text and lyrics. Hecky was impressed by the writers' credits and intrigued by the title, *The First Day at School.* He recalled Steffi's and my first days at school. The anticipation was filled with a blend of excitement, accompanied by anxiety. He knew that all children experience this to varying degrees when they leave the comfort of their homes and mothers to venture into the world of the classroom, new friends, and a teacher on whom they must rely for protection and whose rules they must obey. This topic had never been addressed on records.

The script contained narration about how nice it will be to go to school and have friends and activities hence, not to have to say, "Mommy, it's raining outside. What will I do today?" Mommy won't keep saying, "Junior, stay out of the cookie jar. Johnny, do this. Missy, do that." Lively songs described the "merry classroom with flowers and pictures hanging on the walls," and the "teacher, kind and sweet as she can be." Delightful songs expressed the fun the children would have playing store. "While you're buying peas or selling cheese, you'll be learning your numbers too." Another upbeat tune enticed listeners with images of writing on a blackboard.

Hecky told Dinah that he thought mothers would welcome this record enthusiastically, as the first days at school were often as hard for them as for the child. "Dinah," he asked, as a parent himself, "who hasn't seen a mother's tears as she turns to leave her little one for the first time while the child takes a major step toward growing up, especially as the child cries, 'Mommy don't go'?" Hecky touched the right chord in Dinah, who had her own little daughter, Missy. "You will make history with this record, Dinah. This topic has not been addressed on record or radio or TV, for that matter."

In addition to *The First Day at School,* Hecky sent her other material saying, "I have also observed that some of the Gay '90s songs such as 'Daisy Bell (On a Bicycle Built for Two)' and 'Little Annie Rooney,' are very much loved by young children. I have encountered a number of youngsters who sing 'Daisy Bell' with the same relish as 'Mary Had a Little Lamb,' and dozens of mothers have asked me to record this song."

Hecky suggested a 10-inch album with two songs per side, including "Daddy Wouldn't Buy Me a Bow Wow," and "I Don't Want to Play in Your Yard." "I believe this is another record that has excellent commercial potentialities, and with you singing it, it should be tops," he told Dinah.

Demos of all the material were sent to Hollywood for Dinah to listen. She liked what she heard and agreed to the recordings. The lullabies were put to rest and plans made to meet when Hecky would be in L.A. in November for 10 days. Musical arrangements would be decided, "A First Day at School" recorded, followed by the album of the four much-loved and familiar songs. He also wrote to Dinah, "Incidentally, the jacket design for 'The First Day At School' was submitted to me for approval a few days ago and I was delighted with it. I'm sure you will be too."

As late as 1939, records were packaged in a plain photo album style. One looked the same as another with nothing to attract the eye, not even a photo of the artist. Beethoven's Fifth Symphony looked no different than his Ninth Symphony or Mozart's opera *The Marriage of Figaro*. A children's 78-rpm record of a song appeared the same as that of a story. Alex Steinweiss, a young, innovative, and talented artist changed this and made record shopping as appealing as book browsing.

Steinweiss was a student at Abraham Lincoln High School in Brooklyn, where Leon Friend, the visual arts teacher, encouraged him and a few other talented students to design school publications, posters, and signs. The Art Squad, as these students were called, submitted work to many publications. When he was just 17, Steinweiss showcased his work in *PM Magazine*. After winning a scholarship to Parsons School of Design, he became an assistant in 1937 to Joseph Binder, the Austrian-born designer whose influence permeated Europe and the U.S. Binder applied reductive compositional principles derived from cubism and De Stijl to his posters, and designed these for the New York World's Fair in 1939, and later for such agencies as the National Defense, the United Nations, and the American Red Cross. He also designed covers for *Fortune* and

Graphis magazine. His clients included American Railroads, American Airlines, A&P Iced Coffee, *Fortune*, and *Graphis*.

The recently established Columbia Records hired Binder's assistant, Alex Steinweiss, as their first art director. Looking at the simple albums standing on shelves with only the spines showing, most often packaged in sets of three or four records in brown paper sleeves between their plain pasteboard covers, Steinweiss envisioned a much more creative way to promote the record sales by displaying covers with colorful and appropriate artwork on shelving that would allow the records to lay flat, cover exposed. His first cover design adorned a Rogers and Hart album of songs. It showed a theater marquee with the composers' names in lights. His designs developed into a style that reflected poster art of geometric patterns, folk art, and his unique, curly, hand-drawn lettering. They brought the classical music he loved to life. Record sales soared, and Steinweiss, copyrighting his particular lettering as "Steinweiss Scrawl," designed approximately 850 album covers.

Colorful, eye-catching album covers were part of the overall production when Hecky began his job at Columbia in 1949, and the Columbia art department had to submit the jackets for each recording to him for his approval. *The First Day at School* had a black background with white lettering, evoking white chalk on a blackboard. The lettering resembled that of a child first learning to print letters with, as children are wont to do at first, a few letters reversed. A drawing of a schoolhouse and the face of a little girl reflect the artwork of a young child. A smiling Dinah Shore appeared in the lower right corner. Her smile suggests a friendly, welcoming teacher. The combination of Dinah Shore and the topic of the first day at school was definitely a winner. The record sold well and made history in the record business because of the importance and broad appeal of the topic it addressed. Dinah Shore was pleased and willing to consider future recordings. She now trusted Hecky's suggestions. No longer filled with rancor, their friendship blossomed.

CHAPTER 7

Another "Gene" and a Hunter

· · · · · · · · · · ·

All indications pointed to "Rudolph" becoming a standard annual classic for the holidays. Gene Autry's name was practically synonymous with Rudolph's.

There was another Gene that Hecky respected, who had a pleasant voice and demeanor, acting talent, was an incredible dancer, and, as my mother commented frequently, "donned a winning smile, had bright eyes, and absolutely breathtaking looks. If you have Dinah," she would say, "I can have Gene Kelly. My dream is to dance with him someday."

"Well, you better start brushing up on your technique, honey," my father jested.

"My dear, Mr. Kelly, I am sure, will simply sweep me off of my feet," my mother defended her position.

My mother could not contain her joy when my father announced that he had written a story with songs for three- to five-year-olds for Gene Kelly to record and found two other suitable stories in order to make a 10-inch LP album. He also wanted Gene Kelly to sing a selection of nursery rhymes for toddlers, and could hear him telling the haunting story of "The Pied Piper of Hamlin."

"HunEEEEy—my darling!" My mother, knowing she would meet Gene Kelly—nothing would keep her away from the studio—held my father lovingly and waltzed him around. "Your job gets better every day."

I had a soft spot for Gene Kelly too. What young girl wouldn't want to dream of a man in her grown-up future who could sing, dance, and smile like the dashing sailor in the movie *Anchors Aweigh*? My sister's worship of Gene Kelly was akin to God, and she would be in New York when he recorded for our father.

"Our whole family will be at the studio to meet him, won't we, Dad?" I had to know right there and then.

"We'll have to see, Juddie."

"See what, Dad? You've gotta be kidding. Trust me, it's a fact accomplished. You can't say 'no' to us on this one." I shook my pointed finger at him like I'd done, according to Aunt Pauline's husband, my uncle Mickey, since I was three years old.

"HUHney," my mother's anticipation had to have an immediate answer too. "Judy's right! Oh my, there is surely a silver cloud behind every rainbow."

"What?" My mother's malapropism caused my father to laugh uproariously. Her linguistic mix-ups increased when she was excited. "Honey, you mean, behind every cloud there's a silver lining."

"I think I meant a pot of gold. Oh, what's the difference, you know what I mean."

· · · · · · · · · · ·

In order for Gene Kelly to record for Columbia, permission was required from his contracted film company, MGM. They granted it. The grand day came when Steffi, my mother, and I went into that magical studio again. Special enchantment filled the air today. I thought my mother would float to the ceiling as she walked. She had a bounce in her step like a balloon blowing up and down in the wind. When Gene Kelly heartily shook her hand and looked her straight in the eyes saying, "Well, Lillian Krasnow, if it isn't my pleasure to meet you," I thought she would literally elevate. He then focused on me, putting his arms upon my shoulders as he said, "I heard your father call you Juddie. Is that your name?"

"No, it's Judy."

"Well, Judy, Judy, Judy," he said repeating the famous line from Cary Grant. Oh my God, I thought. Hollywood is really here in front of me.

Then Gene turned to my teenage sister. In a gentlemanly fashion, he took her hand and said, "And you must be Hecky's eldest. I've heard you were his inspiration to write for children. Well, well, well, may I kiss the cheek of such an inspiration?" As he went to kiss her cheek, Steffi turned her head meaning to place her cheek in a very kissable position, but Gene Kelly's lips touched her face before the cheek was turned. His kiss landed on her nose. That was it! For two weeks, Steffi adamantly refused to wash her nose or anything near it that might wash away that precious kiss. If she had to blow her nose, the tissue was held at the bottom touching only her nostrils. My mother admonished her about not washing her nose in light of her budding acne, but had to stop when she asked herself what she would be doing if Gene Kelly had planted a kiss upon her nose.

The recording began. I had attended enough recording sessions by now to sense how a confident and good artist could make the process a simple joy, sending waves out that enveloped everyone present and filled the room with the mysterious ambience of an almost spiritual creativity. Gene's voice would elicit any child's attention, and any adult's for that matter. He could pull all listeners into that story trance where time and space are suspended.

Hecky had written a tale, *The Cranky House*, in which songs served to tell part of the story. He wrote it under two names, Peter Steele and Hecky Krasno, dropping the "w," which he often did. In this story, a family drives to their new house. It isn't new, and it looks rundown. Its door squeaks. The windows creak. Litter lies on the lawn. The roof looks shabby. The paint is dull. When the children, Janie and Ronnie, complain, the old, tired house hears them and engages in all sorts of ways to keep them out. Finally, the father says they will simply have to renovate everything. Various workmen arrive and do their jobs. As each does his work, the cranky house grows angrier, threatening to "shake and pout and blow them out." The workers sing songs that tell what tools they use and how and why. Gene Kelly sings each of these. Repetitive and catchy words draw young listeners into singing along.

The Plasterer:
On my board I mix my plaster.
Clister, claster. Clister, claster.
I can work a little bit faster,
For I am the plaster master.

The Plumber:
With my wrench I tear away
Rusty pipes too old to stay.
With my wrench I screw in tight,
New pipes that are clean and bright.

The Carpenter:
Zzizazood, Zzizazood
This is how I saw my wood.
Wrap-a-rails, wrap-a-rails
This is how I hammer nails.

The Painter:
I can paint a house, I can
Stirring paints here in a pan.
I stir paints of every hue
Yellow, red and green and blue.

When the work is finished with its roof to basement makeover, the family comments on how beautiful the house is. Janie and Ronnie talk about how happy they are to live here now. The house hears their kind words and feels loved. It is not so cranky anymore and says, "Maybe it's better to be happy and bright," another little moral to the story to encourage a positive outlook rather than a chip on the ceiling—or shoulder.

The second story tells of a cuckoo bird who feels imprisoned in his clock and wishes to step out just once to see what it is like to fly from tree to tree as he has seen other birds do while gazing out the window. Ultimately, he returns to the clock, tired from all that flying and happy to sing his song to help others wake up and get through their day.

In the third story, Gene Kelly tells of a beautiful kingdom where everything is painted in vivid colors. The birds, chipmunks, fawns, and all the animals are very sad, for the king has passed a law that no one can dance or sing. Gene plays his whistle and dances right to the king's palace. There he finds a tiny mouse wearing a huge crown and looking miserable as he sits upon his throne. The mouse king has passed the law, Gene learns, because a king must do everything better than his subjects. The sad king can neither dance nor sing. Gene tells him that both dancing and singing would make him happy. "When you feel happy you can make up your mind to do anything you want as long as you keep trying. If you are happy, others will be happy in your company." The king tries and succeeds at singing and dancing, abolishes the law against song and dance, and the land is filled with joy.

The session went quickly and well, too quickly for my mother, sister, and me. We could have sat in the studio for the rest of our lives hearing and watching Gene Kelly. My mother danced around the house for days afterwards, and Steffi finally washed her nose for fear that her adolescent pimples might overrun it and Gene Kelly would not want to kiss such a nose should they meet again.

During Show and Tell at school the day after the recording, I proudly announced that I had met Gene Kelly. I quickly gained celebrity status myself simply from this association. Teachers and students alike, and the parents who heard from their children about Gene Kelly (hence about Mr. Krasnow too) began to hold my father in very high regard. These Jews might not be so peculiar after all.

. . . .

The stars began to roll into my father's studio. After Gene Kelly, Hecky had another actor, author, and famed hunter lined up for recording: Frank Buck. Frank Buck was considered in the same league and held equal fame as the Lindberghs, Babe Ruth, and the Dempseys. This esteemed adventurer wrote the bestselling book *Bring 'Em Back Alive*, and acted in the movie based upon the book as well as in other daring adventure movies about brave men confronting dangerous animals. Buck was the model for the character Carl Denham in the legendary film *King Kong*. He agreed to Hecky's request to record for children.

Hecky wrote the script for the record under the names of Peter Steele and Hecky Krasno and composed the music with Spencer Odom. The script was based upon a segment from Buck's bestselling book and would be sold on four sides of 78-rpm vinyl in album form with a cover like that on the book. Its title was *TIGER, Bring 'Em Back Alive*. The suspenseful story about capturing and bringing a huge, ferocious tiger back alive from the jungles of Malaya to an American zoo would now be heard by children too young to read the still-popular book originally published in the 1920s.

Attitudes towards zoos and animals were very different in the 1950s. Today, with the animal activist movement, Buck is often called "notorious hunter." Yet, unlike hunters who killed for sport, Frank Buck refused to shoot an animal unless it specifically endangered someone's life. He made sure that, in transport, the animals were treated humanely. His 40-acre Frank Buck Zoo was the first open zoo where the animals could roam, and this set the precedent for the open zoos of the future. His zoo served as a resting ground for retired circus animals, and when the animals died of old age and other natural causes, their bodies were given to New York's Museum of Natural History for exhibits and research.

Merrill E. Joels narrates the story on the record. Joels was a well-known radio, television, and screen actor, board member of the Screen Actors Guild, and, later, author of a book published in 1969, *How to Get into Show Business*. Joels plays the role of Captain Harry Curtis, the real-life captain who sailed Frank Buck to and from many of the exotic places he went hunting for animals to bring back alive for circuses and zoos. The record begins with the boat having docked in Malaya, where Buck is looking for a tiger. Ali, a messenger from the local rubber plantation, arrives on the dock telling Buck that a tiger has just killed a cow. The workers want to shoot the tiger, but Buck persuades them to build a trap instead: a pit just deep enough so the tiger can't leap out, but dug into the soft earth so the animal will not be injured. This done, the tiger is baited and does fall in. The scene is filled with the sound effects of a roaring tiger and frightened men. Frank Buck lassoes the animal, then, with the help of the workers, lowers a cage upon it. Buck jumps into the pit to secure the cage door only to discover that the workers have not brought nails. Holding the door shut as the tiger pounds against it, nails are finally delivered, and Buck crawls out of the pit shaken, but alive.

The adventure does not end there. While sailing with the tiger on the boat a storm comes up. The power of the wind and waves sweeps through the lower deck and breaks the tiger's cage. On a ship with passengers and crew, a tiger now roams free. Captain Harry Curtis is ready to kill the animal, but Buck pleads with him not to. He concocts an idea about how he can cage the tiger again. Only if he fails can the captain shoot the animal. Single-handedly, Buck lures the tiger down the stairs into the sailors' mess hall, shooting blanks into the air to scare the tiger into moving forward. He has already placed the cage in the room. Once the tiger is in the room and the door is closed, Buck climbs into the dumbwaiter one floor above holding his lasso. He falls out of the dumbwaiter into the mess hall unseen by the tiger, lassoes the pacing animal, and calls for the sailors to enter and place the cage on top of it while he holds the rope with every ounce of strength so that the animal cannot move to leap or turn its head to bite. The tiger is caged and is, indeed, brought back alive. Sound effects, vocal incantations, drumbeats, and a Malayan chant bring the events to vivid life.

I attended this recording and recall looking at Frank Buck and thinking that he looked dignified, like an upper-crust man from England. Perhaps it was his mustache, or that even though he wasn't wearing a pith helmet, I couldn't look at him without seeing one upon his head. I attempted to conjure up images of Mr. Buck in exotic places, creeping through jungles in search of animals. Meeting Frank Buck was different from meeting a celebrity like Gene Kelly or Dinah Shore. I felt like I was shaking hands with a character that had stepped off the pages of the Rudyard Kipling stories that my father and Uncle Phil read to Karen and me frequently. I wondered how anyone could be so courageous as to lasso a tiger.

As my father was writing the script, he consulted with my uncle Phil regarding the psychological aspects of the story. Phil, as always, offered his input and served as editor. Our fathers asked Karen and me how we would react to hearing that the tiger had eaten a man working on the rubber plantation, not a cow. In Buck's book, the tiger had eaten a man. The workers wanted no mercy for the tiger, only for it to be shot. Karen's and my reaction was like that of the men: it would be hard to hear about a tiger that was known as a man-killer and be fascinated by it in any way other than a morbid one. Just the mention of a man being eaten gave me bad dreams and a sleepless night, hence my parents one, too, as I kept them up with my fears of the prospect of what it must be like to be eaten alive. Phil and Hecky decided that on the record for children, it should be a cow the tiger eats.

TIGER was Frank Buck's last recording. He died from cancer before the album's release on April 17, 1950. Shortly before his death, Frank Buck sent my father a Norman Rockwell sketch of himself with the message, "For my friend 'Hecky Krasno' with best wishes and sincere regards, From Frank Buck."

CHAPTER 8

Josef Marais and Miranda

. . . .

On December 18, 1949, my mother, Helen, Karen, Jean, and I were meeting my father at his office, going out to dinner where Phil would join us, and then, to a concert at Town Hall. Two international balladeers, Josef Marais and Miranda, who in a few short years had won great acclaim as concert artists, were performing. Josef, born in South Africa, grew up on a sheep ranch in the expansive African Veld. On the ranch, an old Hottentot named Koos captured Josef's imagination with many stories of how things came to be and why they are as they are: stories about the great Raincow in the clouds making thunder as he stamped his hooves; how the insect the praying mantis, really a god, could turn himself into anything he wished; and of the Serpent of the Rivers, who could cause or end drought. Without Josef's realizing it, Koos influenced what Josef, a studied classical musician and ethnomusicologist, would ultimately pursue as a career. Thanks to Koos, about whom Josef wrote a book published by Alfred Knopf, *Koos the Hottentot*, our family would now attend what had been advertised as a unique concert not to be missed.

Josef had met Miranda when he was broadcasting a program for Voice of America that included his renditions of songs of the African Veld with his Bushveld Band. Miranda, half Dutch and half French had left the Netherlands with her two young children when Hitler's rise to power made it unsafe for them to stay. Her mother had been an opera singer and, like Josef, Miranda had extensive formal musical training. Josef hired her as a Dutch translator for Voice of America. It wasn't until three years later that he learned she also sang. Miranda asked if she could hear Josef and his Bushveld Band perform at a club. From where she sat, she spontaneously joined in harmonizing. The pleasing sound resulted in Josef inviting her to sing some songs with him and his band. Thus, their duet began, not only as singers but eventually as husband and wife. After many club and college performances where they were received most enthusiastically, the two decided they wished to pursue a career together as concert performers. In 1946, they dared to rent Town Hall, and though the seats were not full, the reviewers raved about this charming couple, their refreshing repertoire of international songs, and the fact-filled and fun dialogue. By 1949, they were traveling around the world performing, and had appeared in a scene in the popular movie *Rope of Sand*, starring Burt Lancaster, Claude Raines, and Peter Lorre.

My father heard Josef and Miranda on the radio and on the two albums they'd recorded for Decca. Their international focus appealed greatly to my father, who had created quite a furor in Hartford when he organized meetings supporting Dumbarton Oaks and the formation of a League of Nations, believing that the future of humankind necessitated peaceful discussion, planning, and working together with respect. Hecky felt certain children would love the international flavor of Josef and Miranda, and, more importantly, that exposure to the sounds of the music, languages, and instruments from other lands would help youngsters gain tolerance for other cultures. Hecky arranged for a brief meeting with Josef and Miranda after the concert. They, of course, knew of the success of "Rudolph," the hit of the season, and were curious to meet the man who had produced it.

The night of the concert, Helen drove our family to the Yonkers train station in her big, green Hudson. Snow was expected, and we didn't want to drive home all the way from the city if the weather turned bad. We boarded the train, always a special treat, and rode to Grand Central Station. In warm weather, we sometimes walked the distance from Grand Central to my father's office. Now, we'd take a taxi, the classic Checker cab with its little folding seats so we could all fit. Karen and I loved to pull open these unfolding seats. This act provided us with never-ending excitement. As the chair bottoms lifted and we pulled the backs of the seats up, this mechanical abracadabra created magic for us as if a rabbit had jumped out of a hat. No sooner had we plunked our eager bottoms on the seats when pop!—they became a covered wagon jogging us along a mountain path. We were now '49ers traveling westward or, pop!—Cinderella in her pumpkin-turned-coach on our way to the ball in spite of the wicked stepmother and sisters. We zoomed on motorcycles or transformed into jockeys riding the winning horse in the Derby, or cowgirls holding on tight as the bucking broncos we'd mounted tried to throw us off in front of the cheering, anxious crowd at the rodeo. Every time we sat upon these miniature chairs, our ride in the traffic became an exciting adventure.

We finally reached our real destination, my father's office. We walked through the turning glass doors framed with gold, and were ushered to the elevator where the friendly elevator operator took us up to the seventh floor. The greetings we received and the obvious respect paid to my father made me feel we'd truly arrived at the king's castle, found the treasure, or won the prize. His office had a window looking out over 7th Avenue. His shelves were filled with books on the record business and the psychology of children, thanks to Phil. A record player sat on the shelf to the left as one entered, and lying near it were huge tapes of recordings, acetate demos, and piles of songs sent to him for review. On the shelf behind his desk stood framed photos of my mother, Steffi, and me, and a family shot of Phil, Helen, Karen, and Jean. Hanging on the wall was a family classic of Sarah, Harry, my father and Al, as babies, and, as we children were told, Uncle Bob growing within his mother.

After greeting all of us warmly, which my father always did no matter how busy he was, he tended to last-minute business, turned off the lights in his office, closed the door, said goodnight to the pool of friendly secretaries, and put on his hat and coat. We went down in a different elevator operated by an equally friendly elevator operator.

As we walked down the chilly streets of the Big Apple, car, taxi, and bus horns blew. We felt the rumble of the subway underground and heard its muffled click and clack upon the tracks each time we passed an iron grill upon the sidewalk. Billboards shimmered under flickering lights. Mannequins waved to us from store windows. Dreams of future weddings were inspired as we walked past window displays of bridal gowns. Sparkling jewels caught our gaze in the windows of fancy jewelry stores. People hustled and bustled along the sidewalk or climbed off of buses, arms filled with packages, as more stepped onto the buses clamoring to reach the few empty seats. Aromas wafted out of restaurants, initiating our noses to the smells of foods from other countries with their curries, hot peppers, cumin, peanut oil, garlic, tahini, pastrami, and the familiar scent of charbroil à la the U.S.A. Karen and I became acutely aware of the accents, attire, and languages of people from all over the world. To us, it was exotic to be foreign. Thus, we began our game of talking gibberish, certain that all those passing us were listening to us and, of course, thought we were from some foreign land which they could not even guess.

"Gishookie fazikoli?" Karen asked me a question.

True to my long-winded nature, I answered, "Z-shoopie penoogie lagoona preshunta. Ahzo pelatee gelatee fekatee poolwaby zacootie."

"Hapakorty." Karen didn't mince words.

We'd carry on these conversations block after block, chests puffed high with the incredible importance of our foreignness. Perhaps we were ambassadors' children.

This night, our conversation in our own foreign tongue ended abruptly as we passed a store window with a display of Santa, Santa's sleigh, several elves, and Rudolph standing next to Santa. "Hey, Daddy," I cried out in glee, "Rudolph's there!" He smiled his big grin that caused his eyebrows to lift nearly up to his hairline. My father's eyebrows pointed upwards because they lacked hair from the point at which eyebrows curve and come down again. With those bushy half-eyebrows of his, if his smile weren't so warm, his eyes a soulful blue, and his demeanor pleasant, my father could well have had the Mephistopheles-like look of Jack Nicholson.

Looking at the Christmas-themed window display, Karen's, Jean's, and my excitement grew, for Christmas was almost here. We'd be true to our Jewish heritage and light the Hanukkah candles, get Hanukkah geld, eat latkes, and play the Dreidle game. On Christmas morning, however, we'd wake up and look for presents. We firmly believed in Santa Claus. Not having a chimney or fireplace, Santa hid our gifts somewhere in the basement or on the first or second floor. The fact that we saw our parents buying and wrapping gifts, and we helped wrap gifts that they bought for us to give to them did not deter us from the suspension of disbelief that miraculously, Santa annually made his visit from the North Pole. Each Christmas Eve, I would sleep with Karen and Jean upstairs, though we didn't sleep. We listened for every hint of sleigh bells and the clip-clop of reindeer hooves. We'd peek out into the hallway for a hopeful glimpse of the man with the bowl full of jelly belly and the long, white beard. That we never got this glimpse only magnified the mystique of his visit.

The "hiding and seeking" of gifts was our parents' compromise with living in a town—and nation—where we simply could not escape Christian holiday celebrations. A Christmas tree, which we often pleaded for, was absolutely forbidden. In our neighborhood such a tree symbolized a belief that Jesus was definitely the Lord and Son of God. Hecky might record Christmas songs, but in our personal lives, we had to maintain our identity and pride as Jews and give no hint of succumbing to our Christian neighbors' hopes for our conversion.

. . . .

On the billboards of Town Hall, a picture of a striking woman and a distinguished-looking man holding a guitar captured me. I'd seen them on the Decca album covers, but here, the posters of them looked life-size. The woman, Miranda, had on a gown, jewelry, and makeup. Her animated smile hosted a slightly crooked tooth. Her eyes appeared like two brightly shining lights. The man, Josef, wore a dark suit and a bow tie. His lips were lined with a distinguished pencil-thin mustache. When I thought of balladeers, Woody Guthrie with his workers cap, short jacket, and dungarees came to my mind, or Pete Seeger in casual pants and a checkered shirt open at the base of his long neck with its prominent Adam's apple that was as much a part of his iconic look as the five-string banjo hanging upon his shoulder. I saw Susan Reed with her flowing, long red hair wearing a bohemian dress, and Jean Ritchie and her clan clad in Appalachian Mountain attire. I wondered what we were in for tonight with a woman in a gown and a man in a suit and tie. Please, not a boring longhair event, I thought.

We entered the concert hall and went to our front-row seats in the balcony, where my father thought Karen, Jean, and I would be able to see better up high and with no one sitting in front of us. The lights dimmed and then spotlights came up in full, shining on two people who looked like they belonged at a formal ball.

"Welcome, everyone, and thank you for coming this evening," Josef's pleasant voice and perfect diction housed in a British accent filled the hall.

"Yes," Miranda put in her two cents with a less formal, delightful sounding accent. "It would be sad to sing to the walls, so thank you from me, too—for coming here tonight."

"We travel to many, many cities, and when we do, we like to sing limericks we've written especially for those cities. We'd like to share some of these with you." Josef began strumming his guitar and sang, "There once was a poet in Delhi."

Miranda's voice echoed, dancing off Josef's like a crystal clear bell, "In Delhi."

"Who wrote a poem upon his wife's belly," Josef maintained a serious face as the audience laughed.

"Wife's belly," Miranda chimed with an impish, questioning expression.

"He was put into jail without any bail . . ." Josef sang the words with great import.

Miranda's eyes widened like huge saucers as she sang, "'Cause he stole all the words right from Shelley." She nodded her head and grinned.

The audience laughed and applauded heartily. It was evident from their opening words that Josef and Miranda did more than sing. Josef played the straight man to Miranda's jesting. I sat spellbound already.

"I grew up on a sheep farm," Joseph told the audience, "and on this farm lived an old Hottentot named Koos. His stories filled my imagination with wonder as he told me about creatures and sky gods and why and how things came to be. And he taught me this song."

"He didn't teach it to me, I am sorry to say." Miranda piped in. "I wasn't there. I was in the Netherlands being half French and half Dutch, and now I'm American."

"Well, thank you for sharing that, Miranda, but what does that have to do with the song?"

"I want to assure the audience that I can sing the song with you, for you see, even though I wasn't there, you taught the song to me, Josef."

The audience laughed again. Miranda's humor bordered on the ridiculous, like a foolish clown taking him or herself very seriously. Her timing was masterful, as were Josef's august responses. I sat entranced by their rapport and Miranda's animated facial expressions, huge, expressive eyes, and the way she moved her mouth as she spoke with her Dutch accent. I lived not far from Rip Van Winkle territory, the Catskills, and I heard stories about the Dutch, their ice skating on frozen water, wooden shoes, windmills, and Hans Brinker, the little boy who plugged up a leaking dam with his finger. Now an enchanting woman from the land of windmills and Hans Brinker was before me, talking, singing, and being very funny.

The song they now sang was, "I Am a Jolly Hottentot." Their harmonies were beautiful. Their renditions posed a combination of folk songs with a definite classical air. Their knowledge of music was evident, their charm immediately endearing.

"Our next number," Josef announced, "is called 'Pity the Poor Patat.' *Patat* is the Afrikaans word for sweet potato. Centuries ago it meant ordinary potato. In Flemish, a sister language, *patat* still means ordinary potato. In modern Afrikaans, a potato is known as an *aartappel*."

"Or as in French, as I am half French, an apple of the earth," Miranda added.

I listened to this song and wanted desperately to sing it, to play my own guitar and sing harmonies with Karen. The air around me seemed to vibrate with something much larger than anything I understood. My hairs stood on end. I felt my heart race ever faster as the program continued. Miranda yodeled in a song called "Fideree Fidera." Her voice literally danced, leaping here and twirling there. Joseph sang a Scottish ballad after translating the literal, guttural Scottish so the audience would understand the song. The two explained the history of a song, "The Zulu Warrior," and sang using their voices percussively, creating sounds I'd never heard any singers use. They sang in French, Dutch, and Afrikaans. When they sang a song called "Mountain Is Far," Miranda's haunting harmonies sent chills up and down my spine. She played a big pair of maracas with African decorations hanging from them. Her voice rang throughout the hall accenting Josef's notes in higher octaves.

I turned to Karen. She turned to me. "You too, Karen?" I asked. She knew what I meant.

. . . .

After several encores, the audience filed out, and we went backstage. Meeting Josef and Miranda in person was like meeting two larger-than-life creatures. I felt like two angels had entered my life and brought me a message. It was a visceral feeling, and I knew, after hearing them, my life had transformed in a wonderful way I couldn't yet fathom.

My father had no doubt that he must record with Josef and Miranda. Josef and Miranda were irresistible storytellers and singers who could not help but capture a child's attention. They set up a meeting to discuss when, how, and what would be recorded. A deep friendship would blossom from this alliance. Josef, as a child and young man, had been quite a virtuoso on violin. He and Hecky shared a love of this instrument and the two were equally refined and gentlemanly. Both adored their wives. Miranda, like Lillian, abounded with warmth and energy.

. . . .

In the spring of 1950, Josef and Miranda recorded an album with Hecky as producer: *Songs of the African Veld,* also known as "the zebra album" because of its yellow, white, and black striped cover. Karen and I insisted upon going to at least one of the sessions for this recording.

We couldn't sing "Old MacDonald Had a Farm" without imitating them, Karen harmonizing and me carrying the melody. We'd pretend we had an audience, and introduce our songs with a back-and-forth dialogue inspired from these two balladeers. Helen took us to Sam Ash Music store in the city, where we bought maracas, a drum, a triangle, and tambourine to play as Miranda played accent instruments. I'd sit at the piano and play chords, but something inside told me I'd need a more portable instrument like Josef's guitar, and that Karen would play the accent instruments.

Hearing Josef and Miranda in the studio only added to the magic spell they'd cast upon us since the concert. For the first time, I saw an Umbira, an African instrument played as the two sang a song called "Umbira Melody." Josef picked up on my fascination as I asked him many questions about it. A few weeks later, an Umbira arrived in the mail with a note from Josef and Miranda. "With this Umbira, may you sing and play many Umbira melodies."

When the zebra album was released, Karen and I played it until it was worn and scratchy. We learned the songs and harmonies of each and every song and developed our own interactive dialogue to segue from song to song and to inform the audiences we would soon entertain.

CHAPTER 9

Success Creates a Market

. . . .

S uccessful projects had been recorded and several others were in the works as Christmas of 1949 approached. Things looked good for Columbia and for my father as he actively paved the way for a full, quality-filled catalog of children's material. But the trial of "Rudolph, the Red-Nosed Reindeer," hence known as Hecky Krasnow vs. Goddard Lieberson, was about to go to the jury. The song had been released September 1, 1949, and sales were already high, but airplay of Christmas songs wouldn't be in full swing until Thanksgiving was over. Holidays, not yet in the total clutches of the advertising market, were truly celebrated one at a time. Pilgrims, the *Mayflower*, turkey, stuffing, sweet potatoes, and the big Thanksgiving feast ended before thoughts turned to the Nativity, Christmas trees, Santa Claus, his relentless, hard-working elves, Mrs. Claus, and the faithful eight reindeer. Who knew that a ninth reindeer would soon forever alter the lineup, pulling jolly old St. Nick's sleigh from the North Pole all around the world?

Children everywhere wrote their lists of desired gifts as postal workers sorted stacks of letters addressed to the North Pole. No thought was given to the possibility of fog interfering with Santa's annual mission. America's highways were still two-lane roads. Still, word of a new song spread from disc jockey to disc jockey, radio station to radio station, and household to household: word about a reindeer with a wondrous, red, glowing nose who saved Christmas from a potential disaster that didn't threaten the planet, but only the joys associated with Santa delivering gifts. It was a far more innocent time, indeed.

It was also a time that romanticized the West. Cowboys like Gene Autry, the Lone Ranger, Roy Rogers, and Hopalong Cassidy were heard on the radio, supplied subject matter for popular comic books, and with television entering households, became the heroes of these new visual adventures. With Gene Autry recording for him, Hecky could capitalize on the obsession with cowboys, their battles against evil as they fought the gun-slinging villains who terrorized towns, and their bravery amidst attacks by angry Indians whose land and way of life were threatened and destroyed.

When we first moved to Yonkers, my mother met a woman named Sherry Walsh, who became her lifelong friend and confidante. Sherry's husband, Henry, was a writer and historian who wrote the plays *The Salem Witch Trials* and *The Signing of the Magna Charta* (written with Robert Louis Shayon). These aired on the television program *You Are There*, hosted by Walter Cronkite. Henry also worked for CBS radio and television writing historical documentaries and segments for the Edward R. Murrow programs *Hear It Now* and *See It Now*. Henry and Hecky became good friends and began collaborating on children's material. My father, as a Columbia employee, could not collect royalties as Hecky Krasnow. He wrote with Henry under the pseudonym of Peter Steele.

In spite of his first, strained meeting with Gene Autry at the "Rudolph" recording, my father liked him, recognized his talent and popularity, and believed that children would like not only songs, but also stories told by Gene. Television shadowed the future, and there was talk of a new program called *Melody Ranch*. In it, Gene would be a singing cowboy and U.S. Marshal, who, while riding upon his smart and faithful horse, Champion, would sing. If the sales of "Rudolph" continued and proved Hecky's gut instinct about the song correct, Hecky felt it should be immediately followed by a story with Gene that could be purchased as soon as Christmas and New Year's were over.

Henry and Hecky created *Champion (The Horse No Man Could Ride)*. In this audio adventure, Gene Autry stumbles upon a ranch carrying a saddle, bridle, and backpack, and looking tired and dusty. He explains to the rancher that his horse had an accident, and, sadly he had to shoot him. "Feet weren't made for walking," he tells the cattleman. "That's why God made horses."

"I reckon you're looking for a new horse," the rancher concludes. He tells Gene about Joe Stockton, a neighbor who ran into hard times when a steer knocked him off a horse and injured him so badly that he can't ride anymore. "With three little children and a wife to support, he sold his horse to me," the rancher informs Gene. However, good as the horse had been to his former owner, the charging steer spooked the once faithful horse. "Now no one can get near him," the rancher explains. "He's known as the meanest critter around. Why, I'll give him to you for nothing if you can perform the impossible and ride him off the ranch."

Gene looks at the horse and says, "Mighty fine-looking horse. He looks like a Champion to me." Gene decides to give the horse a try. He asks to speak to its former owner, Joe Stockton, and learns that the horse responds to whistling. The morning arrives when Gene attempts to mount the critter. Hanging onto the horse's neck for dear life, Gene is dragged all over the corral as worried ranchers look on. He lets go, barely making it over the corral fence in a life-saving leap. Slowly, he enters the corral again, this time standing stoically while staring directly into the eyes of the horse. The horse stands still, whinnying and stamping his feet. Gene whistles rhythmic tunes. When the horse hears these, it appears as though a tear is forming in the frightened critter's eye. Gene gently talks to him and whistles more. The horse is subdued and allows Gene to mount.

Gene tells the rancher, "You made a bargain with me—I tame him, you give him to me at no charge, but I won't take him without paying Joe Stockton for him." He gives a grateful Joe Stockton the money. "Whatcha gonna call him?" Stockton asks. "Champion," Gene replies.

"He is a Champion," Joe says. "He saved my life from that steer."

Champion, a horse that would become as loved as its rider, now had a story. As for Hecky and Henry, their creation made top of the charts in the trade papers as recommended children's fare. Parents flocked to buy another item with Gene Autry, who by Christmas had indeed achieved "Rudolph" fame.

Champion had been recorded in New York on December 3, 1949. Gene and his wife Ina were in town for his big annual attraction, the Flying A Rodeo presented at Madison Square Garden. My mother, father, and I had gone to the rodeo as his guests, sitting with Ina in the Autry box. There, like so many others across the nation, I fell in love with the Wild West, with cowboys, roping steers, riding bucking broncos, cowboy attire, and Champion. Gene Autry's entrance into our lives opened up a whole new world of entertainment for me. At this stage of my life, the rodeo was even more exotic and exciting than the Barnum and Bailey Circus, which our family had also seen at Madison Square Garden. I had dreams of running away with the rodeo, of singing country-western songs, of riding horses and wearing the cowgirl outfits that dazzled my eyes and imagination in the spectacular rodeo parade around the arena.

The recording of *Champion*, which I attended, was the first time I heard a story recorded live. Reading their scripts, the actors transformed time and place and created a new present filled with excitement. As I had at the recording of "Rudolph," I experienced the thrill of the sound effects man generating an array of mood-provoking audio. Falling men, screams, and the whinnying of a wild horse painted images of corrals and both frightened and brave people in my mind. How could Gene Autry not become everyone's hero as he risked his own life to help Joe Stockton? The studio was truly a magical world where imagined stories became reality. I went home and read books aloud, giving different voices and accents to all the characters as I'd heard the actors in the studio do.

. . . .

While *Champion* was being recorded, "Rudolph" filled the airwaves. The song took off far faster than Santa's sleigh. People clamored to record stores to purchase their copies. It was a song recorded with children in mind that appealed to all ages and crossed over all musical genres. The jury, made up of the entire population of the United States, decided in favor of "Rudolph" and, unknowingly, applauded Hecky's gut instinct to record it. Gene Autry would now look at any song Hecky asked him to record. Composer Johnny Marks raked in his unexpected huge sums in royalties and, overnight, went from being an unknown songwriter to an extremely rich and famous one.

My father thought that selling Rudolph in the form of a stuffed animal would be a good idea. Columbia agreed and found a manufacturer and an appealing design. Rudolph came to life in a cuddly, reddish-blond reindeer shape with a bright, button-sized ball of a red nose. Gene Autry personally gave one of these dolls to me and told me, "Say thanks to your father." Promptly, of course, I was taken to a professional photographer to be captured forever with the creature that had created such an overnight phenomenon.

Thanks to "Rudolph," Karen and I began our paid careers as child actresses and promoters. My father enrolled us as members of SAG, the actors guild, and, in keeping with true family tradition, we became union members. We stood in Gertz's Department Store in New York City cuddling and kissing Rudolph dolls as we happily danced, hopped, skipped, and jumped from department to department encouraging shoppers to head straight to the toy department and buy this wonderful hero.

By the end of the Christmas season, "Rudolph" had made history selling two million records, becoming the first record ever to go platinum. It was the biggest seller Columbia Records ever released. At a celebratory party, Goddard Lieberson praised Hecky. "History has been made in the record industry thanks to the gut instinct of a man who has not even been with the company for one year. Hecky Krasnow, I hope you have more such gut instincts. You have pulled Columbia out of the red and opened the door for a thriving future in children's records, one that I hope will continue to entertain children, and as we have seen with 'Rudolph,' their parents and grandparents as well."

At our three-family abode in North Yonkers, the entire family was thrilled. Harry had called to say, "I'm so proud of you, my son. I knew you could do it."

My father received a $500 bonus that Ted Wallerstein had seen fit to present to him in thanks for bringing Columbia to the forefront of all record companies with this historical step forward in media history.

The success of "Rudolph" was certainly something our family wished to celebrate, and celebrate we did. Helen, Phil, Karen, Jean, Sylvia,

Bernie, my parents, and I went to our favorite Italian restaurant: Louie's Pizza Parlor. Owners Louie and Luigi put on quite a show tossing pizza dough back and forth before a glass window as they made everything fresh, including genuine Italian mozzarella cheese.

My uncle Al, his wife Libby, and cousins Merle, Dede, and Jerry came to New York from Hartford to join in the celebration. "Ah, my brother's a big *macha*," Al said, using the Yiddish expression for an important person. "You produced a major hit, Hecky! Here's to more such hits." He lifted yet another glass of wine in yet another toast.

As we ate our delicious pizza and pasta, Louis and Luigi put "Rudolph" on their record player, even though Christmas and New Year's was now over. The song still played on many a radio station, prolonging the season and its merriment throughout the month of January. Louie came to our table and put his hands on my father's shoulders and made a toast to Hecky while telling the other patrons, "Deese iss dee man who geeve us RRRudolph weeth his rrred nose. Brrravo! Mr. Krrrassnow!"

· · · · · · · · · ·

Returning to work, the celebratory weekend over, reality set in for my father. Easter was coming, another holiday to be reckoned with. It isn't enough to have one hit a year. Now the public would expect more. How would Hecky live up to the success of "Rudolph?" A song like that comes maybe once per century. "Rudolph," however, inspired numerous would-be and genuine songwriters to try their hand at creating another such lovable character. My father came home on many a night with demos or sheet music in order to share his laughter. People sent in poems and songs telling tales about everything and anything: Dogs who flew while barking glad tidings to those on Earth; hamsters that could run around the world delivering urgent messages faster than they could run on the treadmills in their cages; beavers who gave up building dams to build houses for the poor (Habitat for Humanity would have loved these critters); and, of course, the proverbial chickens that laid golden eggs and saved poor Bobby or Susie from starvation.

Fortunately, two songwriters had their own ideas about just how to appeal legitimately to the public. Their names were Steve Nelson and Jack Rollins. They contacted Gene Autry with a song for the Easter holiday coming soon, a song about a rabbit named "Peter Cottontail." Gene directed them to Mr. Krasnow, explaining that he was his children's record producer and would decide what to record. "But you can tell Hecky that I'll do it if he likes the song."

Nelson and Rollins, who thought "Rudolph" to be a sublimely simple and rather stupid song, realized that there were reasons the character zeroed right in on the hearts of people. One of these was that he enabled those long-waited-for gifts to be delivered. People love receiving gifts and rewards for good behavior often come in the form of gifts. Though rabbits in folklore are notorious tricksters like Brer Rabbit or likewise in Beatrix Potter's Peter Rabbit, why couldn't a rabbit inspire good behavior too? Here comes Peter Cottontail . . .

Here comes Peter Cottontail
Hopping down the bunny trail
Hippity, hoppity
Easter's on its way.

Bringing every girl and boy
Baskets full of Easter joy,
Things to make your Easter bright and gay.
He's got jellybeans for Tommy,
Colored eggs for sister Sue,
There's an orchid for your Mommy
And an Easter bonnet, too.

Oh! Here comes Peter Cottontail
Hopping down the bunny trail,
Hippity, hoppity,
Happy Easter day.
Here comes Peter Cottontail,
Hopping down the bunny trail,

Look at him stop, and listen to him say:
"Try to do the things you should."
Maybe if you're extra good,
He'll roll lots of Easter eggs your way.
You'll wake up on Easter morning
And you'll know that he was there
When you find those chocolate bunnies
That he's hiding everywhere.

Oh! Here comes Peter Cottontail,
Hopping down the bunny trail,
Hippity, hoppity
Happy Easter day.

In one simple song, the enticements of Easter are presented with the message of "you'll be happy if you do what you should." This song was not about an underdog gaining recognition, but it had all the other elements of "Rudolph"—a hopping, caring critter bringing happiness, gifts, even chocolate, and making Easter a holiday to be anticipated eagerly and celebrated joyously. My father liked it. There was no doubt that Gene Autry was the one to sing it. His melodic, on-pitch voice gracing the airwaves again so soon after "Rudolph," Hecky was certain, would cause the song, like "Rudolph," to cross over from children's to pop fare.

Easter fell on April 9, 1950, and prior to its arrival, Karen and I were called upon once again as department store actresses, this time to hop around with our darling stuffed bunnies with their buckteeth and festive outfits. What excitement it was to be on the "cutting edge" of these hits and know that my father was behind them. I put my heart and soul into those little hippity, hoppity dances. I could now fall asleep peacefully while cuddling a reindeer with a red nose and a rabbit with a cottontail.

"Peter Cottontail" became the second record to sell two million records and go platinum. Hecky had been at Columbia one year. *Champion*, released shortly after "Rudolph," had worked its way rapidly to the top of the *Billboard* charts as a children's must, and parents filled their children's Easter baskets with the story of a horse and a song about a lovable, generous rabbit. Henry Walsh and Hecky got together each weekend again and wrote *Gene Autry at the Rodeo.*

In this exciting adventure, Jay Coleman, a young cowboy, wants to help his father, who's met up with hard times, and his mother, who has been ailing for quite some time. If he can remain on the most ornery steer in the rodeo, the Texas Cyclone, for 10 seconds, he can win $1,000. Jay meets up with Gene at the rodeo and, when he tells Gene his plan, he is reminded by Gene that he isn't even 16 yet, and would not be allowed to ride the steer if those in charge learned his true age. Gene warns him that few who have ridden the Texas Cyclone have come out whole or even alive. Jay promises not to ride, but breaks his promise. The Texas Cyclone throws Jay. True to rodeo bravado, the rodeo clown distracts the audience with humorous antics as the daring pickup team rescues Jay seconds before the charging animal is about to gore him. The young lad suffers a broken leg and cracked ribs. Gene, realizing how very desperate things must be in the Coleman household for this young boy to risk his life, signs up to ride the steer. If he succeeds, he will give his prize money to Jay. The audience watches tensely as the steer bucks, twists, jumps, and turns. It's a close call, but Gene succeeds in remaining on its back for those needed 10 seconds. Jay goes home with the $1,000.

There is a recurring theme in this story and that of *Champion.* They are stories of courage, kindness, and generosity. These stories reflect the best in children's entertainment: an exciting story that teaches, through action and example about helping others. Since cowboys were heroes to children in the 1950s, Gene Autry took to heart that his recordings, television programs, and movies always had to keep the youngsters in his audiences in mind. He must set only a good example. This was Hecky's philosophy in his choice of what to record and not to record. Gene and my father's friendship grew beyond the recording studio. Each had great mutual respect for the other.

. . . .

With the incredible success of "Rudolph" and "Peter Cottontail," envy stirred within "Uncle" Art Satherly and Don Law, Gene's country-western producers. For years they had been guiding Gene Autry and his music along a highly successful and popular path. They had some gold records along the way, major hits like "Back in the Saddle Again," and "Tumbling Tumbleweeds." In 1947, Gene Autry recorded a song he'd written with Oakley Haldeman in 1946, "Here Comes Santa Claus." His inspiration came from children happily crying out those words during the Christmas parade down Hollywood Boulevard, where Gene rode Champion. The song was Gene's first Christmas release and proved to be a huge commercial and artistic achievement that expanded his genre.

Then Hecky entered the scene, and overnight, with an intended kid-disk, Autry's *children's* record producer made industry history with "Rudolph." The relationship between Satherly, Law, and Hecky was tense. The idea that Autry made more success in a few months with children's fare proved a threat. Hecky assured Satherly and Law that this would not interfere with Gene's career as a pop and country-western singer. Such fame and popularity could only make people want to buy his other records too. Autry's record sales in the adult fields did increase, but they would never achieve what his children's songs did. Fortunately, after many meetings, phone conversations, and correspondence, my father turned what could have been an extremely ugly working situation into a positive one, always letting Satherly and Law know what he had in mind for Gene's recordings, always inviting them to attend the sessions and listening to their input, and using the bands that were associated with Gene's adult recordings: The Carl Cotner Orchestra and the Cass County Boys. Hecky was good at handling interpersonal relations. He could put himself in the shoes of others and ask how he would feel in their place and how he would wish to be treated. This was fortunate, for another major children's hit sung by Autry would soon cross over into the field of pop and become a huge hit.

. . . .

Fairy and folktales abound in stories of snow creatures that bring love and happiness to people, then, having accomplished this, either melt or disappear. In some of these tales, childless couples become parents when a boy or girl made of snow comes to life. The child grows sad and silent as warm weather approaches, and the parents encourage the child to go out and play with other children. The child obeys and never returns. If the parents are lucky, the child shows up the following year. In other tales, handsome princes made of ice beg for the kiss of a beautiful young maiden in order to break the spell of an evil snow queen who has frozen them and forced them to live through spring and summer in her clutches in the frozen poles of the planet.

Jack Rollins and Steve Nelson had heard these tales and combined them with another factor: imitation. What works is good to repeat in another form. Rudolph goes away for a whole year. Why can't another character do the same thing? The two sat down and wrote another song with Autry in mind. Hecky liked the catchy tune of "Frosty the Snowman." The lovable, friendly creature created by simple, endearing lyrics was a sure winner. Following "Rudolph" would not be difficult with a fanciful snowman in the picture. Hecky believed this song would be the next Christmas season's big one. He knew that the idea of a snowman coming to life as a silk hat is placed upon its head would appeal to the wishes of anyone who has made a snowman. Time, effort, and love go into every snowman built, not to mention corncob pipes, button noses, scarves, vests, jackets, hats, even mittens. How nice to have fantasies about our snowman's personality come true in a song! Children and parents alike would relish the idea of a snowman enjoying a glorious winter day sledding and ice-skating with them. The warm but somewhat sad feelings felt as the Christmas holiday season ends are expressed when, in the song, warmer weather comes, and Frosty must say goodbye in order to go to a colder climate. But he promises to return when the weather turns cold again, just like the certainty of the holidays returning next year.

The song "Frosty," recorded on June 12, 1950, in Hollywood, did not go platinum as did "Rudolph" and "Peter Cottontail," but it became the season's top new hit, crossing over to the pop-music lines and selling nearly one million records. In 1950, Golden Books, inspired by the song, put out a children's book written by Annie North Bedford and illustrated by Corinne Malvern. The book, like the song, proved a great success and furthered sales of the song each Christmas season.

"Rudolph" continued to sell over one million records in its second season. Columbia Records was the leader in the parade of Christmas songs once again.

CHAPTER 10

A Rhino Named Rhumpy and a Tuba Named Tubby

ecky often consulted with Phil about the psychological aspects of various scenarios from which to create
stories that would be meaningful entertainment for
children. The two men found infinite possibilities in their
imaginations and conversations. One of the stories that grew
out of this dialogue was called *Rhumpy the Rhino*. Recorded by
Columbia in 1947, with Hecky as producer as well as lyricist
and composer under the respective names of Peter Steele and
Hecky Krasno, it became a children's classic of its time and was
released and promoted again when Hecky began his full-time
job at Columbia.

Rhumpy is an ungainly, clumsy rhinoceros unable to keep
up with the other animals as they dance at their jungle celebrations. Rhumpy becomes a grumpy bully to compensate for
his feelings of inadequacy. This causes the other animals not
only to dislike him, but also to fear him. Their rejection of him
makes Rhumpy meaner and grouchier. An understanding jungle sister, Ella the Elephant, visits Rhumpy. "If you would only
give yourself a chance, Rhumpy, you could figure out how to
dance." She admits, "You can't do pirouettes like the birds or
prance like an antelope, but you can dance like a rhino. Come
on, you can make up a rhino dance." Rhumpy decides to give

it a try. With Ella's encouragement, Rhumpy creates the Rhino Hop, goes to a party, and teaches the dance to all the animals. They like it. Rhumpy is pleased, bullies less, and as he feels better about himself, shows how nice he really is. Rhumpy becomes friends with the others, and everybody in the jungle is happier.

. . . .

At Columbia, my father was preparing to record a new version of *Tubby the Tuba*, a popular story already recorded for other companies, including by Danny Kaye for Decca, and at Columbia, by Victor Jory. It was another tale of lack of self-esteem, rejection, and acceptance. A tuba tires of his oompah, oompah melody. He longs to play high and fast like Peepo the Piccolo, or lyrically like a violin or flute. Wandering sad and forlorn along the river one night, Tubby meets a bullfrog that commiserates and explains how no one wishes to hear a frog's serenade either. Yet, the frog must sing all night, and he does. Tubby listens with his tuba-trained, perfect-pitch ears. He learns the frog's song, and his new friend encourages him to play it for the orchestra. "Remember, Tubby, even low is beautiful." At orchestra rehearsal the next day, while waiting for the conductor to enter, Tubby practices the melody learned from the frog. The other instruments attempt to hush him before the maestro arrives. However, they don't silence him soon enough. The conductor hears Tubby's plaintive song, finds the tune beautiful, and debuts the piece with the entire orchestra accompanying Tubby.

Paul Tripp, the writer of *Tubby*, would narrate the story. The eclectic and eccentric composer, George Kleinsinger, would conduct the orchestra. Paul had written the popular children's book, *Tubby the Tuba*. He met composer Kleinsinger prior to WWII, when he performed in the Kleinsinger opera *Victory Against Heaven*. After the war, when Tripp returned from the services, the two collaborated to develop *Tubby* into a story with music. The first recording of *Tubby* took place in 1945. Now, in 1950, Columbia would put out a new version with Hecky as the producer. *Tubby* was to be the first recording in a long-term series created by Hecky to introduce children to instruments of the orchestra.

My father thought I would enjoy the recording and allowed me to attend. It was at this session that *Tubby* (and tubas) irrevocably entered my life. The tuba looked to me like a super-large version of the pipes under our bathroom sink. Until this moment, I had no idea how expansive human facial cheeks could be when filled with air. The tuba player blew into the bulbous instrument with equally bulbous cheeks that inflated and deflated to the rhythmical notes he played. He looked like a squirrel that had stored helium rather than nuts in its cheeks. If a basket could be hung from even one of these inflated cheeks, one could travel in it around the world in 80 days or less.

Electronic keyboards were not yet part of the music scene. I experienced the real thing: genuine piccolos, clarinets, bassoons, flutes, kettledrums, violins, and violas. All the instruments of an orchestra filled the studio, along with their musicians and what seemed like endless rows of black music stands and scores written on pages of rustling paper. Kleinsinger's hair bounced up and down on the top of his head as he and his baton danced, dipped, jumped, and swayed to the music. He conducted Tubby's melodies with his whole body so expressively that he looked like a tuba in human form. He readily became a piccolo or a kettledrum too.

Tubby, the bullfrog, and all the instruments were literally coming alive as imagination in the form of story and music brought them to life, each with his or her own personality, voice, and spirit.

. . . .

On April 24, 1949, Paul Tripp's television program, *Let's Take a Trip,* aired on CBS-TV. Dressed like a train engineer in striped coveralls and an engineer's cap, Paul, alias Mr. I. Magination, blew his slide whistle and took viewers to such places as Ambitionville, Inventorsville, seaports, factories, and multiple states and foreign countries to see how people worked, lived, ate, danced, and sang. There was even a journey to "I Wish I Were Land," the topic of the brief ditty that always followed the program's upbeat theme song: "I wish I may, I wish I might, take the trip I wish tonight." Mr. I. Magination blew his slide whistle. Simple, early television visual effects made the train boarded by him and his guests appear as though it was actually going through a tunnel. The train emerged in the place designated for the day's particular journey. The program's content of adventure and education proved a winning one, and during its successful run, Tripp won a Peabody Award.

The recording of *Tubby the Tuba* opened the door for much future collaboration between my father and Paul Tripp. Many episodes from the television program were recorded, and after the program was no longer on the air, the format became the basis for trips taken via records. Paul recorded *Spaceship to Mars*, Mars being a favorite preoccupation of my father's and one he wished to share with children listening. Paul later recorded several segments and songs for the innovative and extremely popular *Now We Know* series, initiated, directed, and produced by Hecky and written by Hy Zaret and Lou Singer.

Karen and I graduated from hopping around department stores with stuffed Rudolph dolls and bunnies to performing as actresses with Paul Tripp both on record and television. I'd always had a fascination with pioneers and the westward movement, so I was thrilled to be a child crossing this country in the album, *All Aboard a Covered Wagon*, recorded May 29, 1951. If I couldn't cross the country in a genuine wagon, I could now do it through acting. I helped to light campfires, escaped an Indian attack, and found gold in California. I felt as though I'd returned in a time capsule when the recording was over and I realized my attire was not a long calico dress and bonnet, but a calf-length skirt, a blouse, orthopedic saddle shoes, and newly applied, train-track metal braces. Ray Carter and his orchestra provided the music for this album. It had a square dance ring to it and an air like the western music that always caught my eager ears while watching cowboy movies.

. . . .

My father's working relationship with Paul Tripp was in its infancy at the time of the recording of *Tubby the Tuba*. It was also the beginning of his recordings with George Kleinsinger. Kleinsinger's antics in the studio were genuine, and they paid off. *Tubby the Tuba*, in its new version, received acclaim in all the trade papers. George Kleinsinger, who had been going through a dry spell of sorts, dabbling with jazz, and not knowing quite which direction to next take his music, achieved much attention and accolades for *Tubby the Tuba*. It was his first genuine success. He was grateful and decided to show his thanks and celebrate by having a party.

Kleinsinger lived in the Chelsea Hotel at 222 West 23rd Street between 7th and Eighth Avenues in Greenwich Village. Built in the early 1880s, this 12-story, Queen Anne-style, red brick hotel with ornate balconies and room enough for 40 families was the first co-operative apartment complex. It soon became part of a growing center for culture. Nearby were opera houses, vaudeville theaters, and playhouses. The 20th century was ushering in a new theatrical era. The hotel's list of guests included poet Dylan Thomas; writer/actor Brendan Behan, who befriended George Kleinsinger; Arthur Miller; Thomas Wolfe; other notable literati, artists, musicians; and, in the 1960s and '70s, folk and rock stars Bob Dylan, Leonard Cohen, Jimi Hendrix, and Janis Joplin. Though its reputation was classy price-wise and its lobby appeared like a gallery in a museum with its colorful and offbeat art, it had a somewhat seedy ambience. The ghosts of many alcohol-induced deaths, like that of Dylan Thomas, and a couple of suicides added to this ambience. However, it was the perfect place for George Kleinsinger.

He rented a penthouse apartment on the twelfth floor, where he could transform his abode into a lush jungle. His precious grand piano stood amidst tanks of tropical fish, including an aquarium of piranhas. In the corner, a waterfall flowed and splashed, while free-flying birds roosted wherever they desired. Their droppings graced the apartment like white, green, and brown paint thrown upon a canvas.

George Kleinsinger was an odd but sociable man, and his apartment was a melting pot for all kinds of characters from the respectable, conservative, conformist, and reputable to the offbeat, liberal, eccentric, and disreputable. His array of animals included pythons, mice, insects, birds, an ocelot, a ferret, and, of course, monkeys. He fancied himself Father Nature.

After an intensive study of plants of the tropics, the amount of heat and light they required, and the amount of rain it would take to keep them alive, he created a mini-Amazon rain forest in the living room, parlor, and den. Only the kitchen and bedroom had standard furniture. The jungle rooms were adorned with seats that looked like logs, and the living room had one big couch and chair upholstered with fabric of a jungle motif. Fountains fed small running streams that watered the foliage. The soothing sound of trickling and running water permeated the apartment. The overall plan was idyllic: a homegrown Garden of Eden.

George Kleinsinger was a relatively unknown composer prior to Columbia's highly successful release of *Tubby the Tuba*. Now he was receiving calls from potential collaborators. He wanted his assortment of friends to celebrate. These included my mother, father, Steffi, and me. Steffi was more interested in a party with her teenage friends and decided not to come with us. I wouldn't miss visiting the jungle I'd heard about. I had been intrigued by the conductor who had taken on the attributes of the instruments he had conducted at the recording of *Tubby*. The Tripps, of course, were also invited. Kleinsinger had told Hecky that he wished for him to meet a talented lyricist named Joe Darion. Darion was relatively unknown at the time, but Kleinsinger thought he had great potential. No one knew then that in 1965, Joe Darion would pen "The Impossible Dream."

Kleinsinger had an idea for a musical version of *Archie and Mehitabel*, based on the long-running cartoon by Don Marquis about a cockroach news reporter and his beloved alley cat, Mehitabel. He hoped Joe Darion would work with him to create it. George invited his usual fascinating mixture of people, including some military buddies from the 2nd Service Command, ASF, with whom he'd served during WWII, and some old pals from his years as music director for the Civilian Conservation Corps camps.

George, unfortunately, discovered a terrible problem prior to the party. Father Nature was not an easy job, and the balance of nature in his jungle apartment had gotten totally out of hand. While his monkeys screeched, he noticed that his ferrets, rather than his pythons, were chasing mice. The pythons showed signs of digesting mice, as their tubular shapes bulged along various points and they slept. What George realized is that the mice had somehow performed a coupe. They had taken over, and nature was certainly not in its usual harmony. There wasn't a corner of the apartment or a kitchen cabinet that didn't harbor these little white and gray creatures. Firstly, this was not good for his jungle. Secondly, he knew his guests would not enjoy mice at their feet and, heaven forbid, in their laps. He called a knowledgeable friend for advice. He was told to go immediately to an aviary shop where they sold rare insects. He was to purchase three or four of these highly useful insects, which apparently attacked mice, but not birds. The birds flying around the penthouse would be safe. "I also suggest you buy several mousetraps, at least for the kitchen cabinets," he was told.

Matters improved between the traps, the insects, and the snakes now awakening with renewed appetites. Things seemed under control, at least to Kleinsinger's concept of control. Walking among mice, insects, screeching monkeys, flying, cackling birds, and slithering snakes was a daily experience for him.

The evening of the party arrived. The caterer and hired crew placed platters of food on folding tables rented for the occasion. George selected music for the three jungle rooms: the Faure Requiem at the lead of the classical music that would play in the den, the Almanac Singers and other folk music in the parlor, and jazz played intermittently with good ole *Tubby* in the living room. Food would be eaten buffet style, while two bartenders would generously serve drinks from the bar built into an exotic display of plants and trees.

My mother, father, and I had driven to the Village and found a parking space not far from the hotel. We walked to its entrance, where a doorman let us in after finding our names on the list Kleinsinger had given to him. We took the elevator, which stopped on the sixth floor. The door opened. My father pushed the button to the twelfth floor again. The door closed and took us down to the lobby.

"Honey, you must have pressed the down button," my mother said. My father pushed 12 again. The elevator stopped at the sixth floor. He pushed the "close door" button. We returned to the lobby.

We got out. My father asked why we couldn't get to the twelfth floor. The doorman informed us that the elevator wasn't working properly. "I called for its repair, but they are not coming until Monday."

"Well, is there a service elevator, sir?"

"Yes."

"Can you please take us to the twelfth floor in the service elevator then?"

"No."

"No?" My father was obviously annoyed. "And why not?"

"The elevator operator called in sick. You will have to go to the sixth floor and walk up the rest of the way."

"That's ridiculous," my father roared. "My wife has a heart condition. She can't walk up six flights of stairs."

"HUHney," my mother was a peacekeeper at any cost, "it's not the man's fault. Keep your voice low when talking to him."

My father was not about to become subservient to this ridiculous situation, but he lowered his voice a few decibels. "Sir, you must know how to operate the elevator. Can't you take us?"

"It's against the rules, Mister. I am the doorman. The elevator operator does what he does. Union rules, sir."

"In a situation like this, I am sure the union would bend its rules for one night."

"Maybe, sir, but since those are the rules, I never learned how to operate the elevator."

"Well, at least you're a union member. Good for you." My father then turned to my mother and me. "Honey and Juddie, we are going home. Kleinsinger or no, I will not have you, my darling, walk up six flights of stairs."

"HUHney. We've driven all the way from Yonkers. I want to see that jungle, and so does Judy. If I could give birth to her, I can walk up six flights of stairs. We got here early. We'll go slowly."

"I think this is a terrible mistake, honey."

"Let's at least try. If I find it too hard, I'll let you know."

We got back in the elevator, which, as it had done before, opened its doors as it automatically stopped on the sixth floor. We all started the ascent on wide metal stairs covered with dust that seemed not to have been washed or wiped since the hotel had been built. It was a warm, spring evening, and ventilation was at an all-time low. My mother's smile was fading, and that vein in her neck was showing its signs of pulsating visibly.

"HuhNEY!" My father spoke noticing the vein. "This is ridiculous. I won't let you get sick over a totally inadequate elevator system. We are all mature enough to bear disappointment. We are turning around and going home. I'll explain to George."

"ANYONE ON THE STAIRS?" A voice echoed. "It's George here. I understand the elevator isn't working properly. One of the bartenders came late and told me. I know how to operate the service elevator. If anyone is there, go back to the sixth floor. I will meet you there and take you up."

"George, its Hecky here. Thank goodness. We were about to turn around and go home. Lillian has a heart condition."

"HUUUney," my mother gasped. "I don't want the world to know."

"Oh, for heaven's sakes, so you have a heart condition. That's not a crime."

"But I'm not sickly."

"That's obvious to anyone who meets you, honey. Don't worry. Okay?"

"Hooray!" I chimed as we found George Kleinsinger waiting for us when we emerged from the dust-ridden stairway. "Now I can see the jungle. Maybe I can hold a monkey."

"You certainly can," George replied and then led us through an equally dusty hallway to the service elevator. He opened the doors of crisscrossed wood with a key, and we walked in. "I am a man of many talents," he told us, "including operating elevators. The man who usually does this is terrified of snakes, so he taught me how to operate this elevator so I can transport my menagerie up and down without him."

We finally reached the twelfth floor, and George led us to his jungle. I felt I'd entered another world entirely, another life: Juddie of the jungle. Humidity from the jungle brought beads of moisture to my forehead. George excused himself to go and bring some other guests up on the elevator. While gone, he assigned one of the catering crew to the job of host. The man, dressed in black-and-white waiter's attire stood tongue-tied and terrified as a monkey tugged at his pants leg with sharp nails while making very unfriendly noises.

I stood there in total wonderment at this veritable jungle. Tarzan movies could be filmed here, and I fully expected Tarzan to give his call and swing from a tree. I'd gladly be his Jane. As the monkey tugged at the man's pants, I drifted off into a fantasy world with Tarzan. I returned abruptly to reality as my eyes focused on my mother. She stood frozen, arms in the air, a look of terror on her face. The monkey had let go of Mr. Waiter, whose pants had a distinct tear, and had now grabbed onto the leg of Lillian Krasnow. His sharp nails had already made an ugly rip in her stocking. My mother was not an animal lover. However, she could not be mean to animals or ignore such a human-like creature. She regained her voice and as though soothing a baby, she looked down at her ankle and into the little capuchin's eyes and spoke, "Such a sweet thing, yes, such a nice boy—or are you a girl?" Since the monkey was wearing a diaper, it was hard to tell. "Coochie, coochie coo." My mother extended her finger to tickle the critter's chin. At this gesture, the monkey bared its teeth and made such a loud screech that my mother screamed. The vein in her neck responded accordingly.

At this precise moment, more guests arrived. The monkey disappeared into a tree. We were introduced to Joe and Helen Darion, strangers who would become close family friends and Joe, another of Hecky's collaborators. The Tripps arrived too. So did three women in black attire, black makeup around their eyes, and long, straight hair. They smelled like sweet smoke and an acid-like perfume I later learned was called patchouli. Another woman who entered with this particular elevator group seemed totally lacking eyebrows and drew them on with dark brown pencil though her hair was bleached the color of champagne. Her cheeks were bright pink dots of rouge, and her lipstick was equally bright. She looked ancient and wore an outfit reminiscent of a Russian czarina. She put out a cold, blue vein-ridden hand to shake hello. The wrinkles on her face were so deep they would smother a caterpillar, of which there were plenty in the apartment. When she said hello, her spittle sprayed all to whom she spoke. Apparently, she had been a well-known opera singer in Vienna in her youth.

Next, a young woman entered, and, at the sight of her, George Kleinsinger took on the strut and air of a male peacock fanning its colorful tail. Charlene, as she was introduced to us, had Marilyn Monroe-like bleached blond hair, a bright red dress, very long and very false eyelashes, and lips shaped like a heart by the application of lipstick as red as her dress. Under the lipstick, the true lines of her real lips could be seen, and this made her look as though she had two upper and two lower lips. Charlene had a bosom that, as a developing girl, I could not help but gape at. Unfortunately, for any personality she might have, this bosom would definitely serve as a detraction. All eyes were drawn in the direction of her chest. Kleinsinger lavished her with attention and affectionately called her "Charlie" for the rest of the evening.

"Time to get drinks, folks," Kleinsinger called out. "Then, I will give the grand tour."

The drinks flowed. Ice crackled in glasses of scotch on the rocks and gin and tonics, and some Amazonian liqueur that soon had tongues wagging and giggles flying. With drink in hand, George Kleinsinger took us on the tour, telling us about each plant, bird, snake, monkey, all the flora and fauna he'd imported, planted, and cared for. He was literally in his element.

I was the only child there and very absorbed in the exotic tour. The adults, however, were jumping, slapping various parts of their bodies, scratching, and mumbling "damn its," even an "Oh, shit." Kleinsinger appeared oblivious. "Isn't it incredibly beautiful?" he repeated after almost every brief lecture on a given plant or critter.

When the tour ended, we were invited to partake of the gourmet Peruvian food, including *cuy*, which we were told was a popular dish made of roasted guinea pig. We all passed that platter restraining our gags, except for one of the women in black. At my persistent questioning about their look and smell, my father told me the three women in black were beatniks, "an artistic, subculture against the mainstream considered both beautiful for their artistic and political views yet beaten down as outcasts and known for smoking marijuana, an illegal drug." This beatnik ate several poor roasted guinea pigs with relish. If beatniks ate guinea pigs, I vowed never to become a beatnik.

Once we had filled our plates with what we could tolerate as edible, the Tripps, Darions, and my parents sought a comfortable log to sit upon in the parlor where the Almanac Singers energetically sang a Woody Guthrie tune. Hungry, and happy to be sitting at last, our relaxation was short-lived as an army of huge, frightening bugs began to crawl across the floor. This was my mother's worst nightmare come true, for she hated bugs with a passion. She swore that, if she didn't love my father so much that she wanted to lie next to him in their graves after death, she would have herself cremated and give no bugs the satisfaction of dining on her dead body.

We heard screams from the other rooms followed by the sounds of plates dropping and silverware clanking. George Kleinsinger loudly announced, "Don't worry! Trust me. Mice were overrunning my place this week. These bugs go after mice, not people. You are all safe." But George Kleinsinger realized that, though the mice were now far less in number, the insects had reproduced rapidly. Perhaps he had balanced one part of nature, but now a new imbalance existed in this precious jungle of his. How would he get rid of the insects? In the presence of us, his guests, he called his knowledgeable friend, projecting his voice so that we could all hear how he was in control of the situation. Hanging up, he announced that he would have to buy a particular bird that ate these insects. He gave a brief lecture about how this keeps check on that, and that keeps check on this. Nothing, at this point, could convince the rest of us that in a penthouse Mother Nature could work efficiently as she could out in the wild.

My mother tried to remain calm, but her pulsating vein was getting a good workout this night. Helen Darion smiled and conversed, all the while looking up, down, and around to insure she would not be attacked by surprise. She and Joe were two of the smallest people I'd ever met. Joe stood about five feet tall and looked like his parents might have been leprechauns. Helen stood less than four feet. Her petite frame seemed dwarfed by her shiny, lush, thick black hair. She was a dancer. Unnoticed at first with its silent movements, suddenly Helen realized a huge python had slithered out from under a bush and was headed straight toward her. She leaped up, as only a dancer could, onto a large rock behind the wooden log she'd been sitting on. A large insect had leaped with her, for she had been about to swat it off her leg before python terror inspired her graceful but terrified jump. "Joe, my God!" She yelled, as her high-pitched voice, topped with a heavy New York accent, pierced the air. "Get up here with me. I've heard adult pythons can eat a big deer. You and I are smaller than a big deer."

George heard this and came running in. "Samson," he spoke to the snake, "come here." He bent down and lifted the huge creature that wrapped itself around his arms and waist. The snake wasn't slithering about any longer. The ferret ran by, hissing and chasing the bugs. A mouse jumped onto my mother's plate, and she responded instinctively by throwing the plate in the air. Its contents landed on her hair, dress, and the floor.

"That's it," my father said, standing to put his plate down on a rock. A tree frog leapt onto the plate, which fell, trapping the creature underneath. "I think it's time for us to leave. Juddie, honey, let's go." At that moment, a curious bird flew into the melee, landing on my back. Startled, I screamed and dropped my plate of food. The insects were having a field day with the gourmet food. Everyone made a beeline to the front door, grabbing pocketbooks, suit jackets, attempting to be polite, saying, "Thanks, George. Congratulations on *Tubby*!"

Then we heard the nasal tone of Charlene's voice. "Are you crazy, George? That snake will strangle you. George Kleinsinger, why on earth do you have this live jungle? You could get fake trees and stuffed and wooden animals, even statues."

That was one too many for an already mortified George Kleinsinger. He'd given parties when nature was in balance, at least in relative balance. People enjoyed coming to his place. "Fake plants, you say?" He screamed at Charlene. "Statues? You don't understand anything!" The peacock stance he had taken with Charlene up until now abruptly ended. "Leave, Charlene. Leave!" As we approached the stairway, we heard George Kleinsinger mutter despairingly, "Fake trees? Statues? Is she crazy? Well, there's one woman gone out of my life." Then his door slammed shut.

"Well, hail to *Tubby the Tuba*," my father said as we got into our car and drove towards home. Our little house in Yonkers, bug-, snake-, mice-, and monkey-free, felt wonderful when we walked in. My mother immediately showered. When she emerged, clean, safe, and happy, the vein in her neck keeping a steady rhythm and barely showing, she said, "Honey, your job is crazy!" We laughed ourselves to sleep that night.

. . . .

CHAPTER 11

Rosie Becomes a Household Name

. . . .

n 1948, a popular radio personality named Arthur Godfrey debuted a television program that ran for 10 years and kept its place in the prime Top 10 programs for the entire decade. *Arthur Godfrey's Talent Scouts*, which aired Monday nights at 8:30 P.M. EST, helped launch the careers of some of the era's truly talented and beloved performance artists. The list of these celebrities includes Pat Boone, Tony Bennett, Eddie Fisher, Leslie Uggams, Lenny Bruce, Steve Lawrence, Connie Francis, Roy Clark, and Patsy Cline. A sister program, *Arthur Godfrey and His Friends*, brought many of the talented artists launched on the *Talent Scouts* program into homes across America weekly: stars like Tony Marvin, The Chordettes, The Mariners, Julius La Rosa, Lu Ann Simms, The McGuire Sisters, The Toppers, Haleloke and more. All the performers were clean-cut young people, and perhaps that is why Arthur Godfrey did not accept Elvis Presley or Buddy Holly. Their personas and music may have been a step ahead of what was desired and acceptable in the late '40s until the mid-'50s.

When Arthur Godfrey was a young teenager, his father left. He and his mother, an unsuccessful entertainer, found themselves impoverished. Arthur took odd jobs, even traveled around as a hobo, until he served in the United States Navy from 1920 to 1924 as a radio operator. Further radio training came when he served with the Coast Guard from 1927 to 1930. Leaving the Coast Guard, he became a radio announcer until a car crash left him hospitalized for several months. During his recovery, he listened to the radio and felt that most radio announcers were stiff, formal, and didn't speak to the public listening to them. When he returned to the airwaves, he decided that his manner would be friendly, relaxed, and informal. He would speak as though he were speaking to just one person. With his warm voice, intimate style, and sophistication mixed with down-home Southern warmth, people listened to him and loved his programs.

When he ventured onto the television screen, his friendly manner combined with his freckles, wavy, bright red hair, and inviting smile endeared him to viewers across the nation. He quipped humorously with his sponsors, putting aside scripts and using his own words to describe the products. He promoted only those items that he liked and would use himself. He refused to advertise things that he personally would not endorse. In 1953, after an operation, Godfrey gave up smoking. Chesterfield had been a major sponsor of his programs. He refused to continue to promote smoking and said he would simply find another major sponsor—and he did. His advertising quips added spice to the programs and turned out to be a more effective sales pitch than those written by advertising firms. Arthur Godfrey played the ukulele and sang a song or two in between the talent competitors. Later, Godfrey was inducted into the Ukulele Hall of Fame. The Hawaiian shirts he donned along with his ukulele playing added to his colorful personality.

On *American Idol*, the 21st century talent show, some very talented wannabes manage to remain on the show for several weeks, and one even wins amid some very untalented wannabes. On *Arthur Godfrey's Talent Scouts*, agents, other scouts—including mothers (as with Patsy Cline)—brought their discoveries to a New York theater to perform before a live studio audience. The majority of those who performed were not simply wannabes. They were extremely talented professionals looking for their break into show biz. The quality of talent the American public viewed and heard on Godfrey's program was of the highest caliber. An applause meter responded to the audience's assessment of the performers. The public enjoyed being the judge of top-notch talent and often had a difficult choice to make. Even those who did not emerge as the winner were often signed to contracts with record and film companies. CBS and the sponsors loved the program, for it cost from twenty to thirty thousand dollars less to air than most shows.

By 1951, *Arthur Godfrey's Talent Scouts* topped the Nielsen Ratings as the highest rated television show for 1951–1952. *I Love Lucy* surpassed it when the show appeared on TV in 1952, but the *Talent Scouts* remained close in second place.

Hecky knew that Arthur Godfrey's name and picture on a children's record would sell well. Godfrey was happy to oblige with certain stipulations. He came, in effect, as a package. The Archie Bleyer Orchestra of his programs would have to accompany him, and his "friends," The Mariners and The Chordettes, likewise, if backup singers were needed. This posed no problem. Hecky knew it would only add to the appeal of the record. Godfrey recorded "The Tubby the Tuba Song," which increased sales of the complete story of Tubby. The flip side to the Tubby song was a ditty by Jack Winters and J. Fred Coots called "Tweedle Dee the Clown." These were followed by Godfrey reciting the Clement Moore poem "'Twas the Night Before Christmas" with the Bleyer orchestra in the background and on the flip side, a lively rendition of "Jingle Bells" with both The Mariners and The Chordettes adding their harmonies.

I was at the recording of the Christmas numbers. The studio was bustling with the orchestra and the two vocal groups. Godfrey stood out like a bright red light on an ambulance or police car. Mild-mannered and sweet as he appeared, that flaming red hair, the Hawaiian shirt he wore to the session, his smile, and deep baritone voice shone through the bustle. He sat upon a stool and smoked one unfiltered Chesterfield after another. His rosy-cheeked, freckled face seemed enveloped in smoke as he lifted his chin toward the ceiling and blew smoke rings while waiting for one or another thing to be set up in the studio: an orchestra adjustment, sound effects experiment, another microphone being placed for The Mariners and The Chordettes. He made my father's dependence upon cigarettes seem mild as he lit one from the remainder of the butt just smoked. Almost everyone in the studio smoked. The intrigue of those little sticks of tobacco was overwhelming. It seemed part of the glamour of the celebrity and musician life. In later years, when my mother had to have a heart operation, she was asked after a lung X-ray, "When did you give up smoking?" "I never smoked," she replied. Second-hand smoke was not a known fact yet.

Godfrey puffed away, even while recording whenever a phrase allowed a quick inhale and exhale. He'd simply turn away from the microphone so the sound would not be heard. He also brought his ukulele. Maybe he could add its sound here and there. But Christmas and a ukulele, ingrained in the public's consciousness as having a sunny, Hawaiian sound, did not mesh. Godfrey sat puffing Chesterfields and strumming his uke during breaks. I couldn't take my eyes off of him. He seemed the epitome of jolly, totally relaxed, a person all my school chums had heard about, a name that rolled off the tongues of nearly everyone in the nation. Here I was in the same room with him, hearing and seeing him recite a poem I loved, and hearing him sing the ever-sung "Jingle Bells." At the end of the session, my father let me go out of the control booth to speak with him. We had been introduced before the session began.

"Do you like this little instrument of mine?" He asked me holding up his ukulele.

"Yes. I'm taking piano lessons, dance lessons, and I wanted to play the harp, but my parents told me I am too impatient and it's too expensive to rent or buy. I think I will take guitar lessons."

"For a young girl you sure make long sentences." He had summed me up well—the *pisc* or "mouth" of the family. "Would you like to strum my ukulele?" He asked.

"Wow! Yes!"

"Let me show you a simple chord." He showed me with his fingers, then handed me the instrument, placed my fingers where they should be, showed me how to strum with my right hand, and la-de-da—I played my first chord on a uke. I began singing "On Top of Old Smokey," a folk song I knew and one that was now a hit on the radio sung by the Weavers.

"That's enough now, Juddie," my father said as he came out of the control booth. "Let Mr. Godfrey go."

"Your daughter's got talent, Hecky. Maybe she'll make it onto the show someday."

"We'll see," my father answered in a voice half mixed with a vaguely punitive sound. That was his tone and answer when he had inner questions as to which way my life should or shouldn't go.

After this encounter with Arthur Godfrey, I became obsessed with the ukulele. My school friends oohed and aahed when I told them that I had played Arthur Godfrey's ukulele. I dreamed that I could be a child star on the *Talent Scouts*.

. . . .

In 1948, a young singer who had been touring with the big band of Tony Pastor and harmonizing with her sister Betty made a solo appearance on *Arthur Godfrey's Talent Scouts*. Her name was Rosemary Clooney. She sang the song "Golden Earrings," which she'd been singing with Pastor's band. She competed, among others, against a young man whose stage name was Joe Bari, whose birth name was Anthony Dominick Benedetto, and who later became known as Tony Bennett. Rosemary won as the applause meter soared to its highest mark and stayed there as the audience continued to show their appreciation of this young lady's vocal talent. Columbia Records wanted to sign her up immediately, but they would have to wait until May of 1949, when she would turn 21 and could sign her own contract.

Rosemary Clooney was born in Maysville, Kentucky, to an alcoholic father and a flighty mother who preferred the road and a handsome sailor to motherhood. Rosemary, sister Betty, and brother Nick, spent their childhoods being passed from one relative to another. At age 13, their mother took Nick with her, and the two girls, no longer able to live with their aging grandmother, were on their own. Their lunches at school were purchased with the refunds from soda bottles they collected. Their voices saved them. They won an open singing contest, and the two were hired for a weekly radio show and paid $20 each per week. Word of their talent spread, and soon, their uncle George Guilfoyle became their guardian and manager as they traveled, singing with a variety of big bands and ending up with the Tony Pastor Band. Relatives and friends said of the two sisters that Betty was the decisive one and Rosemary the one with talent. Rosemary felt like she was betraying her sister when she set off on her own path to fame and stardom, but Betty claimed she just wanted to have a family and be at home with no one asking for her autograph.

Rosemary Clooney signed her contract with Columbia on May 24, 1949, the day after her 21st birthday. The popularity of big bands was slowly waning, for it was costly to transport so many musicians and their instruments to gigs from town to town. More and more, the talented singers with these bands were in demand as solo artists, their voices taking the lead with just enough instrumentation to back them. Like many of these artists, Rosemary Clooney was known in the specific towns where she had performed with the Tony Pastor Band. Her name was not yet known across the nation. It took time and the right songs to create a hit. Rosemary's early pop recordings at Columbia were not significant hits.

She began recording for Hecky on March 9th of 1950 with a song called "I Found My Mamma." Its flip side was a song that would bring Rosemary Clooney's name into homes across the nation and in England, where it also aired on the radio, crossed over from children's to pop, and sold hundreds and thousands of copies. The song was "Me and My Teddy Bear," written by J. Fred Coots.

After composing many famous songs like "I Still Get a Thrill (Thinking of You)," "Love Letters in the Sand," "You Go to My Head," and "Santa Claus is Coming to Town," Coots was having a dry spell. He struggled for months to come up with a new hit that would pay the bills that his well-to-do lifestyle now demanded. While preparing to take a three-week vacation, he went to the attic in his large Westchester home to get a suitcase and his golf clubs. There he tripped over an old beaten-up teddy bear that belonged to his daughter Gloria. Looking at the one-eyed, mangy-looking creature with one leg almost gone as sawdust poured out of its now torn fur covering, he remembered how Gloria loved that little bear. She would dress it up and place it in a kneeling position each night so it could say its prayers with her. Touched by his memories and inspired, he went to his piano, and in less than one hour, "Me and My Teddy Bear" was written.

J. Fred Coots put his vacation down south on the back burner and headed straight to Hecky's office. He played it for my father, who was in constant search of songs that could follow "Rudolph." He thought that "Me and My Teddy Bear" had the right appeal. He set up a recording date for that very afternoon and called upon Percy Faith to arrange the orchestration for a novelty seven-piece band. He called Rosemary Clooney to come to the office at once so that Coots could teach her the song. Surveys, like the one done during Hecky's and Dinah Shore's lullaby controversy, continued to show that female voices were not as popular among children, for they were reminders of mother, with whom the children spent most of their time. But Hecky felt that Rosemary's voice would be perfect for the song. When she arrived, he advised her, "Sing with clarity and directness and without hint of maternal sweetness. Just tell the story as you sing the song."

The recording session began at 4:00 P.M. with Percy Faith as the conducting maestro. Within one hour, the recording was completed and the tape rushed to the Columbia Plant in Bridgeport, Connecticut for pressing. Early the next morning, 2,000 vinylite records were on their way to disc jockeys and jukebox operators all over the country. "Me and My Teddy Bear" was Rosemary's springboard to prominence. That 2,000 multiplied rapidly as the song worked its way into the homes and hearts of families across the country. So did the name Rosemary Clooney.

. . . .

Easter vacation arrived. My father had been at Columbia for one year, and he now could take his first two-week vacation. He and my mother decided that we would take a trip to historic Yorktown, see the Liberty Bell in Philadelphia, and head on to Williamsburg, Virginia, to see historical reenactments, houses, and shops, as they were in colonial times. I was spellbound by history and felt the ghosts of the brave and many wounded soldiers at Yorktown. I thought deep and hard about those freezing cold men that George Washington led across the Delaware. The Liberty Bell brought tears to my eyes as I thought of our founding fathers and the democracy they wished this country to become. Our celebration on the Fourth of July at Granny and Grandpa's beach house, where Grandpa set off firecrackers, would now have new and deep meaning for me. As for Granny and Grandpa, my parents explained the historical places we were witnessing often in relation to my grandparents and the dream that America offered to them and to all the immigrants who poured into this country to escape tyranny, poverty, and oppression. Young as I was, I felt connected to this land and its government and felt that each and every one of its inhabitants counted and could make a difference.

Then we reached Williamsburg. My excitement knew no end as I felt I had walked into the colonial past. The blacksmith's shop gave me insight into what my grandfather's work had been in his youth, and I was fascinated with the tools, the hot, bending metal, the wooden building, and the attire of the blacksmith. In the silversmith's shop, the story of Paul Revere was told as we watched silver take shape into a cup and a vase. Lunch was a super treat at The Kings Arms Tavern with its dark wood atmosphere embellished by hanging lanterns, food and drink served on plates like those in colonial times, and silverware with fork prongs larger than any with which I'd ever eaten. The hot deep-dish apple pie had a cream sauce that filled my father with totally contagious joy. Warm apple pie was something his stomach always welcomed without negative effects. We left our plates spotless of any remnant of food.

After lunch, we went to the information center for further pamphlets and maps of the general area. Lunch, and the breakfast preceding it, had moved its way through my digestive system. The ladies' room was my next stop. I had heard about segregation. I had learned some things about the Civil War. I knew the words Ku Klux Klan, and they sent shivers down my spine. I had nightmares after Aunt Helen took Karen and me to Sam Goody's record store on 47th Street, where I bought the Josh White album that contained the song "Strange Fruit," about lynching in the South. Poplar trees only held one association for me after hearing the song. In my house, lynching, separate areas on buses and trains, separate schools and restaurants, and separate toilets for blacks and whites seemed unimaginable. I had learned that they existed, but they were not yet part of my actual experience, not until Williamsburg,

Virginia. Here, the crack in the Liberty Bell took on a whole new meaning for me.

As I looked for the bathroom, I noticed two ladies' rooms. One said, "White Only." The other said, "Colored Only." I stood there wishing I could shed my skin like a snake. I felt totally ashamed of being white as I viewed for the first time, right before me, segregation. I did not want to go into the White Only bathroom. I didn't want to stoop so low as to be a white person who wouldn't share a bathroom with a colored person. I would take my stand and protest by entering the one marked Colored Only, which I did. As I entered, the black women inside nervously pleaded, "Chile, get out of here! You're in the wrong bathroom. Get out before it's too late."

"I want to be here. I don't want to go to the white bathroom. It isn't right."

"Lord, have mercy, chile! A guard will surely have seen you. Get out quick!" A tall, hefty black woman took my shoulders, turned me around and pushed me toward the door.

I wouldn't leave. "I don't care if I get in trouble." The thought of going to the white bathroom made me want to throw up, and I felt like I might.

"Chile, it isn't you that'll get in trouble. It's us."

"But you didn't go into the white bathroom. I came in here."

"That's not the point." More women surrounded me pleading anxiously for me to leave.

The door opened, and my mother, who suspected what I'd done when she couldn't find me in the White Only bathroom demanded, "Judy, get out of here right now!" The vein in her neck pounded like an accordion in the hands of a fast polka player.

"But you told me segregation is wrong. I don't want to be with the whites in the bathroom."

A guard appeared at the door. "What's this commotion?" The women in the bathroom grew silent. I could practically hear their hearts pounding as the scent of fear in droplets of sweat permeated the air. My mother smiled her charming smile amidst her terror and spoke before the guard could get a word in. "Officer," she said as she yanked me by the arm so hard I thought my arm was torn off, "Forgive us. My daughter can't read very well."

"But she can see."

"She was on her way out." She dragged me out and smiled at the officer. She mingled with the crowd but kept looking back at the Colored Only bathroom to make sure he didn't go in and arrest the women. She wouldn't leave until she was sure of it. Then she took me to the door of the White Only bathroom, opened it, pushed me toward a stall and said, "Hurry up and do what you have to do, and don't ever do what you did again. You could have gotten those women into terrible trouble." I noticed a tear trickling down her cheek.

The rest of the vacation and all the way back to New York, I asked question after question about those two bathrooms, about slavery, about that mean word, segregation. It was difficult for me to understand how the women, and not me, could have gotten into trouble because I went into their bathroom. My parents bought me the Signet biography of Harriet Tubman, which I read night and day. This only raised another question. "Why couldn't the women in the bathroom do something like Harriet Tubman?"

"Change doesn't come overnight," my father tried to explain, "And you need a network, an organized and large group like the Underground Railroad for change to take place. Many people and leaders are working on ending segregation, but it will take time."

. . . .

When my father returned to work, "Me and My Teddy Bear" had already become a hit. We heard it time and again as we drove from place to place on our trip. On April 18, Rosemary recorded four more songs by J. Fred Coots: "Little Sally One-Shoe," "Little Johnny Chickadee," "Peterkin Pillowboy," and "Who'll Tie the Bell (On the Old Cat's Tail)." Again, Percy Faith conducted the band. Coots wrote to Hecky, "Have a good time and look for me upon my return from Washington. And again, my deep appreciation to you for the nice things you have been able to do for the new Coots tunes."

. . . .

It was the end of May. My father had recorded four more songs with Burl Ives including "The Little White Duck," which, like "Me and My Teddy Bear," won the hearts of the American public and was played by disc jockeys on the pop stations, praised in the trade journals, and reached the top of the charts for recommended children's fare. Hecky was due to leave for Hollywood the first week in June. The last week in May, two of Rosemary's aunts, whom I assume were the Jeanne and Rose she wrote about in her autobiography, came to visit her in New York. Rosemary took them to the Columbia offices. She introduced them to the people with whom she was working. It was Friday, in the late afternoon. My mother and I were at my father's office, for the family was going to see the Broadway musical *Peter Pan*, starring Jean Arthur. It had just opened on the 24th of April at the Imperial Theater where we'd meet Helen, Phil, Karen, and Jean.

Rosemary walked into my father's office. It was the first time I saw her in person. She didn't look like a glamorous star to me, but like a pretty, plain, simple girl who came from one of those states where they grew wheat and corn. She looked wholesome, and her smile held no guile. It was open and trusting, a beautiful smile that made me feel like the sun was shining right through her and out into the room. Her aunts appeared wholesome too, like people you might see at a country fair. Though women in the 1950s wore gloves, hats, and carried small, leather handbags, the gloves and hats on these two women struck me as more pronounced. Perhaps it was the way they clutched their pocketbooks demurely with both hands holding them at their waists. When shaking hands with my father and mother, they simply released one of their hands from the leather purses with their snap tops of gold-colored metal. After shaking hands, the other hand returned to the purses. They wore shirtwaist dresses and somewhat matronly pumps. Both wore hats that looked like little saucers sitting upon their heads, and each hat was secured with a hatpin.

Rosemary and my father had established a father/daughter-like kinship from the start. Hecky was 17 years her senior. Though her relationships indicated that she was attracted to older men, with Hecky there was no romantic inclination. She sensed in him his gentleness and honesty. He spoke to her in a doting fatherly way and treated her with respect and kindness. She responded to this gratefully. Her aunts picked up on Hecky's protective trait. Jeanne said, "Mr. Krasnow, take care of Rosemary here in this Big Apple. She's a small town girl, and a big city like this can be dangerous and tempting."

"I'll do that. I'll make sure Rosemary is just fine," my father assured them. My mother promptly invited them for dinner during the week. They accepted, and the date was made for Wednesday evening. We all said our goodbyes, as we had to allow time for dinner before going to the theater.

. . . .

We ate at a restaurant where I enjoyed one of my favorites, a hot turkey sandwich with mashed potatoes. Then we met the Eisenbergs at the Imperial Theater, where Karen, Jean, and I sat entranced. I couldn't separate Jean Arthur from the character she played, and she and Peter Pan became irrevocably intertwined in my mind. *Peter Pan* began a new round of artistic creativity for Karen and me that would last for several years. Helen and Phil's living room became our own Imperial Theater. Each time we saw a new show, inspired, we came home and developed our own production. We'd make tickets, charge 10 cents, invite the neighbors and friends (who actually came), and, hence, brought Broadway to 143 Douglas Avenue.

Our scenery was made from a variety of items stored in our large basement and sticks, stones, leaves, and flowers collected from our yard. We acquired costumes from raiding our parents' closets. Our music resounded from Helen's Knabe piano, the percussion of pots, pans, and spoons, my ukulele, an Autoharp my parents bought me, and the recorders we learned to play at Mrs. Wachtel's School of Music. We attended this wonderful music school in the Bronx each Thursday night. Here we thrilled to play drums, xylophones, zithers, bells, even a balalaika, and about as many instruments as sound effects men had gadgets.

After seeing *Peter Pan*, we felt we must somehow be able to re-create the scene where Peter and the children fly, as we'd sing the song "I Can Fly." I watched this scene in the theater with great curiosity. Though it was camouflaged as well as the technology of the day could do, I couldn't help but notice the wire attached to Jean Arthur and the others' backs. Out of everything in the show, those wires caught my attention more than anything else. I looked at the ceiling on the stage and spent a good deal of time throughout the musical trying to decipher the mechanism that enabled Peter, Wendy, and the others to fly. I wanted such a wire for my back so that I could experience the sensation of flying. In Karen's and my production, I came up with the idea that Jean, being younger and smaller than Karen and me, could be Tinkerbell. At least she could fly. Karen agreed. "But how?" she asked.

"We can take a rope, tie it around Jeanie's waist, and hang the rope from the chandelier in the living room. Jean can then flutter there as Tinkerbell."

Helen saved the chandelier, and Karen and I were spared the rod. While in her kitchen preparing lunch, Helen heard peculiar noises and Jean's cry of, "I'm scared." In the knick of time, Helen flew into the living room before Karen and I let go of Jean who was now strung up on the small lighting fixture with it's six ornate glass decorations covering the light bulbs within. Hence, Tinkerbell, alias Jean, fluttered and said the few lines we assigned to her standing on a chair.

. . . .

Wednesday arrived, and my father drove the car to work and later drove Rosemary and her two aunts to our house. My mother had made roast beef on the new rotisserie my father had bought for her in advance of her upcoming birthday on May 15. Her cooking was sublime, and she knew how to use seasonings to make dishes that were uniquely Lillian's. Salad and roasted potatoes dressed with the roast's drippings accompanied the meat. A lime Jell-O aspic filled with carrots and pineapple added color to the meal.

Though our house was small, it was welcoming. My parents collected interesting items ranging from sketches by friend and artist Joseph Margolis to exotic vases from Turkey and the Orient. The top of the Chickering piano was covered with a quilted piece of material that Aunt Pauline's husband Mickey, who had served in WWII as a butcher for Allied soldiers stationed in India, gave to them. On this, an assortment of unique knick-knacks rested, including brass candlesticks inlaid in orange and turquoise, purportedly from Russia and given to my parents by Sarah.

Rosemary and her aunts looked at all the objects and the many books upon the shelves my father had built in both the living and dining rooms. "This is like visiting a personal museum," Rosemary said. "And it's so good to have a home-cooked meal like this. I feel like I have a mother and a father in you, Hecky and Lillian. If there is anyone I know for sure I can trust in this business, Hecky, it is you."

It was a truly pleasant visit. Helen, Phil, Karen and Jean joined us after dinner. Rosemary was impressed with Phil's wit and understanding manner. Karen and I sang a few Burl Ives folk songs for Rosemary and her aunts. I now had a ukulele of my own and supplied basic chords and rhythm. At around ten o'clock, my father drove the three women to the train station. Before leaving, all three thanked my mother and father for an evening that, as they all commented, "felt like being at home with family." Jeanne said, "We will go home with our hearts at rest knowing our niece has you two wonderful people here to keep an eye on her."

CHAPTER 12

A Bitter Divorce

Grandma Sarah had essentially raised Steffi, who had moved back with us in autumn of 1950 to begin high school. Sarah doted upon Steffi as the first grandchild, and she had many dreams for her. She encouraged her to grow up be an intelligent, independent, educated woman. When Steffi moved in with us, my parents and I had bonded in our new home and new life. Steffi never truly became part of the core family that Hecky, Lillian, and I had become. Perhaps out of resentment that Lillian was never a "first mother" combined with the two having very different temperaments and outlooks, Steffi and our mother rarely saw eye to eye on matters.

I looked forward to having my sister again and thought it would be great to share a room. In Hartford, Steffi had taken care of me, played with me, and saved money from her allowance to buy me gifts, including a memorable and expensive talking doll whose short life ended as neighbor and playmate David Traub smashed its head to see if it had a brain that enabled it to talk. Often Steffi vied with my mother over matters of how to discipline me, with Steffi on the sterner side. I had only good expectations about her moving in. I didn't foresee any glitches.

There was one closet in my room, the one we would now share. The closet had a door in the center no larger than the door to the entrance of our room. It had a right and left corner defined by two parallel walls about three feet from each other. There was room for the clothes to hang, but not enough room to stand before the clothes in order to see them. To get to something on either side of the opening where each item was visible, I had to push the middle things to the left, or, conversely, to the right, then pull the items on the right and left towards the center. This worked fine with just my clothes in the closet, with blouses on one side, skirts for school on the other, and my shoes lined in a row in the center.

When Steffi arrived, she had gone through a transformation. She didn't even look like the sister I'd left behind. She was taller, and she had breasts. My sister wore a brassiere! She had developed into a pubescent teenager. As such, she took the liberty to push all of my clothes to the right of the center door and to place her clothes to the left and, of course, her most prized outfits smack center. She warned me not to dare touch them unless, of course, I wanted to die. I obeyed my sister and dutifully accepted my dark, crowded corner in the closet. However, I was enraged at the intrusion. With my blood at its boiling point, ignited by my inherently dramatic nature, I threw a ferocious tantrum of shouts, tears, stamps, and stomps like a two-year-old but added a developed barrage of words. "Go back to Hartford. I am moving upstairs with Karen. She's my real sister anyway!" To my mother, I flung the worst insult of all, one that always touched a raw chord. "Helen is a better mother than you!"

At this point, my father entered. "Mind what you say, Judy! That is your mother you are speaking to. I won't tolerate disrespect toward her. Get yourself under control. This is a big change for all of us, especially for your sister. We all have to make adjustments, but it is well worth it to have Steffi with us again."

"Thank you, honey," my mother said and returned to trying to gain some control over the situation. "Calm down, calm down, Judy," she implored trying to keep her voice soft and steady. "Just think, Judy, if you move upstairs you'll have to share a closet not only with Karen, but also with Jean."

My mother was not talking to me in her normal manner. She appeared nervous, and that telltale vein in her neck fluttered. She acted awkward with Steffi and I sensed that she had to get to know her. She had talked about how wonderful it would be to have her family totally intact with Steffi's return and how nice it would be with her two daughters together. Life wasn't turning out according to her vision.

My mother forever strove to maintain peace at any price. Strong of character as she was, she sought to please people, rather than aggravate them. She shied away from confrontation. I acquired this trait, except when it came to matters of social justice for others. The closet incident was not settled by discussion and compromise. Steffi was simply given the majority of the space in the closet. I told myself that I was making my sister happy. Doing mitzvahs (good deeds for others) was emphasized in our family.

My father aborted another of my tantrums. He enjoyed carpentry, something he was not allowed to engage in during his youth, and now threw himself into it with joy and pride in his rare spare time. He appeased my frustration by building Steffi her own dresser and me a headboard with a long, big shelf where I could pile everything I had piled atop the dresser before Steffi's arrival. He also built a desk in the room where, more often than Steffi, I did my homework because, more often than not, Steffi was off at some girlfriend's house.

Steffi had her own frustrations. She truly hated leaving Hartford. She was also at an age where, whether in Hartford or Yonkers, she would have begun to move toward greater independence and separation. To her, Yonkers was as much about her gang of girlfriends and the endless hours they spent discussing hairdos, sex, and boyfriends, as it was about life at home.

By 1951, Steffi had met Gerry Schamess, whom she would eventually marry. Steffi and Gerry had their own life, friends, and activities. They often included me in these activities. They introduced me to the beautiful and eccentric music of falsetto singer Alfred Deller and his Renaissance consort. Jon's Scandinavian Shop in Greenwich Village was another hangout of theirs, and here I bought the warmest sweater I ever owned and smelled the delicious cinnamon spiced Scandinavian grog. As we wandered the streets of Greenwich Village, I familiarized myself with its cafes and the growing interest in folk music. Steffi and Gerry took me to Pete Seeger and Weaver's concerts. I even befriended the duck that lived in the bathtub in Gerry's apartment near Columbia University, where he was getting his master's degree in psychology.

Most often, though, Steffi went her way, and the rest of us went ours. I was far more focused on activities with Karen, our mutual friends, dance and music lessons, and my ever-increasing involvement in my father's work and his and my mother's social life as a result.

. . . .

Hecky and Lillian had become good friends with Helen and Burl Ives. One evening, I, too, was invited to the Ives' Westchester home. The door opened, and Helen, a lovely, smiling lady greeted us with a warm, "Hello, well come right on in." The floors in front of me and to the right and left of me were wide slats of shiny, blond-colored wood. Their shine caught my eye and immediately made me feel that the Ives' house was a place with a sunny atmosphere. To the right of the foyer was a living room with a rustic wooden coffee table and a stone mantelpiece around a fireplace. Over the fireplace hung two guitars, one with a polished brownish-black finish and the other with a pinewood front and rosewood sides and back. The brownish-black one cast a spell upon me. I longed to have an instrument that looked like that. As I gazed at it, an ongoing conflict between my parents and me was resolved. I had been told that I could study another instrument along with my piano lessons. In the moment that I laid eyes on Burl's brownish-black guitar, I knew I would learn to play the guitar.

Burl Ives greeted us dressed in a black shirt and pants. His girth was modified very little, if at all, by the wearing of black. His belly, smile, sparkling eyes, and beard made him a definite second to Santa. If Westchester were the North Pole, I would have said that, without doubt, I had met this icon of childhood fantasy and gifts.

"Hecky and Lillian, it's so good to have you here. And Judy, you are a colorful sight for the eyes." My mother had bought me a skirt in keeping with her idea that she wished to dress me like a gypsy, an endearment she often used: "My little gypsy." The skirt could have matched Jacob's coat of many colors but, rather than stripes, had swirls of every color in the rainbow. "Come in. Come right in."

We followed Burl. To the left was a dining room, again with welcoming furniture: a wooden dining room table that looked like it had been made by elves in the woods, not unlike the table I imagined Snow White ate at with the seven dwarfs. In this instance, however, the table was not scaled for the comfort of dwarfs. Tonight I would be eating with a giant. Burl and Helen gave us a tour of their comfortable, lived-in, modestly large house, furnished simply. It had an open, uncluttered appearance. Consequently, the paintings, sculptures, and knick-knacks truly accented the corners, tables, or shelves they occupied. After the tour, we sat down to a wonderful meal of roast beef, potatoes, hot breads with lots of butter, and a variety of vegetables. First, Helen served a soup whose hearty aroma caused me to imagine that this was something knights around King Arthur's table would have eaten. I tasted it, closing my eyes and fancying myself to be just such a knight, and finished it plus a second helping. Here, at the Ives' table, I initiated into my almost nine-year-old existence a lifelong love of French onion soup.

After dinner, we went into the living room. Music, playwright Arthur Miller, the success of "The Little White Duck," museum exhibits, and new Broadway musicals comprised the content of the discussions. The name Joseph McCarthy entered the conversation frequently along with words like "communist list," "Cold War," "Red Scare," "vicious senator," "terrifying." The Iveses and my parents became quite agitated, especially when they talked about artists and writers on some list.

"Well," Burl Ives said, "I make a move that we talk about a more pleasant topic. Judy, I see you've been eyeing that guitar over the fireplace since you walked in. Do you play guitar?"

"No, but I can play several chords on the ukulele."

"I have one." Burl got up, went into another room, and came back with his ukulele. He handed it to me and I sang my usual "On Top of Old Smokey," which he'd just recorded for my father and then "Buckeye Jim," the sweet lullaby from his album *Animal Fair*.

"If you can play the uke so well and sing like that, I think you could play the guitar."

"I want to, Burl. Mom and Dad have said I can study another instrument along with piano. Of course, I have to promise to practice piano every day."

"But of course," Burl said.

Then I turned to my parents. "Mom and Dad, I knew as soon as I saw the guitar hanging over that fireplace that the guitar is what I will learn."

"Burl," my father said, "If you have solved our problem with my Juddie, I will be forever grateful. Our daughter Steffi bought an album with folk singer Susan Reed, *Songs of the Auvergne*."

"That's one of my favorites," Burl commented. "So let me guess, Judy, you want to play the harp."

"Yes, you are right. I love the sound of the harp, and I want to learn all the songs Susan Reed sings. I already know all your songs from *Animal Fair*. I want to grow up and sing and play something, but my parents say I am impulsive and change my mind a lot."

"Well, you are very young still. It takes time to know what you really want to play."

"My daughter is a very talented pianist," my mother piped in. "I think she should stick to the piano and perfect her talent on this instrument. Her teacher, Kenneth Wentworth, says she could become a concert pianist."

"Ah, Lillian, it takes more than talent to perfect anything. It takes a love of whatever it is you do or play." Wow! I thought. Burl Ives understands me! "From what I have seen of your daughter when I met her at the studio and here again tonight, she loves folk music and also enjoys singing. Maybe you have a budding troubadour."

"Well her second choice to the harp is the lute," my father said. "Maybe you are right, Burl, though I've told my Juddie that if she wants to be a Julian Bream on the lute her life wouldn't be much different from that of a concert pianist."

Burl Ives went to the mantelpiece. He lifted that enchanting brownish-black guitar off the wall, sat down next to me and showed me the C chord. He handed me the guitar. I placed my fingers where he instructed. The sound was a bit muted at first. "Hold your wrist up in the same way you do when you play the piano. That way you won't muffle the strings."

I did as he instructed. He taught me the G chord, and then the F chord, which was the hardest. That would take practice. I knew right there and then: guitar it would be!

That week, I spoke with my friend Arthur Lee, a fellow student, bike rider, and play- cowboys-pal as handsome as any real cowpoke. Arthur lived nearby on Bellevue Avenue. He studied guitar. He gave me the number of his teacher, Mr. Riggoli. My father called and spoke with him. I'd begin lessons in two weeks. The next weekend my parents took me guitar shopping. Still not trusting that I would follow through with these lessons, they purchased the cheapest guitar we could find that, once tuned, remained in tune. It didn't resemble Burl's enchanting one, and the strings certainly didn't feel as smooth and low to the neck as Burl's guitar. The action on the instrument was dreadful, and its strings were not nylon. This guitar, called a steel-string guitar, had strings made of catgut, the very thought of which made my stomach turn and my guilt rise. The strings made my fingers bleed, but I told myself this was the penalty I must incur for a cat having been slaughtered so that I could play the guitar. I never missed a lesson with Mr. Riggoli, and I practiced daily, until my fingertips cried out for me to stop. Ultimately, calluses developed, and I could play for longer and longer periods of time. In a matter of months, I knew several chords and strums, and spent hours singing. Frequently, Karen joined me, adding her sweet harmonies. We enjoyed singing, and for Karen at the time, it was infinitely preferable to being upstairs in her own house.

. . . .

Aunt Helen had grown quite bitter over the past several months. Mild-mannered Phil had been the brunt of much of this bitterness. Phil enjoyed the time he spent with Karen and Jean, and, since I was always with them, played games with us, answered our many questions of wonder, and read us books we relished. One favorite was entitled *First Man*, and told about the evolution of life forms on Earth and of man from apes to human. The book raised some eyebrows and spurred controversy in its reviews 25 years after the famous Scopes Trial regarding Darwin's *Origins of Species*. The book fed Karen and me with fascinating thoughts and an equal number of inquiries, which Phil answered, thrilled with our interest. In return, he asked us questions of psychological import like, "If you could be something other than what you are, what would you want to be and why?"

"I think I'd like to be a tree," I volunteered. "A tree is strong. It is beautiful. It dances when the wind blows its branches and leaves. It always hears music because birds sing in it, and trees live for a very, very long time and know the secrets we don't know."

Karen answered, "I would want to be a monkey, a chimpanzee, because it is the closest thing to a human with its brain. I would want that because I want to be something very intelligent."

Phil probed further. "Judy, what is it about strength and longevity that appeals to you?" He asked Karen, "Why do you feel it is necessary to be intelligent?"

This was our life with Phil. He made us think about truly interesting topics. When he and Hecky were together, it was a special treat. We were a talkative family, and conversation was one of our early-learned skills. Whether Hecky and Phil took us to the Bronx Zoo, a museum, The Adventurers (a Nathan's hot dog eatery with games to play), or to the Louis Untermeyer Estate Park, we always returned with exciting new thoughts and fun stories to tell. Of course, there were times when Phil and Hecky became so engrossed in their own conversations that they tended to forget they were not alone on the planet.

One time we were headed for Hartford to celebrate Passover at Grandma Sarah's. We all piled into Helen and Phil's green, tubby-bodied Hudson. I sat up front between Phil and my father, who drove. Phil turned the radio to a classical music station. Soon he and my father were talking. I switched the station to a country one that was closer to folk music, and the funereal Requiem on the classical station was boring me. Just as Patsy Cline came on with her hit "Crazy," Phil's ears caused his fingers to turn the knob back to the classical station.

"Juddie," my father's voice followed Phil's fingers, "I don't want you listening to that junk."

"But I like it, Daddy."

"Well learn to unlike it."

"Why?"

"Because the singers whine and moan over broken hearts, cheating, and too much drinking down at the bar."

"And the majority of them support Joseph McCarthy and his absurd allegations and lists," Phil added.

"They never sing about the guy you just mentioned," I pleaded.

"Believe me, if things get worse, they will. End of conversation. Now let your father and I talk."

"Why can't I listen to what I like while you talk? That classical music is putting me to sleep."

"It won't harm you to get some sleep," my father responded. "You'll be staying up past your bedtime tonight."

"That's not a good answer," I said, shaking my pointed finger at him.

"Put that finger down, and do as I say."

I tried to change the station a couple of more times on the long ride to Grandma's. Somehow, deep as they were in conversation, Phil and my father always perked up to the change I made in the radio's sound.

Along route on the two-lane highway, one lane in each direction, we stopped to fill the car with gasoline and, more importantly, to use the bathrooms. Gas stations were few and far between. I was the first one in—and out—of the ladies' room. I walked to the gas pumps where I assumed I'd find the big green Hudson. The Hudson wasn't there. I walked around the left side of the little store at the station. No hint of the Hudson. I walked around the whole building until I came to a small parking area. The car was invisible. As the others ambled out of the bathroom, I told them I couldn't find the car. My mother and Helen figured out just what had happened. Phil and Hecky had filled the tank, climbed back in, started talking again, and drove off oblivious that not one of us had returned to the car. I pondered deeply over how their reveries could leave us abandoned at a gas station, but when I switched the radio to country music, their reveries could be interrupted.

For what seemed an interminably long time, my mother, Helen, Karen, Jean, and I talked. We drank sodas from bottles, put the bottles back, and got a nickel for each bottle returned. We went to the bathroom again. We talked. We walked. We drank more soda. We ate Hershey bars purchased with the nickels from the returned soda bottles. We went to the bathroom again.

Two hours later, that tub of a Hudson rolled back into the gas station. My father and Phil got out of the car somewhat sheepishly.

"Honey, I am sorry, genuinely sorry," my father said before my mother could open her mouth. "Phil and I were so involved in discussing a new idea for a record project. We thought you'd all returned to the car."

"New idea, shmoo idea!" My mother wasn't interested in any ideas right now. "What if it had been winter? We'd be frozen by now. How can you just drive off without checking to see if everyone's accounted for?"

"I'm sorry, honey, really sorry. As I said, wait until you hear this new idea. It's a winner!"

"Winner, shminner! Helen and I should tie the two of you up in the backseat and do the driving ourselves, better yet, tie you to balloons and let you float up to the clouds where you belong!" Then, angry as she was, her relief that they had at least returned and the ridiculousness of the circumstances caused her to burst out laughing. She laughed so hard that Karen, Jean, and I began to laugh too.

Helen, on the other hand, smoked like an angry chimney and yelled two hours worth of pent up fury at Phil. "You incompetent, selfish man. This is the way you care about me and your children?" Helen's bitterness could sour many a moment that could benefit from a little sugar, not lemon.

Then, before we all piled into the car once again, my mother said, "You drank so much soda, Judy, you'll have to pee again. Go now before we get on the road."

"What?" I cried. "So they'll leave us waiting here again?" I meant it as a joke, or maybe I really wondered if our trip to Hartford would be spent at a gas station.

My words must have touched my father's sense of responsibility. His guilt over his irresponsibility barked back at me, "Judith!" He never called me Judith. I was scared. "Judith, I will ask of you please to keep your always eager mouth quiet! Everything is under control now."

As always, he'd ask, "Is everything under control?" or he'd state, "Everything is under control," usually when he felt everything, particularly he, was out of control.

"Just go pee!" my mother implored. "I will stand here and make sure they don't drive off again."

I did my mother's bidding and returned to my tempting place between my father and Phil, smack in front of the radio dial. Now I was truly tempted. If they could drive off without us, maybe they would be so involved in discussion that they would now not notice the country music. I got to hear one whole song and nearly half of another before their alert ears picked up the signal and ended my music ecstasy.

Over the next several months, Phil and Helen quarreled incessantly. During this time, a huge box was delivered to the house. Karen, Jean, and I watched as it was carried in through the garage and placed in the basement. Two muscled deliverymen removed what looked like a small shed. Its outside was made of a cotton-like substance, while its inside was silver-colored and shiny. It looked like a house one might encounter in a fairy tale when lost in the woods. One of the deliverymen attached a wooden bench that stretched around three of the inner walls. There were no shelves, no drawers to store things, nothing but the wooden bench. Phil, who had ordered this whatever-it-was, tipped the men handily.

"What's that?" Karen asked. "A playhouse for us? Thanks, Daddy."

"It's not a playhouse for you or anyone, Karen. It's an Orgone Accumulator. It will make you healthy if you sit in it."

"Will it get rid of poison ivy? I hate it every summer when I get poison ivy so bad that my eyes can't even open."

"It might build up your defenses against poison ivy. It does wondrous things."

This magical box did become a playhouse for us. Each day, after running around outdoors after school, Karen, Jean, and I would find time to bring our dolls, coloring books, cards, and checker game and spend hours inside this strange edifice. When Steffi was at home and wished for privacy, she monopolized the orgone box claiming she had homework to do, and this was the only quiet place in the house to do it. On weekends, Phil had first dibs and spent many hours in there. My father joined him, and there, the two collaborated on ideas for my father's projects.

Helen had her own reaction. "Orgone, my eye! It's just another excuse, Phil, another excuse for you not to spend time with me!"

Helen was not entirely wrong, but Phil's obsession with orgone was not an excuse not to be with Helen. Phil had become deeply involved with the supporters of psychologist Wilhelm Reich, whose experiments led this controversial doctor to believe that a universal and biological energy that he called orgone did exist and had definite curative effects, particularly on cancer. Reich, a German psychotherapist who emigrated from his native land to Forest Hills, New York, was quite famous for his book *Character Analysis*. The book received acclaim for its theories about the relationships between mental and physical health as well as between sexual repression and neurosis. Reich recognized a direct link between negative mental states and ensuing physical illnesses. He was the first therapist to encourage his patients to express deep emotion in sessions by screaming and weeping, a practice that is fairly common in psychotherapy today.

Reich used the scientific method—a hypothesis, experiments, and control groups to draw conclusions regarding orgone. He attempted to observe the orgone phenomenon under many varied circumstances. Based upon his observations, he built his box with metal walls on the inside and cotton, an organic material, on the outside. He simultaneously did a great deal of research on T cells before and during the onset of cancer. He believed orgone could help to regulate these and lessen, possibly prevent, and be helpful in the cure of cancer. In 15 cases using cancer patients, between 1941 and 1943, all were in the advanced stages. All spent time in Reich's Orgone Accumulator. Their sessions were timed, for Reich believed that too much exposure to orgone could also create harm. Three patients died within the time their doctors predicted. Six of the patients lived between five to twelve months longer than predicted. The remaining six patients were still alive in 1943, when Reich wrote his paper on the experiment. All of his patients claimed that sitting in the orgone box greatly alleviated their pain and lessened their use of morphine drastically.

Reich did many other experiments, and the results of these and his concept of orgone created much controversy, scientific politicking, and envy. Were many of his theories proven true, other theories that for years had been solid pillars in scientific circles and the halls of academe would be proven false. Those who were proponents and teachers of these theories as absolute truths would look foolish. Ultimately, Reich was imprisoned in 1957. Most of his equipment and written research was destroyed, leaving huge numbers of his followers horrified, and the world unable to continue, particularly in cancer research, from where he left off.

. . . .

Phil was dedicated to Reich and his research. He knew the Orgone Accumulator could not harm any of us, and it might truly increase our health. The entire family used it. My mother tried it, but found her health did better if she could spend hours on the phone talking to Sherry Walsh, who, for her, proved a far better therapist than Wilhelm Reich. My father spent daily time in the Accumulator hoping it might help his Crohn's. Unfortunately, we did not have enough time to find out if it would help Crohn's victims or prevent Karen's annual summer bout with poison ivy. Helen, in an effort to share Phil's interest in Reich and the healing powers of orgone, spent time with him in the Accumulator. More often than not, however, she would emerge from it furious. Helen suspected something. And she was correct.

Phil had been married before to a woman named Miriam. Miriam was a follower of Reich and attended the same meetings as Phil. Here, she and Phil met again. The two shared their dedication to the Wilhelm Reich movement. Their passion for Reich and orgone rekindled their passion for each other. Helen knew and tried desperately to save her threatened marriage. Not only was Phil her husband but he had also become an ingrained Krasnow family member. To Hecky, he was a soul mate, friend, and collaborator; to Lillian, a brother; to me, a second father. If Helen and Phil were to divorce, it would not just be a couple breaking up. It would be a divorce that created a tidal wave throughout the family.

Phil came home less and less. Karen and I often tried to calm Jean's tears of fear, and I attempted to keep Karen from crying along with Jean. Helen's uncontrolled anger aggravated the tears as she screeched over the phone when Phil called. "Don't bother coming home. I hope *she* likes you in bed. You're not man enough to be a husband in or out of bed. Don't think you'll see your children very often. A man who is so untrustworthy doesn't deserve his children. I don't need you, Phil. Hecky lives right downstairs. Now there's a man who knows what it is to be loyal and faithful! You bastard!"

A pall fell across the first two floors of our three-family house. The pain was palpable in the air itself. Phil moved out. "You remain friends with Phil, Hecky, and I'll never speak to you again," Helen gave her ultimatum.

My mother, while coping with her own deep sorrow and anger over the situation, had to deal with my father, who grew deeply depressed. Inwardly, he was battling the choice Helen had given him, but he knew his friendship with Phil must, of needs, end. He began to lose weight though he ate well. The stress of losing Phil aggravated his Crohn's and landed him in Montefiore Hospital in the Bronx with a horrific bout with involuntary anorexia.

At home, Helen wept each night, holding Karen, Jean, and often me, saying, "We'll manage. We'll get by. You'll see. We will all be happy again."

CHAPTER 13

A Red Caboose, a Harpsichord, and Horn & Hardart's

. . . .

n the early 1950s, television was still a relatively new technology. It was emerging from its childhood into its adolescence and finding its identity in society. Increasingly, it crept into the homes across America. However, channels and programs were few, and radio still hung on to the last couple of years of its golden age. Even as radio personalities began to also be seen on television as they transformed their radio formats for a viewing audience, radio still dazzled the ears and ignited the imaginations of adults and children alike through exciting, familiar, and beloved programs.

On Monday evenings, hearts would race to the sounds of adventure. *Faster than a speeding bullet! More powerful than a locomotive! Able to leap tall buildings at a single bound! Yes, it's Superman—strange visitor from another planet who came to Earth with powers and abilities far beyond those of mortal men.*

Superman flew through the airwaves and out of the speakers of radios into virtually every household. So did the call of the *Lone Ranger*, "Hi-Yo, Silver!" *The Shadow* cackled, "Who knows what evil lurks in the hearts of men? The Shadow knows!" *Dragnet*, laden with suspense and mystery, elevated the pulse rate of each and every listener.

Names like Burns and Allen, Jack Benny, Groucho Marx, Abbott and Costello, Amos 'n' Andy, Ethel and Albert, Fibber McGee and Molly were part of the American consciousness. Comic strip characters like Archie Andrews, Popeye the Sailor, Li'l Abner, and Little Orphan Annie came to life over the radio and sent kids everywhere to the local news stores to buy the comics and read them regularly. Gag shows, mysteries, and soap operas were heard like books on tape. Listening was a satisfying, humorous, and thrilling form of entertainment.

Children would awaken on Saturday eager to hear stories told with animated voices and evocative background music on programs like Nila Mack's *Let's Pretend* and Jon Arthur's creation, *Big Jon and Sparkie*, also titled *No School Today*. Karen and I would get up well ahead of the start of these programs, eat our Kellogg's Rice Krispies, and plunk down in front of the radio in Helen's living room. Though monaural, the radio had two speakers, one on each side of the three-foot-wide wooden cabinet that housed it. My ear leaned on one speaker, Karen's on the other. On *Let's Pretend*, "Pretenders" re-enacted both adaptations of classic fairy tales and original fantasies. Here we were inspired to be honest and courageous, and to "live happily ever after" as we heard Hans Christian Anderson's *Goose Girl, Jack and the Beanstalk, King Midas and the Golden Touch, Robin Hood, Cinderella, Beauty and the Beast, Aladdin and the Wonderful Lamp, Chinese Nightingale*, and many, many more. Our heads filled with images of castles, forests, magic carpets, genies, poor children, kind rescuers, damsels in distress, and knights in shining armor.

We'd talk about these stories with our friends, who equally relished Saturday morning and the radio programs that entertained while continuing to educate us when we were not at school. The programs expanded the horizons of our imaginations and inspired us to become proficient readers of storybooks, comic books, and just about any kind of book we could tackle by ourselves.

When *Let's Pretend* ended, the gripping music of "The Teddy Bears' Picnic" would ready us for an adventure with Big Jon and Sparkie on *No School Today*. We were compelled to tune in each and every week to hear the elf-like voice of Sparkie as he convinced Big Jon to listen to what he had to say. We'd hear Yuki the cab driver help solve the mysterious events that grew out of the program's intriguing themes. We simply had to find out what happened when the wealthy widow Daffodil Dilly was kidnapped, or how the "Canine Mutiny" was resolved. This program was, in effect, a child's introduction to reading Agatha Christie mysteries in the future, or analyzing clues Sherlock Holmes might find. As we listened, we learned very definite civics lessons of right, wrong, and acceptable behavior towards others. Big Jon and Sparkie ignited our interest in nature through episodes like "Sparkie Finds a Bug" and "Sparkie's Mysterious Butterfly."

One episode of *No School Today* grew out of a song that Hecky contracted Big Jon and Sparkie to record, "Little Red Caboose." The lyrics derived from a common rhyme often recited by children.

> Little Red Caboose chug, chug, chug
> Little Red Caboose, chug, chug, chug,
> Little Red caboose behind the train, train, train, train
> Smokestack on its back, back, back, back
> Never looking back, back, back, back
> Little Red Caboose behind the train.

Ray Carter and his orchestra, through chromatic notes starting slowly and increasing in speed, along with the sound effects man using a gadget that looked like a mixture of a bicycle pump and an oilcan, created the sound of train wheels moving and the train whistle blowing. Sparkie, whose elf-like voice was actually that of Big Jon (who created most of the voices on the programs), not only sang but also spoke on the record. "Children, we're coming to a hill. Let's help the caboose push that train." As Sparkie made chugging sounds, children listening couldn't help but participate. Sparkie asked them, "Are you having fun? Hold on tight—here we go!"

When the song was released in October of 1951, records quickly cleared the shelves as parents bought them not only for their children, but to hear for themselves. Big Jon and Sparkie captivated old and young alike. The song remained on the charts for several years and sold in large numbers when the radio episode with the song was aired.

The reverse side, too, became popular. In "Run, Rabbit, Run," Sparkie sings about how Friday on the farm is "rabbit pie day." He sings of how he wakes up early to warn his friend the rabbit to stay clear of the farmer's gun and "run, run, run." The simple melody with its running rhythm repeats accompanied by sounds of a rabbit chomping carrots and bunny feet scurrying as Sparkie calls out to the rabbit to run and says the farmer will "get by without his rabbit pie." Hecky's collection of *Billboard* and *Variety* clippings has many reporting on these two popular songs.

· · · · · · · · · · · ·

The year 1950 ended with "Rudolph" selling millions of more records. On January 6th and 13th, with Christmas now over, *Billboard* showed that for 10 weeks, "Rudolph" held the number one place. "Frosty the Snowman" had been on the charts for 12 weeks and held second place along with another Johnny Marks song, "When Santa Claus Gets Your Letter." Things were going very well for Columbia, for Johnny Marks, and for Hecky, whose choice of songs proved to be just what the public wanted to hear.

In January, Rosemary Clooney recorded the song "The Land of Hatchy Milatchy." It had a pleasant catchy tune with lyrics about a wonderful place, where "lollipops grow right up out of the ground, merry-go-rounds are made of sugar and spice, the moon is made of strawberry ice; and if you should run and you trip and you fall, the ground's made of rubber—you'll bounce like a ball." The song was a good seller along with Rosemary's first pop hit at Columbia also recorded in January, "Beautiful Brown Eyes," which eventually sold 400,000 records.

Burl Ives's "Little White Duck" moved its way up to number five on the charts. Easter came, and "Peter Cottontail" held the number one place for all of March and April. Another tune, sung by Gene Autry climbed to number four, "Sonny the Bunny." Hecky wrote this song with Tommy Johnson, the songwriter who was the inspiration for the character who sold his soul to the devil to play guitar and became one of the Soggy Bottom Boys in the 2000 movie *Oh Brother, Where Art Thou?*

Hecky participated in a big promotion for "Sonny the Bunny" at Macy's. So did Karen and I. We walked around the store cuddling little Sonny Bunnies while an adult dressed in a large Sonny costume shook hands and posed for pictures with shoppers. Toddlers, often frightened by large renditions of animal characters, hesitated to shake hands with such a huge rabbit. Some even cried. Karen and I stepped in to let them pet our smaller rabbits. We danced with our bunnies as "Sonny the Bunny" played over the loudspeaker system. Growing used to this extroverted life of performing in department stores, and well-practiced in circle dances from family gatherings, we encouraged the children to join hands and dance along. They accepted the pecks on the cheek from our little bunnies, while Big Sonny went to the older children and signed autographs. Many Sonny Bunnies and records of the song were purchased.

A Macy's executive, who had reserved a table for us at a busy delicatessen, treated us to lunch at the popular place. Karen and I fed our bunnies juicy pickles and lean corned beef. "I think carrots and lettuce might be more to their liking," my father reminded us, concerned that our attempts to feed these adorable stuffed animals might leave unsightly grease stains. We still had an afternoon of work ahead of us.

In April, Rosemary Clooney recorded *Songs from "Alice in Wonderland,"* much in demand by parents and their children for years after its release. May came, and another of "Peter Steele" and Henry Walsh's stories came out: *The Story of Little Champ* with Gene Autry, about a little colt that looks and acts just like Autry's famous Champion. *Billboard* wrote, "For cowboy fans, movie and TV, this is first rate material."

. . . .

On June 6, 1951, Rosemary Clooney recorded a song for Mitch Miller, head A&R man for the pop department. She balked at recording it for weeks, feeling it was gimmicky, insincere, and had ridiculous and tastelessly suggestive lyrics. She knew that her friend and colleague Frank Sinatra had left Columbia because of the low quality of material Mitch

Miller had given him to sing and wondered if this might be a decision she, too, would have to make.

Mitch Miller had an instinct for songs with a gimmick. The track he now wanted Rosie to record was just such a song. He believed that one couldn't remain a prima donna in this business and get ahead, and he believed Rosemary Clooney was the right singer for this record. He cajoled her, literally harassed her, into singing it. In effect, he let her know that if she did not record it, her career with Columbia might be over. She was becoming savvy enough about the business not to have to be told.

The song was called "Come On-a My House." The creators of the Chipmunks, William Saroyan and songwriter Ross Bagdasarian, wrote it. The song could be likened to a platypus, known as the mixed-up animal with its traits of fish, duck, and mammal. A parody, the song was based on Armenian folk music tradition, orchestrated with a harpsichord played not in the baroque fashion for which it was designed, but in a jazz style. The bizarre song also hinted of a calypso rhythm. Rosemary had to sing what she felt were lyrics that ranged from "incoherent to just plain silly" with an accent that combined stereotyped Italian with a hint of Armenian.

Hecky engineered the recording, and I was lucky enough to attend. When I walked into the recording studio, its magic captured me and I entered into my studio trance, this time triggered by three men setting up a harpsichord. I was studying piano with Kenneth Wentworth. He and his wife Jean, a concert pianist with a rapidly growing reputation, had moved to North Yonkers and built up quite a student clientele. They were a handsome couple, played duets together, were very politically active in the local branch of the Democratic Party, and Jean was pregnant, always a romantic notion for me.

Johann Sebastian Bach was my favorite composer. The Hungarian and more contemporary composer Bela Bartok held second place. When I saw a harpsichord in the Columbia studio, I went into a near-ecstatic state imagining Bach playing it—and me playing Bach upon it. I knew that Mitch Miller held the reigns over this recording, not my father. I had been told that I would have to just sit in the control booth and behave myself. However, I couldn't help but pester my father with,

"Daddy, Daddy, p-l-e-a-s-e, when the recording is over, can I at least *touch* the harpsichord?"

"We'll see, Judy, we'll see." Uh-oh, he called me "Judy." That doesn't bode well, I thought. I resigned myself to the joy of simply being near the instrument and watching and listening as Stan Freeman, keyboard whiz and would-be comedian played it.

Tension permeated the recording studio from the start, though Mitch Miller in his forever-buoyant manner attempted to eliminate the negative vibes. Everyone sensed that Clooney was ill at ease. Her sweet smile and radiance were absent, likewise her air of confidence.

Hecky played with the soundboard, working on the harpsichord, which proved challenging. The instrument could not have the formal and muted sound as though being played in the concert room of a royal palace. It needed "bite," as my father called it, resilience, and a more modern, upbeat sound. His fingers slid the levers here and there until what he heard in his earphones indicated to him that the music coming from the instrument would jump out and grab its listeners.

The red warning lights for anyone trying to enter went on, "Recording in Session." Take one was aborted. "A little heavier on the accent, Rosie," Mitch Miller instructed her.

"Take one," my father called out again for the second time, for a take was when the complete song was recorded, not stopped before it was finished. Take one wasn't right. Neither were takes two, three, or four. In between these, there were several aborted takes. This was turning into a long session. Ashtrays filled and needed emptying. Musicians lifted their bottles of soda and coffee cups and took sips or gulps. Mitch Miller plastered his smile on to try and keep things jolly. But they weren't.

Rosemary's usually rich, warm, and vibrant voice did not have the accent or lively tambour that Mitch wanted. With each aborted take, she grew more discouraged. Mitch, known for presenting meaningful scenarios to his singers, ones that could paint a picture that would fill them with the necessary emotion for the song, was not succeeding with Rosemary. Things picked up somewhat when he told her to sing it as though she were inviting the boy in the song into the house because she was going to marry him. Rosemary Clooney, however many relationships she may have engaged in her few short years in the Big Apple, found it necessary to view each one as though this was *the* man in her life, her true love, the one she would marry. The era's dichotomy between good and bad females demanded that a good female would only have a relationship and, of course, sex, with a man she'd marry, and preferably only have the sex after marriage. The bad woman would simply have relationships for pleasure without concern about commitment.

Take four (actually take 13 if one counted the aborted takes) still did not have the sound Mitch wanted, though it was far closer than the others after he had presented Rosemary with the "marry the boy" image. Hecky, who up until now had remained silent, spoke. "Let me go talk with Rosie, Mitch." Mitch, though he highly respected Hecky and recognized his talent as a producer, looked at him disdainfully. Mitch always needed to assert himself as the "alpha" male. In the lineup today, Hecky was the engineer, not the producer. He was to communicate with the board, not the artist.

Hecky, sensing Rosemary's discomfort overlooked Mitch's disapproving expression. He left the board and went into the studio. Placing a comforting arm upon her shoulder, he said, "Rosie. You're thinking too much. Detach yourself from the song. Sing it like a kid's song. Let your voice just flow as you tell the story. The song is not the story of Rosemary Clooney. It's someone else's story, and that someone out there might love its message and thank you for being able to express it for them."

Hecky returned to the booth. "This better work, Hecky," Mitch said to him.

My father arranged a few levers and turned the reverb up slightly on both the harpsichord and the vocal mike. He turned the volume in Rosemary's earphones up thinking the louder sound might also infuse some energy into her rendering of the song. "Take five," he announced. Stan Freeman plunked his fingers on the harpsichord keys. The other musicians kept their tunes and time. Rosie smiled as she sang the story that Hecky had assured her wasn't about her and that others might enjoy. Take five finished the session. Mitch Miller, Rosemary Clooney, and all the others, Hecky included, were relieved.

As they animatedly talked, slapped each other's backs, and lit up cigarettes of relief, I snuck out of the control room and into the studio, where I promptly began to play upon the harpsichord. It was different from the piano, but I quickly caught onto its high action keys that plucked rather than hammered the strings. I felt like I was engaging in history as I played phrases I had memorized from J.S. Bach.

I heard Mitch Miller's voice coming from the control room into the studio. "Judy, it cost $200 to rent the instrument from the Juilliard School of Music. That is not a toy." He didn't tell me to stop playing, so I didn't. I couldn't. I was lost in the sound of my fingers producing the sounds of Bach upon a harpsichord. My joy knew no bounds until the crew who had delivered it asked me to get up, for they had to put it on the truck.

After the tape was wound and placed in its box, the board turned off, the studio nearly empty and ready for the next session, my father informed me that we were going uptown to eat at Horn & Hardart's cafeteria, and then to visit my mother briefly, though, since children were not allowed into hospital rooms unless they were the patient, I would have to sit downstairs in the lobby. What did I care? First a harpsichord, then Horn & Hardart's: a child's dreams come true.

. . . .

One of Columbia's studios stood on the first floor of a skyscraper on the southeast corner of 57th Street and 6th Avenue not far from the main offices on 57th Street and 7th Avenue. The building next to it housed a Horn & Hardart's Automat. New York City was the original home of Horn & Hardart's Automats, which sold nickel cups of coffee during the Depression and post-war years. Opening in Times Square on July 2, 1912, the menu offered only buns, beans, fish cakes, and coffee. As time went on, the menu increased to Salisbury steak with fluffy mashed potatoes; beef stew; creamy rich pot pies with freshly baked, thick pie crusts, succulent chicken chunks, peas, and carrots in a tasty thick sauce; macaroni and cheese made with genuine cheddar; rice pudding with raisins and big, chewy grains of rice; and a host of other taste-bud treats and desserts. Horn & Hardart's was the first restaurant at which one could eat without being served by waiters or waitresses.

With all of the fast foods around today, there is no fast food or cafeteria that can compare with Horn & Hardart's. Even mother could not make such delicious macaroni and cheese as one could get from putting two quarters into the slot at Horn & Hardart's. Macaroni and cheese was my choice now. My father gave me several quarters. I heard the metal of the money drop securely into place, saw the green light come on, opened the little glass door, and pulled out a hard china dish. Steam rose from the piping hot dish and carried the aroma of the macaroni and cheese to my very happy nose. My stomach responded, growling with anticipated delight. When I'd savored each bite and finished this delicacy, I excitedly rose again and walked to the large glass bins that offered a colorful tapestry of desserts. I put more quarters into another slot, heard them drop into place with great satisfaction, opened the little door with its gold-colored handle, and removed a delectable, hot deep-dish apple pie, its crust filling the air with the smell of risen yeast and freshly made whipped cream on top of vanilla ice cream that smelled and tasted as if the vanilla beans had just been picked and the cow was standing right by milking itself and making fresh ice cream for each bite.

My father mmmed and aahed as he ate his favorite main course—hot, chunky chicken pot pie—and smacked his lips in glee over his piece of deep-dish apple pie. "Juddie," he said, "this is the life. This is the life."

How right he was! And how proud I felt. I imagined that everyone knew he was none other than Hecky Krasnow, producer of "Rudolph, the Red-Nosed Reindeer," and that he had just engineered a recording with Rosemary Clooney. Little did either my father or I know that "Come On-a My House" would soon become the number one song across the nation and make Rosemary Clooney into one of the most famous singers of her time.

CHAPTER 14

Television, Cowboys, Marbles, and McCarthy

. . . .

The first week in October of 1951 arrived with further successful record releases. "The Little Red Caboose" chugged along on the trade paper bestselling children's charts. "Rudolph" remained at the head of the lineup and indicated that it would again reach the million or more mark by the end of the season. Hecky recorded several other Christmas tunes with Autry: "Coming Down the Chimney," "Poppy the Puppy," "The Three Little Dwarfs," and "Thirty-Two Feet— Eight Little Tails." *Billboard* wrote of "Coming Down the Chimney": "Here's a powerful follow-up by Autry to his two previous Christmas hits, 'Rudolph' and 'Frosty.' Tune uses the familiar music to the verse of 'Jingle Bells,' the Autry name is powerful with the moppets, the lyric is pop material. It all adds up to a strong piece of Christmas wax."

The song, "The Little Engine That Could," was praised as a "good bet for the market" with its smart packaging and a story "sung with feeling" by Burl Ives. Likewise, the tongue twister "Old Witch Old Witch" ("she lived in a ditch and rode around on her hickory switch") was called a "pop tune possibility with a tune sure to attract the kids." Burl also recorded the widely sung "Twelve Days of Christmas," and a song, "Grandfather Kringle," written by Hecky under the pseudonym of Stephen

Gale. *Billboard* called this song ". . . a fine piece of yuletide material which includes a retentive melody, story line and yodeling. Could make lots of noise this year."

Josef Marais and Miranda's album fare was now being heard as singles. *Billboard* praised "Bulu the Zulu" saying, "Josef and Miranda have fashioned a swingy little melody into a pop tune with a story line, whose rhythm and melody should appeal to kids. A fine performance."

Of "Fideree Fidera," they commented, "Light, singable tune, easy for kids to follow, which tells of all the things children like to be—firemen, Eskimos, etc. Very well done."

Rosemary Clooney's renditions of four tunes from Disney's *Alice In Wonderland* received praise and climbed the charts. "The Syncopated Clock," by famed composer and orchestra leader Leroy Anderson, became a children's hit and crossed over to pop. Rosie recorded "Suzy Snowflake," another of Jack Rollins and Steve Nelson's creations. Its tune, once heard, left listeners humming. Its words gave an endearing persona to a tiny snowflake, making Suzy as lovable as Frosty. By December, the song had sold 250,000 records and crossed over to pop. On the heels of this success, Rosie's renditions of "Willie the Whistling Giraffe," about a giraffe who couldn't talk until he swallowed a whistle, and "Dandy, Handy and Candy," another "little bears" story, were singled out as highly worthwhile and well done.

Ray Heatherton's 25-cent minidisk, produced by Hecky, of the *Alice In Wonderland* story with non-Disney original ditties grew in popularity. Heatherton, father of Joey Heatherton (who would later become a well-known celebrity in her own right), performed in musicals such as *The Desert Song, Anniversary Waltz,* and *Babes in Arms* and hosted a children's program that first aired on WOR-TV, Monday evening, October 16, 1950. Called *The Merry Mailman,* the show entertained its viewers with games, songs, stories, comedy, crafts, hobbies, puppet skits, magic tricks, and interviews with performers and personalities who offered engaging educational segments. By 1951, the show had a large following. Hecky knew that the record industry had to work hand in hand with television, its programs, and its stars. If he was to stay one step ahead of the game

with television's increasing children's fare, it was time for him to purchase a television at home.

. . . .

Just before my ninth birthday in December of 1951, Karen, Jean,
and I watched with great excitement from the dining room window
while awaiting the arrival of the delivery truck. When it pulled up,
parked on the hill, and two men rang the front doorbell, our anticipation
was intense. What new wonders would this delivery—a television—
bring into our life? We stood in a corner of the small living room as the
men clad in heavy winter clothes put a plank on the stairs leading to the
front door entrance and rolled a huge box up the incline. The box would
not fit through the entrance from the outer foyer into the living room.
With knives, they cut the tape sealing it, removed a big white-blond
wooden cabinet, placing it onto a dolly, and maneuvered it into our
dining room. It took several twists and turns, pushes, pulls and shoves
until it was in place in the space my father had made for it between the
black-and-gold painted bookshelves he'd built on the left side and the
black-and-gold, glass-shelved curio cabinet mastered by his hands on
the right side. The men pulled tape off two doors the length of half the
cabinet, opened these doors, and exposed a dark, gray-looking screen.
They connected wires, fidgeted with knobs, and adjusted a contraption
they called an aerial, which sat atop the cabinet. Finally, a clear picture
filled the small, 10-inch screen. Now done, they cleaned up their trail
of cardboard and plywood, and took the dolly back to the truck. My father tipped them generously and thanked them as they left.

The men left the set on after adjusting it, and we children sat in
wonder as little black and white dots formed pictures and the speakers
brought voices to our ears. Treble frequencies made the voices sound
somewhat like Karen's and my voices when we connected tin cans with
a string and spoke to each other from my downstairs windows to her upstairs ones; but the combination of picture and sound, tin-like or not,
was thrilling nevertheless. For the first few days, Karen, Jean, and I sat
totally bedazzled as we experienced the Lone Ranger, Tonto, Hopalong

Cassidy, Gene Autry, and Champion with our eyes, rather than with our ears pressed to the speakers of Aunt Helen's radio. We sang along with "Its Howdy Doody Time," and the Mouseketeers' "M-I-C-K-E-Y M-O-U-S-E." Howdy Doody, that smiling freckle-faced puppet prankster became a Monday through Friday ritual along with Claribel the Clown and Buffalo Bob, the host with a smile as wide as Howdy Doody's. Little did Hecky know that the man in Claribel's costume, one Mr. Bob Keeshan, would, in years to come, be another feather he would put in Columbia's cap as well as his own.

In the evenings, sitting with our parents, we laughed uproariously at the *I Love Lucy Show*. I tried to imitate Lucy's facial expressions and other gestures, praying my hair would turn bright red. From the Lucy show, I also learned a lot about guile and beguiling: how women must connive in order to get what they want. Lucy, of course, made this not-so-funny reality of the era hilarious.

In the late afternoon, Mr. Oliver J. Dragon, the single-toothed puppet who looked more like a lovable alligator than a dragon, and his friend, fellow puppet Kukla, visited on that little screen. Kukla resembled a small boy in spite of the fact that he was bald and had a nose akin to Rudolph's, though it appeared more like a brightly painted red door-knob than an actual light. And what a friend we had in host Fran, a sweet, understanding woman who could have been anyone's favorite schoolteacher, grandmother, or aunt. She conversed with Ollie, Kukla, and other characters, like Fletcher Rabbit, Beulah Witch, Colonel Cracky, and Madame Ooglepuss about various topics of interest and issues of immediate concern.

Each Sunday night at 8:00 P.M. sharp, my parents, and, of course, Helen, Karen, and Jean, gathered in front of the massive square television cabinet to watch *The Ed Sullivan Show*. This was variety show entertainment at its very best. It catered not to the lowest common denominator, but brought the highest quality performers into homes from opera stars to comedians, pop singers to glamorous actors and actresses. Names on the weekly shows included the likes of Renata Tebaldi, Danny Kaye, Dean Martin and Jerry Lewis, Mario Lanza, Kate Smith, Frank Sinatra, Bing Crosby, Bob Hope, Loretta Lynn, Johnny

Cash, and many, many more. Later, when rock 'n' roll entered the scene, groups whose music and members would become classics like Elvis, The Beatles, and The Mamas and the Papas also made appearances. With Ray Bloch and his orchestra and the talented June Taylor Dancers, this hour of television flew by leaving us eagerly awaiting the next Sunday night. None of us knew in 1951, that in 1955, Karen and I would appear on the esteemed *Ed Sullivan Show* with another of Hecky's hits.

. . . .

The year 1952 witnessed the FCC-approved UHF Channels (14–83) and headlines that read, "International TV Is Here." France, Belgium, and Great Britain were lined together to telecast the same programs for a full week. Color television was in its experimental stage and would take several years to be both reliable and affordable enough to be in family homes.

Though we certainly looked forward to our routinely watched programs, Karen and I, like most other children, were not preoccupied with television. There were few channels, and what aired on these channels was either children's or family fare. Outstanding history and news reporting programs such as *You Are There*, hosted by Walter Cronkite, and *See It Now*, brought history and news to life and made even us youngsters think about the past and present and what it would bring for the future. The wholesome content, representative of the times, did not include any foul language, scantily clad or nude people. Couples like Lucy and Ricky had twin beds, and Lucy's pregnancy was the first ever to be written into a script and shown. Television added to the engaging entertainment we already had with radio, records, and an occasional Saturday matinee at the town's one movie theater (where harried ushers tried to keep order with an audience of popcorn munching, paper airplane throwing, laughing, and talking kids and the few bullies that always attempted to terrorize the rest of us). Television helped to ignite our already vivid imaginations. It inspired action: new games with friends.

Two more Jewish families had moved to North Yonkers and Karen and I, as well as our parents, consequently found new friends: Karen

Miller and Jill Spitzer. With them, Wendy Wolf, and our Christian friends Patty Mason, Mary Edie, Billy Whelman, Billy Reid, David Smith, Barbara Jenson, and Dorkas Murray, we watched TV. Not everyone had a television set, so my family's dining room was often filled with eight to ten of us, with television viewing a social event. My mother supplied home-baked cookies or her famous fudge squares, a mixture of fudge in a semi-soft state filled with nuts and the very definite taste of vanilla extract, which clinched their delectability.

We'd watch our selected program of the day for half an hour, an hour at most, then run outside for a yo-yo contest doing the double spinner, walk the dog, cork the bottle, and other tricks we attempted to master. Some days we'd focus on our beautiful glass or stone marbles and trade purees that looked like jewels from the treasure chests of pirates. Other days it was softball. Our field was the top of Trausneck Place, and the catcher always had a good run if he didn't catch the ball and it rolled or flew down the steep hill.

However, it was perhaps the cowboy episodes we saw on television that inspired us the most. In one, a brave cowboy broke his arm and rode the range with his arm in a sling. We took turns tying scarves around our necks and placing our arms in these fabricated slings pretending to be brave, broken-armed cowgirls and cowboys. Other times, arms healed, we'd mount our bikes, give them a name suited for a horse, and galloped on them to the empty lot next to our neighbors, the Abeschers. Here, nearly every day, with our cap guns in their holsters, cowboy hats upon our heads, and cowboy boots with fake spurs, we'd run, ride, climb trees, and envision ourselves to be the characters we saw on the televisions entering more and more of our houses. We felt wondrously at home on the range in the empty lot, where a large, lone weeping willow tree stood among tall grasses. Camouflaged by grass and the long, thick, drooping foliage of the tree, each of us could attack unseen and hide from the enemy. We could even climb into the weeping willow and sit upon a branch hidden and ready to make an attack from above—just as we saw it happen on television.

I still see our scenarios. . . . Black garden snakes slither in the grass. They become rattlesnakes and their dangerous venom adds tension to our western scene. Shots ring out as the sunny breeze blows across the lot carrying the skunk-like smell of caps. Handsome Billy Reid with his gorgeous blue eyes is the gun-slinging bandit come to the peaceful prairie town to cause trouble. Our *Zie* Posse is ready and waiting: Eye*zie* for Eisenberg, Mill*zie* for Miller, Kra*zie* for Krasnow, Bill*zie*-2 for Billy Whelman, also the town sheriff. More shots! Adrenaline races in all of us, the same heart-pounding excitement we feel when the TV pixel screens draw us into their visual adventures. I run and lean against the willow tree, cautiously looking left and right, my finger on the trigger of my gun raring, ready, and eager to fight for justice in a town upset by the arrival of a bandit. Is there a shadow among the blades of grass, perhaps the shadow of Billy Reid? (Why is it the gorgeous guys are always the bandits?)

I don't see anyone. Maybe it's just the sound of grass blowing. I venture away from the tree trunk, bending so the grass is at eye level, just as I witnessed Gene Autry do on TV. I see no one. Quickly, I return to the tree, lift my foot onto the gnarl in its trunk and hoist myself onto the lowest branch. With some height, perhaps I can see what is going on in this town, seemingly silent as the air before the snow falls. I barely gain my balance on the branch when the silence is broken.

"Hold the fire!" The voice of Billzie-2 carries across the field. Billy Whelman is steadfast, sure-footed, confident, tall, and broad of build: a boy soprano rendering of John Wayne. His authoritative, monotone voice calls out, "I've . . . got . . . him!"

Billzie-2 walks towards the open part of the field where we, the posse, can see him. I climb down from the branch running toward the sound of Billzie-2's voice. Everyone leaves their hiding spots revealing where they have been. We all keep our guns ready, just like on television, as we walk to the spot where Billzie-2 holds handsome Billy Reid. We must be alert. You never know what sly, clever moves such a bandit might suddenly attempt. Billzie-2 pushes Billy Reid somewhat roughly, just like we've seen on our new television screens.

"Dandy McHandy," Billzie-2 says with authority like Hopalong Cassidy, "You'll never bother this town again!" Big and bland as the color of wheat from head to toe, Billy Whelman—*Sheriff* Whelman, is the hero of the day. "No," the Sheriff says, "Without my posse, without all of you surrounding and cornering this villain, I could not have done it!"

Another day has passed where, inspired by a new medium, Posse *Zie* conquered evil, and good is the victor! The shadows on the sundial we made tell us that it's time to go to our respective homes. Scattering over the field, we run in all different directions.

That night, as I pull the pink table and benches out of their hiding place in the kitchen wall and set the table, my father turns the new television on. Edward R. Murrow, who eventually would come to be known as the most distinguished figure in the history of American broadcast journalism, appears on the screen. The night's news brings tales of real guns, real shootings, and Senator Joseph McCarthy.

Hecky's mother, Sarah Wohl Krasnow, with brother Al on her lap, Hecky at age 2 ½ in middle, and father Harry Krasnow, 1912

Program of Hecky's violin debut at age 16 in Hartford, CT, 1926

Hecky and Lillian's wedding, July 5, 1929

L-R: Uncle Phil Eisenberg, Steffi (age 4), and Hecky in Battery Park, NY, 1940

Hecky and Steffi at Chickering piano in Hartford, CT, 1941

Our house in Yonkers, NY, at 143 Douglas Avenue

Book cover of A Guide to Children's Records, *by Hecky and Phil, which landed Hecky his job at Columbia, 1948*

L-R: Jackie Robinson, Hecky Krasnow, and Pee Wee Reese, publicity photo at the recording of Slugger at the Bat, *July 19, 1949*

Judy at age 7 with Rudolph doll given by Gene Autry, December 1949

The Modernaires, famous quintet that recorded The Glooby Game *in 1949 and other pieces later; inscription says, "To Hecky—Thanks for all the wonderful things you did for us. The thing we all like to do is make records with Hecky!! The Mods"*

L-R: Uncle Art Satherly, Don Law (Autry's country-western producers), Gene Autry, Hecky, NY, February 1950

Album cover of The First Day at School, *with Dinah Shore, 1950*

Dinah Shore, inscription says, "To Hecky, Who made the first day at school a pleasant day." 1950

L-R: Hecky; Gene Kelly; front with music, Lehman Engle, famed conductor and composer; actor Stanley Carlson, 1950

Hecky, Sonny the Bunny, and Macy's store manager at "Sonny the Bunny" promotion party of record and doll, 1950

In the studio: Burl Ives at piano (center), Hecky Krasnow (right), and an instrumental trio, 1950

Paul Tripp, actor, writer, Mr. I. Magin-ation on award-winning TV program Let's Take a Trip, *and author of* Tubby the Tuba. *Inscription on photo: "For Judy, A real special wish from Mr. I. Magination (Paul Tripp)," 1951*

Frank Buck, hunter and author of Bring 'Em Back Alive, *inscription says, "For my friend 'Hecky Krasno' with best wishes and sincere regards. From Frank Buck."*

L-R: Hecky, Rosemary Clooney, and Gene Autry at the recording of the song by Johnny Marks to Clement Moore's poem, "Twas the Night Before Christmas," 1952

Hecky in the studio with an unfiltered Chesterfield—characteristic pose, 1953

Front, L-R: Hal Frederick, Percy Faith; Back, L-R: Hecky, Pat Blunda; St. Louis, MO, July 24, 1952

L-R: Jimmy Boyd and Judy (age 10) in the studio, 1952

1949, Columbia Records

1951, Columbia Records

1952, Columbia Records

1955, Columbia Records

1955, Columbia Records

1956, Columbia Records

L-R: Bandleader Ray Carter, Rosemary Clooney, and Hecky, 1953

In the studio: Hecky, Robin Morgan (Dagmar on I Remember Mama *TV show), guitarist and bandleader Tony Mottola, 1953*

L-R: Hecky, Paul Tripp, and Ray Carter in the studio, 1953

Johnny Marks, composer of "Rudolph"; inscription on photo says, "To a Real Friend—Hecky Krasnow—Since meeting you I have forgotten my ABCs and learned my RSTs—Rudolph, Santa Claus and Thank You—Johnny Marks," 1953

Josef Marais and Miranda, international balladeers. Inscription on photo: "To our dear friend Hecky, looking forward to more and more exciting collaborations. Josef Marais and Miranda."

In the studio: Hecky in back, Art Carney in front, 1954

Josef Marais, Judy, and cousin Karen Eisenberg, who sang with Judy on records and in their own folk duo, 1954

Judy and guitar, 1954

Burl Ives, inscription reads, "To Hecky— whose gentle hand led this singer in paths proper, progressive and prosperous. Best wishes. Burl" (given to Hecky when Ives returned to Columbia after the downfall of Senator Joseph McCarthy), 1954

Hecky and his sister Helen, 1954

Karen and Judy doing "A Trip Around the World in Song" on the Let's Take a Trip *TV program, 1954*

Tom Glazer, folk singer and songwriter, inscription says, "For Hecky—Without whom . . . and I don't mean maybe. Gratefully—Tom Glazer," 1955

Sheet music of "The Captain Kangaroo March" (Lee Herschel is Hecky's pseudonym here), 1955

Let's Take A Trip *TV program: Ginger McManus; Hecky (back); Pud Flanagan; recording engineer; Art Carney (standing); Sonny Fox (leaning over board); cameraman (right), October 30, 1955*

The Blue Jeaners recording "I'm Gettin' Nuttin' for Christmas," 1955. L-R: Judy, George Werner, Ricky Zahnd, Angelo Roselli, and Karen Eisenberg. Back: Hecky in the booth

Captain Kangaroo's Dance-Along Songs *by Hecky (as Lee Herschel and Leo Israel as Leo Paris), 1956*

L-R: Judy (age 14), Lillian, Hecky, and Steffi, 1956

At a party with friends, L-R: Aaron Copland, pianist Bennett Lerner, Leonard Bernstein (photo taken by Hecky), 1969

Hecky returns to chamber music, April 1975

Hotel Montclair
New York

Dec 16 —

Dear Mr. Kraznow,—

My uncle Harry has showed me your letter. If you will call me up after Christmas we can arrange a date when you can play for me.

Yours cordially

Aaron Copland

Letter to Hecky from Aaron Copland

CHAPTER 15

Bookworms

Senator Joseph McCarthy masterfully played upon people's fears as tensions increased between Russia and the United States during the escalating Cold War. History would later call McCarthy possibly the "greatest demagogue in the history of America." He cunningly manipulated the press and gained fame as his name appeared regularly in the headlines reporting his claims that a core of communists had infiltrated the United States government with the intent to destroy democracy. According to McCarthy, communists permeated the army itself, and, if not stopped, there would soon be a military coup. McCarthy brought this country into one of its darkest moments as fear, suspicion, prejudice, and paranoia prevailed in an atmosphere that fostered the loss of basic democratic freedoms.

To McCarthy, anyone who read left-wing books, performed in plays by left-wing playwrights, had ever attended communist or socialist meetings, or had been in favor of the Russian Revolution was suspect of disloyalty and of being a communist. He claimed that communists infiltrated unions, and he attempted to destroy the lives of many union leaders and members. Jewish professors, particularly psychology professors, were suspected of engaging in subversive activities. Many of these professors were fired by their administrations, which feared if they didn't fire them, the universities would be forced to close. Many professors willingly relinquished their long sought-after positions for fear of being investigated by the House Un-American Activities Committee. Authors, actors, filmmakers, playwrights, and artists of all kinds came under McCarthy's scrutiny along with homosexuals, deviants, alcoholics, and former fascists.

Reporters who dared to question McCarthy's statements and tactics were branded as communists, and the press increasingly lost more of its freedoms. If one had neighbors who held alternative points of view, the right action would be to report this to McCarthy's committees. After all, these neighbors were not only disloyal Americans, but dangerous to freedom. Many friendships fell victim to the possibility of one's own acquaintances spying on them. From 1950 to 1954, Senator Joseph McCarthy reigned. A word from him against someone could be enough to ruin that person's career. McCarthy's whims and interrogations destroyed the lives of many.

．．．．．．．．．．．

Columbia was known as the most progressive and experimental of the major record companies. Several Jews made up its ranks including Ted Wallerstein, Goddard Lieberson, Percy Faith, Mitch Miller, and Hecky Krasnow. With the advent of McCarthyism, many at Columbia lived in fear of being investigated or called to testify before HUAC and, if they refused to name any colleagues or friends who may (or may not) have attended communist meetings, read the books on McCarthy's extensive forbidden list, or engaged in any suspicious activities, they could be blacklisted.

Several of the Columbia employees from the top on down had, indeed, attended socialist meetings at one time or another or favored the revolution in Russia that would not only end the rule of tyrannical czars and their anti-Semitic pogroms, but also the inequities of the peasants versus the royalty. In principle, they viewed communism in Russia as a potential liberating force. None of these idealists imagined that Stalin would grow out of the revolution, religion of all kinds would be banned, and that Soviet artists and writers would be subject to government control. Their initial support of the downfall of the czars did not mean they wished for revolution in America. Similarly, having supported Henry Wallace's progressive platform in the 1948 presidential race, as well as more socialistic programs like national health care, government-owned transportation, and civil rights for blacks, certainly was not a wish for an end to the cherished freedoms and rights guaranteed by America's Constitution and Bill of Rights.

On June 21, 1950, McCarthy published a list called *Red Channels*. This list gave the names of 151 entertainers with alleged communist affiliations. This publication essentially began the blacklist. It included such names as playwright Arthur Miller, director John Huston, singer Lena Horne, actress Jean Muir, conductor Leonard Bernstein, composer Aaron Copland, folk singer Pete Seeger, writer Orson Welles, and actor José Ferrer. Anyone, by virtue of association, could be called to testify against those on the list, and, if they didn't, they were sure to be blacklisted. Rosemary Clooney, who had recently met José Ferrer and had been seen in his office, could have been suspect under the rules of Senator Joseph McCarthy.

Henry Walsh, Hecky's faithful collaborator on Gene Autry stories, was blacklisted and laid off from CBS-TV. He could no longer write for *You Are There* and the Edward R. Murrow show, *See It Now*. (Murrow, so popular with the American public, would eventually be instrumental in McCarthy's ultimate downfall.) Sherry Walsh had to find employment under her maiden name and hope that her connection with Henry, namely that she was his wife, would not be discovered. Hecky feared that his association with Henry would backfire on him. However, true to his ethics and determination to stand up for freedom, he continued their artistic association and friendship. Columbia Records continued to let Henry write for them.

In 1950, the FBI investigated actress and Columbia recording artist Judy Holliday. She won acclaim in roles like ditsy Billie Dawn in *Born Yesterday* and dumb blond parts such as in *The Marrying Kind* and *On the Town*. Goddard Lieberson advised her, "All you have to do is answer the questions like a Billie Dawn—be that scatterbrained blond. They won't know how to handle such diversion and they'll fall for it."

Taking his advice, Holliday's response to her inquisitors sounded like a genuine comedy script:

Mr. Arens: When was the last meeting you ever attended of either Actors Equity, Screen Actors Guild, or the American Federation of Radio Artists?

Miss Holliday: Years and years ago.

Mr. Arens: Have you had any active participation in the affairs of those organizations in the last few years?

Miss Holliday: Oh, no; years ago.

Mr. Arens: Miss Holliday, during the course of your session here with the Internal Security Subcommittee have you been treated courteously and fairly?

Miss Holliday: Yes.

Senator Watkins: You are not saying that because of any fear of coercion?

Miss Holliday: No. The fact that I am nervous is not because of this, it's because I get nervous whenever I get a parking ticket.

Judy Holliday was not blacklisted from the movie business. However, guilty by the association of having been investigated, she could not perform on radio or television for three years.

Burl Ives was listed in *Red Channels*. At the end of 1951, Burl, suspect because he had performed in Arthur Miller's play, *Death of a Salesman*, knew he would be called before HUAC to testify. He left Columbia and returned to Decca, in part because Decca had a far more conservative reputation. In order to save his thriving career, he made the decision not to remain silent, but to give the requested names and information.

My parents and the Iveses had become close friends, frequently visiting and attending plays and other events together. On January 30, 1952, Helen Ives sent a letter to my father.

> Dear Hecky,
> The world revolves and in its course the only constant thing is change. At this particular change in our professional life, I want you to know that Burl and I remember all your friendly cooperation with a good deal of affectionate warmth, and hope

that the severing of our official ties won't necessarily mean we won't see each other from time to time.

Love,
Helen

When Burl Ives appeared before HUAC and testified against Arthur Miller and Pete Seeger, among others, my parents could not find it within themselves to remain on friendly terms with the Iveses. Though they did much soul searching as to what would happen should my father ever be called before the McCarthy committee to testify against friends and/or colleagues, or blacklisted for meetings he and my mother had attended in the past, they knew that they could not do what Burl had done. Whatever the cost to them, they could not put others in a precarious situation in order to save themselves.

Our usually warm, relaxed, everyone-doing-his-own-creative-project household was now permeated by a nerve-grating tension. My parents never allowed their threatening physical ailments to interfere with their positive outlook that things would always turn out okay. Now, and not because of these conditions, they acted threatened, as though held at knifepoint with little hope of escape.

Our house had comfortable but small, compact rooms. Sound carried from the living room, dining room, and kitchen to my bedroom, which stood at the end of a short hallway that led to the dining room and kitchen. Usually, I would fall asleep hearing my mother at the piano and my father playing his violin, their love for each other reflected in their duets. Now the sounds of anxious talk brought upsetting words to my ears. Old friends whose names I remembered from our years in Hartford began to pop up with relative frequency—Dr. Herb Schwartz, his wife Rosalind, their daughter Susan, the Littles, Jack and Ruth, and their daughter Janet, whose weak heart made her into a near-invalid.

"Honey?" my father's voice said as though asking a question. "No matter what happens, you agree, don't you, that we will never under any circumstances reveal a name?"

"Of course!" My mother's voice conveyed utter disbelief that my father would even question or doubt her on this topic. "If they accuse us of treason—like Julius and Ethel Rosenberg—my mouth is sealed! With McCarthy accusing universities of being hotbeds of communism, I am worried about Phil, divorce or not. What a perverted mind this McCarthy has to think that intellectuals are most often communists. Since when has thinking become dangerous? People of great intellect and thought founded this nation. What does the damned stinker want—a nation of stupid, non-questioning, non-thinkers?"

My mother never cursed. I shuddered under the covers.

"You're preaching to the choir, honey."

"Look what has happened to people. Look at Burl Ives. How can people betray others like that? Arthur Miller kept quiet. Pete Seeger kept quiet. Copland, Bernstein—oh, this whole thing makes me sick. It's no different than Russia silencing its artists."

"My dear," my father answered, "people have different cracking points, and demagogues know just how to put the dynamite into the cracks to make them explode."

Oh, God. Is someone going to blow us up? My room echoed with my heartbeat.

"Are you forgiving Burl?"

"Absolutely not, but I think he is doing us a favor by severing his relations with us at the moment. He is the one who has been called before HUAC, not you or me. Honey, I know you are nervous about next week— and rightfully so. Not everyone has FBI agents come to their house to ask questions. I won't be here to answer questions because, well, you know how my blood boils. I wouldn't give names, but I'd say things that would rile them. Helen just doesn't come across like a nice little housewife, and she's divorced—a reason to question her morality according to the great *pro-family* man, Mr. McCarthy. It's a hard burden to place upon you, but I know you can handle anyone with your charm, grace, and smile."

What is Mommy going to have to do all alone? My pillow grew wet with tears.

"'Mind over matter, Lillian.' That's what I keep telling myself. Hah, would they laugh if they knew about how my brother Harry died."

"They probably do. If they ask you, your imagination is so vivid, you'll tell them a story they will never forget, and it won't get anyone in trouble. By the way, honey, Phil is coming on Saturday to visit the girls, and he and I are going to burn many books, including those still upon Helen's shelves upstairs: all those that might be construed as evidence we have read about socialism or communism or that might give suspicion that we have attended party meetings. There are 30,000 books on McCarthy's list purportedly written by communists, pro-communists, former communists, and anti-anti-communists."

"Burn the books?"

Mommy's choking! A loud gasp traveled to my terrified ears.

"HONEY, NO! You can't burn books. My God, these are a lifetime's collection. Burn books? I can't imagine burning books, any books. What is the matter with this country? This is a witch hunt!"

Help, please, God! Are they going to burn us like those Salem witches on that program Henry wrote? My room felt filled with monsters.

"I know it's a witch hunt. Do you think Phil and I want to destroy these books? It is a dark time in America, when every principle upon which this country was founded is being violated. McCarthy's afraid of communism? He should open his eyes to the fascism and the tyranny he is creating in this once-upon-a-time land of the free!"

I heard my mother crying. She didn't cry except at sentimental movies, weddings, and at finishing books that totally absorbed her. My mother was a source of constant strength. Now she said, "Oh, honey, I'm scared. This Joseph McCarthy situation is like Hitler rising right here on our own soil. Snitch on your neighbors. Snitch on your friends. Don't dare speak out the truth or the government will come after you and ruin your life." My mother's voice rang with fury now. "How is it possible that a simple sentence from that rotten man could be sufficient to ruin a person's career? How could *anyone* listen to his suggestion that John Lewis and the striking miners be drafted into the army and court-martialed for insubordination and shot if they refuse to mine the coal? How does McCarthy get away with putting the lives of homosexuals in danger when evidence points to the fact that he himself is a homosexual? How does his severe drinking problem, poker games to raise money for his campaigns, and lies about his noble missions in the Marines go without notice, without check?"

What's a homosexual? What are they talking about? The sweat on my forehead mingled on the pillow with my tears.

"Honey, again you are preaching to the choir. Demagogues, afraid of their own tendencies, make scapegoats out of those whom they should help. I can only say that the fear of going hungry, of not having a job, of having one's career ruined, of having no way to pay for one's house, for clothes or food, or to support one's children intimidates many. If only FDR's words would once again ring in the minds of Americans—'There is nothing to fear but fear itself.' Now, instead, we have a man who wants nothing more than for people to be afraid. With all that's going on across the ocean in Korea, Russia, and Eastern Europe, McCarthy's scare tactics have convinced the American public that the danger lies right here on our own shores, that within our own government communists are plotting to rid everyone—including themselves—of the blessings of the freedoms they enjoy. It's insane! He's even manipulated Congress into forgetting that it is supposed to have an open mind and serve as a check and balance. Americans have been bamboozled. They are scared enough to believe these lies."

I lay in my bed, unable to fall asleep, hearing my parents' voices and their words. What was happening in this country that I had fallen in love with in Yorktown and at the Liberty Bell? Even in Williamsburg, Virginia, where I had witnessed how very wrong segregation was, I had been profoundly affected by my parents telling me that here in America we could make changes, that in my lifetime they were certain I would see an end to Jim Crow.

I felt like I couldn't breathe. A horrid memory entered my head. It mixed with the names my parents were mentioning like Roz and Herb Schwartz. It was September 4, 1949. Herb, Roz, and their daughter Susan came all the way from Hartford to go to a concert with us. We drove to a park where we all piled into a school bus and drove through beautiful countryside to Peekskill, New York. The sun shone through the early signs of an autumn breeze, and leaves were no longer as bright green, but speckled already with shades of orange and red. The open windows on the bus let in the homey scent of firewood burning. The Schwartzes had brought their straw picnic basket lined with blue, yellow,

. . . .

and white material that reminded me of a dress I'd seen a pioneer woman wear in a storybook. We had our own picnic basket. The odors of cold chicken, boiled eggs, peanut butter sandwiches with grape jelly, the vanilla from my mother's fudge squares, apples and bananas wafted out when Roz and my mother opened the baskets on the bus to get Susan and me our beloved Baby Ruth candy bars and bottles of Welch's grape juice as a snack en route.

I'd been told we were going to hear Paul Robeson, whose rich baritone voice I had heard on records. My parents explained to me that Mr. Robeson was a black person, and, like Jackie Robinson, spoke out and dared to take action to let America know that it could not be a true democracy until all of its citizens were treated with justice and allowed equality.

"Juddie," my father told me, preparing me for the concert, "Paul Robeson has been speaking out against the many lynchings that have happened recently in the South. Because he campaigned for a man named Henry Wallace in 1948, a man who believed in equality, Mr. Robeson has received death threats from the Ku Klux Klan."

"Why, Daddy? Why?"

"Fear, Juddie. Fear of that which is different. Fear that those different from you might actually be just as good as you, just as capable. It's also what you're taught. If a child is taught to hate a Negro, that is all they know. Hate and lies and fear are the worst enemies of people."

"Daddy, I've heard you talk with Mommy about the concert. Something about it was supposed to be in August, but it was going to be violent or something. I'm scared."

"Yes, it was supposed to be in August, but there were threats against Robeson's life. After that, 2,000 union members and others have promised to make a human ring around the grounds to stop any prejudiced person from causing trouble. The police are going to be there too."

"Why should there have to be guards and police?"

"Whenever there's a crowd, police are there."

"Yeah, Dad, but not 2000 guards."

"Well, you see, Juddie, Paul Robeson told a reporter in Paris, after singing at the World Peace Conference there, that it is unthinkable that Negroes go to war and give their lives to fight for America only to come home to a country where they can't use the same bathrooms or water fountains, go to the same schools, or sit at the same counters or seats in restaurants, that they must sit in the back of buses and can't get the same good jobs or equal pay as white people. And then he said that the Soviet Union, in just one generation after its revolution, has given people of color full and equal rights and dignity. So, now, because he spoke a truth and pointed out that a communist country treats Negroes humanely, they are calling Mr. Robeson a communist. People who hate communists and believe Senator McCarthy are now attacking Paul Robeson. It is a hard time now, my Juddie, a very hard time. But if we are intimidated and don't go to the concert, prejudice and wrongs will continue. We must make a statement by going. Paul Robeson is a great singer with noble principles."

After my father told me these things, the words of a song I'd heard the Weavers sing made sense to me. "Wasn't that a time? Wasn't that a time, a time to try the soul of Man? Wasn't that a terrible time?"

Now, lying in my bed, I could once again hear the voice of Paul Robeson singing "Ol' Man River." I tried to let the sound of the music in my head lull me to sleep, but other refrains he'd sung played in my mind. "I dreamed I saw Joe Hill last night, alive as you and me. . . . Madam I have come for to court you, your acceptance for to gain. . . . We are climbing Jacob's ladder." Then the images returned, images I had pushed down and attempted to block out: images that came back in the form of nightmares. Images of the concert in Peekskill.

Cries of "Communist Nigger" rang through the air. The circle of union guards fought with hundreds of men, who appeared seemingly out of nowhere. The police helped these men and swung their billy clubs at the union guards. Brutes, whom we learned were hired thugs, began beating the people sitting on the grassy hills. "Traitors, communists, Reds," they cried as they swung clubs, used fists, and even kicked old people as they tried to get up from the ground.

Our picnic baskets were open, and we were holding plates of chicken and potato salad on our laps while sitting on blankets Roz and my mother had laid out for us. The music, gorgeous day, and surroundings had been idyllic just moments ago. Now, Susan and I were told to drop our food and take our parents' hands and run.

"We've got to get to our bus," Herb Schwartz instructed us in a frantic tone of voice. He and Roz held Susan's hand and ran towards the top of the hill and the parking lot.

"HONEY!" My father yelled over the screams and crying of hundreds of people and the jeers of the thugs taunting us. "You go ahead as fast as you can. Stop only to catch your breath. I will take care of Judy."

"Daddy," I cried, terrified, "the picnic baskets . . ."

"Forget the baskets." He grabbed my hand and pulled me. I had never seen my father run so fast. My mother was just ahead of us. She stopped for a moment and staggered, holding her chest where her heart was. "Honey, mind over matter," my father yelled to her. "And remember, it is bus number five." My mother put her hands at her side, lifted her chin toward the sky, and resumed a climb at a pace that would have killed her had she not been the determined person she was.

My father and I ran, zigzagging between billy clubs and people lying on the ground pleading for mercy as they were hit, kicked, and called words that my Catholic friends said people go to hell for when they die. Then I saw a little girl fall. "Daddy, that girl will be killed." Over the screams, my father yelled, "There's a child on the ground. Pick her up someone," but his voice blended with the many, some of whom were probably yelling the same thing as their heads turned back in the direction of the fallen girl. My father looked to see if we could quickly turn around go to her rescue, but the throngs of people running for their lives grew thick so fast that we could not even see the child anymore. Turning around and running back would have been a feat only Superman could accomplish. I prayed her parents were by her side and had picked her up. The thought of people running over her made my stomach heave.

We reached the top of the hill. Dust and rocks from the dirt road leading in and out of the park were flying through the air as cars and buses tried to speed out of the park. The thugs threw rocks at glass windows, and if a car was going slowly, they opened doors and pulled people out. Other cars and buses sat lopsided in the grass as their tires had been slashed and the windows smashed. People screamed from inside these vehicles as billy clubs swung through the broken windows. Stones, hurled with hate, hit peoples' heads. Blood splattered. My father dragged me, panting and ashen.

"Where's Mommy?" I cried, but he didn't answer. He just kept pulling me, even though I was running as fast as he was. We ran into a parking lot and saw a big number 5 on a school bus. "Come on, Judy, run for your life," my father gasped. We reached the bus. "Mommy," I cried as I saw her hanging onto a pole right near the front bus door. Seeing her made me run even faster. My father leaped onto the first stair. He pulled me into the bus, and the driver pushed the button to close the door. It wouldn't close because people were standing on the stairs, and my father and I were in the path of the door.

My mother cried out, "Squash in, everybody. Please, that's my husband and daughter!"

People pushed against each other and my father and I did too. There was barely room for rib cages to move in and out simply to breathe. The bus doors closed, and the driver floored the gas pedal. We took off speeding. A rock flew through the window, narrowly missing my mother's jaw and hitting the man next to her in his stomach. He screamed in pain and fear but had no room to double over. The bus driver went even faster. The stones now hitting the windows were those from tires racing over dirt and gravel. The dust flew in from the broken window. From the angle at which I was squashed between my father and strangers, I faced my mother. She looked like death warmed over, and that vein pulsated in and out, in and out. Her eyes were closed. Tears ran down her cheeks. I didn't think she'd survive. My heart pounded in my chest. Air in the bus was virtually nonexistent, and I was certain I'd suffocate.

The bus with its skilled and brave driver finally reached safety on the road back to Yonkers, but wouldn't stop until we were far from the grounds upon which the riot had taken place.

We learned later that two men were discovered with high-powered rifles on a hilltop at the concert grounds The police couldn't refuse to arrest them, for that would have been an obvious blatant failure of their duties, enough of which they'd already shirked: that the marksmen got onto the grounds to begin with proved questionable. We also learned that the thugs were fully prepared to kill Paul Robeson and his bodyguards.

Robeson's guards discovered this plot and knew the only way to get out alive was to drive through the surrounding woods, thick with trees, a creek, hills, gullies, boulders, and sharp rocks. The five men drew straws as to which of them would drive. The one who drew the shortest straw would sit at the wheel and heroically maneuver the car through the treacherous paths to save the life of Paul Robeson, himself, and the other four.

As my parents talked of the man named McCarthy and witch hunts, I couldn't get the images of the riot out of my mind. Terrified, I got out of bed and went to my parents.

"You are crying, my sweetie," my mother said, taking me into her arms.

"What is going on?" I asked. "Why does everything feel so scary and awful?"

My mother held me in her arms and caressed my back. She rocked me back and forth. I could hear her heartbeat and was glad and comforted that she was alive and holding me. "Judy," she said, "life is like one big book, one great novel. It has good chapters and bad chapters, happy and sad chapters, but it is such a good story that you are compelled to go on to the next chapter and the next and the next. You feel sad when it nears the end because it is so interesting. But who knows, when it's over, maybe there's another good story that begins somewhere else."

The sound of my mother's voice as my head rested on her chest, with its soft and comfortable bosom, lulled me. My eyelids could no longer stay open. My father took me back to my bed. He sat on the edge while covering me and said something about having always to be vigilant about democracy and that pendulums swing back and forth but end up in the middle again. I fell asleep.

. . . .

Saturday arrived and Phil with it. Karen, Jean, and I were happy to see him. He talked with us, played a few rounds of Go Fish, and read us a few books. Then he said, "I have work to do with Hecky now."

A wooden garbage shed stood in the far left corner of our backyard. My father and Phil had built it. Its picket-fence style and dark green paint gave the appearance of a small playhouse. It had enough room for six large steel garbage cans, two for my family, two for Phil's, and two for the Buddingtons on the third floor. Phil and my father took four of these cans. As the bookshelves in our respective living rooms grew gaping holes, the books tumbled into the cans. With the books in, Hecky and Phil lit a fire. The ashes of thousands of written words flew out of the red flames, snapping, crackling, and bursting into the air above the rims. Helen and my mother wept at this fiery spectacle as they looked out of the sun porch window on our first floor.

Karen, Jean, and I simply could not comprehend what was happening. Books, a sacred commodity in our family, were our friends. In between our mothers' tears, the two cleaned the shelves and with frenzied motions, filled the gaping holes left by the removed books. Every knick-knack, framed photo, and vase that could be found now sat where revered books had once set the ambience for curiosity and knowledge. "That should do it," we heard Helen say. "Now the shelves don't have noticeable spaces. Even those would create suspicion."

Karen, Jean, and I had recently planted a vegetable garden on the plot of land that bordered the back door of the house, our enclosed sun porches, and the garbage shed. It lay under a Chinese maple tree separated by thick hedges from the bordering sidewalk at the top of Trausneck Place. Jean's carrots were doing better than anything Karen and I had planted, though Karen's and my beets and celery were showing hopeful signs of emerging. Our planting had drawn thick, juicy earthworms to the soil.

Phil and Hecky had moved the cans out of the shed and were burning the books on the cement walkway leading to the back door. The garden was about 12 feet from where the flames spewed forth. Why were our fathers getting rid of books? Why, as we'd been told, were men going to visit Wednesday and ask questions? Why were our mothers crying?

Karen, Jean, and I were not prone to harming animals, but Karen now said with sinister glee, "Let's dig up worms. Look, I got one."

"That's huge," I commented, and before I knew what was happening, Karen ran over to the flaming garbage cans and threw the worm in. It exploded with a huge popping sound. Karen laughed.

"You try it," she said, and dug up another worm. It was the size of a baby snake only fatter. She threw it into the fire. The same exploding popping sound filled the air, followed by her laugh again.

There was something macabre in her actions and her laugh. It proved contagious. I dug out a huge earthworm and tossed it into the fire. I laughed. Jean caught the sinister mood. The three of us depleted the earth in our newly planted vegetable garden of what must have been every garden's dream of health: oxygenating worms. Each squiggling critter met a fiery death in the devil-possessed furnace lit by the antics of Senator Joseph McCarthy.

Hecky and Phil, who had taught us reverence for all living creatures, made no attempts to stop us from this vicious venture. They were absorbed in going in and out of the house carrying books and tossing them into the fire, and they seemed to be in a nervous hurry to do so. Their eyes darted this way and that, fearful that the neighbors would get wind of what they were doing and report them to someone.

"Children," finally Phil called us over. "We love you very much. If anyone asks you what Hecky and I have been doing this afternoon, you just answer that we were burning some old, unnecessary rubbish—shoes too worn, clothes too torn, and outdated magazines, plus a pile of leaves that accumulated around the side of the house."

"Got that?" my father piped in. "No more, no less. If they keep questioning you, say you have to go home, and immediately come inside."

"Whatever you do," Phil continued, "don't mention that we were burning books. Please, Karen. Please, Jean. Please, Judy. This is serious business. Don't mention books."

We continued digging for what we now called *bookworms*, our laughter filling the air each time another innocent worm died, popping in the flames like a pricked balloon.

·　·　·　·　·　·　·　·　·　·　·

For the next several days I heard my father rehearsing with my mother, rehearsing lines for the men due to visit, men called the FBI. My mother scrubbed more windowsills, countertops, and dishes than I'd ever seen her scrub in my entire lifetime. She couldn't sit still. When she spoke with Sherry Walsh on the phone, or any other friends, she talked small talk, not her usual interesting conversations. She said nothing about what was happening. It was the era of party lines, with operators whom we all came to know and who knew us.

The men came on Wednesday. A teachers' meeting that my parents had not known about when told which day the men were coming meant that Karen, Jean, and I were home from school. My mother instructed us, "First you will say hello to the men and be as polite as you always are. Then, ask if you can go play, just like you always do. However, do not, under any circumstances, come out and interrupt for anything, and that means *anything*."

"What if we're choking to death?" I asked.

"Death is the only thing you can come out for—and that doesn't mean fake death. There are to be no 'boys who cry wolf.' You might want to open the trundle bed and play tent under there," my mother said. "No coughing. No singing. No burping. No farts. Silence, please. If the men insist on looking around the house, be pleasant, but don't answer any questions except to say, 'I don't know,' unless they ask what grade you're in or something that most people ask when they first meet you. If they mention names like the Schwartzes, zipper your lips. Don't say anything. If they ask you anything about Phil or Henry tell them Phil is your father and uncle and Henry is a friend. That's it. Lips zippered."

Wednesday came and two men arrived. My mother introduced us and then shooed us off to the bedroom. Through the walls I could hear their voices. They sounded polite but intimidating. I heard my mother's voice waiver. One after another, the words that came out of her were, "No. No. No." She must have gotten hold of herself, for the tones that rang, albeit softly through the closed door, began to sound like my mother at her most charming. I heard the men laugh. The manner of the conversation grew less threatening. I could hear her offering them cake and coffee.

Karen, Jean, and I opened the trundle bed. We climbed under and were playing tent. We decided, since we had to remain silent, that we would make it part of our game. We would be quiet in order to hear the footsteps of grizzly bears creeping up on us in our imaginary forest. However, neither ghosts nor bears occupied my mind. All I could think of was that the dust bunnies made me want to sneeze. My stomach, churning with fright, made me want to make very loud farts, but I remembered my mother's admonishment, and held all that air inside. I thought I would explode like the worms we'd thrown into the fire.

Finally, the door to our room opened. "Come on out," my mother cried with a sense of joy and relief in her voice. "You did a great job. You children were perfect, just perfect." She sighed, clapped her hands, then held them in a prayer position. She looked up toward the ceiling, but I could tell she was looking through the ceiling at something far higher. "They've gone!"

That night, my father hugged my mother innumerable times. Phil called and congratulated her on a job more than well done. Helen said, "We knew, if anyone could do it, Lil, it was you! You are probably the only person in the history of an FBI investigation who managed to get the guys to sit down with you over a cup of coffee and cake and ask *your* advice about their marriages and children."

CHAPTER 16

A Tribute at the Rodeo

. . . .

Gene Autry was born on September 29, 1907, in Tioga, Texas, and raised in both Texas and Oklahoma where the town of Gene Autry is now named after him. His grandfather and mother encouraged him to sing as they sang hymns and psalms to him. His first work wasn't singing, but bailing and stacking hay on his uncle's farm. Then he worked as an apprentice on the railroad. At age 12, he purchased his first guitar for $8.00 from a Sears and Roebuck catalog. Once he learned to play, he sang wherever he could: in school assemblies and plays, at fairs, and in small local clubs. He liked to sing and continued to do so when he worked as a telegraph operator earning $150 a month, a comfortable salary in the 1920s. Late one rainy night, humorist, actor, and author Will Rogers walked into the telegraph office and heard Gene singing while strumming his guitar during the telegraph's momentary silent spell. "You should be heard, young man. You've got a fine voice there," Rogers encouraged him.

A year later, Gene Autry went to New York City to audition for RCA Records. He met Art Satherley, who advised him that with the numerous recording artists RCA had in its roster, Gene would get lost. Satherley guided him as he signed up with American Record Company (ARC), which would eventually become Columbia Records. Gene formed a band and signed on Carl Cotner, a talented fiddler as well as musician on several other instruments. There were others in the band slated for thriving careers, like Mary Ford and Merle Travis. By the 1930s, Gene Autry was a popular country-western singer with several recordings and hits to his name.

He could read lines in scripts well too. When citizen groups were complaining about the amount of violence in B-grade cowboy films, Gene Autry was hired to overdub dialogue that gave the movies a different focus. Most of the cowboy film actors could ride well and were adept at stunts but could not act. Gene Autry rescued many films from these deficiencies. As his popularity grew and he himself appeared in movies, his directors realized that his forte did not lie in portraying imaginary characters. He was brilliant at simply playing himself: a genuine, nice, singing cowboy who cared about others. This was the Autry appeal.

In the late 1940s, after serving in WWII, Gene Autry started what developed into his famous Flying A Rodeo, named after his Flying A Ranch in Berwyn, Oklahoma. The rodeo grew in popularity and soon traversed the country appearing in grand halls, including New York City's Madison Square Garden. Gene Autry's Flying A Rodeo had all of the showmanship and excitement to fill Madison Square Garden's seats with an eager audience just waiting to see the feats of cowboys and cowgirls, the parade with acrobats upon bareback horses, the bucking broncos and bulls upon which cowboys attempted to stay for a grand 10 seconds, and the daring clowns ready to pull fallen riders to their safety. By 1951, "Rudolph" had sold millions more copies, as had "Frosty." Gene Autry was gaining fame as the Christmas Cowboy. In 1951, in December, this Christmas Cowboy brought his rodeo to the Garden. The pageantry outdid any Christmas gala imaginable.

My father and our family were Gene's special guests. We had a catered meal in his dressing room. The steaks tasted as though the bull had grazed on the best grass the good Lord could grow and the steer had just been slaughtered right on the farm. Gene and Ina knew of my father's propensity for hot apple pie, and this was served for dessert. The apple slices were huge and fresh. Wherever the food came from, it had to be a restaurant or a catering service as fine as the ritzy Delmonico Steak House of Gilded Age fame.

We finished dinner, and Gene took us to say hello to Champion, a truly beautiful horse with his rich, cream-colored mane and the classic white streak running from his forehead to the tip of his nose. Champion's groom was busily preparing him for the night's performance. Pre-show excitement buzzed in the air. In the stalls of Madison Square Garden, horses whinnied and bulls snorted. In the area of the dressing rooms, those working behind the scenes ran hither and thither to get cleaned and pressed costumes to the right artists. We were allowed to watch cowgirls as makeup artists applied the various shades of theatrical face paint and coiffed hair into tousled styles plastered with sprays and fortified with hairpins that would withstand the jostling and jolting of riding horses. The combined scents of makeup, perfume, hair sprays, cow and horse manure, hay, and the sweat of cowhands grooming the animals lent an air to this performance like no other theater in town.

Returning to Gene's dressing room, I was about to embark on one of the most memorable treats of my life. "Judy," he said, "how would you like to see my wardrobe? Come on, let's have a walk in my closet."

After my closet shared with Steffi at home, I couldn't imagine how one could take a walk in a closet, but this was Gene Autry inviting me, so I said, "Sure! That sounds like fun."

It was here that I learned another characteristic that differentiated cowboy Gene Autry from others like the Lone Ranger, always in his same cowboy attire and mask, or Hopalong Cassidy, forever looking ready for a long ride on the range or like he'd just returned from one. Gene Autry set a fashion trend for singing cowboys and for country music performers that continues today as witnessed in the bangles, baubles, glitz, and glamour at the Grand Ole Opry.

I followed Gene into the closet. "This is a closet?" blurted out of my mouth. "This looks as big as the whole first floor in our house!"

"A show is a show, Judy. I sweat a lot under those lights, and I don't like to be seen in the same outfits all the time. There are people who come back several nights to see the rodeo. I need lots of changes, even during just one show alone."

My eyes were drawn upward to the top shelves. Perhaps it was all the white there. In the past, Gene had worn varied hats of different colors.

Now, his own hats bore his particular symbol: a double crease on the top of his white Stetsons. Most people own one or two hats. Here in this closet lay hat after hat after hat lined up in rows on shelves that ran along three sides of this vast room called a closet. Gene saw me stare, my eyes roaming from one shelf to another and back again.

"Hats are hot to wear. My head sweats a lot. I like the feel of a clean, dry hat. Even if the audience doesn't know my head is hot and sweaty, I do; so I change my hats constantly throughout the show."

My eyes went to the poles under the shelves. Except in huge Alexander's Department Store in the Bronx, where my mother and Helen always took us kids and themselves for the greatest in bargain shopping, I had never seen so many shirts hanging together in my life. The pastel colors had a sheen to them. The embroidery looked like the fine crafting of an artist. The buttons appeared to be made from the same thing that lined the inside of the big shells sitting on the mantel at Granny and Grandpa's beach house.

"Those shirts look so shiny, Gene. Are they polished like shoes?"

Gene laughed. "No, sweetheart, no one polishes shirts. They are made of silk. Have you ever read about silkworms? They produce the compound this material is made from sort of the way that spiders spin webs. Here, touch this, and feel what it's like."

"Amazing!" I said. "I'm touching a shirt made out of worm spit, and it's just so soft and smooth and nice."

"The buttons are made out of the inside of oyster and abalone shells. We call it 'mother-of-pearl.'"

Now I understood why the buttons looked like those shells. Eager to see everything in the closet before we'd have to go out because showtime was nearing, I looked below the shirts. Row after row of colorful cowboy boots intensified my growing shoe fetish, which was inspired by playing with my twin aunts' exotic shoes found in Grandma's closets and attic, two-toned shoes from the 1930s with a toe hole and a thick, layered sole with a high heel. Now, before my eyes, were so many boots that I yearned instantly to collect cowboy boots, to wear several different pairs each day, to run through the lot and climb the weeping willow tree donning boots just like Gene Autry's. And the spurs! Some were already on the boots.

Others, like the hats, lined a long row stretching from one end of the closet to the other. They sparkled like silver stars on a cloudless night and bore Gene's initials and the Flying A insignia. Gene's many colored cowboy boots, with their intricate designs carved into the leather, permeated the closet with the scent of cowhide, and this mingled with Gene's cologne. I stood in Madison Square Garden with Gene Autry in the enormous closet where he kept his clothes. In that moment, to me, this man was the nicest, most dapper, fanciful, and best cowboy in the whole wide world. Oh, dear God, I thought. If only I could grow up to be a singing cowgirl with a closet like this and clothes made of silk. God, listen, I'd give up the silk just to have all the boots with the spurs. I'd even have only one hat if I could have all those boots.

And so my thoughts went until Gene broke my reverie, "Judy, we'd better go out. It's time for you and Mom and Dad to go up to my box and sit, and for me to get myself ready for the night's performance. Can you keep a secret?"

I didn't answer because I had no idea what marvelous secret Gene might share, hence if I'd be capable of keeping it. Then, quickly I thought of what a terrific thing it would be to share a secret with my favorite cowboy, so I said, "Sure I can."

"Well, I won't tell you exactly what it is. I want you to be surprised too. But I intend to surprise your father tonight. You'll see how."

"Just don't let him ride a horse. He's never been on one," I answered, a bit scared at the thought that somehow my father might end up part of the rodeo.

"Oh, no, no, I am not going to have him ride anything. You'll see what it is. But don't tell him there's going to be a surprise. That's our secret."

"It's a deal."

We joined the others, and I zippered my lips regarding the surprise. I couldn't imagine what it would be, and for once, my imagination conjured a blank slate. But I couldn't help but spew forth my ecstatic description of the closet tour. I had emerged from it with something new to pester my parents about: "Please, PLEASE let me get more cowboy boots. Please!

"We'll discuss this further at home," my father said in a tone that signaled me to save my imploring for a different time and place. My mother and father thanked the Autrys for the dinner. I thanked Gene for the tour. "Break a leg," my father said to Gene, and the two of them hugged each other. We walked out with me saying, "Why did you tell him to break a leg?"

We sat in Gene's box so close to the arena that I could see hoof marks in the dirt upon the rodeo floor. Cowboys mounting bulls in the chutes were within eyeshot as were the spangled riders lining up for the grand opening parade. The orchestra played. The announcer introduced the great singing cowboy, founder of the Flying A Rodeo, and its star horse, the faithful and beloved Champion. The spotlights illuminated the arena and out came Gene Autry in his white Stetson, embroidered silk shirt, designer pants, and a pair of those magnificent boots with their jewel-like spurs. He sang, "I'm back in the saddle again, back where a friend is a friend . . ." The crowd cheered and the applause echoed throughout the huge Garden.

My heart pounded with excitement as a whole parade of handsome cowboys dressed to the hilt pranced out on their horses along with cowgirls in outfits whose sequins reflected the lights as they twinkled and bounced everywhere. I loved the country-western songs and twangs on guitars, mandolins, and fiddles. Here it was okay, no Hecky or Phil turning the dial to something else. I envisioned myself upon one of those horses doing an arabesque as I rode bareback in the parade.

The rodeo proceeded with daring acts. Cowpokes mounted bucking horses and bulls, many falling, others remaining on the wildly moving animals for the required number of seconds. The crowd cheered exuberantly. The riders who fell created tension as to whether or not they'd escape the hooves of the animals. Meanwhile, the antics of the rodeo clowns elicited laughter amidst danger as the rescue teams risked their own lives with a still loose charging bull or maddened horse. Acrobats performed thrilling contortions on galloping horses, and the background music provided just the right ambience to augment what our eyes witnessed. Terrific! But I kept thinking, what is the secret Gene is going to reveal?

The answer was soon to be revealed as Gene Autry rode out on Champion again, this time singing a medley of his now famous Christmas songs, including "If It Doesn't Snow On Christmas," "He's a Chubby Little Fellow," "Frosty the Snowman," "When Santa Claus Gets Your Letter," "(Hard Rock, Coco and Joe) The Three Little Dwarfs," and "Thirty-Two Feet—Eight Little Tails," all selected for recording and produced by Hecky.

After singing, "Thirty-two feet and eight little tails in all/See 'em canter, hear ol' Santa call, 'Merry, merry Christmas to you all,'" Gene stopped. Immediately, he said, "Don't worry, folks. I haven't forgotten our friend, Rudolph. With us here tonight, is a very special man, a good friend of mine, my children's record producer, who brought you the songs I've just sung and *Champion, The Horse No Man Would Ride,* and *Gene Autry at the Rodeo.* I'd like you to meet the man without whom that endearing song, 'Rudolph, the Red-Nosed Reindeer' would never have been recorded." The spotlight swirled around to Gene's box and shone upon my father. "Hecky Krasnow, will you please stand up. Folks, Johnny Marks wrote the wonderful song, but it was Hecky Krasnow who decided it was a song you'd all love to hear. Without him, our friend Rudolph would still be waiting to be heard. Thank you from all of us, Hecky, for a song we love."

As my father stood, the applause echoed through Madison Square Garden. Over it, Gene began singing "Rudolph." Champion pranced around the arena with Gene singing as he rode. When he reached the area in front of the box, he lifted his white, double-creased Stetson off his head and tipped his hat to my father, who stood again and waved back. The entire audience joined in singing the song.

This public honoring of my father was the secret Gene had shared with me. I looked at my father and saw the huge smile on his face. When he sat down again, he took my mother's hand. I heard her say, "Oh, honey, how very exciting!" He turned his head towards me and put his arm around my shoulder tapping it in time with the song. I was glad to feel that tapping. It reminded me that I was not dreaming. This was a dream come true.

CHAPTER 17

Parties and Payola

. . . .

My father's office stood between those of arranger, conductor, and composer Percy Faith and conductor and arranger Mitch Miller. Percy Faith orchestrated and conducted the music for many of Hecky's productions. In the late '20s, Faith began arranging pieces for hotel orchestras and, later, for radio in his native Canada. In 1945, he moved to New York City, became an American citizen, and conducted the scores for several popular radio shows. He worked at Decca, RCA, and became part of the Columbia A&R staff in 1950. Inspired by an old folk song, he wrote the Guy Mitchell bestseller, "My Heart Cries for You." Other hits followed, including "The Song from the Moulin Rouge." His fame grew, and his income rose accordingly.

Mitch Miller was playing piano by age six. When he graduated from the Eastman School of Music in Rochester, where he'd met another student named Goddard Lieberson, the Rochester Symphony hired him to play oboe. He honed his talent as a soloist with the CBS Symphony. At this time, he also played oboe with famed conductor Andre Kostelanetz and with the Budapest String Quartet. As director of Mercury Records Popular Music Division, he was responsible for several big hits by vocalist Frankie Laine, including the highly popular "Mule Train." When country songs began to cross over to popular music—with songs like Pattie Page's hit, "Tennessee Waltz"—Mitch Miller hopped on the bandwagon and arranged songs like Hank Williams's "Hey Good Lookin,'" turning them into hit records for Frankie Laine and Joe Stafford. When he moved to Columbia, he continued to create hits for in-house artists as the pop music department's A&R man, and as a Columbia artist himself, recording several hits under the title of *Mitch Miller and His Gang*.

The 1950s were notorious for payola, a practice that was outlawed by the federal government and that led to several major federal investigations. Payola included bribing disc jockeys to play records whether or not the public called and wrote requesting that the particular tunes be played. Demanding a piece of a song from the artist or writer in exchange for recording it, practiced by many an A&R man or producer, constituted payola. One or a few select publishers dominating B-sides in order to make big bucks from the popular A-sides also classified as payola. Videola, television's form of payola, involved producers of television programs selecting the theme songs for money and excluding public opinion from the decision. Top disc jockeys could earn as much as $35,000 a year from payola, a very sizeable sum in the 1950s.

When Frank Sinatra left Columbia, he accused Mitch Miller of engaging in payola. He claimed that the poor quality songs Mitch gave him to sing were the result of his refusal to pay to sing the good ones. Sinatra went so far as to write and call various members of Congress about Miller. There are biographical reports that claim Mitch Miller did, indeed, engage in payola schemes. Other reports claim he stayed true to his word once deals were made and contracts signed with writers and artists. In a phone conversation with him in November of 2006, he said he refused to become involved with rock 'n' roll in the '60s because one could not be in that field without engaging in payola and he would have gotten Columbia in trouble were he to do so. He stated that he didn't need to be paid by artists. His contract with Columbia gave him 50% of royalties on what he produced and Columbia the other 50%. That amounted to one cent for him, and one cent for Columbia at the time.

At Columbia, the choices Mitch made as an A&R man brought in millions. Though his salary was $25,000 per year, he also earned royalties with his band as a recording artist. The artists and the songs he selected for them to sing resulted in one hit after another: Johnny Ray's "Cry";

Jo Stafford's "Jambalaya"; Tony Bennett's "Cold, Cold Heart"; *Mitch Miller and His Gang*'s rendition of the Israeli tune, "Tzena, Tzena"; "The Yellow Rose of Texas"; and "The Colonel Bogey March" from the hit film *Bridge Over the River Kwai.* These were just a few of the songs that fattened Mitch's bank account. Mitch Miller selected songs that became hits for other Columbia artists, including Doris Day, Frankie Laine, Rosemary Clooney, Mahalia Jackson, and Jerry Vale. When it came to selecting the right songs for the right artists and ones that the public would demand, Mitch Miller was to Columbia's pop music what Hecky was for children's music. However, pop music had a far larger audience and didn't have to rely on holiday crossovers to make the megabucks from airplay and consequent purchases; and Mitch was able to draw upon his own talent as a bandleader and singer to earn big sums of money. In essence, he was both a Columbia employee and a Columbia recording artist.

Hecky respected Mitch as a musician. At several informal social evenings, Hecky played his violin, Mitch his oboe, jazz A&R man George Avakian's well-known violinist wife her violin, and other musicians their violas and cellos. Chamber music afforded a lovely respite from the constant search for new hits that would bring money to Columbia.

Both men shared a love of classical music. Mitch respected Hecky's uncanny instincts as an A&R man and the quality of his projects. Their easygoing rapport as office neighbors, along with Percy Faith, made for a friendly, casual work environment. Hecky and Mitch truly appreciated their capabilities in their respective fields.

Yet, Hecky viewed Mitch as a wheeler and dealer, a business aspect with which Hecky was not comfortable. Mitch's reputation in the business as a gimmick pusher, as someone who would sacrifice quality lyrics or melody for an attention grabber worked well for Columbia and for Mitch, as the public loved the schmaltz of "The Yellow Rose of Texas" and the innuendos of "Come On-a My House." For the adult public, from Hecky's viewpoint, such schmaltz and gimmicks were okay. Children, on the other hand, should never be manipulated or fooled. Honesty, integrity, and the highest of quality were standards that must be followed.

Hecky refused to engage in payola. If a song he produced was ultimately in demand, he wished for it to be so by virtue of its own merit. There was talk within our family when "Rudolph" came upon his desk that Johnny Marks, after two years of rejections, offered Hecky 25% if he would only record it. Hecky liked the song and, if indeed this is what occurred, he could not bring himself to accept what he considered a bribe. Hecky's brother Bob implored him regarding "Rudolph." "If you think this little ditty is going to be a hit, for God's sake, accept Johnny Marks' offer. Even better, buy the damned song from him!" Bob had founded COIL, the first under-the-floor heating systems and grew tough after the Mafia threatened to break his knees badly enough to cripple him for life if he didn't do their bidding. Somehow, he found a solution and walked unharmed until his dying day at age 87.

Hecky suspected that Mitch engaged in some payola schemes, if not constantly, at least upon occasion. Mitch reminded Hecky of his brother Bob, and, to a degree, of his brother Al, who had taken over much of Harry's National Iron Company and had become a millionaire. Though both brothers ran union companies and paid and treated their workers well, Bob and Al thought in terms of profits, as did Mitch Miller. Hecky thought of music, stories, good singers, and quality musicians. He knew he had to bring in the bucks for Columbia and was obviously succeeding. For himself, he desired money—or at least to live without worrying about it, but he could not wheel and deal. He was not a salesman, as his stints in the hardware and haberdashery businesses had demonstrated. Inwardly, still the coddled violin prodigy, he found it difficult to hustle his own creations. He could defend what his heart believed in and what his gut instincts assured him were wise choices, as he had defended "Rudolph" against Goddard Lieberson's admonitions. He could not play games, and the record industry was filled with them. When he signed his contract, either out of a newcomer's ignorance, or simply accepting the terms for the start, he remained Columbia's company employee, creating and recording projects that belonged to Columbia, and necessitating the use of pseudonyms (not considered payola or unethical) in order to collect royalties on any songs he wrote. No 50-50 deal for him.

Hecky was reminded of his decision regarding "Rudolph" when he visited Gene and Ina Autry at the Palm Springs mansion they now owned, thanks to that red-nosed reindeer. The fact that Johnny Marks could dwell wherever and however he pleased forever reminded Hecky that such wealth would not be his if he continued to follow his conscience—but he did. Hecky's success could not be measured by wealth and fame, society's ultimate stamp of achievement. At times, the lack of these reminded him of his violin debut at age 16 that left him behind to watch other violinists achieve fame, wealth, and glory. These moments made temporary inroads upon his self-esteem and knowledge of his own success at Columbia. Perhaps one of these times reared its head when New Year's Day of 1952 was ushered in at Mitch Miller's large, elegant home, built during the Revolutionary War in Stony Point, Rockland County, New York.

. . . .

My mother, father, Steffi, and I drove along the winding, wooded roads of the New York Palisades in our moderately priced, two-door car to Mitch's home. There, a young man requested the keys and, after helping us out, drove the car to a parking place on the grounds. At the door, we were greeted by a man dressed like the butlers who opened doors at the mansions I'd seen in movies and some television shows. We were led into a room with a bar, uniformed men tending it, and tables filled with tempting appetizers. There, Mitch greeted everyone and talked with his characteristic energy and confidence, his lips always turned upwards in a smile as though all was well with the world and always would be. As he greeted us over the sound of many people's voices, men and women in black uniforms with little white aprons politely interrupted conversations to ask if we wished for hors d'oeuvres from the tray. I happily helped myself to more pigs in blankets than I'd ever eaten in my life and downed enough fried shrimp on toothpicks to develop a lot of karma with those crawling creatures of the sea. Finally, drinks and food in hand, the guests wandered into other rooms while wishing each other good things in the upcoming year. The guests included Goddard Lieberson,

Rosemary Clooney, Percy Faith, and Frankie Laine. Frances, Mitch's wife, alternately socialized and disappeared to make sure all was running smoothly in the kitchen.

I thought Grandma and Grandpa's houses in Hartford and at the beach were large. It seemed to me now that three or four of each of them would fit into this home. There were windows everywhere, and looking through them at the thin blanket of snow that lay upon the ground, it seemed the lawn stretched endlessly. In the living room, a fire roared and crackled in the huge fireplace with its mantel decked with objects that looked like some I'd seen behind the glass cases at the Metropolitan Museum of Art. Adjacent to the foyer, which was large enough to constitute being a room itself, lay another room. In it, a Steinway piano shined as though polished for hours. This room, though furnished with items evocative of musical endeavors, felt like a den one might sit in after an active day at a British foxhunt. I felt like I was in one of the palatial mansions Sherlock Holmes visited to investigate a murder.

"Daddy," I said to my father at one point, "Is Mitch Miller a duke?"

My father laughed. "No, Juddie. Americans don't become dukes or duchesses. Mitch earns a lot of money."

"Why don't you? You work at Columbia too."

"I haven't been doing what Mitch has been doing as long as he has been doing it," my father answered. "Give it time. I'll write a hit song yet." Those last words were ones I would hear for years to come.

I left my father's side to join Steffi, who was talking with Mitch's daughter, Margaret. I didn't really listen because my mind was imagining the day that my father finally earned as much as Mitch and we had a house like this. I was lost in my thoughts as I designed my bedroom with a huge closet and a room big enough to practice my interpretive dances without always having to push aside the mahogany coffee table, fortunately bearing legs resting upon little wheels not unlike those on my roller skates.

My reverie ended as a gong reverberated and it was announced that we should all come into the dining room. "Hey, Mom and Dad," I commented as we walked past a living room, den, office, and some rooms I couldn't name but called "extras," "is this like the homes you used to play duets in during the Depression?"

"Kind of, but not quite," my mother responded. "This house has taste. You can feel Mitch and Frances in it. You can tell he's a musician by the paintings and various knick-knacks. The ones we played in were gilded in gold and silver. All you could feel was the decorators who designed them."

"Besides," my father said. "If there were starving people outside, you can be sure Mitch Miller would see to it that as many as he could feed would be fed."

The dining room was long and large, the table laden with colorful food: meats, vegetables, salads, fish, bread, rolls, and fruits. The aroma was gamey, as though the meat had been hunted fresh. A rare roast beef carved by a man wearing a chef's hat seemed a favorite of all those gathered around the table. I preferred my mother's roasts cooked in her little rotisserie and not quite so bloody looking. The table had the air of a work of art with each dish decorated to look like a flower, fish, leaf, or just a design made from herbs and other garnishes. Servers stationed along the table told us what each dish contained and served us what we requested. Round tables and chairs were set up in the foyer outside the dining room for us to sit. We found ourselves sitting down with Rosemary Clooney and Frankie Laine. This was the first time I'd met him. "I just love your song, 'Mule Train' so much, Mr. Laine. I love the sound of that whip. It makes it so real."

"Compliment the producer—Mitch—on that, Judy. I just sing."

Frankie, who was soon to record some children's songs for Hecky, seemed a jolly fellow. He had a broad grin and smiled a lot. Rosemary Clooney was her usual sweet self. She made several references to the actor José Ferrer during the course of the evening. Those present, my father included, seemed a little uncomfortable when she spoke of him. Comments like, "Rosie, be careful." "Rosemary, you are aware of his reputation as a womanizer." "His poor wife, I sure wouldn't want to be in her place." "Rosie . . ." Rosemary insisted no one should worry, that there was nothing between them but friendship and a mutual appreciation of theater and music. I saw her eyes light up and her cheeks blush every time his name was mentioned.

The other children and I finished eating before the adults and, with our tummies now more than full, we warmed up to one another. We left our seats and went off to share our names, tales of school, teachers we liked and didn't like, and television shows we mutually watched. We burst into songs from the television programs fast becoming a new unifying pop culture.

Frances Miller gave us a deck of cards. One of the boys had learned some card tricks from his uncle. He showed signs of a budding magician as the others of us wondered how it was possible for him to know what card we had actually picked. Having seen the young boy's bag of tricks about three times over, the girls and I danced around the spacious house to music playing in the background. Eventually, the gong bonged again, and Mitch called everyone for a champagne toast. We kids were given the famous drink of the day: Shirley Temples made with ginger ale and topped with juicy, overly sweet maraschino cherries.

"Here's to the New Year," Mitch said, holding his champagne glass in one hand and his other arm wrapped around Frances' shoulder. "May all of us be happy and in love, like Frances and me, and may those of us here tonight continue with the great successes we are all bringing to Columbia."

Goddard Lieberson, now president of Columbia, emitted a loud, "AMEN!"

The guests talked a bit more, then one by one, we asked for our coats, brought to us by a uniformed man and woman. Our respective cars awaited us as we walked out the front door into the chilly night scented by pine trees. The car keys were handed back to us.

On the ride home, my father said, "I hope Rosemary comes to her senses. She talks about that bum, Mr. Ferrer, with a little too much familiarity for comfort."

"He is a good actor," my mother said.

"There's apples and cherries, honey. Right now, you are mixing them. A good actor doesn't necessarily make a good man."

"What a house," I heard my mother say. "Frances won't have to lift a finger cleaning up, and you can be sure Mitch won't vacuum."

"HUHney! I like to vacuum," my father said defensively. "It gives me a satisfying feeling to see crumbs and other dirt just whoosh up into that machine."

"Well, warm up your vacuuming muscles, honey. The next Columbia party falls upon us. I think I'll make veal scaloppini. Mmmm, that would be good with asparagus hollandaise. No, too much sauce. Just plain asparagus."

"It's months away, honey. Why worry about it now?"

"I'm not worrying, I am planning. There's a difference. Besides, I want to show them that I can cook as well as any caterer."

"Your food, honey, is far better than any caterer or restaurant, believe me. You make chicken—the best chicken in the world—and you'll have to cook 50 chickens because there won't be a piece left."

"Well thanks, but I think it's going to be veal—veal is classier."

In the back seat, my eyelids were closing as I fell asleep against my sister and her warm coat.

. . . .

Mitch Miller's New Year's toast brought good tidings for children's records. Arthur Godfrey delighted youngsters with two new releases sung in his inimitable style. In "Bullfrog on the Bank," he sang about the meeting of the bulldog on the bank and the bullfrog in the pool. "The Animal Fair" brought to 78-rpm the classic song about the monk who jumped on the elephant's trunk. "Peter Cottontail" returned for his Easter visit, remaining high on the charts for weeks on end. Rosemary Clooney added to the Easter fare with "Eggbert the Easter Egg," while "Me and My Teddy Bear" continued to enchant millions of teddy bear lovers. "The Little Red Caboose" chugged along, creating a lot of steam.

In spite of the increasing fear-mongering of Senator McCarthy, Hecky and Henry Walsh came out with another Gene Autry special: *Stampede.* This story included details about the southwest and was written in radio script style. An article in a prestigious educational publication, *Elementary English,* stated, "Perhaps its real value, however, [referring to both *Stampede* and *Champion*] lies in its entertainment value for boys and girls. It is possible that we in education would motivate greater interest in the books of Will James, Marguerite Henry and others if we employed such recordings as *Stampede,* which, because they do give pleasure, would help bridge the gap to books and the entertainment they also provide. . . . Experience has shown that recordings such as Autry's will serve as avenues to books."

Another of Hecky's 1952 projects, *New Music Horizons,* inspired an article. These 12 albums contained songs for children of preschool age with the goal of developing the innate music in them. Each album was complete unto itself. Each was also part of a carefully worked-out musical program researched and created by leading American music educators. The content of the albums allowed preschool children to sing, play, and dance along. "Sleepy Songs" helped a child get ready for his or her nap. Topics included "Singing Games," "Community Helpers," and "Animal Friends." The article states, "Children will love them all, and parents and teachers will find them perfect for use with one child or for an entire group. This is an excellent disking, conceived, performed and recorded with taste."

William Keene, a popular actor and narrator who performed on Broadway, television, and radio, lent his seasoned and animated voice to one of the most delightful recordings and stories my father ever recorded. With Gail Kubik's orchestra providing the captivating music, Keene tells the story of Benny, a beaver who does not like to gnaw with his teeth and build dams, but instead, likes to create percussion with his tail. The beavers in the forest are not pleased with such eccentricity. Beavers are supposed to do what beavers do. Benny is ostracized and forced to leave beaver camp. As he wanders away forlorn and destitute, he sees a band of hunters headed right for the beavers. He whips out his percussion instruments and begins a solo that would put Gene Krupa to shame. The hunters run out of the forest terrified. Benny becomes the beavers' hero and opens up a music conservatory where beavers come to study bird calls, snare drums, bass drums, cymbals, and many other marvelous percussion instruments. This story diverges somewhat from the underdog theme and gives praise to those who are different and don't quite fit in. *Variety* wrote, "Here is a musical story that is absolutely wonderful. . . . The modern Stravinskyesque music is great; the story in rhyme is cute-as-a-button and will appeal to older kids. Yet, the use of percussion instruments as part of the story line should hold the interest of the youngsters. A fine item."

. . . .

Hecky was now collaborating with a lyricist named Leo Israel, who most often used the pseudonym Leo Paris, perhaps because it was a less controversial name than that of the newly formed country of Israel, surrounded by hostile neighbors who vowed to undo all the United Nations had done by establishing it. With Leo Israel/Paris, one could only conjecture. Leo had written a number of records for Young People's Records and the Children's Record Guild. Leo's wife Sylvia was a dedicated first-grade teacher, and the two combined her knowledge of young children with his flare for writing clever and hilarious lyrics. Leo also worked with conductor Rudolph Goehr, and the two had written several pieces for Young People's Records. Leo definitely had a sense of the absurd. Hecky and Leo made a very productive but odd couple.

Leo was a broad-boned man with a mustache. His thick-rimmed glasses looked perpetually fogged, and the black plastic frames were more often than not broken and patched together with tape. Leo stood about 6 feet tall. He always looked rumpled. He smiled a lot, laughed heartily, and grew totally exuberant and jolly when he'd come up with some humorous and witty verses.

Hecky was a meticulous man. Spots on his glasses were promptly wiped away. He always looked well-groomed and smelled of refreshing cologne and aftershave lotion. Hecky met deadlines and would often become exasperated when Leo didn't meet these same deadlines. Yet, the two worked well together.

Leo was a kind man, but very much the absentminded professor. In this regard, my father may have found some piece of Phil returned in the form of Leo. Though his intellect, knowledge of literature, and use of language was brilliant, Leo could not match Phil's refinement and grace.

We often visited the Israels at their apartment. The families became friends. Sometimes we'd have dinner together at one or another's homes or go out to eat, see a movie, or attend a concert. The Israels were a close-knit family with their own very definite dynamics. Leo had the characteristic of a child genius with a mind far ahead of his emotional development. He seemed a perpetual child more than a parent in charge. Sylvia teeter-tottered between being his wife and his mother. Their eldest daughter, Laurie, held the position of parenting both her mother and father. Jared, the middle child, was subjected to two women who, long before the era of women's liberation, freely spoke their minds and had no difficulty acting as boss to him and the other family members.

I liked Jared. He enjoyed discussing all kinds of topics that fascinated my inquisitive mind, and he differed from the boys I knew in school, who viewed girls in the far more demeaning manner characteristic of the '50s. Jared was sandwiched between his elder sister and his younger sister, Deborah, a cute, punchy kid who did just as she pleased, I think primarily in an effort to stay clear of the family antics surrounding her. She was my age, and we became good friends, reading books, playing checkers and monopoly, mothering our dolls, or twisting our bodies as we attempted to perform acrobatic feats. Steffi and Laurie, the same age, got along fairly well. Both shared a love of literature and writing. Leo and Sylvia's political background matched Hecky and Lillian's. If there is one thing that stood out in the Israels' abode, it was the sound of language: everyone talking about something at the same time like birds in a tree loudly cackling and declaring their territory. In the case of the Israels, it was cackling to expound the never-ending ideas that ran through all of their heads nonstop.

The Israels' apartment was in perpetual disarray and smelled of sweat and fried food. Sitting down on the couch or chairs in the small living room challenged anyone who wished to rest their legs and feet. The room, dwarfed by the floor to ceiling bookshelves lining each wall, literally bore the weight of the written word. The shelves tilted. Most were concave. Others that began at a proper height from the shelf below at one end slanted like a seesaw at rest by the time they joined the shelf below at its other end. Like a stack of dominoes, they looked about to topple at any given moment.

In order to sit, we'd first have to clear the couch and chairs of papers, magazines, and various board games. Finally seated, there was always the concern that if we moved and created even a minor vibration, an item from the surrounding shelves would fall upon our heads. One item dislodging itself could cause an avalanche of written materials to cascade down. The visits were lively, and the discussion always sent me home with new things to think about or espouse.

Leo, without doubt, was a mad genius. If I could have seen his brain, I am certain it would have looked exactly like his bookshelves. Yet, out of all the disheveled mess, came highly original, brilliant lyrics that painted wonderful and amusing scenes that inspired equally original and delightful tunes in Hecky's compositions. As Leo, when writing with Hecky, most often used the last name of Paris, Hecky most often used the very Jewish sounding pseudonym, Lee Herschel. At the time he was born, Herschel was the standard name written on the birth certificates of Jewish boys whose foreign-speaking parents the nurses could not understand. That was the name on Hecky's birth certificate, changed later to Hermann.

Leo and Hecky had just completed recording a series designed to give firsthand experiences through aural illusion. In this series, listeners visited *Skyliner Flight 35*, *Hook and Ladder #99*, and *Tugboat Peter Moran*. Portable tape machines were now in their infancy and, as a result, Hecky and Leo spent their days recording the story of the ins and outs of flying, traversed around New York City on a fire engine, and pushed a ship in New York's harbor as they sailed with the crew on a tugboat.

My father came home from each of these days like a little boy whose heroes were pilots, firefighters, and captains of ships. He literally glowed with excitement as he described sitting in the cockpit, watching the pilot as he started up the engines, hearing the whir of the propellers, the sound of the wheels coming up. At dinner, he announced with utter joy, "Flight is a wondrous invention. It is amazing how that heavy, steel bird can lift off the ground. The pilot was so calm, cool, and collected.

Oh, Juddie, you would have loved it. Wait until you hear the record and can imagine the day I've had."

When he arrived home in the evening of the day he'd spent riding on Hook and Ladder #99, he had experienced the embodiment of every boy's dream come true. "I heard it, actually heard the fire bell clang, and saw, with my own eyes, the firemen slide down the pole. I felt the thrill of going to a fire as the sirens screeched and the truck sped, tooting its horn for traffic to let it through. They are so, so brave, so brave!" Years later, I would know firsthand the thrill and excitement my father experienced as I had been asked by some firefighters to write a song about them, "the unsung heroes," and spent a day doing just what my father had done. The song, "This Could Be the Night," became the anthem of the New York City Firefighters Union in the '70s.

The tugboat totally awed Hecky. "You can't imagine what it is like to be on a boat that, relatively speaking, would be the size of an ant compared to the boat it was pushing: a genuine giant. The tugboat must move so accurately at angles, and the way the tugboat captain and the ship's captain work together, each steering his vessel so the whole thing works is simply amazing, I say amazing!"

Billboard heard these audio adventures and expressed its own enthusiasm.

Here's an idea that seems like a sure winner. Simply, it's to offer the realistic aural illusion of an airplane, fire engine, and tug boat at work with all the incidental sounds that are produced in the process. They are remarkably realistic. And no background music is allowed to interfere with the illusion. The plane flies from New York to Los Angeles, a fire is put out and the tug helps dock an ocean liner. Listeners (adult ones, too, incidentally) will feel they are participating in the action. In addition to being entertaining, the disks get across plenty of information. They should catch on quickly.

* * * * * * * * * * *

This series came out in September of 1952, on the heels of a productive springtime of releases including additions to *Baseball Tips from the Stars.* This time it was tips on pitching by Bob Feller, fielding by Phil Rizzuto, catching by Yogi Berra, and batting by Ralph Kiner. Narrator William Keene followed *Benny the Beaver* with *Johnny Brown Who Turned Green*, about a boy whose day at the circus was spent overeating. He ate so much that he turned green. The story's undercurrent was a lesson about greed.

Gene Autry recorded the first in a series called *Heroes of the West*, with a story about the Gold Rush and the life of Kit Carson. Josef and Miranda blended their harmonies for the "moppets" with "BooBoo the Baby Baboon" and an album, *South African Folk Songs for Children*, including songs like "The Zulu Warrior" with its rhythmic words as Josef sang "I kama zimba zimba zayo," and Miranda's vibrant voice reached its uppermost register and chanted back, "I kama zimba zimba zee."

When November rolled around, "Rudolph" was still selling more millions. Gene Autry and Rosemary Clooney combined their warm voices for Hecky in another Christmas song composed by the now legendary Johnny Marks, a song adapted from Clement Moore's poem, "The Night Before Christmas." *Billboard* selected the recording to be listed as one of its choice picks along with *Benny Goodman 1937–'38 Jazz concert, No. 2 Album*; Jo Stafford singing with the Paul Weston Orchestra, "Keep It a Secret"; and Doris Day singing with the Percy Faith orchestra, "The Cherries." *Variety* called Gene and Rosie's song a "Best Bet" and wrote, "The Autry-Miss Clooney rendition gives it an all-age appeal."

The season didn't end with just these. With Jack Rollins and Steve Nelson's expert songwriting, Gene Autry's popular voice and persona, and Hecky's right-on gut instincts, another beloved character entered the national consciousness and spread awareness of caring for our forests and being forever vigilant about the danger of starting forest fires.

CHAPTER 18

Westward Ho!

. . . .

In 1950, the Capitan Mountains of New Mexico were aflame as a strong wind swept a major fire along the ground between the trees. A ranger in one of the fire towers to the north saw the flames and alerted the nearest ranger station. As the fire spread ever more rapidly, forest rangers, army soldiers, workers from the New Mexico State Game Department, and civilian volunteers joined forces to gain control of the raging fire. It was a difficult task, for each time the fire was contained in one spot the wind would push it across the lines.

A lonely bear cub had been spotted wandering near the fireline during one of the lulls in the fight against the fire. Those near the scene stayed away from the cub thinking the mother would be close behind. She never appeared, and the firefighters finally rescued the little critter. He became known as Smokey Bear and soon won fame as a cartoon character promoting forest fire prevention.

Smokey's name changed when songwriters Jack Rollins and Steve Nelson needed an extra beat for their song, "Smokey *the* Bear." Depicted as a ranger with a hat, shovel, and a pair of dungarees, the song tells how Smokey can sniff fires miles away and asks those visiting the forests to listen as he explains how to prevent forest fires. He points out how trees are great for kids to climb on and they're beautiful to see.

If you've ever seen the forest when a fire is running wild
And you love the things within it like a mother loves her child,
Then you know why Smokey tells you when he sees you passing
     through,
"Remember . . . please be careful . . . It's the least that you can do."

The song, another of Hecky's projects, was recorded with Gene
Autry in Los Angeles on July 7, 1952, and became a consistent popular seller and was heard in nearly every forest fire prevention campaign.

. . . .

Columbia not only paid for my father to travel to L.A. for his summer's work in 1952, but also paid for our family to join him. My parents
decided to combine my father's vacation with his going to L.A. The
four of us would drive across the country sightseeing as we navigated
plains, hills, valleys, mountains, and the desert in the new two-tone,
gold-and-brown Nash Rambler my parents had just purchased.

The car had two front seats that folded down to create two beds,
which served no purpose for a family of four but proved a great game
for Karen and me when the car was parked in our driveway. It was an
affordable and popular automobile and considered one of the safest; a
strong point for my parents, who'd never driven across the Rockies and
always feared tire blowouts, a not infrequent occurrence before the era
of radial tires.

Since we'd be driving across the desert, my father bought a bag made
from jute and lined with tightly woven cotton to hang on the back
bumper. The bag held water and as the car was in motion, the breeze
cooled the water, which would keep us hydrated as we drove in degrees
over 100. My mother had learned to drive but was not really comfortable
at the wheel. She would spell my father on the flat, rural surfaces of the
Plains states. He would do the city and mountain driving.

We took off in our Rambler in mid-June. Steffi packed a supply of
books and began to read them the moment we drove away from Douglas
Avenue. I began looking out of the window as soon as we left, excited

by the opportunity to see every inch of 3,000 of planet Earth's miles. My nose was constantly pressed against the back window on the left side of the car.

We drove for hours every day, stopping at diners with jukeboxes hanging on the wall of the booths we sat in. For one dime, you could hear three songs. There were 200 choices on each box. At one table, I put in a dime and pressed 200 buttons. They all played. I didn't want to leave until I'd heard every song, but my father said, "We have miles and miles to go, Juddie. Now say goodbye to the jukebox and come to the car." I tried this trick in every diner across the country, but I never hit the jackpot again.

Washington, D.C., was our first stop for sightseeing. I wondered who would be in the White House come November. My parents were working hard for Adlai Stevenson, who was running against General Dwight D. Eisenhower. I had already sealed hundreds of envelopes for Stevenson mailings at the local Yonkers Democratic headquarters. I looked forward with great excitement to the day I could vote. For days, I mulled over a fact I learned at the Abraham Lincoln National Park in Hodgenville, Kentucky: that for being anti-slavery, Lincoln's parents were rejected by their Baptist church. My mother drove the miles and miles as we passed the cornfields of Kansas. Throughout Kansas, I imagined I'd see Dorothy and Toto, the Tin Man, Scarecrow, and Cowardly Lion. If I saw a black cloud in the distance, I prayed it wasn't a tornado.

Finally, we reached Colorado. We'd never seen mountains of such height and breadth. Steffi and I were asked for the first time ever to please be quiet in the car so my father could concentrate on driving. There were no guardrails on the narrow mountain roads and often one car would have to back up or go forward to find room to pull aside so the oncoming car could fit to pass. Frequent scenic stops gave my father time to rest his jangled driving nerves. At these stops, he indulged his hobby, one for which he'd won several blue ribbons in contests: photography. In between focusing the lens, pushing the picture button, and changing roles of film, Steffi and I heard the constant cry of his other major concern besides driving on mountain roads. "Girls, get away from the edge! Rocks can slip. You can lose your balance."

We didn't walk on loose rocks, and when we lay on our bellies with our eyes looking down over a ledge, we knew we wouldn't fall. We pretended to slip and disappeared from sight. Our parents' frantic screams finally brought them to the edge of what seemed to be a huge cliff with a sheer drop. Though relieved to find us crouching and laughing on a huge ledge where we were in absolutely no danger of falling, they were not amused. However, they stopped telling us every step of the way to stay away from ledges.

In the Rockies we stayed in a tent-like cabin with canvas sides and a wooden floor. It combined the rustic with comfort and had a shower and flush toilet, the latter a necessity in traveling with someone with Crohn's. It was here at the edge of the woods that I saw a deer. I stealthily walked toward her, obviously a doe, for she had no antlers. She didn't run. When I was about 10 feet away, I spoke softly to her. "Don't worry. I won't hurt you. I'm just a kid who wants to be your friend." I was certain the deer understood because she didn't run. She didn't move at all, except for her ears and nose continuing to twitch. I walked closer and reached my hand out to caress her neck. She didn't flinch. Then, she turned around and slowly trotted through the woods.

I followed her along a path that led to a clearing, down a hill, through some tall grasses, and further down a slope. There the deer went into what appeared to be a small hut camouflaged by branches. I peeked in and saw a litter of three fawns. The mother looked at me and showed no signs of fear. I sat down and watched the babies nurse. When they finished, she got up and came to the entrance of the little hut. I put my hand out, and she licked it. I crawled inside the hut and petted the fawns. She came in and placed her warm body near them.

I sat there in wonder at being inside the home of a doe and her fawns until I realized that the sun no longer shone its rays through the hut's entrance. I went outside and saw the exquisite sunset from atop the Rockies. I had no idea where I was. I had been so concentrated on the deer when I'd followed her to her dwelling that I hadn't observed any landmarks along the way.

The beautiful mountain sunset quickly moved over the majestic mountains, and utter darkness set in. My stomach began to churn with fear. The mother deer must have smelled its scent. She came out of the hut and began to lick my arms and face. I knew tonight I would not sleep in the comfortable cabin in the woods. I would sleep in the home of a mother deer and her fawns. I felt my stomach growl and out of my pocket pulled a half melted candy bar I had taken with me in case I got hungry playing with the other kids I'd met on the campground. I ate it quickly and followed the deer back into the hut. As I lay down beside her warm body along with the fawns, I thought of my parents. *Oh, boy, this will make looking over mountain cliffs with Steffi seem like nothing.* How would I ever be found or how would I ever find my way back? Maybe in the daylight I could figure it out. Right now, exhausted from fright, I lay next to the deer. Her body warmed me in the chilly mountain night and I drifted off to sleep.

The sun shining through the hut's entrance woke me in the morning. I went outside, pulled my jeans down and peed. I looked around for any familiar grounds that would tell me this is the way I got here and allow me to go back the way I came. Never having been in the mountains before or having befriended a deer, it didn't occur to me that her footprints might lie in the dirt under the grass and be a clue to the path back. I saw a tree and climbed it thinking that maybe higher up I could see my way back, but the tree wasn't all that high, and the land surrounding me seemed to stretch in every direction with no signs of cabins or a lodge. Then, I heard the sound of human voices. "JUDY, ARE YOU THERE?"

I crawled out of the hut and saw them: a park ranger, my parents, and sister. "I'M HERE, OVER HERE!" We mutually ran towards one another. "Shush," I said. "Don't scare my friend. She's a deer with new babies."

That didn't stop my parents, who grabbed me as their tears of relief dripped down their cheeks. The hugged me, one on each side, caressed my hair, held my face in their hands, and looked at me as though inspecting what changes might have occurred as the result of whatever had happened to me. "Where have you been? How could you do something like this? Do you know how terrified we've been? What is wrong with you? We love you." More hugs, squeezes, kisses, and inspection.

I wanted to cry but all the fear I'd held in since the sun had gone down last night and all the guilt I felt now only came out in these words: "I made friends with a deer. She took care of me last night."

"Juddie, oh, Juddie, oh Juddie," my father put his arms around me even tighter. I thought he would squash me with his hug.

The ranger turned to my parents. "This is definitely a first in my career, oh, not lost children, but a deer that makes friends with a person."

My father had his camera, a permanent fixture around his neck. "Well," he said, "we might as well capture this unique nightmare for posterity." Click! Click!

"Bid your new friends farewell," the ranger instructed. "The main office is waiting to see if you've been found. You've created quite a stir on the campgrounds. I'm just glad to know it's a deer and not a bear you encountered." The image of a bear coming after a meal of deer, fawns, and a chunky little girl ran through my unwitting head. I shuddered.

"The kids you'd been playing with told us you went off with a deer," my sister said. "That's how the ranger knew where to begin looking."

"We followed the deer's tracks," the ranger explained. "Then we found some piles of deer spoor. That's what finally turned us in this direction."

"What's deer spoor?" I inquired.

"Deer poop," the ranger answered.

I never loved poop so much as I loved that deer poop. I kept asking myself if they would have found me were it not for the *spoor,* a new word to add to my growing vocabulary.

. . . .

The wonders of the Painted Desert, the Petrified Forest, and the Grand Canyon left an impression upon all of us regarding the utter beauty and grandeur of America's land. Between these sights and Emma Lazarus's poem, "Give me your tired, your poor, your humble masses yearning to be free. . . ." which my mother recited as a ploy to get me to practice Chopin's Prelude in D Minor on the piano at home, my patriotism couldn't have peaked higher.

In contrast, driving through Navajo territory, we stopped at a roadside stand to purchase some artifacts and jewelry. As Steffi and my parents looked at the offerings, my wanderlust led me into conversation with the most ragged, emaciated girl I'd ever seen. She noticed the jute water bag hanging on the Nash bumper. "My mother sick, very sick," she told me. "No water. Very dry these days. Some water for my mother? Some food?"

I untied the water bag and then opened the back door of the Nash. We had packs of Life Savers to keep our mouths moist for our soon-to-occur jaunt over the Mojave. There were peanut butter and jelly sandwiches too. I took a few of these, some packs of the Life Savers, and slung the jute bag over my shoulder and followed the girl a short distance up a hill to a hovel the likes of which I couldn't have imagined. Six near-naked children sat on the dirt floor. The littlest, a boy of about 18 months, cried while a girl who looked around four attempted to calm him.

On a bed made out of a soiled, woven blanket, lay a woman so skinny I thought I gazed upon a living skeleton. The girl got a ceramic cup and held it out for me to pour water from our jute bag, which I did. She held her mother's head in one hand and slowly dripped droplets of water into her mouth with the other. "She very hot. I think she going to die. We all scared. We so hungry. Thank you for food and candy."

"I have to go," I said. I went back to our car.

"Where have you been now?" My mother's patience with my disappearing acts was growing shorter by the day. "And why is the water bag on your shoulder and not hanging on the car?"

"Mommy, come with me. Please. We can't let the woman die." The tone in my voice indicated to my mother that something was very wrong, and she followed me. When she saw the scene in the hovel, she stood as though frozen.

"No money, no food. Nothing, and father die," my Navajo acquaintance said.

My mother fumbled in her purse and took out a $20 bill. "Here," she handed it to the girl. "Maybe it will feed your family at least a few meals." She grabbed my hand hard to indicate that I should come with her immediately.

At our car, she took the bag of food we had in the car and handed it to me. "Give this to her. Don't go too near her. No hugs."

"Why? What's wrong with hugging someone goodbye?"

"The mother could have TB, meningitis—*strep*, for God's sake. Judy, if your throat begins to hurt even at all, you better tell me right away." Sore throats scared her, for one had permanently damaged her heart. "Go on now. Give her the food and come right back. I said *right* back."

The girl and I waved to each other as she stood a sad figure on the hill, and we drove on.

Driving across the Mojave, we wrapped ourselves in wet towels and refreshed our jute water bag at every few-and-far-between gas station we found. Reaching the welcome hills of California, we all burst into song ". . . Did you ever hear tell of Sweet Betsy from Pike, who crossed the wide prairie with her lover Ike . . ."

After more than two weeks on the road before the advent of interstate highways (to be promoted by Eisenhower, who would win November's election), the Roosevelt Hotel seemed truly a palace. I signed up for swimming lessons with the gorgeous 16-year-old lifeguard, even more gorgeous than Rock Hudson and Tony Curtis, at the luxurious pool. I diligently followed his instructions and became a skilled swimmer for life.

. . . .

On July 5, we visited the Autrys at their Palm Springs home to celebrate my parents' 23rd anniversary. Gene gave us a tour of his mansion closets. He seemed to enjoy giving tours of his wardrobe, whether here or at Madison Square Garden. If I thought I'd seen anything at the Garden, his closets here were each mansions unto themselves. I don't think I could have counted high enough to list how many shirts, pants, boots, hats, and spurs he owned. We got a tour of the beautifully landscaped grounds, which had a lovely fountain surrounded by a cactus garden. For all their wealth and Gene's fame, he and Ina remained two of the most easygoing, warmest, friendliest, unassuming people. An evening with them was casual and relaxing even in their mansion. Ina and Gene presented my parents with a set of luxuriously soft, mint-green towels with the initials HLK. The bath towels were large enough to almost classify as blankets. One has lasted to this day and resides in my linen closet as a warm memory.

A couple of days later, Columbia arranged a private tour of a Hollywood set. We saw editing rooms, costume warehouses, and watched the filming of a scene in a B-grade war film. It was a warm day, and what we saw didn't paint a very glamorous picture of the art of filmmaking, at least not from the actors' point of view. Extras dressed in soldier uniforms lay on the streets of a set of a bombed city. The scene was filmed over and over again, and finally, to fix whatever kinks were causing the numerous takes, the soldiers were told to remain lying in their positions in the sun. Stagehands periodically sprinkled them with water. Bottles of catsup had been poured over them to look like fresh blood. It dried and caked in the California summer sun, so, along with the water, the actors succumbed to the repeated dousing of catsup.

The next day, my mother, Steffi, and I said goodbye to my father and headed for a visit with his twin sisters who had moved to San Diego.

. . . .

Hecky now focused on his recordings. One of the artists he'd record was a young boy named Jimmy Boyd. He had red hair, freckles, wore checkered flannel shirts with dungarees, and topped it all with a straw cowboy hat. He looked like he'd stepped right off the farm. His wholesome, healthy, happy appearance was just what America wanted amidst the growing Cold War and Senator McCarthy's hunt for communists. His wide, winning grin could make the most pressed and pressured momentarily forget their problems.

After his birth on January 9, 1939, Jimmy Boyd lived an impoverished childhood until his father, forced to leave the family for a long period of time in pursuit of work, became an accomplished finish carpenter and moved with his family to Riverside, California. When Jimmy was seven, his nine-year-old brother Kenneth said to the bandleader at a country-western dance their parents had taken them to in nearby Colton, "You should hear my little brother sing and play the guitar."

When the bandleader, Texas Jim Lewis, agreed and Jimmy sang and played, the crowd responded with wild enthusiasm.

Later, when the family was in Los Angeles, little Jimmy auditioned for Al Jarvis, who had a talent show on KLAC-TV. Jimmy appeared and won. The program received over 20,000 enthusiastic responses to the young boy's performance. Jimmy became a regular on Jarvis' daily five-hour talk show on the station: *Make-Believe Ballroom.* It wasn't long until Jimmy was asked to appear on *The Frank Sinatra Show* on CBS.

Hecky knew this young man was already very popular and could only become more so. The public loved adorable, talented children, as evidenced by Judy Garland in her 1939 appearance in the movie *The Wizard of Oz* and Shirley Temple, still a child making movies that drew crowds to the theaters. Columbia, at Hecky's urging, signed Jimmy Boyd to a contract. In January, Hecky recorded a duet of "Dennis the Menace" with Jimmy and Rosemary Clooney, and "Tell Me a Story" with Jimmy and Frankie Laine. Both songs quickly rose on the trade paper charts and crossed over from children's to pop.

Inspired, Hecky wrote a song under the name of Steve Mann called "There's a Little Train a-Chugging in My Heart." It was recorded on February 18, 1952, and sold over 100,000 records in both the children's and pop fields: not the gold record hit Hecky might have wished for, but a hit nonetheless, and it only served to raise Jimmy Boyd even higher in the public's consciousness.

I had seen Jimmy Boyd on television and fallen head-over-heels in puppy love with this freckle-faced, cute boy. I insisted on going to the February recording. Norman Luboff was hired as the arranger for the session, and his chorus sang backup. Three other songs were also recorded. There wasn't much time to talk with Jimmy between songs and takes, but the publicity photographer took a photo of us together. I loved to smile, but as he stood so close to me, I feared opening my mouth with the train-track braces that had been put on my teeth. These were not par for the course in 1952. Orthodontia was a new form of dental care. However, being in such close proximity with Jimmy Boyd, I couldn't help but smile.

. . . .

. . . .

When Jimmy was one month short of turning 13, a song by Tim Connor called "I Saw Mommy Kissing Santa Claus" came upon Hecky's desk. He knew it would appeal to children as well as adults.

> I saw Mommy kissing Santa Claus underneath the mistletoe last
>   night
> She didn't see me creep down the stairs to have a peep;
> She thought that I was tucked up in my bedroom fast asleep.
> Then, I saw Mommy tickle Santa Claus underneath his beard
>   so snowy white;
> Oh, what a laugh it would have been if Daddy had only seen
> Mommy kissing Santa Claus last night.

Who could resist the delightful message the song's lyrics delivered, especially when sung by Jimmy Boyd, with his boy soprano voice made even more charming by its country-western twang? "Use that voice to the hilt," Hecky knew, "before puberty transforms it into a man's voice."

The song, recorded on July 7, 1952, was released in October. It sold over two and a half million records in its first few months. This was a record industry phenomenon in 1952. When sales like this occurred, the artist was presented with an Oscar of sorts: a gold record that was actually made of gold. Jimmy Boyd had received two of these from Columbia. When sales of the song reached over three million, Columbia presented Jimmy with a silver-mounted saddle because he loved and owned horses. Like "Rudolph," the song went on to sell huge numbers of records each and every Christmas. Little did Hecky know then, that long after his demise, future generations would hear and buy the song via the Internet. Since its initial release in October of 1952, the song has purportedly sold over 60,000,000 records.

After we returned to L.A. from San Diego, I got to see Jimmy Boyd again at a lunch date in which my father, Boyd, and his manager set up dates to record other songs in New York. Already promoting the farm boy image, Jimmy Boyd always appeared in public in his jeans, checkered shirts, cowboy boots, and hat. He was the only child in the nation allowed to wear such attire to school and to keep a hat on in the classroom.

Plans were made for Jimmy to record several songs in the beginning of 1953, including solos of already favorite tunes like "Rudolph," "Frosty," "Silent Night," "Jingle Bells," and "Winter Wonderland." While the adults planned his next steps, Jimmy and I talked. We both loved horses. I told him about the blue ribbon I'd won in a horse show at Camp Windham, where I went for a month each summer from the time I turned seven. He played the guitar, and so did I. We commiserated about how much our fingertips hurt when we first began to play and felt each other's callused fingertips. We both enjoyed the applause of an audience. He loved the excitement of the recording studio, just like me. When we said goodbye, he gave me a kiss on the cheek. Oh my God! He kissed my cheek. In keeping with Steffi and Lillian's Gene Kelly episodes, I refused to wash that spot for weeks and even attempted to keep that cheek out of the water for my last few swims in the Roosevelt pool supervised by the handsome lifeguard.

. . . .

We planned our route driving home so that we'd go through the San Bernardino National Forest, where Gene Autry was filming *Blue Canadian Rockies*. In this beautiful setting of mountains and Joshua Trees, I watched a human double for Gene and a horse double for Champion trot down a hill about 20 times until the director was happy with the shot. A makeup artist dabbed Gene's face with what made him appear to have grime on it, powdered it, and placed his hat upon his head just at the right angle. Gene mounted the real Champion, and, now, the real Gene on his real horse trotted down that hill, said his few lines, and it was a take. When we visited, I had told Gene about my blue ribbon at the camp horse show. After the scene was filmed, he asked if I wanted to ride on Champion.

"Ride on Champion? Are you kidding? YES!"

He helped me mount the horse, not wanting to readjust the stirrups before the next scene was shot. He handed me the reigns, patted Champion, and said, "Take this little darlin' for a ride."

We went up and down the hill and around the back of it, turned and came down the hill again. That was all there was time for, maybe two, maybe three minutes upon Champion's back before the shooting of the next scene began. For me it seemed a wonderful eternity. I couldn't wait to tell Karen and all my friends. I kissed Champion's nose when I got off and gave Gene a hug.

. . . .

We headed home and drove through Texas. In a diner filled with men in cowboy boots and 10-gallon hats, a genuine cowpoke sat down at the table next to us. He and his buddy ordered fried rattlesnake. He heard my loud voice as I said, "Daddy that man is going to eat rattlesnake. How can anyone eat a snake, especially a poisonous snake?"

Before my father could respond, the cowboy turned to me. "Whah, sweetheart, rattlesnake is ayabsolutely deelish-eeous. If you lived around heah, you'd be eatin' it too. Cain't be poisoned bah it. A deyad snake cain't produce venom. Ahl give you a tayaste when it comes."

"Thanks, but . . . no," I answered.

"Whah you must hayave heard thayat saying, 'When in Rome, do ayas the Romans do?' Give it a trah, and you'll be able to go hoahme and teyall your friends you tayasted a genyuwiyane Teyaxas dayalicacy."

"You're very generous, but I don't think I can taste a snake." When his plate came, the thought of what he was eating made my stomach churn. My big, juicy-looking, genyuwiyane Teyaxas Longhorn beef hamburger went almost untouched.

We visited the Alamo, and I heard about a man named Davy Crockett who fought there. Little did I know that Davy Crockett, à la Fess Parker, lay in Hecky's future. I also learned about knife-swinging fighter Jim Bowie and finally understood the words "bowie knife," which I'd heard Woody Guthrie, Pete Seeger, and the Weavers sing in labor songs.

Our last stop was Lancaster County, Pennsylvania, home of the Amish. "I wish I could wear long dresses and ride in a buggy pulled by horses," I told my mother.

"You, Judy?" My mother laughed. "I have to battle with you just to wear a skirt anyplace we go. You're fixated on jeans and the life of a tomboy."

We ate at Leshers Inn, where we sat at a huge table with total strangers and passed huge platters of fresh and colorful foods. The spinach was so large it could have been picked from a stalk akin to Jack's beanstalk. Our host cleared away the main meal and then brought the largest pie I'd ever seen and explained that this was the famous shoofly pie of the region.

"You see," she said, "flies gave it its name. As wives would set the pies upon windowsills to cool, the flies would swarm by for their taste of the treat. 'Shoo, shoo fly, don't bother my pie,' they'd have to say. Soon, it became necessary to close the window and just let the pie cool indoors. So now, you may taste this wonderful dessert."

I feared, as I looked at the lumps and bumps protruding through the crust, that some flies had not gotten their bite and flown away free. But one taste of the pie at my father-the-pie-lover's insistence, assured me that, even if there were flies within, there was nothing in the world more delicious than shoofly pie.

After an exciting, mind-expanding journey, we drove into our driveway on Douglas Avenue. We spent a weekend unpacking, shopping, and doing laundry. Come Monday, life resumed its normal routine. For me this included attending further recordings by Jimmy Boyd and a popular newcomer and talent scout winner on Arthur Godfrey's show, Lu Ann Simms. It also meant singing with Karen at more local places and events, promoting a new doll for a new song, and asking questions of young genius Mozart on Hecky's new series, *Introduction to the Masters*.

CHAPTER 19

A Little Red Monkey and a Marriage

· · · · · · · · · · ·

Τ he short shelf life of seasonal songs had proven to be far
longer than imagined and it seemed they had several
lives to boot. "I Saw Mommy Kissing Santa Claus"
catapulted young Jimmy Boyd into international stardom.
"Suzy Snowflake" "tapped at windowsills and showed she was
in town" daily. Autry and Clooney's duet of Johnny Marks's
adaptation of the Moore poem, "'Twas the Night Before
Christmas," broadcast hourly over radio stations everywhere.
"Rudolph" had by now sold well over 11 million records and
continued to sell more.

Jazz, growing in popularity, entered the lives of young lis-
teners as Hecky developed further projects. The jazz artists
Hecky recorded included Tony Mottola on guitar, Bobby
Haggart on bass, Lou Stein and Stan Freeman on piano, Terry
Snyder on clarinet, Charlie Magnato on accordion, and Specs
Powell on drums.

RCA Victor had come out with a phonograph for children
designed solely for playing 45-rpm records. These records
were less expensive than the 10-inch 78-rpms or the increasing
number of LPs. Goddard Lieberson wrote a memo asking
Hecky to come up with a solution to the phonograph-for-kids
competition. Hecky responded, "Spending money on a record
player that can only play some, not all of the vast selections

out there, to me as a parent would seem a waste of money. Since Columbia is the leader in the innovation of LPs to begin with, I think we should design a phonograph that plays all three speeds: 45, 78, and LP. If designed correctly, the juniors and missies will easily catch on to how to play which record on which speed."

Lieberson, now trusting Hecky implicitly, followed this advice. Columbia's phonograph far exceeded RCA's 45-rpm in sales and added to the money pouring in from the children's catalog.

. . . .

In the 1950s, the arts were recognized as an essential part of a child's education, and music was included in the curriculum from kindergarten through high school. Students were taught to read music right along with letters and words. To augment music lessons, Hecky created a series about the lives and music of the classical masters. Mozart was the first to be depicted in the series, which would include Haydn, Handel, Beethoven, and others.

The series' narrator, Milton Cross, hosted the Saturday afternoon broadcasts from the Metropolitan Opera House and was known as "the voice of the Metropolitan Opera." Rudolph Goehr, world famous conductor, led the symphony. Sally and Lee Sweetland, who provided singing voices in movies for Hollywood stars who could not sing, lent lyrical sounds for opera arias. Sandy Fussell, a dwarf with many performance credits including Disney, was the voice of the young masters. I was hired as the child who asks Milton Cross questions. In an article on August 15, 1953, *Billboard* wrote, "Columbia Records is prepping a new line of kiddie disks for release next month called 'Introducing the Masters.' The move is part of a general broadening of the label's children's catalog, under Hecky Krasno's direction. . . . The series will feature the music of classical composers and contain dramatization of the lives of the writers. . . . Krasno has also pacted Tom Glazer for a series of activity records for pre-school children. . . . Lu Ann Simms, too, has been signed to cut kiddie sides."

As one of Arthur Godfrey's "Little Godfreys," Lu Ann Simms's voice, popularity, adorable appearance, and sweet personality resulted in three celebrity dolls modeled after her. Hecky felt it was time to add Simms to the roster of recording stars. Her first four songs, recorded in May of 1953, were featured in *Billboard's* "New Records to Watch." *Variety* wrote, "Lu Ann Simms: 'I Just Can't Wait 'Til Christmas' . . . bears watching in 1953's Yule song spread. It's a lilting item with a solid lyric and should be able to keep ahead of the Xmas pack via Lu Ann Simms' charming cut. She gives it just the right flavor."

The Daily News commented in this blurb, "ARTHUR GODFREY and 'Hecky' Krasnow, Columbia's Children's Record chieftain, are raving about the kiddie disc debut of pert singer Lu Ann Simms of the Godfrey troupe. Lu Ann has waxed 'Sandy The Sandman' and 'Little Rag Doll' and the pairing looks red hot!!"

Hecky also signed on folk singer Tom Glazer, who had his own program on ABC radio, *Tom Glazer's Ballad Box*. He wrote songs that spoke to the hearts of Americans everywhere and became part of the nation's consciousness, songs like "A Dollar Ain't a Dollar Anymore," "Worried Man," and "Old Soldiers Never Die." His songs were sung by folk singers including the Weavers and later, Bob Dylan. Glazer, always an outstanding children's performer, dedicated much of his folk career developing quality material for his young audiences. In the 1960s, he would compose the major hit, "On Top of Spaghetti." For Hecky, Tom Glazer recorded songs with titles like "Train to Toyland," "Jump-A-Jingles," the classic Guthrie tune, "Put Your Finger in the Air," "Dr. Snif-fleswiper," "Friendly Doctor Drillum Fillum," and "Bonito the Barber."

Tom Glazer's folk songs, Lu Ann Simms's sweet tunes, and *The Story and Music of Mozart* hit the market within months of each other. *Record Retailing* wrote of all three in November of 1953,

> *The Story and Music of Mozart* has the ideal combination of dramatization, the use of juvenile actors, instruments of the period, questions and answers (done most naturally and delightfully), and above all, a top-notch narrator (Milton Cross) and first-rate musical performances. . . . On the less erudite

side, though none-the-less enjoyable, we have Lu Ann Simms and Tom Glazer. Miss Simms' slow pace is good to help the children learn the words of songs. . . . Tom Glazer is without doubt a top children's artist. His first release is for the very young listener, and he performs in his usual come-along, play-along style. Parents and teachers will surely get an enthusiastic response from the little folk in nursery and kindergarten.

. . . .

Hecky, under the pseudonym of Stephen Gale (and still in pursuit of composing a hit song), collaborated with Jack Jordan and wrote a lively tune with Rosie in mind, "The Little Red Monkey."

Look at the monkey, funny monkey, little, red monkey acting
   so fidgety
Look at the monkey, funny monkey, little red monkey, cute as
   can be.
Where is her Mama, Papa, sister, brother, cousin, rest of the
   family?
Little red monkey on her ownsome, very lonesome monkey is
   she.
If you get her into a zoo, she'll do all of her tricks for you.
Won't you drop her a line or two inviting her to the zoo, for if
   you do,
She'll be a happy, snappy monkey, little red monkey acting so
   merrily.
I hope you like this little red monkey, for that little red monkey
   is me.

The song climbed high on the charts. (Popular in countries around the world, it still brings in constant royalties today.) The Knickerbocker Toy Company, under the trademark of Liliputian Bazaar, manufactured a doll for the song: a hurdy-gurdy player's monkey with a little square cap, a bow tie, and a suit resembling snug baby pajamas with a tail. The monkey's perpetual smile and impish look fit the lyrics of the song perfectly. Again, Karen and I danced holding Little Red Monkeys in our hands throughout the Liliputian Bazaar, a store on 5th Avenue and 51st Street. We were becoming seasoned performers having recently added to our growing list of credits *All Aboard a Showboat with Mr. I. Magination*, another recording with Paul Tripp that took listeners down the Mississippi River. We performed our Josef and Miranda-inspired duets at venues including the Neustadter Home for the Aged, Hartman-Homecrest Home for the Blind, and a local Yonkers Orphanage.

Hecky, under the pseudonym of Lillian Kay, joined with composers Tommy Johnston and Milton Pascal and wrote "Betsy, My Paper Doll," recorded by Rosie. *Billboard* noted that Christmas had become the peak children's record selling time of the year. However, things were changing as manufacturers' interest in the accelerated market for kid-disks increased. *Billboard* comments, "Columbia, for example, has tied in with McCall's magazine to issue *Betsy My Paper Doll* as sung by Rosemary Clooney. The combined name value of the label, magazine and Miss Clooney should make this a big item."

The song promoted sales of a paper doll named Betsy McCall. She came with a cut-out wardrobe that occupied young girls like me for hours. I loved my Betsy. She had a round face with huge eyes, and dark wavy hair. With her extensive wardrobe, Betsy was an early Barbie. However, she looked like a young girl, not a young woman with measurements guaranteed to make girls dream of a figure they could never have. Along with "Betsy," *Singing Time with Gene Autry*, an album of his children's hits to date—including his latest, "Freddie the Little Fir Tree"—and another song by Tom Glazer, "Train to Toyland," were singled out in an article titled "Clooney Entry First in Class."

. . . .

While Betsy occupied little girls across America, internationally famous José Ferrer occupied Rosemary Clooney. While in college, Ferrer had known that he wanted to be an actor. After a walk-on part on Broadway in 1935, he was called for bigger parts and quickly gained a reputation for his versatility. His credits included *Charlie's Aunt,* Iago in *Othello,* the Dauphin opposed to Ingrid Bergman in *Joan of Arc* in 1948 for which he received an Oscar nomination for Best Supporting Actor, a Best Actor Oscar for his starring role in the movie version of *Cyrano de Bergerac,* and another Oscar nomination for his portrayal of painter Toulouse-Lautrec in *Moulin Rouge* in 1952. He was brilliant, handsome, seductive, and relentlessly pursued those women he wanted. From the moment he saw Rosemary, he became intrigued with her, though she was 16 years his junior, perhaps part of the intrigue.

Those close to Rosemary sensed that she was about to do something that none of them felt wise. Rumor had it that Ferrer's wife, Phyllis Hill, could stand his infidelities no more and intended to get a divorce. Hecky felt towards Rosie as though she were a daughter of his. He wanted only the best for her and to see her with someone who would appreciate what a talented and fine human being she was. He took her to lunch at the Russian Tea Room.

Located on the south side of 57th Street near Carnegie Hall, the Russian Tea Room first opened serving glasses of tea with cherry preserves to Russian émigrés. In 1932, it became a full-service restaurant and gained a reputation for its gourmet Eastern European specialties and classy service yet casual atmosphere. Its popularity grew to where it averaged serving 2,647 pounds of caviar, 5,884 liters of vodka, 8,000 pounds of beets, 15,867 pounds of sour cream, and 43,860 pounds of lamb per year. The Russian Tea Room was a favorite among those who worked at Columbia.

I had eaten lunch there with Goddard Lieberson, my father, mother, and Burl Ives. Ordering chicken kiev, I thought this dish must be what my grandparents had grown up eating since they were from Kiev. However, as I ate my chicken kiev, I gazed upon the unique and colorful delicacies the others had ordered, served upon elegant china by waiters in impeccably clean and tailored uniforms. They served us as though we were royalty. It occurred to me then that the food cooked at the Russian Tea Room was more along the lines of what the czars ate. There was no way that Russian peasants like Sarah and Harry could have indulged in such elegant dishes. I became inquisitor to my conscience as I obsessed,

"Would I want to live like the mean, horrid czars so I could eat chicken kiev, or like the poor peasants?" My first answer appeased my conscience: the peasants. As Lieberson, Ives, and my parents conversed, the battle within me raged. Finally, the answer came. "Everyone should be able to partake of the good life. Dishes like chicken kiev should be shared among all of humankind." With that, I relished my lunch and left the plate empty.

The day my father took Rosie to the Russian Tea Room, he had no illusions about the potential success of his mission. "Love is blind," my mother had said to him. "Love sweeps one away. Love not only is blind, but worse—stupid. Love doesn't listen."

"HuhNEEEY, you sure sound down on love. Is that what you think about our love?"

"No, honey. We knew each other for a while. We fell in love—not off the cliff."

"I have to try with Rosemary," he insisted. "Ferrer will make her miserable."

"He isn't even divorced yet. Don't jump to conclusions."

"Mark my words, he will be, and before the ink dries on the divorce papers, he'll have convinced Rosemary that she is the only one for him."

Over a delicious lunch, Hecky tried to at least persuade Rosemary not to do anything rash. "Think about it, Rosie. Men like Joe don't change. Each woman he temporarily falls in love with thinks, 'Oh, it will be different with me, I'm the right one for him.' But it won't be different. Men like him can be passionate, but they can't love, I mean truly care and stick with it in the harder moments. Think of what a loving, interesting, but stable life you could have with Dante DiPaolo. It's obvious you love him in your own way and he adores you."

"Hecky, you are so kind, so good to me. Joe is married. I have time to think. I promise I will take to heart what you are saying. I think about Dante and how he fits in with my family beautifully. I know he'd always be there for me. As a dancer on Broadway and in Hollywood movies he understands the life of an artist. Joe does too, of course."

"Yes Joe does—for himself. But he wants loyalty from his women. When apart, he can do as he pleases, but not the woman. I fear he will begin to restrict you, Rosie, clip your wings. Pardon my bluntness. I'd love to wish you nothing but what you want, but I don't think what you want is what you'll get with Joe."

"I'm thinking of all sides, Hecky, really. No matter what happens, you and I will be working together for a long time to come. The most joyous moments in my career are those when I record for you, for kids— no gimmicks, just forthrightness. I think I've proven that the theory kids don't like women's voices just doesn't hold water."

"I never thought it did, Rosie. Psychiatrists and their theories can take things to extremes at times."

"Don't worry about me, Hecky. Please. Things will be okay."

. . . .

Phyllis Hill Ferrer went to Mexico for a quickie divorce in July. On a day when Dante was visiting and playing lovingly with members of Rosemary's family, and when he cooked a genuine Italian spaghetti dinner for them all, Joe called to say the divorce from Phyllis was final. Looking out the window as Dante romped in the pool laughing with nephew Nicky, Rosemary almost unpacked the suitcase she'd readied: but she didn't. On July 13, 1953, Rosemary Clooney married José Ferrer in Durant, Oklahoma, a town near Dallas where he'd be performing that night, and a town that didn't require a waiting period after obtaining the marriage license. The ceremony took all of 10 minutes in a judge's office. Joe's agent and Rosemary's manager were present. Immediately afterwards, they had to leave for Joe's performance. Love's ultimate destruction and the slow, insidious downhill path Rosie's life would take seemed impossible as newspapers, magazines, radio, and television reported hot romance, the kind of glamorous story they seek as the public soaks up stardom, the royalty of America. Hecky heard the news and was crestfallen.

"Maybe they'll be happy," my mother tried to soothe my father, who felt like one of his own daughters had eloped with a charlatan.

"Let's hope. I find it hard to be the cockeyed optimist you most often are, honey."

Shortly after the hoopla died down, while in France upon their honeymoon, Joe already had a paramour.

José Ferrer exhibited all the traits of a classic misogynist. These men seek the mother-love they feel they never fully received. They compensate for this lack through sexual conquests, multiple relationships, and the inability to genuinely commit. In order to bolster themselves, misogynists demean traits, characteristics, and the talents of their wives. Hecky knew Joe was a jealous man and that there was friction regarding Rosie's excellent singing voice and Joe's not always reliable one. It wasn't enough for him to be the superb actor he was. It would not surprise Hecky if, in time, Joe would want to prove that he, too, could sing children's songs. His name would sell records, but could he sing for kids? Erudite, somewhat snobbish about his education and the type of high-class roles he played, could he just let loose, not preach, and sing honestly for the younger set? Hecky kept his eye out for songs that might be suitable for Ferrer when the time came. For now, he and those at Columbia reveled in the successes of Rosie's renditions of "The Little Red Monkey," "Betsy My Paper Doll," "Little Glow Worm" and its relative, "Little Joe Worm (Son of Glow Worm)," and, with Christmas on the horizon, Rosie's pleasing version of "Winter Wonderland."

.　.　.　.　.　.　.　.　.　.　.

While Rosemary Clooney basked in her love for José Ferrer, in Yonkers, Helen had fallen in love with a charming doctor from Quebec by the name of Jacques Lifshitz. When asked about him, Karen and I would only give his first name, for his last was an embarrassment to say, and we'd be accused of cursing by our Catholic classmates. We likened the situation of Helen's possibly marrying him to a Marais and Miranda song about Johnny Pieriwiet, with the "J" pronounced like "Y."

Johnny Pieriwiet, Johnny Pieriwiet, he doesn't like his name,
Johnny Pieriwiet, Johnny Pieriwiet, he's Johnny full of shame.
To the girls he's a treat, as he walks down the street;
They all whistle and bleat, Johnny Pieri, Pieri, Pieriwiet.

Jacques, whom we called Jack, was extremely nice to us children. Though in their hearts no one could replace Phil, my parents enjoyed Jack. The entire Krasnow clan liked him. Jacques, a doctor at St. Johns Riverside Hospital in Yonkers, had various French contacts both from Quebec and from France. Two of these people were a couple, Pierre La Berry and his wife Marie. They owned a quaint French restaurant called La Berry's off Eighth Avenue on 43rd Street in the city. La Berry's became another family dining room for us whenever we celebrated something special, from an anniversary, birthday, or graduation, to success with a song. Tonight we were en route to the Ziegfeld Theatre. First, we'd eat at La Berry's and toast to my mother's upcoming birthday.

Our family had seen the musicals *Peter Pan, Brigadoon, Guys and Dolls, Where's Charley?, The Mikado, The King and I, Oklahoma, Pal Joey, Kiss Me Kate*, and *The Pirates of Penzance*. We had seen Katherine Dunham's dance troupe and Spain's flamenco virtuoso, José Greco, when his dance company made their debut New York performance in 1951. Karen and I, inspired by José Greco and the troupe of beautiful, dark-haired, gorgeously costumed flamenco dancers, treated our neighbors to our own version of the flamenco experience. Donning wide, colorful skirts Uncle Mickey had bought us in Tijuana, castanets Helen had taken us to Sam Ash to buy, and flowers in our hair picked from our garden, we danced up a storm. I strummed upon my guitar flamenco-style as we stamped our feet and twirled and whirled while singing and shouting many "oles" in our attempt to sound vibrant and Spanish like the singers we'd heard in Greco's company. The United Nations and air flight was slowly opening up the world to its global nature, and the arts were the perfect way to share humankind's diversity.

Tonight, it was a balmy May spring night, and again, we were going to enjoy a Broadway musical, this time the famed and acclaimed *Porgy and Bess* by George and Ira Gershwin, based on a novel by DuBose Heyward. The music in this historical production, with its controversial past (and now called the "True American Opera"), was the first to mix technical classical form with jazz. The cast included famed Leontyne Price and William Warfield.

Uncle Al and his family had come from Hartford to join us. As the entourage of Krasnows walked down Eighth Avenue towards La Berry's, we reached the corner of 46ᵗʰ Street. Al, an extrovert with a prankster's sense of humor, a generous heart, and a heavy drinking habit, stopped behind a man dressed in cowboy attire walking in front of us. The man had a guitar slung over his shoulder. Around his neck was a harmonica.

Al tapped him on the shoulder and said, "Sir, excuse me, please do me a favor. I have two nieces." He pointed to Karen and me. "They're terrific singers. I'll make it worth your while if you play and let them sing right here."

"I have a gig in a restaurant I have to get to," the man answered looking at Al as though he was a typical New York City street nut.

"Come on, just a couple of songs. You won't be sorry." Al's manner was convincing.

"Well, okay, but just a couple of songs. What do you girls sing?"

This moment was so unexpected that our heads were blank and we didn't answer. My father piped in, "Sing 'On Top of Old Smokey,' 'The Fox,' and 'St. James Infirmary.'"

My father was our coach, so we dutifully obeyed. There, on the corner of 46ᵗʰ Street and Eighth Avenue, the musician played, and Karen and I sang. A crowd gathered and continued to grow. There wasn't room enough for the people on the sidewalk, so they stood in the street. Horns tooted while windows opened to hear the music.

Al took off his hat and with his eyes closed said to the crowd, "Money for the blind, please. Please, give money for the blind." People could see how well-dressed he was, but they took money out of their purses, wallets, and pockets and dropped it into Al's hat. At the end of our third song, as the crowd applauded, Al opened his eyes and said, "Our musician isn't blind, but he's one good struggling musician. He and the two singers are grateful for your generosity. Thank you all." He counted the money, which came to $100. He gave $10 to me, $10 to Karen, and $80 to the guitar player, whose name we never learned.

"Thank you. Thank you," the musician said. "This is double what I get paid for my gig. This is crazy. And by the way, you two girls are going to go places." He disappeared into the many people walking down Eighth Avenue.

"You are out of your mind, Al," Libby, Al's wife, said.

"Hey, the guy earned a lot of money tonight. I did a mitzvah for him."

We arrived at La Berry's, located on the lower floor of a town house, walked down the concrete stairs surrounded by plants and bounded by ornate bronze railings. We entered the cozy restaurant with its genuine French ambience. Pierre, wearing a beret-like chef's hat came out of the kitchen along with his wife, a short, round, jolly woman, to greet us. I salivated from the aromas in the place: the yeast in the homemade breads and pastries, the garlic sauce for the escargot. I sat next to my aunt Libby, an overweight, overly sweet woman whom I couldn't help but love for her kindness, her humor, and the problems she had being bipolar in a time when no one knew what the condition was or fathomed the suffering it caused. "Forgive me if I can't remember," she'd say to us. "Since I was institutionalized and had shock therapy, my memory is definitely not what it used to be."

With lip-smacking delight, Libby indulged in a large bowl of turtle soup. The seeds for ultimate vegetarianism were planted in me. I could clearly see the dismantled pieces of turtle floating in the steaming liquid. I could not release this image from my head until the tray of French pastries smelling of cream, cinnamon, pistachio, and chocolate were placed in front of us to select our particular choices. Full, happy, and toasts to my mother's 43rd birthday said and done (she'd now lived three years beyond what doctors had direly predicted when she was but a teenager), we said our goodbyes to Pierre and Marie and set off for the Ziegfeld Theatre.

After seeing the magnificent and deeply moving *Porgy and Bess*, Karen and I worked hard on another of our home productions. I always got the male roles. Insisting upon realism, to portray crippled Porgy I bent my legs into an old pair of my father's pants and bore the pain in my shins as I turned my metal roller skates backwards to cup my knees and rolled around this way in lieu of the padded cart William Warfield had the luxury of using at the Ziegfeld. Each show Karen and I attended on Broadway opened our minds to a new aspect of life. Our homespun performances inspired us to attempt to walk in the shoes of those whom we had seen and heard.

. . . .

While we were obsessed with *Porgy and Bess*, a recording session produced by Hecky took place that would bring another huge hit at Christmastime. In Oklahoma City, the zoo wanted a hippopotamus. John Rox, a composer and author, wrote a song called "I Want a Hippopotamus for Christmas." A 10-year-old regional star in Oklahoma, Gayla Peevey, hired by Hecky, sang the song. Hecky thought that even if people couldn't particularly warm up to hippos, known to be slow, large, and dangerous, the title alone would catch the curiosity of the public. Additionally, the song would be part of a promotional blitz asking children to send in their pennies, nickels, and dimes to raise money in order for the zoo to acquire the animal. What child and animal lover could resist helping a zoo in one of the American states to add to its interesting animal population? The song became a huge hit and the $3,000 needed to purchase and transport the baby hippo named Matilda, was, indeed, raised.

Gayla recorded more songs for Hecky including "Angel in the Christmas Play," and "Got a Cold in the Node for Christmas." She and Jimmy Boyd became the darlings of the Christmas season.

. . . .

"Rudolph," still the number one darling, had now sold 14.5 million records. This amounted to nearly three million per year. *LIFE* Magazine wrote the following tongue-in-cheek article about "Rudolph" that concluded with a genuine message. It couldn't have been a better tribute to why Hecky fell for the song to begin with and why Gene Autry finally decided to record it.

RUDOLPH AND THE STINKERS

Some two million recordings of the song about **Rudolph, the Red-Nosed Reindeer** were sold over the Christmas holidays, and we hope that the little boys and girls who played the record and heard it over and over again on the radio will stop to reflect. The reindeer around Rudolph, so the kids should note, were all too human in their behavior. They discriminated against Rudolph for not being just like every other reindeer in the herd. They called him the reindeer equivalent of wop; they drew the color line against his nose:

Came Santa Claus, a nice old fellow who had the sense to see that Rudolph had a special gift—his luminous snoot. Santa put that gift to work guiding his sleigh through the foggy night. In a twinkling Rudolph became fashionable. Reindeer bigwigs delighted in showing him off at the reindeer equivalent of the Stork Club. The run-of-the-sled reindeer began shouting his praises, not because they really loved Rudolph but because Rudolph was suddenly a Big Shot.

Ponder the lesson, children, that is here. Kick other people around just because they're different in some way and, like the mean reindeer, you'll be shown up as a bunch of stinkers. Get that into your noggins and the world will be a better place when you grow up.

CHAPTER 20

Veal Scaloppini

My mother had begun her New Year's Eve party planning on the way home from Mitch Miller's house at the bash that ushered in 1952, and had not ceased planning since. Steffi and I were part of her catering service, which consisted of her, Steffi, me, and my father as bartender and later vacuum chief. Veal scaloppini had caught her fancy riding home on the hilly Palisades from Stony Point to Yonkers and it captured her imagination in her final menu decisions. "Here," she said as she handed me a pestle with which to pound the veal. "We have to tenderize it even further, so just hammer way. Steffi, you have the chocolate tooth like me, so I give you the honor of mixing the fudge square batter. By now you should have it memorized."

"Great!" I whined. "I get to pound bloody meat while she gets to lick chocolate."

"Quiet, Judy. No kvetching allowed. This is a family project."

In later years, en route to the life of a vegetarian, I'd look back upon my further torture of that already abused little calf. Now, I had to do what my mother said. "Your next job, Judy, is to be careful with this knife and cut off the thick part of the stems of asparagus."

"Mom, why couldn't you take advantage of the new frozen asparagus? You make it for us. Why can't you make it for guests?"

"Young lady, I don't like your attitude. You don't serve frozen food to guests. People's moods are reflected in what they cook, and I don't want your sass in my cooking."

"Then maybe I better bow out of this before it's too late."

"Judy," my sister now entered the growing conflict, "be quiet and help."

"Yeah, easy for you to say, miss chocolate fingers."

"Mom," Steffi said, "I told you from the time she was born that you didn't discipline her enough. Judy, there are important people coming here tonight, and you better pull yourself together."

"Your sister is right. No winding yourself into a tantrum now. This will be fun. Since when did you become so lazy that you find cooking and helping me so taxing?"

I wanted to play softball, to be outdoors, to climb a tree. It wasn't the cooking that bothered me, or helping out. My mother wasn't smiling. Her *farbissener* look permeated the room: the look of anxiety, bitterness, the pinched lips, points of the lips turned downward. Her nerves danced in the kitchen air. This didn't feel like a happy occasion to me, but a worrisome one. My mother liked to cook. She liked to entertain. However, she was a people pleaser, and her concern about whether she would sufficiently give pleasure to her guests filled her with tension. I nipped my tantrum in its rapidly blooming bud and pounded the veal and cut the asparagus tips, all the while absorbing every step of the recipes unfurling before my eyes, knowing that someday, like my mother, I would fuss to please in the kitchen too. Perhaps this was the unknown source of my irritation.

The clock ticked. My father came home with rented folding chairs, set them up in the living and dining rooms, took out the liquor, dusted the furniture, and puffed up the couch cushions. My mother's vein in her neck indicated elevated levels of activity. The kitchen was dreadfully hot and clouded the small window over the kitchen sink with vapor. My mother pulled the stepladder in front of the sink, climbed upon it, and opened the window. "Open the kitchen door," she said. "We need more air." Steffi obliged. With little counter space other than the table we pulled out from the wall, along with its benches, one on each side, we had to juggle platters, pots, mixing bowls, spatulas, and spoons from one spot to another to make room for the banquet in preparation.

Guests for the evening were the Mitch Millers, Percy Faiths, Paul Tripps, Liebersons, Josef and Miranda, the Israels and their daughter Deborah, George Kleinsinger and a new date sure to add spice to the evening, the wife of and composer Meyer Kupferman, whom my father and mother had met through Henry Walsh (as Henry and Kupferman both taught at Sarah Lawrence College), and Jean and Kenneth Wentworth, our piano teachers and friends who played on the third recording in the *Masters* series, this one about Chopin. Of course, Helen, Karen, and Jean would attend, and Jacques Lifshitz too. Likewise Steffi's beau, whom I considered to be my older brother, Gerry Schamess, who had arrived early and pitched in, helping my father with any lifting and furniture moving that had to be done.

Our living room had space for two people to sit on side chairs and four on the couch. One more could sit upon the piano chair designed after those in Mozart's time. There was room for about six bridge chairs crowded between and in front of the other furniture. The dining room had a daybed/couch, which sat about three people. There was room for a bridge table and four chairs, or no table and about six folding chairs. Twenty-seven people in all would fill our home tonight. As my mother cooked, she had second thoughts about having invited so many all at once. She mumbled, "I couldn't have the Millers without the Faiths, the Tripps without Kleinsinger, the Kupfermans without the Wentworths or visa versa. . . ."

"Mom," Steffi responded to the muttering, "It's too late to change things. It will all work out. It always does. Stop beating yourself and relax." You could hear annoyance in her voice. To help, she had given up a party with her peers. She didn't mind helping but she did mind being subjected to our mother's worries.

"I love your father," my mother said, "but I don't understand how everyone coming here can have catered parties and big homes, but not us." I had never heard my mother say this before.

"That's not true," Steffi said. "The Israels' apartment is smaller than our house. The Wentworths have a modest house that, yes, is larger, but they have kids and hardly any furniture. They couldn't pay a caterer."

. . . .

"You don't have to list it all, Steffi. I'm talking about those at Columbia. What will Goddard Lieberson think?"

"He's been here before, and he's coming back. That says something," Steffi reminded her.

The delicious smell of food cooking in the kitchen spread throughout the house. I'd sampled the sauce my mother made for the veal, and any anger I held at having to help was promptly dissipated by its taste. "Mom, just keep quiet and keep cooking. The way to everyone's heart is through their stomachs, and you have the key." This brought a smile to my mother's face, and those turned down points of her lips finally changed to an upward direction as she remembered that it gratified her to feed people with her flair for concocting unique and scrumptious cuisine.

"Go change your clothes, girls. The guests will be here soon."

"You go first, Mom," Steffi suggested.

My father walked into the kitchen. "Honey, this is going to be a feast no one will forget. Tell me what to stir or watch, and I will do so as you change your clothes." My mother hesitantly showed him what to do, for my father couldn't even boil an egg without the result being either liquid or too hard to chew. She turned all burners low, put on the kitchen timer, and said, "When this buzzes, just stir this pot so the sauce doesn't stick to the bottom."

We changed our clothes, and none too soon, for the doorbell rang. The Tripps had arrived. Soon after came Josef and Miranda. Four of my favorite people in the world were now at our house. Soon the others came, and the volume of so many voices in such small quarters buzzed through the air creating a lot of animated energy. My father enlisted me as his assistant in serving drinks. While I waited for the next round I said, "Daddy, admit it. I am the son you never had."

"No, Juddie, you are the daughter I have."

"But admit it. I am like a son."

"No, you are my daughter, and I love you."

"But I do things with you that a son would do."

"You do things with me that daughters do."

"But I take after you."

"So?"

"So that's what I mean. Sons take after their fathers."

"So do daughters. Now go give these two gin and tonics to the Tripps."

After drinks and my mother's homemade hors d'oeuvres, which included little blintzes filled with cheese both crumbly and chewy at the same time, it was time for dinner. Steffi and I dutifully placed the food upon the table. Helen and Karen helped. The table looked beautiful, for my mother had decorated the platters with greens, radishes, and other colorful and artistically placed herbs and vegetables. She was a master at making gelatin aspics with various fruits and nuts. Tonight's glistened like emeralds and rubies with orange crystals inside. She told everyone what each dish was, and left them to help themselves, which they heartily did. Everyone managed to find a place to sit while they held their plates of white china with a gold rim and a motif of birds on a branch bearing berries. They placed these plates upon white cloth napkins on their laps. My mother had dutifully stayed up until well after midnight the night before and polished each piece of sterling.

The conversations in the two rooms didn't allow for individuals to have corners in which to discuss different topics so everyone conversed together. Goddard Lieberson shared experiences of being a student at Rochester's Eastman School of Music with Mitch, who shared his stories too. Percy Faith told stories of growing up an immigrant in Chicago and the joy of being able finally to play with top-notch jazz musicians. Josef engaged everyone with his tales of boyhood in South Africa. Listening to him felt like sitting around a campfire in a tribal village as the masterful storyteller revealed the tribe's history and myths. His eyes twinkled and danced. His beautiful speech and gentle voice sounded like the most magical music one could hear. I could not take my eyes off of him as I soaked up each detail of the stories, each facial gesture, lift of the eyebrows, and tone used for the different characters in the tales. Miranda's comments and stories of her childhood in the Netherlands and travels in other lands made the world a place I wished to see every inch of and if I couldn't, I could imagine through stories like the ones Josef and she now told.

George Kleinsinger filled everyone in on the progress of his jungle. "There's always something to balance," he reminded those of us who had attended his bug-ridden party. His present lady friend was buxom, young, wore bright orange lipstick, had dark brown hair, a low-cut blouse and commented after each story was told, "This is spec-TAC-ular! I've never been to a party like this where people really talk about things, you know, I mean *ree-aal* things."

My mother had succeeded on the pleasing level in so far as the victuals, for each guest maneuvered through the crowded chairs and a few people sitting on the floor in order to get seconds, even thirds. Among those sitting on the floor were Paul Tripp, Gerry, and Kenneth Wentworth, who insisted they didn't mind.

Dessert and coffee would wait until Jean and Kenneth Wentworth gave a brief piano concert of duets from the Chopin recording and a few other pieces they'd selected, but first, Karen and I would sing a few songs. We opened with our rendition of the folk song "The Fox." Inspired by Josef and Miranda's international fare, we followed this with our interpretation of how the song might be sung in other lands using accents and a few percussion instruments from these lands: Spain, Israel, India, the Soviet Union, and Japan. "Mountain Is Far," learned from Josef and Miranda came next. Karen played maracas. One of our favorites was an English ballad, "Three Jolly Rogues of Lynn," a spoof which we appropriately sang tongue-in-cheek. We ended with the popular "Tzena, Tzena" and sang as everyone clapped along and joined in on the chorus.

The guests loved it. Josef and Miranda offered much praise and a couple of sage suggestions. Paul Tripp said, "Hecky, Judy and Karen are pros. I think we should take a trip around the world in story and song on my program. Let's discuss it during the week after I speak with the producer."

"Wonderful idea," Josef commented. "Music is the universal language and would make a terrific lead-in to visiting other countries to see how the people live, go to school, dress, and eat. I think it's a marvelous idea."

Karen and I looked at each other, squeezed hands, and were unbelievably excited about the prospect of being on *Let's Take a Trip*. Recording with Paul was a joy. We'd already been paid actresses in the 1951 recordings of *All Aboard a Covered Wagon*, *Digging for Gold with Mr. I. Magination*, and *All Aboard a Showboat with Mr. I. Magination*.

Appearing on Paul Tripp's television show would be a first for us—television, wow!

Our song medley over, it was now time to hear the Wentworths, a delightful couple, very talented, and very much in love. Kenneth, about 5'11", and a bit stocky in build, had a mustache and goatee, and dark brown hair, which he wore in a fuzzy crew cut. Jean was freckled with long, red hair, which she braided, pulled back, and wrapped in a bun in the middle of the back of her head. Big metal hairpins often slipped out of this two-foot braid, and pushing them back in became a characteristic gesture of hers. She had twinkling amber eyes and a somewhat crooked smile over one crooked tooth. All put together, she exuded an impishly endearing look. An extremely talented pianist, Jean had performed at Town Hall, and was gaining more and more recognition. Steffi, Karen, and I, in addition to studying piano with Kenneth, who excelled as a teacher, all babysat for their children.

Sylvia and Deborah Israel settled into their folding chairs and sat near Helen, Karen, and me in the corner of the living room under the arch that led into the dining room. Our chairs were next to the wooden cabinet my father had built to house our phonograph and records. We were elbow-to-elbow. The dining room windows were opened a hair, for it was a cool night, likewise the living room windows. The concert began.

Jean and Kenneth were well into a Chopin Prelude upon our Chickering baby grand when a terrible odor spread throughout the small living room. It seemed to have begun right next to the record cabinet where Deborah sat. Jean and Kenneth were thoroughly absorbed in their playing while the rest of us tried to remain as attentive as we'd been prior to the odor. I noticed my mother sitting near one of the living room windows. Her happy hostess face had a look of consternation. The smell finally dissipated. She looked relieved. However, the bad smell emerged once more. My mother kept looking at the window near her. I knew she was thinking about opening it wider but knew her motion and the sound of an opening window would disrupt the playing and bring more attention to this embarrassing situation. Everyone sitting in these tight quarters had, of course, figured out the cause of the odiferous scent and that Deborah was its source. Bodily functions of this nature embarrassed my mother terribly. The look on her face sent her voice going through my head as if I could read her mind: *After all the work I did, all the trouble I went to cook, to make a decent party, have a concert too, and all they will remember is that someone kept passing smelly wind.*

Though the room filled with the bad smell, everyone maintained polite concert hall silence. Sylvia Israel leaned over to Deborah and, trying hard not to be heard, whispered in her ear, "Deborah, stop farting."

Unfortunately, the sound of her voice carried. Lips quivered around the room as everyone tried not to laugh and to pretend nothing had happened. Having finished a Chopin duet, Jean and Kenneth had just begun a piece by Bartok. Deborah scented the room again. Sylvia, angry now, whispered unintentionally louder, "Deborah, leave your chair and go to the bathroom!"

"How can I do that?" Deborah, whose whisper was almost as audible as her naturally loud voice, said, "There's no room to get up and out of here." She was right, for chairs were to each side, in front, and in back of her.

I felt really sorry for her. My piano lessons had familiarized me with the Bartok piece being played, and I calculated how many more farts Deborah might asphyxiate us with before the piece ended and she could politely disrupt all those seated in her path to go to the bathroom. My calculation was just about right minus one. At the end of the piece, everyone applauded, I think more out of relief that a break could now be taken and the culprit leave the room, than for the rendering of the piece, which was outstanding. Those of us near Deborah, rose from our seats, moved, and opened a path for her to run to our one, small bathroom. No one mentioned the odiferous concert, and when Deborah returned, Jean and Kenneth played another piece by Meyer Kupferman. The applause indicated the appreciation of talent of both pianists and composer.

Coffee and dessert were served, and, indeed, it seemed as though Deborah's gas had permanently faded from the memory of the evening as everyone became engaged in interesting conversation again. No one seemed to want to leave, and they remained until well after midnight, always a statement about whether or not guests are having a good time.

As each couple left, they commented on what a fun evening it had been. "I haven't enjoyed myself this much at a social gathering in a long time," Goddard Lieberson commented.

"No phony cocktail conversation here," Mitch said. "This is the real thing."

"Lil," Miranda said as she hugged my mother goodbye. "Do you share recipes? That veal scaloppini was superb."

Others said "Amen," to Miranda's comment.

Ruth Tripp announced, "I think Lillian is the hostess with the mostess."

Some days later, Helen found a souvenir shaped like an athletic trophy that she gave to my mother. It said "Hostess With The Mostess."

. . . .

At the office the following Monday, Hecky happily accepted heartfelt comments about what an interesting, pleasant evening it had been and what a terrific chef Lillian was. Then he was off to the 30th Street studio to record Artie Malvin. Malvin, a versatile, lively, amusing man sang and worked as a vocal contractor, arranger, and composer. When he joined the Army Air Corps in 1942, Glenn Miller, then a newly appointed major, formed a band of uniformed men and recruited Artie Malvin. Malvin became one of Miller's Crew Chiefs, the male vocal quartet that Miller used for almost all of his vocal numbers. His experience with Miller and his baritone contribution to the Crew Chiefs was a gold key that opened doors for him as a session singer in New York City when the war was over. In the '50s, his credits included the highly popular *Pat Boone-Chevy Showroom* series. Hecky thought his voice and personality would definitely appeal to children.

Malvin, like the other celebrities recording for Hecky, sang Christmas songs like "Silent Night," "Up on the Housetop," and "Santa Claus Is Coming to Town." These were recorded with the Tony Mottola Orchestra. Mottola, one of the most respected studio musicians of the era, played with the Jackie Gleason Band, Frank Sinatra, and later Doc Severinsen on the *Tonight Show*. The growing numbers of artists recording the holiday repertoire simply added to the sales. The public seemed insatiable for them. Malvin, like the others working for Hecky, made his mark recording other numbers too including "Peewee the Kiwi Bird," "Over in the Meadow," and *Let's Form a Rhythm Band*, an album for preschoolers and toddlers sung with Sally Sweetland.

Production was in full swing with the popular quartet The Mariners, regulars on *Arthur Godfrey's Friends*, recording songs with titles like "The Ancient Mariners," "Skidilee Gumbo," "The Monkey Band," and "Toot, Whistle, Plunk and Boom." Rosie's list of songs grew. Hecky wrote "Ting-a-Ling-Ling, Here Comes the Ice Cream Man," for her, inspired by our neighborhood ice cream vendor who, each merry springtime signaled his daily visits with the bells ringing on his truck. We children dropped balls and bats, interrupted marble games, put the kickstands down on bikes, and ran to get money or took it out of pockets for this daily exciting event. With jokes and laughter, this neighborhood icon sold Hershey-coated vanilla or chocolate ice cream pops, creamsicles of rich vanilla ice cream covered with orange ice, almond crunch bars, and double raspberry, orange, lemon, and lime popsicles sticks. Cracker Jacks could be bought in boxes with a mystery prize, and fudge or butterscotch sundaes were available in pleated paper cups from which they were eaten with a thin wooden spoon that look like a miniature canoe paddle. No one questioned the affinity for children held by the ice cream man. Most often, he was a father himself, often an immigrant, who found a pleasant way to earn a decent living during the warmer months of the year.

Tom Glazer continued to delight children with his growing number of discs. His frequent concerts kept his records in the limelight, and parents flocked to buy them for their children. Josef and Miranda added *Folk Songs from Around the World* sung in English and languages from the lands of the songs, and *Dance and Whistle* with titles like "It's a Mosquito" and "Yodel with Me." Popular artist Bob Hannon recorded several songs for an album that included, of course, popular Christmas tunes and also Americana songs such as "I've Been Working on the Railroad," "Going to Boston," and others that had now become classic children's fare: "The Little Engine That Could," and "The Little Red Caboose." Hannon appeared as a regular on radio and television shows including *The Jack*

Benny Program, Red Skelton's *Raleigh Cigarette Program*, and an annual Yuletide program on which stars like beloved Eddie Fisher sang.

Haydn would follow Chopin and Mozart in the *Masters* series, and *Billboard* wrote of this and further plans for the series: "Columbia's big kiddie push this fall is believed to be three integrated 'good music' series. . . . The three series are entitled 'Introducing the Masterworks,' 'Introducing the Instruments of the Orchestra,' and 'Introducing the Masters.' 'Introducing the Masterworks' will feature well-known excerpts from longer works recorded by Columbia's key Masterwork classical artists— Sir Thomas Beecham, Andre Kostelanetz, etc. The first release includes selections from 'The Nutcracker Suite,' 'Carmen,' and 'Swan Lake.'"

Billboard also mentioned that plans were underway as "kiddie record chief, Hecky Krasno, readied the market for releases by Red Buttons, José Ferrer, and Art Carney."

. . . .

Joe Darion, whom Hecky had met at the infamous George Kleinsinger party, had joined forces with Kleinsinger and written the successful off-Broadway-turned-Broadway operetta now called a musical, *Archie and Mehitabel.* This imaginative musical about a journalist cockroach and a scrappy, hot siren alley cat endeared these unlikely creatures to the theater-going and record-buying public. Darion and Kleinsinger continued collaborating and wrote songs for some of Hecky's artists. Joe also wrote the theme song for famed comedian Red Buttons's television program, *The Red Buttons Show.*

In the beginning of his career, Red Buttons, a comedian and actor, often joked about a show in which he was to appear in 1941, a play called *The Admiral Had a Wife.* This was scheduled to open on December 8. The story, a farce, took place in Pearl Harbor. After the Japanese attacked Pearl Harbor on December 7, the play was cancelled. Buttons always drew a laugh as he claimed with a straight face, "The Japanese only attacked Pearl Harbor to keep me off Broadway." Red Buttons made it onto Broadway several times thereafter and also to the Borscht Belt, where Robert Alda played straight man to Buttons's hilarious antics. Buttons's television program, which began in 1952, introduced a saying that became part of the nation's consciousness, inspired by Joe Darion's song: "Strange Things Are Happening." Sprightly Buttons never failed to give a shot of adrenaline as well as laughs to audiences as, in each show, he hopped around singing, "Ho, ho! Hee, hee! Ha, ha!— Strange things are happening."

Hecky thought the "Ho, Ho, Hee, Hee" song would be fun for kids, and hired Red Buttons to record it. This session was one of my choices to attend. It was difficult for Red Buttons to sing the song without hopping around. Since the sound faded and then got louder with each move away from and towards the microphone, Hecky insisted that he stay in range of it. Red Buttons was a little man, and all I could think of, unoriginal as it sounded, was, "He is just as cute as a button." He solved the microphone problem by bouncing up and down in place, elevating himself upon his tip-toes, lowering himself down to flat feet again, and moving his hands in staccato motions. Confining himself in this way gave him the appearance of a marionette. I'd seen brilliant French mime Marcel Marceau and thought that if Red Buttons put on mime makeup, he would have given an equally superb performance.

Joe Darion attended the session. Later his wife Helen joined him. My mother, also a Red Buttons fan, was there. After the session, we all went to eat at a Chinese restaurant. Red Buttons was as funny in person as on television. We laughed throughout the dinner in between visits from customers who recognized Mr. Buttons and wanted his autograph. The chef came out to meet him and, totally pleased to have such a famous person at his restaurant, followed up with a platter of the "House Specialty" fit to feed an army. In between laughing at Red Buttons, I looked upon Helen with great admiration as she used chopsticks adeptly, even to being able to hoist upon them a few last remaining grains of rice. She showed me how to use them, but I realized it would take practice, and the food was too delicious, and I was laughing too long and hard to concentrate on the skill of using chopsticks. After dinner, filled with warm tea, good fortunes as predicted in the fortune cookies we all read aloud, we said our goodbyes. Red Buttons gave me a hug and kiss. All the way home I sang the "Ho, Ho, Hee, Hee" song until my parents not so politely asked me if I'd please sing another song.

The Darions and my parents got along with ease and shared much in common. A friendship developed between them, and soon we were visiting at their little apartment on West End Avenue. Their kitchen was tiny. Only two at a time could fit in it. The Darions were so small that, to me, this seemed ideal for them. Their kitchen door opened onto a stairway. There was no place to put garbage outside of the door, and Joe had to walk to the sixth floor in order to dump the garbage into the incinerator chute. Joe was mildly bow-legged, and as he walked down those stairs he resembled a waddling duck. Joe and Helen were jolly people with delicious senses of humor. When Joe spoke, his quips were like listening to cleverly written poems. Helen expressed everything through movement. Emphatic, graceful gestures punctuated her verbal expression. The Darions had no children, and Helen spent many hours a week in dance classes and rehearsing with a small company with which she performed. Joe and my father discussed ideas for projects upon which they might collaborate. The two commiserated about how highly creative but totally *meshugeh* (crazy) George Kleinsinger was but that in spite of (or maybe because of) his *meshugeh* tendencies, he was producing some mighty fine compositions.

· · · · · · · · · · · ·

Hecky's instincts regarding José Ferrer and the issue of singing had been correct. While Rosemary Clooney's voice was lauded at home and abroad, she also now ranked as a classy Hollywood movie star appearing in the western spoof *Red Garters* with Guy Mitchell, Jack Carson, Buddy Ebsen, Gene Barry, and Pat Crowley. The film entertained with songs like "A Dime a Dollar," "Man and Woman," and "Good Intentions." Come October, Rosie would be in theaters in the film *White Christmas* along with Vera Ellen, Bing Crosby, and Danny Kaye singing Irving Berlin classics like "Blue Skies," "Sisters," and "Count Your Blessings Instead of Sheep."

Joe began looking for roles in which he could sing and show that he, too, had prowess in the vocal field. The fact that a review of one of his performances in which he sang pointed out that his forte was as an actor and not a singer was not to his liking. This caused friction in an already tense marriage. Hecky had set up a session with Rosemary when she and Joe were due in town briefly before returning to England where Joe was filming. Rosie would record a song written by Tom Glazer and Hecky (under the pseudonym of Lee Herschel), "Let's Give a Christmas Present to Santa Claus." It was sentimental and slow with a message reflected in these words: "Last night I dreamed he sat on my windowsill and gave the toy I'm hoping for—Peace and love on Earth forevermore." It needed an upbeat B-side.

Ruth Roberts and Bill Katz had sent a song they'd written to Hecky, "March of the Christmas Toys." It definitely was a peppy little tune that orchestrated and sung properly, would have children up and marching around wherever they might be. In it, a monkey strums the banjo and blows on a kazoo with a "plinka-plunka-plinka and a zooty-zoot-zoo-zoo." The lion plays the tuba with an "oompah" while another creature plays the flute with a "rootatie-toot-toot-toot." There are fire trucks and trains with their "clangas" and "clacketies," horses with their "giddiyapaties," and jumping jacks with their "paddle-dee-doos." The orchestra and sound effects man would have a heyday.

Hecky hadn't yet thought of a singer for it. Gene Autry's more mellow approach to songs would not do justice to this rhythmic tune about the parade of various toys. Hecky decided to give Joe a try at this one. If his pitch wavered, the song's beat and oomph would compensate. Hecky contacted Joe, who was none too delighted to comply. Hecky hired the Quartones to sing backup and Sid Feller to lead the orchestra. Whatever plagued the personal lives of Joe and Rosie, they were a hot couple to a public that loved romance and glamour. A record with the two of them would surely be a boon to Columbia's coffers.

. . . .

It was an exciting day in the studio as these two internationally famous celebrities walked into the Columbia building on 57th Street. Rosemary and Joe both looked sporting, as though they'd just arrived from a British foxhunt with their English wool sweaters, hats, and shoes. The Quartones consisted of four grown men. Four children joined them today and gathered around Rosemary and Joe as though they were the Pied Pipers of Hamlin. Papers rustled on music stands. Rosie went off in one corner to practice her songs. Joe stood in another and waved his hand as though he held a baton to conduct himself. The smile on his face increased as he grew more comfortable with the song. The orchestra tuned up and then sounded totally cacophonous as each individual instrumentalist practiced his or her part. The air felt charged with energy that would have crackled had it been electric.

When Hecky called everyone to attention and said it was time to begin, it seemed impossible that the results of the songs about to be recorded could be anything but hits. The whole place felt joyous. "March of the Christmas Toys" proved to do what Hecky thought it would: make it impossible to sit still. Even a parent would be inspired to get up and march around the house with a child. Joe sang with abounding enthusiasm and it poured right back out when the tape was played back.

When the song was released, Macy's jumped on it. The *Columbia Record* reported the following:

> New York's world-famous department store, Macy's, has just selected "March Of The Christmas Toys" to be the official theme song of the 1954 Macy Thanksgiving Day Parade. José Ferrer has waxed the tune for Columbia (40317) and it is the only disc available on the song.
>
> A 160-piece band will lead off the procession playing this selection and a band of the same size will bring up the rear doing the same. Radio and television will bring the festivities to millions.
>
> Selection of the theme was greatly influenced by the deep impression made upon Macy's executives by Ferrer's interpretation of the tune. It is the first time an official tune has been set by the store for the annual event.

Back in England, Rosie sent a letter.

> Dear Hecky,
>
> Sorry that I was not able to spend any time with you in New York but as Joe told you, it was really very hectic. I have been having a wonderful time here and the people are just great and very hospitable.
>
> Me And My Teddy Bear seems to be very popular over here as I have had a lot of people mention it to me.
>
> All the best for the New Year. Please give the family all my love. Rosie
>
> P.S. Thank you Hecky Darling for the wonderful brooch. I just loved it. Love to Everyone, Rosemary.

In mid-July, the media would announce to the world that Rosemary Clooney and José Ferrer were expecting their first child.

CHAPTER 21

Goodbye McCarthy, Welcome Back Burl, Hello Art Carney

or nearly four years, Senator Joseph McCarthy had foisted fear and unreason upon the nation. Numerous people had lost jobs, stature, homes, marriages, money, and opportunities due to the senator's unmitigated pursuit of communists. The American public, frightened and bullied at first, began to notice severe flaws in this grand inquisitor and his tactics. Moderate Republicans withdrew their support from him as they saw that his actions were hurting the presidential administration. Initially, Eisenhower would not publicly speak out against McCarthy, for he didn't desire a confrontation that would force him to stoop to the senator's level and "go into the gutter." Such a confrontation would only bring more publicity to McCarthy.

Fortunately for the nation, Joe McCarthy made a huge miscalculation when his research director, J.B. Matthews, published an article called "Reds in Our Churches," purporting that the Protestant clergy was by far the largest single group in the country supporting communist machinations. The public outrage from this could not be quelled.

McCarthy made another big mistake in single-handedly taking on the army with his investigation of the Army Signal Corps Laboratory at Fort Monmouth, New Jersey, in 1953. He accused the army of taking on many Jewish engineers from New York who had been members of the left-leaning Populist Front. The army was less than cooperative, and finally McCarthy gave up, but he wouldn't relent, still attacking others. When he compared General Ralph Zwicker's intelligence to that of a "five-year-old child," he generated further intense hostility from the press and the American public. The army retaliated by accusing Roy Cohn, McCarthy's aide, of trying to force the army into giving special treatment to his friend G. David Schine.

The army/McCarthy hearings were televised, and Americans were able to view firsthand the senator's scare tactics and utter rudeness. There wasn't a day that the television in our house in Yonkers wasn't on. As it had when McCarthy first began his investigations several years before, tension filled our otherwise relaxed abode. Dinner, always a time of friendly talk and discussion, now held our tongues in silence while the sound of the hearings provided the discordant background to our meals. My parents broke the silence when, riled beyond all understanding, they'd slam their utensils on their plates and cry out, "How could he? Is he out of his mind? Good for you, Joseph Welch. Good for you. Get him. Get the miserable tyrant."

Joseph Welch was a lawyer who represented the army. His self-restraint ceased when McCarthy, with a vengeance, attacked Fred Fisher, a young associate in Welch's firm. Welch rebuked McCarthy, "You've done enough. Have you no sense of decency, sir, at long last? Have you left no sense of decency?"

These hearings were McCarthy's swan song. Edward R. Murrow added to the demise with his powerful documentary, which showed how groundless McCarthy's charges were and how the senator bullied, utilized fear tactics, and harassed individuals into providing the answers he wanted from them. Murrow succeeded at this simply by allowing McCarthy himself to appear in the documentary and say what he wished. Murrow also voiced his opinion: "We will not be driven by fear into an age of unreason, if we dig deep into our own history and our doctrine and remember that we are not descended from fearful men, not men who feared to write, to speak, to associate, and to defend causes which were for the moment unpopular. This is no time for men who oppose Senator McCarthy's methods to keep silent. We can deny our heritage and our history, but we cannot escape responsibility for the result."

Over 12,000 people phoned into the program and polled fifteen-to-one in favor of Murrow. By June of 1954, McCarthy's ratings fell in the polls from 50% to 34%.

Inspired by Murrow's documentary, other journalists found their long-silenced voices again. President Eisenhower finally spoke out publicly without stooping to answer the highly unpopular senator: "People in high and low places see in him a potential Hitler, seeking the presidency of the United States. That he could get away with what he already has in America has made some of them wonder whether our concept of democratic governments and the rights of individuals is really different from those of the Communists and Fascists."

On December 2, 1954, the Senate voted to censure Joe McCarthy by a margin of 67 to 22. The reign of Senator Joseph McCarthy was over!

. . . .

With McCarthy out of the picture, Burl Ives wished to leave Decca and return to Columbia. During his years at Decca, the records he'd recorded with Hecky prior to his leaving Columbia continued to sell and constantly remained at the top of the charts. Burl preferred the more open-minded, relaxed yet productive atmosphere at Columbia. There were a lot of apologies to be made, but Burl stood his own ground at the same time. His career had soared ahead in spite of McCarthy, and truth be told, it wouldn't have done so had he not revealed the names and answered the questions asked when he was brought before McCarthy's committee.

Burl and Helen invited our family for a reconciliation dinner. As we drove to the Ives house after a long and painful absence, I sensed that my parents were quite nervous. My mother practiced smiling and rehearsed saying hello while trying to sound natural, not forced. She was about to do something this night that she never believed she'd do: forgive someone who, in effect, acted the role of a scab during a union strike. This situation was even worse. She was about to make amends with an artist whom she admired intensely but who had no regard for, or simply didn't care, how he would endanger the lives of others as he protected his own life and career.

We arrived, parked on the Iveses' driveway, walked to the front door, and rang the bell. Helen opened the door. As my mother entered, Helen extended her arms and held my mother in a big hug. "Lillian, oh, Lillian, it is so good to see you again. I have missed you and Hecky so."

My mother's rehearsal en route was no longer necessary. In Helen Ives's voice, she heard the relief of the end of four difficult years suffered by the Iveses as well. My mother heartily hugged Helen back. Helen was more reserved with my father. She shook his hand. Once she saw that he smiled his warm smile, she gave him a hug too. I was next in the hug line. Looking me over, she commented, "My goodness, my goodness, Judy, last I saw you, you were a child. You've grown into a young woman."

Indeed I had. While my parents had been in California during the summer of 1954, and Aunt Helen took care of me, I had fallen hard on Trausneck Place while roller-skating. I began to bleed. Terrified, I thought I had injured some internal organ. Aunt Helen examined the blood and assured me that I had begun to menstruate. I denied this, not wanting to grow up, and cried hysterically fearing I'd have to be a proper girl who could no longer climb trees, play cowboys, or roller skate. Helen insisted that getting my period would not affect my ability to do these things. I envied Karen for still being free of the mark of womanhood.

Helen Ives remarked upon my maturing as we heard Burl's voice at the top of the stairway that stood opposite to the entrance door and the small foyer. "Ah, so the Krasnows are here again," he said, his voice sounding like a jolly Santa. His appearance matched his voice.

He wore a red flannel nightgown that hung just below his knees. It had a button-up neck, and the buttons were open exposing the golden-brown hair on his chest. The sleeves of the nightgown were rolled up to his elbows. Looking at him as he stood on the uppermost stairs, his belly appeared his most prominent feature. He wore beige slippers that covered his toes and flipped and flopped as he ambled down the stairs. Descending towards us, his beard, jolly smile, and twinkling eyes complimented his belly. Burl could definitely be Santa, I thought. When he reached the bottom of the stairs, he laughed an equally jolly Santa laugh and said, "Forgive this outfit, but the heat in the house makes me warm while Helen is always cool. This is the coolest and most comfortable thing I have to wear."

He took a blue handkerchief out of the pocket of the nightgown and wiped his forehead. "I am so glad you are here," he said putting the handkerchief in a pocket in the nightgown and taking my father's hands in his. "Hecky, I have missed you, really missed you. You are special to work with, and I am eager to be in the studio with you again, let alone just having your company here in my house. Come on in all of you. No need to stand here in the foyer."

We went into the living room. "What would you all like to drink?" Helen asked.

When we'd all given our orders and drinks were served, the doorbell rang and some neighbors arrived to join us for dinner. They had children my age, and they'd brought the game Monopoly and also Chinese checkers. As the adults talked, we children played. Then it was time for dinner. Helen enjoyed cooking and her food indicated this. Burl liked eating, and his food, piled high on his plate, resembled the shape, in miniature, of a mountain. The conversations were, as they'd been in the past, interesting. The adults included the children, and we learned from listening, were encouraged to participate, and offered our questions, reactions, and opinions.

After dinner, the neighbors had to leave for an appointment, but left their son and daughter to play with me. In the parlor off the living room, we plunked ourselves down on the floor and pulled out the Monopoly board. I heard the voices of my parents and the Iveses in the adjoining room and, distracted by Burl's words, I lost the opportunity to buy Park Place.

"All my life, I have worked to become the actor and singer that I have become. Was I to give it all up, start all over, and possibly never achieve this status again and have to find my way in some field that isn't me? Hecky, that happened to many of those who chose silence over speaking out."

"But look what you did to those about whom you spoke out. What about their lives, Burl?"

"Hecky, to tell you the truth, I knew the scoundrel McCarthy was. I thought he'd fall even sooner. I didn't think it would drag on for four years. I didn't think, once he fell, that those affected would still be shunned."

"Burl, it takes a long time for suspicion to leave the minds and hearts of those who have been brainwashed by it. Fear is a terrible thing. Look at the suicides that resulted from lives destroyed in those four years, or two years, or even in a matter of the first few months of McCarthy's reign."

"Hecky, none whose names I gave—Copland, Seeger, Bernstein, Miller, for example, have lost their careers. Yes, it was hard for them while the hearings and interrogations persisted, but now these artists will be back in swing, their talents never doubted to begin with and not ones that can be suppressed forever."

"Pete Seeger and the Weavers—they've been banned from the radio, Burl, banned from television. Thank goodness Canada is still sane and they've had outlets there."

"You'll see. They'll be back in full swing in due time. Hecky, let me ask you this. If you had known for sure that neither you nor Lillian would be able to find employment if you didn't appear before the committee and give names, what would you have done—let your daughters starve?"

"Burl, we each do what we can live with, or at least try to do what we can live with. I am afraid we can't ever see eye to eye on this and to discuss it further will not help. Thank goodness it's over. You want to return to Columbia. Columbia wants you back. We can work together."

Burl Ives returned to Columbia recording singles and albums, all of which sold extremely well, as his earlier recordings had done. The McCarthy years had not made a dent in his popularity. Hecky enjoyed his work with Burl, who was the consummate singer, actor, and entertainer. However, the friendship, though cordial between the Iveses and Krasnows, never regained its initial closeness, as Senator Joseph McCarthy had cast his pall upon it.

. . . .

Variety shows, a source of great entertainment and comedy continued to gain further eager viewers. Popular radio shows transformed into television programs as TV sets entered more homes. Jackie Gleason, actor, comedian, and orchestra leader, transformed his beloved radio show into one of the most successful television programs of the 1950s and '60s. The program included guest stars from all entertainment genres. The mainstay of the program, however, was a comedy skit that later, by popular demand, developed into an early television sitcom of its own: *The Honeymooners.* This series of half-hour skits about the lives and friendship of two miscreants would continue to air for 50 years.

In these hilarious episodes, Gleason played a potbellied, belligerent bus driver named Ralph Kramden who lived with his resigned yet blunt wife played by Audrey Meadows. Ralph Kramden's upstairs neighbor, Ed Norton, a sewer worker (who, by the sound of him had breathed in a few too many noxious fumes) was his buddy. Ralph belittled Ed constantly. Ed, in spite of this bullying and his dimwittedness, frequently shed light on Ralph's problems at work or home. Ed's wife Trixie, played by Joyce Randolph, was uncomplaining to the point of near sainthood. She and Alice Kramden had their own friendship. The interaction between these four, and particularly between Ralph and Ed, made for many unparalleled comedic moments.

Art Carney, a talented actor and comedian, played the role of Ed Norton. His manner of talking, misshapen hat, facial expressions, and body language became part of American television viewers' consciousness. Ed Norton and Ralph Kramden moved into the hearts, minds, and homes of all who watched their escapades and encounters.

Art Carney had participated as an infantryman in the Battle of Normandy. The shrapnel that injured his leg caused him to walk with a limp for the rest of his life, and he incorporated this limp into his portrayal of the endearing character of Ed Norton. As Carney's career developed, the man who became synonymous with the somewhat mindless sewer worker proved himself to be an actor of great depth in serious and

. . . .

touching roles as well as in humorous ones. In 1974, he won an Academy Award for Best Actor for his performance in *Harry and Tonto*, the poignant story of an old man who follows his cat to the afterlife. His roles included Felix Unger in the original Broadway production of *The Odd Couple*.

. . . .

Hecky had some humorous, nonsense songs sitting on his desk. They were definitely not the genre for Clooney, Autry or Lu Ann Simms. Perhaps Arthur Godfrey could pull them off, maybe Artie Malvin or Red Buttons. One night as our family watched *The Jackie Gleason Show* and the "Honeymooners" skit was in full swing, Ed Norton walked into the Kramdens' apartment. Suddenly my father jumped up yelping, "That's it! He's the one. How did I not think of this before? Of course! Art Carney—he's the one!"

"HUHney, you just made me miss the last line. Listen to the audience laughing. Now I won't know what I missed."

"You'll have more to laugh at. Don't worry. Art Carney is the one."

My father summoned us into the living room. He pulled a song out of his briefcase, sat at the piano, and began to play and sing. The song was called "Them," and was written by Al Hoffman and Dick Manning. The singer asks listeners if they have ever seen animals with names like porcudile, crocomingo, nanny duck, elepharoo, pelicapuss, and chimpanzelle. At the end he suggests that even if you look in a dictionary you won't see them because he made them up.

"I love it, Dad. Love, it, love it, love it!" I cried. "Those animals are great."

"Can't you just hear it, Juddie? It's something Ed Norton would sing. He's such a goof." My father knew he was onto something wonderful. My mother and I could only agree.

Art Carney was more than willing to step into the world of children's records. He loved kids and the thought of entertaining them pleased him. The date was set. Carney would record "Them," which would be released in February of 1955, along with a few other nonsense-style songs he'd sing, like "Where Did the Chickie Lay the Eggie?" written by Tom Glazer and Nicolo Paone. These amusing tunes would surely keep the market engaged after the Christmas season's ever-growing list of hit songs. To create anticipation, Carney would record two stories, which could be sold all year round and as Christmas presents.

The first story was *The Bremen Town Musicians*, based upon the Brothers Grimm folktale. In it, four animals are about to be sent away or killed because they are old and can no longer serve their masters well. The rejected four meet along the paths of their escape and discover that they enjoy singing together. In an abandoned cabin where they take shelter, robbers approach. The quartet begins to bray, meow, hee-haw, and crow. Their musical cacophony frightens the thieves away.

Art Carney's masterful storytelling and his facility for creating a different voice for each character totally endeared the bedraggled Bremen Town musicians to listeners of all ages. George Kleinsinger wrote the score for the tale in keeping with Hecky's philosophy that the musical background for a story should simply set the mood, be present only when it truly enhanced the dialogue, and never be of such volume as to distract. Kleinsinger's sense of the bizarre combined with Carney's sense of the absurd melded to create a pleasant, suspenseful, and amusing record.

The second story, *Buzzy Bear's Christmas,* had an inbuilt lesson about bears and hibernation. Buzzy always fell asleep in November. As a result, he missed Christmas. Trying to stay awake, he falls asleep under a fir tree. Passing overhead in his sleigh, Santa sees the tree and descends. He places honey, a fishing rod, and a pail to collect nuts and berries beside the sleeping Buzzy, who awakens in springtime and finds his gifts. Thinking it's still Christmas he greeted everyone with "Merry Christmas." "Well, it might have been 'Merry Easter,'" Carney comments.

Billboard commented that the pacing on *Buzzy* was slow but Carney's fame would sell the disk. Parents bought it, and children listened. They liked what they heard and were eager for further releases by this amusing artist.

When in the studio, Art Carney appeared quiet and serious. As a photo of him with Hecky displays, he would study the script and music with intensity. From the looks of him, no one would guess that he was a comedian. He liked Hecky to stand nearby in order to answer any questions he might have or to approve any changes he might suggest. Carney's experience with *The Honeymooners* carried into the recording studio. Jackie Gleason didn't like rehearsed comedy and never allowed second takes. The script served only as a springboard. The spontaneity of the moment is what made the interaction so funny and alive.

Before recording, Carney studied the script, absorbed it, digested it, and ruminated over it. His somber look transformed into a totally cheerful one once in front of the microphone. Here, his entire body came alive and reflected the smile that grew wider upon his face as he threw himself with abandon into the material at hand. He was a master at improvisation.

· · · · · · · · · · · ·

Art Carney, like Hecky, cared deeply about his family. Their hours in the studio brought these two men together as friends, and it wasn't long until Lillian joined Hecky in the city for dinner with Art and Jean Myers Carney. The Carneys were looking for a place to spend the summer. Hecky and Lillian told them about the Krasnow beach house in Saybrook, Connecticut, and the house next to it, which was up for rent. The Carneys were interested and pursued the lead.

A woman named Mrs. Hubbard owned the house and rented it each summer. In 1954, a strange but nice woman named Miriam had stayed there. She left a lasting impression on all of us, for she had a number branded on her arm. As a young Jewish girl, she'd been spared at Auschwitz while being forced to serve as a whore for Nazi officers. This year, Art Carney and his family rented Mrs. Hubbard's place.

A wide expanse of grass that served as a public walkway extended from the street, which the back of our house faced, continued the length of our long driveway, and on for the entire length of our house. Mrs. Hubbard's house began at an angle to where the front of our house lay. It did not have a large front lawn and stood facing the Long Island Sound with a porch overlooking rocks that led to the water. The walkway between our two houses led to large stone stairs from which the public could walk onto the beach. It wasn't long before someone on the walkway recognized Art Carney. Word spread that "Ed Norton" was staying in Mrs. Hubbard's house. The beach soon filled with curious and excited people.

When Grandpa Harry purchased our house, the land he bought with it extended out into 100 feet of the water. The sandy beach and big rock with an iron ring in the top for mooring boats became our private property. Harry used this fact throughout the Carneys' stay to keep people from ogling each time the Carneys went to sunbathe, swim, or just sit and chat on our lawn. "Shoo, shoo, can't you read the sign," he'd yell to them. "It clearly says 'Private Property.'" The flaw with the private part of the equation lay in the fact that to get to any other part of the beach, one had to trespass over our little section of private beach because the public walkway and stairs had been built prior to my grandfather's purchase.

The beach to the left of our private segment and in front of Mrs. Hubbard's home was comprised of huge rocks. Negotiating these rocks made gawking at the celebrity more difficult when Grandpa hurriedly shooed trespassers off of our private area.

Art and Jean Carney and their young children became part of our extended family. There was barely a meal that they didn't eat with us. Jean and her children joined us when Art traveled into the city during the week in order to appear on *The Jackie Gleason Show*. He was also recording songs for Hecky. Jean and my mother became quite close. Jean seemed happy to have someone to talk to about her husband. Art, as we had observed, was a loving and dedicated father and husband. However, he had a childish side to him, perhaps the source of his incredible talent at comedy. At times, it seemed that he found it difficult to put this side away.

"Sometimes," Jean confessed, "I feel like my husband is my third child. He just doesn't understand that what he thinks is humorous is not helpful, not even funny in a given moment, but just disruptive. And when he's had one too many to drink, a not infrequent occurrence, life is just an amusing thing to him and reason and reality fade away." The

Carneys would divorce in 1965 after 25 years of marriage and remarry in 1980 after Art Carney's 10-year marriage to Barbara Isaac.

It didn't take long for Art and my uncle Al to befriend each other. They enjoyed their drinks—and their pranks upon the rest of us. On the morning of July 5th, my parents' 29th anniversary, to be celebrated with a feast that evening, the two men left in Al's Cadillac and disappeared for a few hours. Al, who often shared his skills as an excellent cook, intended to treat the family to his cuisine this night. Art offered to assist. When they returned from wherever they'd gone and began to prepare the meal, the smell of melting butter, garlic, basil, dill, and fish whetted all of our appetites. We kept going into the kitchen to see exactly what the delicious party menu offered. Al and Art, now in command of the kitchen, gave few answers and insisted that the rest of us go swimming, sit out on the lawn, sit on the porch of Mrs. Hubbard's, or go into town. "Plain and simply," Art told us, "get lost! We have major things to accomplish."

Before dinner, they closed the doors that led from the kitchen to the dining room and from the dining room to the living room. No one was allowed upstairs, and anyone upstairs had to come down, for the stairs ended in the dining room. Off of the dining room was a small hall with a bathroom. This little hall could be entered from the garage or the side of the house near the outdoor shower where we all washed away the sand and salt after swimming. Art and Al closed the door from this hallway to the dining room. We children tried peeking in the dining room windows, but Al and Art had closed the shutters to block our view. The dining room was now totally off limits. We knew Art and Al were up to something. The suspense was overwhelming.

At last the moment arrived when we were allowed to enter the mystifying dining room. To herald us in, Art played a harmonica while beating on a little gong that my uncle Mickey had brought home from India when he served there as a butcher for the army during WWII. "Come one, come all, come big and small. Come to the dining room for a treat and be prepared to stand at the head of the table," he cried out in one of the many voices and accents he could muster in a flash second.

By now the curiosity of all the family and friends who had come to celebrate eagerly brought us to the dining room doors like individuals in a mob wanting to be the first to get the best view of a parade or ball-game. Art was still intermittently blowing on the harmonica, banging the gong, and calling out like a carnival barker with emphasis on the words, "Stand at *the head* of the table."

Grandma's white linen tablecloth, used for special occasions, covered the large table now opened to its capacity with all three sections extended. Platters of seafood, including bright red, cooked lobsters given to my grandfather fresh by the lobster fisherman whom he knew, created a colorful array of tempting food. Each platter rested upon a large, white linen napkin. In the center of the table lay a sterling silver platter. Upon it, in an upright position with thick, dark-rimmed glasses, a big smile, and a chef's hat, lay Uncle Al's head. There was no sign that his head was attached to his body. My grandmother screamed. Aunt Libby laughed uproariously and announced, "I knew he'd come to a bizarre end—that's Al." My father, camera around his neck as always, took photos.

Art Carney picked up a carving knife and a knife sharpener. He began scraping the knife against the sharpener with great gusto. As he did this he announced in a totally goofy voice, "Along with lobster, lox, and lollipops, you will have luscious brains!"

With true magician expertise, Art had totally drawn our attention to the knife scraping upon the sharpener and the hilarious faces, one after another, he made as he continued to recite ridiculous dialogue. How Uncle Al's head was able to sit upon the platter separated from his body, we'd never know. With a rapid movement, Art Carney took the knife and cut the head. It opened and gray slop-like matter and a red, bloody looking substance poured out.

At this moment, Al walked into the dining room from the kitchen. He wore the chef's hat, still bore the smile, and, of course, his thick, dark-rimmed glasses. He had a glass of scotch in his hand and one for Art. The two clicked their glasses together. "To the head of the table," Art said. "To the great head carver," Al said.

Though besieged by all of us children with questions about how they could have possibly done this great act that we were certain equaled any ever done by the great Houdini we'd heard about from our parents, Art and Al refused to divulge even one clue of their secret. Laughing, merry, and amazed, we ate the delicious dinner and celebrated my parents' 29th year of marriage. Art and Al had not forgotten to buy a beautiful cake.

. . . .

The summer went on with jokes and laughter. Art and his family were packing to leave after their six-week stay. Again, Al and Art disappeared in the Cadillac. This time they returned with three canvas sacks of varying sizes from fairly small to very large. Again, what was in the sacks and what they were up to remained a secret between them. They went to the front lawn of our house, a large lawn that lead to a stone wall and steps that led to a terrace with more stairs that led to our section of private beach. On the upper part of the lawn, Al and Art unraveled a large spool of white thread. They made lanes with this thread, each one running from the foot of the porch with its Corinthian columns to the stone-rimmed edge of the terrace. They made 30 rows that looked like miniature swimming lanes in an Olympic-sized pool.

After lunch, the harmonica and gong summoned us again, and this time, his head not on a platter, Uncle Al added percussion with a spoon as a drumstick upon a huge soup pot. "We are about to witness a race here," Al announced, "the race of the century right here at Kelsey Point in Saybrook, Connecticut."

Art Carney lifted one of the sacks. "In here are the critters that will race."

He opened the sack and held it while Al reached in and pulled out 30 little painted turtles. Painted turtles held millions across the nation captive, as they'd become a major fad as pets. They always remained small, had beautiful natural designs on their shells, and were sold for a mere 10 cents in candy shops, the multipurpose stores which sold candy bars, chewing gum, cigarettes, newspapers, magazines, and comic books—the sustenance of superhero fans, *Archie* lovers, and those of us who gained great knowledge of literature through Classic Comics. The turtles often were painted and shellacked to further augment the look bestowed upon them by Mother Nature. One could not simply buy a turtle, but had to add the plastic bowl to house the turtle, a fake log for it to climb upon to dry off from the water in the bowl, and turtle food. By the time the sale was complete, 10 cents had turned into at least three dollars.

Al handed one turtle to each family member. Some neighbors' children wandered by and were also invited to a turtle and lane as Al and Art assigned each turtle a number that corresponded to the lane. The race included 22 little critters. "Hold your turtle until we say go. Then put it down in your aisle and let it run."

"Ha," Art said in his inimitable Ed Norton voice. "I don't think Mr. Al here has ever heard the story about the Tortoise and the Hare. Get ready, get set and—be prepared to spend, the rest of your life here."

"Don't listen to him," Al retorted. "Turtles always get a bad rap. These little ones can scurry pretty quickly."

"How will the turtles know to stay in their own lane?" Al's son Jerry asked.

"Because when a turtle starts to go, it walks in a straight line."

"We better begin this race," Art piped up, "because me and my family have to leave in three days and it might take that long for the race. Come on, Al, one, two, three . . ."

"Okay, everybody—ready, set . . ." Al revved us up.

"One, two, three . . . GO!" Art finished.

We stood watching as not one turtle moved. "Give it a few minutes," Al said in a confident tone. We gave it a few minutes. No movement. "All of you tap your turtle on the back as though you are kicking a horse with a spur as soon as I say 'Go' . . . Okay—one, two, three, go!"

A few turtles moved about one-eighth of an inch.

"Why just look at those little buggers," Art said shaking his head back and forth. "Hey, Al, we should have thought of this first . . . you know, fed them first. Look at them. Those little mouths look like they're munching on grass."

"Good, it will give them energy for the race. Wait a second. I have an idea," Al said. He went inside and came out with a plate of chopped meat. "Turtles love chopped meat."

"Hey, did you hear that?" It sounded like the voice of Ed Norton again. "Al here thinks turtles like chopped meat. Now I ask you, where is a turtle going to find chopped meat?"

"I am giving it to them. That's how they'll find it. We have to try, Art. We'll put the meat at intervals along each lane. The meat should get them in motion."

"Well, that means the contest will be different," Art insisted. "It means the winner will be not only the fastest walker, but the fastest eater."

Al had sprinkled the chopped meat at various points along the individual lanes. He attempted to place it at equal distances. Before Art and Al began another countdown, several turtles, apparently following their instinct of smell, began slowly creeping forward. Karen's and mine, along with Cousin Jerry's, were among them. Each stopped where Al had placed the tidbits of meat. "Ha, ha, Mr. Carney," Al said, "there's a method to my madness."

The method was definitely not foolproof, for the majority of turtles still stood motionless at the starting line. The turtle in my lane, once in motion, continued. Karen's turtle, in the lane next to mine, also seemed to have overcome inertia. Cousin Jerry's walked towards the finish line too. All over the lawn, aunts, uncles, neighbors' kids, cousins, fathers, and mothers could be heard prodding their turtles to "Giddy-yap, turtle."

Perhaps my turtle wished to escape the madness. Perhaps it got a whiff not of chopped meat, but of the ocean. Suddenly it walked as fast as a little, painted turtle might. Karen's, not far behind, followed suit. Before we knew what was happening, my turtle reached the stone wall of the terrace. It continued walking over this wall and catapulted downwards to the terrace below. It had definitely crossed the finish line. Karen's turtle did the same, only, more cautious and wise, stopped at the edge of the wall. Cousin Jerry's turtle had reached the second round of chopped meat.

"As the proprietor of the winning turtle," Al announced, "Judy, you win first prize." He presented me with a 10-dollar bill.

"Second prize goes to Miss Karen here." Art Carney gave her a five-dollar bill.

Cousin Jerry got three dollars.

"Anyone who wants to keep their turtles, we have the bowls and food." Naturally, all the kids kept the turtles. As for the Carneys, turtle race completed, they packed their car and left a couple of days later. A wonderfully bizarre summer came to its end.

CHAPTER 22

A Doctor, a Bishop, Disney, and a Captain Named Kangaroo

· · · · · · · · · · ·

K aren and I were booked to appear on *Let's Take a Trip*, Paul Tripp's television program, taking viewers on a journey around the world in story and song. The countries we'd visit were South Africa, India, Israel, Spain, Japan, Ireland, and America. We knew songs from all of these lands and even sang some verses in the native languages. We rehearsed daily in preparation for this television debut. On the weekends, my father coached us in our dialogue, posture, how we would have to look at the camera, the height at which Karen should hold the accent instruments she played, how we should move when we had to sing, walk, and talk, as well as, of course, helping to perfect our harmonies and my chord progressions on the guitar.

The day of our appearance arrived in late January. My father took us to the studio where we were excited to see in person the set and people we'd been viewing on television for the past couple of years. Paul and Ruth were there, and we were thrilled to be performing with them. The fact that we'd be seen by millions of viewers nationwide slowly dawned upon us. The producer had drawn upon the New York City melting pot and found children from the various lands to appear in each segment wearing their country's characteristic garb. At home, Aunt Helen took pictures of the television screen as we performed.

It was not yet the global world of today. Men had not walked on the moon and imbued Earth's inhabitants with the knowledge that this is one small planet to be shared by all. Jet planes were in their experimental stage. Different cultures, customs, rituals, dress, food, music, and languages were viewed as exotic. The Cold War raged. School children quickly crawled under desks for air raid drills, haunted by the specter of nuclear war. I was truly glad to be part of a program that would show viewers from coast to coast about other lands, hoping that familiarity would help in the effort to bring peace. Television proved to be a different experience from recording. We were not singing before a microphone knowing that if we made a mistake we could do another take. It was a live performance.

Karen's and my appearance on *Let's Take a Trip* brought us an invitation from the organizer of the United Nations' annual Christmas party to perform at the U.N.'s 1955 family celebration. We accepted the booking. It was our first advanced booking for that many months ahead. Our television debut also led to a call to my father from the producer of *The Robert Q. Lewis Show* requesting that Karen and I appear on the television program for an interview. Lewis, a well-known radio announcer and disc jockey, also hosted the famed game shows *I've Got a Secret* and *What's My Line?* Betty Clooney and Merv Griffin appeared as regulars on the talk show we'd be on, a program that combined comedy, variety acts, and interviews. We'd sing a song and talk briefly about how we began performing together. Josef Marais and Miranda would certainly be mentioned as our mentors.

We also appeared on the *Morning Show*, hosted by Walter Cronkite. Dick Van Dyke often stepped in when Cronkite was away on assignment and later became the steady host of the program. He interviewed Karen and me. Hecky didn't feel the need to coach us for this interview as we had done beautifully on the Robert Q. Lewis program. However, Dick Van Dyke phrased similar questions with a different twist. All went well until he inquired, "And, Judy, how did you become a backup singer for Columbia Records?"

True to my honest nature, I replied, "My father is the head of children's records at Columbia." (Wrong answer)

"And, Karen, how did you come by this childhood career?"

"Judy's father is my uncle." (Wrong answer)

Two wrongs don't make a right, and Hecky received the following telegram that evening, presumably from a family member. MY FATHER IS CHIEF INSPECTOR OF THE VICE SQUAD (STOP) JUST IMAGINE THE JOB I HAVE= DAISY. After this, we were always reminded prior to appearances to focus on Josef and Miranda's influence upon us and how our talents and training since early childhood were the major factor in procuring employment at Columbia and elsewhere.

Our television appearances resulted in invitations for us to perform at schools, nursing homes, community centers, and other venues. We were making fairly steady money, and with my share, I traded in my high action, catgut string guitar for some other beginner to show his or her determination upon and bought myself a Martin acoustic picking guitar.

. . . .

At Columbia, the precarious Cold War presented itself in the form of yet another new project for Hecky. The tension caused by the threat of nuclear war resulted in a growing epidemic of neurosis, paranoia, and other mental disturbances throughout the nation. Employers observed an increase in absenteeism as a result of mental disorders. The nation launched a campaign to encourage mental health.

In 1955, Westinghouse Electrical Corporation reached its peak as its home appliance sales soared during the Eisenhower administration and it acquired scientist and manufacturer Allen Balcom DuMont's WDTV station in Pittsburgh. Funding from Westinghouse was granted to all kinds of projects, including those in the arts. Hecky had previously engaged songwriters Hy Zaret and Lou Singer to write a series called *Now We Know*: songs about scientific subjects for 6–12 year olds. The three agreed to pursue another idea with a somewhat different scientific bent and target age: songs about mental health for the family and workplace. Westinghouse liked the idea, and the Westinghouse Broadcasting Company backed the project, called *Songs for Mental Health*. Upbeat songs with memorable hooks informed listeners that many people experienced psychological problems. The songs encouraged those who needed it to seek help to attain mental health and that this was a wise and intelligent thing to do.

> Ring, ring, oh, ring the bell.
> Ring the bell for mental health.
> Ring, ring 'til all are well,
> Ring the bell for mental health.

> We need more tolerance, more research, and more personnel,
> And we need you to help us ring the bell for mental health.

The project had the input and backing of several well-known psychiatrists throughout the nation. After reviewing the songs, Dr. Benjamin Spock, professor of child development at the University of Pittsburgh School of Medicine and author of *The Common Sense Book of Baby and Child Care*, which became the child-rearing Bible of new parents around the world, wrote a letter in support of the project.

> These "little songs" are a job well done. The music is catchy, the words are friendly and hopeful; the messages are sound. . . . Even when a person is troubled, he hates to think of himself as being in such a bad way that he needs "treatment." But he likes to think, in the words of these "little songs," that there may be someone to "help" him. . . . I never would have thought it possible to put such worthwhile words as "need for research" and "more trained personnel" into songs and have them sound so pleasant and persuasive. . . . I hope everyone in America has a chance to hear these songs, for their own sake and for the great cause of mental health.

Specialists, including the medical director of the National Association for Mental Health, Inc., Dr. George S. Stevenson, and Dr. Julius Schreiber, chairman of the Education Committee for the Association wrote, "When a problem is as tremendous and, at the same time, as neglected as mental illness . . . it is gratifying to know that these songs will reach the public through the great medium of radio. . . . Congratulations to Westinghouse and the contributing artists for such a splendid and timely public service."

Hecky and Charles Grean directed the project. Grean had been librarian and arranger for Glenn Miller for three years prior to WWII and, at the time of the mental health project, was manager for famed singers Eddy Arnold and Betty Johnson, among others, through his talent agency. In the publicity for the project, Hecky's history from violinist through to his present position at Columbia was touted with the added mention that "one of his greatest successes was Autry's 'Rudolph, the Red-Nosed Reindeer.'"

The singers for the project included Sally Sweetland. The information about her noted that her father was the projectionist at the first motion picture house in Los Angeles, that she was only two when she made her stage debut as a dancer in an amateur show, and that she was the singing voice of Joan Fontaine and Joan Leslie in several movies.

Publicity boasted The Toppers—Bob Harter, Ed Cole, Paul Friesen, and Bob Flavelle—who sang "Ring the Bell for Mental Health," "The Mental Health Toast," and "Mountains Can Be Moved." All four Toppers began as individual concert singers but later joined forces, switched to the pop field, and became one of the most well-liked singing groups on radio, records, and television. Guitarist and bandleader Tony Mottola provided most of the accompaniment and was known as one of the nation's ablest electrical guitar players and composers for the instrument. Jim Coy, a popular radio host, narrated dialogue in a couple of the numbers.

The project created a stir by bringing the topic of mental health into homes and offices across America. On radio and television news and talk shows, *Songs for Mental Health* was aired while various psychological problems facing the nation were openly discussed. In a nation where seeking help had heretofore been considered shameful, a sign of failure, and frightening, this record of "little songs," as Dr. Spock called them, had a positive impact.

. . . .

In addition to mental health, people relied on faith and prayer to get them through the uncertain times. By 1952, Bishop Fulton J. Sheen had become a national icon via his radio program, *The Catholic Hour*, which first aired in 1932. Now, he also offered hope through the medium of television with his program *Life Is Worth Living*. It aired on the Dumont WDTV station Tuesday nights at 8:00 P.M. opposite the beloved *Milton Berle Show* and *The Frank Sinatra Show*. Initially, Sheen's program was not considered competition for comedian "Uncle Miltie" or the great Sinatra. It surprised all as it drew an audience of over 30 million weekly. Milton Berle joked about Sheen saying, "He uses old material too."

The bishop ended each show with the message, "Bye now, and God love you!" The program won an Emmy. Evangelist Billy Graham later called Bishop Sheen "the greatest communicator of the 20ᵗʰ century," quite an achievement considering the fact that his high school debating coach had told him he was the poorest speaker he'd ever heard.

Bishop Sheen responded positively when Hecky requested that he record for children. After the first session, my father came home and expressed what a wonderful man he found Sheen to be. "You can't imagine," he told us, "the dignity of this man. He epitomizes what a true holy man is and should be. He surpasses any particular religion. Something thoroughly honest and almost beyond human nature simply emanates from him."

On the record, Bishop Fulton J. Sheen recited poems and prayers with organ music as background. *Record Review* called it a "magnificent record" and commented that "it includes the greatest and simplest of all prayers, namely, "Our Father." The *Review* wrote regarding the Francis Thompson poem, "Little Jesus, Wast Thou Shy?": "It is so exquisite that the desire to quote in full is almost irresistible!" On the second side, in reaction to the poem "Lovely Lady Dressed in Blue," *Record Review* says, ". . . a little child asks Mary to teach him how to pray, as she once taught

Jesus—and the urge to quote at length is very tempting; when you listen to the record, you'll see why!" The bishop's record, like his program, drew many listeners, and record stores continually stocked it.

. . . .

The public sought knowledge along with faith. The *Now We Know* series made a hit in schools with teachers and with parents at home. Written by Hy Zaret and Lou Singer, and sung by Tom Glazer, Dottie Evans, Paul Tripp, and Josef Marais and Miranda, the songs with their catchy lyrics and tunes explained and answered questions evident in titles such as "What's Inside Our Earth?" "Do Animals Talk to One Another?" "Where Does the Sun Go at Night?" "What Is the Atmosphere?" "How Does Television Work?" and "How Does a Cow Make Milk?"

Hecky traveled to Boston to present the series at the Music Educators' National Conference, where 500 special LPs were given to teachers. The records were distributed among children's disc jockeys along with four different 15-minute scripts. Children's television shows were provided with special slides to air about the series. *Billboard* praised it as an ongoing series that expertly combined entertainment and education. The *New York Times* commented, "Some ready-made answers have been prepared for those 64-thousand dollar questions that alert, inquisitive youngsters ask so often about the world around them . . . in a new record series called 'Now We Know.' The series includes 21 lively ditties . . . with some enlightening, tuneful answers to questions about the atom, molecules, radar and television." *Variety* commented, "Columbia Records has come up with a topflight album for the juve market in its 'Now We Know' Package. Sub-tagged 'Songs To Learn By,' the set is a general science course taught to the tune of rhythmic jingles. . . . Hecky Krasnow, Col's kid-division chief, rates a bow for putting the whole thing together in such an expert manner."

. . . .

New projects were at their height in the children's record department at Columbia in 1955 in spite of television's growing place in the homes of Americans. Recordings by television stars served as a major bridge between the media of TV and records. Hecky knew that featuring television artists on vinyl was essential to the survival of the recording industry, particularly where children were concerned. With Hecky at the helm, Paul Tripp's *Let's Take a Trip* program took viewers to visit a recording studio to hear Art Carney recording a new song called "Mama." Another featured artist on the program along with Carney was Sonny Fox, who hosted a successful travelogue/news program for children on St. Louis radio called *The Finder*. He also worked with Paul Tripp on *Let's Take a Trip*, became a cohost, and later hosted the program when Paul Tripp dedicated his time to writing children's books and acting in other venues. Later, Fox would be known for his highly successful children's program, *Wonderama*. On the visit to the recording studio, two well-known children's actors, Ginger McManus and Pud Flanagan joined in the tour. *Variety*, reviewing the program, pointed out that "Hecky Krasnow didn't get too involved in explaining the mechanics of mikes, sound controls and tapes. He kept the info at the level to be understood by juves and the points came across easily." The article pointed out that the history of the release of the very first platter, "Whoopsie Doo," was covered.

. . . .

A child actress named Robin Morgan had won the hearts of the television viewing public in her role as Dagmar on a much loved program called *Mama*. It aired at 8:00 P.M. Friday nights. The cast included Peggy Wood as Marta Hansen and Judson Lair as Papa Lars Hansen. Edgar Bergen and Barbara Bel Geddes were among the cast. The program's theme centered on a Norwegian family living in San Francisco in 1910. The daughter Katrin, played by Rosemary Rice, told the stories in each episode, all of which opened with the family looking through the pages of their photo album and reminiscing about the past.

Robin Morgan recorded two albums of stories for very young children with Tony Mottola providing the musical background. Morgan began her career modeling at age two. By age four, she had her own radio program called *Little Robin Morgan.* By the time she was 11, she had been a model, a disc jockey, an actress, and a beauty contest winner. Not long after recording for Hecky, Morgan would leave the pressures of show business behind and opt for being a poet, magazine editor, and highly influential feminist activist. Her albums sold well and proved once again that television personalities increased the sale of records and the availability of records increased viewers for the television programs on which the actors appeared. Robin Morgan's assistant emailed in December of 2006, "Ms. Morgan does indeed remember your father warmly. . . . He was a kind man and a pro, who didn't patronize her, for which she was grateful."

. . . .

For years, Walt Disney movie soundtracks had been recorded along with the soundtracks of its shorter stories and mini-cartoon episodes. Disney had never recorded individual songs from soundtracks or allowed their material to be recorded by artists other than those associated with the particular Disney productions. Hecky, while on one of his California trips, set up a meeting with the powers that be at the Walt Disney Company. He suggested that many of the songs in the movies would make wonderful solos and should be sung by a wide array of artists. Disney, in a historic move, broke its long-standing tradition and agreed to allow Columbia to engage artists to sing songs from its various productions. The result was a 12-inch LP called *Songs from Walt Disney's Magic Kingdom.* Artists on the album included Dottie Evans, Johnny Anderson, and The Merrymakers.

The association between Disney and Columbia grew when Disney aired what might rightly be called the first television miniseries: *Davy Crockett.* A young actor named Fess Parker became a national icon as he played Crockett, the daring frontiersman who bravely survived in the wild, fought Indians, went to Congress, and joined the fight for Texas and the U.S. at the Alamo. Buddy Ebsen, first hired by Disney to play Crockett, ended up instead as Parker's sidekick, George Russel, when the Disney studios discovered the handsome, charismatic Fess Parker. In the 1960s, Ebsen became a household name as Jed Clampett in the television series *The Beverly Hillbillies*. Parker, irrevocably associated with the character of Davy Crockett, played Daniel Boone in a later TV series, then, with no further roles coming his way because of his typecasting as the two frontiersmen, left showbiz to become a successful businessman in realty and proprietor of the Fess Parker Wineries.

In 1954–55, the Davy Crockett series captured the imaginations of viewers of all ages. The programs were so popular that this miniseries was repeated several times while new episodes were written in which Davy Crockett portrayed a life that could only have been lived on the American frontier. The theme song from the series, "Davy Crockett, King of the Wild Frontier," written by George Bruns and Tom Blackburn and sung by Bill Hayes, became a hit song rolling off the lips of virtually every American.

> Born on a mountain top in Tennessee
> Greenest state in the land of the free
> Raised in the woods so's he knew ev'ry tree
> Kilt him a b'ar when he was only three
> Davy, Davy Crockett, king of the wild frontier.

Video players had not yet been invented. A good way to experience a loved program after seeing it was through listening to it on records. Hecky played upon the popularity of *Davy Crockett* by directing and producing albums with the highlights from the Disney episodes along with the memorable songs from the programs including, of course, the theme song. With cleverly designed, enticing album covers, the records sold in huge numbers.

Fess Parker, like handsome, romantic film stars Rudolph Valentino and Cary Grant, had great sex appeal for females of all ages with his good looks, bravery, rough and tumble lifestyle, and rustic appearance (at least as Davy Crockett). Having just entered my teen years at 13, I dreamed of someday meeting a Davy Crockett of my own. Like the rest of the American public, I could not separate Fess Parker from the man he portrayed. Pioneers, their covered wagons, log cabins, and the courage it took for them to survive had fascinated me for quite some time. Davy Crockett à la Fess Parker cemented my obsession with this era forever. In 1955, I felt blessed to attend the recording session of *Davy Crockett Goes to Congress*. The story appealed to my sense of justice. The combination of the story and the presence of Davy Crockett/Fess Parker created a day in my life never to be forgotten.

Parker was as handsome in person as on television. Charisma surrounded him like a glowing aura. I felt that I was literally in the presence of the great frontiersman. The story unfolded: A Tennessee town where Davy enters a beef shoot and wins over a bully and scoundrel who's been disenfranchising Indian settlers; a decision to become magistrate in order to throw the rascal and his cohorts out; a run for Congress backed by Andrew Jackson, who secretly works against Crockett's efforts to help the Indians; the death of Davy's wife—oh, how very sad for her and such loneliness for him. (I was so absorbed that I fantasized being alive in his time, meeting him, and, of course, with wife number one dead, becoming his wife and living in a romantic log cabin in the wilderness with him.) I insisted on getting a coonskin cap after this session. My father brought one home for me on his next Hollywood trip. I wore it in the house, to play baseball, to bed—wherever I could. I knew how very privileged I had been to meet, shake hands with, and speak with *Davy Crockett* and to hear him perform live.

. . . .

Beginning in October of 1954, ABC aired a program called *Rin Tin Tin* that would continue through 1959. The series starred Lee William Aaker, a child actor whose career began with bit parts in films such as *The Greatest Show on Earth* and *High Noon*. In *Rin Tin Tin*, Aaker played a boy rescued with his dog by rangers after he and the dog survived an Indian raid. He's taken to live with the rangers at a western fort. There, the dog, named Rin Tin Tin, and the boy, Rusty, together accomplish many a heroic feat. The original show dog, Rin Tin Tin was a shell-shocked pup found by an American serviceman named Lee Duncan in bombed-out kennels in Lorraine, France, less than two months before the end of WWI. The dog was named for a puppet called Rintintin that French children gave to the American soldiers for good luck. The Rin Tin Tin of the TV program was no kin of the original dog, but the fame of the name, which produced a line of German shepherds who were trained as performance dogs, continued on.

Billboard announced that Columbia was on its toes with the release of the ABC-TV show, *The Adventures of Rin Tin Tin*. It noted that the project "is being handled by Hecky Krasnow . . . in co-operation with Screen Gems, producers of the TV series." Each original disk would have a six-minute story with background music and would be packaged with an illustrated liner.

. . . .

Hecky kept Columbia ahead of the game when it came to deals with the most popular television programs. He'd heard about a new program soon to air with a host named Bob Keeshan. Keeshan had delighted young audiences for several years as the silent, horn-honking clown Clarabell on the *Howdy Doody Show*. Keeshan left *Howdy Doody* in 1952 and played other clown characters, such as Corny, host of *Time for Fun*, which aired on ABC at noon. He enforced his concern for nonviolent and quality children's fare when he made clear to his producers and sponsors that he would not appear on broadcasts airing cartoons displaying too much violence or ones that perpetuated racial inequality. They listened to him. In addition to the character of Corny, Keeshan appeared on another ABC program called *Tinker's Workshop*. This early morning program in which Keeshan played an Alpine toymaker served as the prototype for the show Keeshan developed with his long-time friend Jack Miller: *Captain Kangaroo*.

Hecky arranged a meeting with Keeshan and Miller. His initial impressions from what he'd heard about the program were thoroughly verified during this meeting. Bob Keeshan proved easygoing. His attitude of respect for children and belief that one should not talk down to them was in keeping with Hecky's own views. On the program, Keeshan maintained his easygoing manner. It was not acted, but a natural part of his character. His costume resembled a generic captain. It had big pockets out of which he pulled interesting items that would lure children into topics like reading a storybook, doing a simple science experiment, or dancing and singing a pleasant song. Hecky had heard about Keeshan's rejection of the increasing trend to commercialize children's programming and of his belief in toning down the loud and overly slapstick style associated with so many hosts for children's shows. This host smiled gently under a big, bushy mustache.

Other kind and interesting characters added to the events on each program. Hugh "Lumpy" Brannum, a farmer in green coveralls, played the Captain's sidekick, Mr. Greenjeans. He also visited periodically in other personas such as Mr. Bainter the Painter, and the New Old Folk Singer, playing a cello as if it were a guitar. Puppets created by Cosmo Allegretti included Bunny Rabbit, the trickster who always got the Captain to give him carrots, and Mr. Moose, who asked riddles and told knock-knock jokes that most always ended with hundreds of ping-pong balls falling from the ceiling and hitting the Captain on the head. Allegretti also acted the roles of the endearing Dennis the Apprentice, Mr. Whispers, Banana Man, Dancing Bear, Miss Frog, and old Grandfather Clock. Every segment of the program—including a brief cartoon, "Tom Terrific"—involved educating while entertaining, whether on a specific topic or about promoting respect for others. Keeshan and Miller spoke of the books to be read on the programs, all the finest in children's literature both classic and new.

Many songs were needed, as music comprised an important part of the program's content. Riddles, nature, jokes, and dances all had to be written into tunes and lyrics in keeping with the program's philosophy. Parents would certainly want to buy records for their children to listen to the delightful songs, riddles, and participatory movement games.

Hecky sensed a kindred spirit in Bob Keeshan, evident in the format of the new program and in the man's words as he spoke about children. Keeshan shared his attitude towards cross commercialization of children's programming. He talked about how television had the potential to either elevate or lower the public's intelligence. He emphasized how vitally important it was to insure that children were not used and abused by this new and growing medium. He stated that the only companies that would be accepted as advertisers were those that manufactured products beneficial to youngsters such as Play Dough and Etch A Sketch. Hecky, sensing that this program would be a popular and long-lasting one due to its sincerity and honest appeal to the needs and interest of children, brokered a deal between the new program and Columbia.

In October of 1955, the trade papers carried the headline "Columbia Inks 'Capt. Kangaroo.'" The details of the articles included the fact that the Captain Kangaroo program was the first of its kind not to be taped before a live audience and not to have children as part of the format like *Howdy Doody's* "Peanut Gallery" of cheering children or Disney's "Mouseketeers." The papers noted that the program had been signed as a "disk property" by Columbia: "The deal, negotiated through Hecky Krasnow, Columbia's kidisks head, runs for two years with a minimum of 16 sides to be cut in that period. . . . Columbia's quick inking of the video show reflects the growing interest among the major labels for video-properties which can plug their disk output."

. . . .

Every spare moment at home, my father sat at the piano productively writing music to lyrics penned by Leo Israel. The two began their many years of writing for the Captain together. The first song they contributed to the program's antics was "The Captain Kangaroo March." With an entourage of the show's familiar characters, the Captain marched around his Treasure House singing,

The first part of my name is in the army,
The second part of my name is in the zoo.
If the first part of my name is in the army,
I'm a captain, yes, a captain, I am Captain Kangaroo!

Our visits to the Israels' apartment and theirs to our house increased. As their books slipped off the shelves onto our heads, I could only think of the ping-pong balls falling upon the Captain's head.

More exciting for me, however, was the fact that Karen and I were hired as backup singers for many of the Captain's recordings. The first of these was the song "Two Little Magic Words." The Captain walks into his Treasure House and reminds us that we forgot two very important words, which open many doors. The song begins.

Captain: There are two little magic words that can open any door with ease. One little word is . . .

Karen and Judy: Thanks,

Captain: And the other little word is . . .

Karen and Judy: Please.

Captain, Karen, and Judy: No matter what you ask for, you'll get what you ask for. . . .

Standing next to Bob Keeshan (with petite Karen elevated on a carpeted stepping stool) and me almost as tall as the Captain felt wonderful. He reminded me of Uncle Phil with his soft-spoken, mild manner. Hecky always relaxed when working in the studio with Keeshan. His shoulders never seemed to slide upwards and reach his head. Those involuntary breaths were nonexistent. His intake of unfiltered Chesterfields was almost nil. Songs were completed in one take.

Bob Keeshan and "The Captain" were one and the same. The nice, gentle, caring man with the delicious sense of humor on-screen was the same off-screen: totally genuine. As Hecky had intuited, the program became an overnight success. Households throughout the entire nation got off to a happy, good start each morning as the Captain said "Good Morning" on television screens while families prepared to go to work and school. Captain Kangaroo became as much a part of the morning ritual as eating breakfast.

For Karen and me, it was thrilling not only to sing with Bob Keeshan, but for us to appear on his program with a couple of other children in an episode where we visited Mr. Greenjeans at his barn and all of us went to the Treasure House to show the Captain some little chicks just hatched from the barnyard. As we marched through the Treasure House singing, Bunny Rabbit and Mr. Moose engaged in their usual antics, and those famous ping-pong balls dropped on all of our heads. The privilege of this moment felt like manna falling from heaven.

CHAPTER 23

Riding the Crest
of the Wave

he year 1955 proved one of the busiest and most productive in Columbia's history regarding children's
records. Another series written by the team of George
Kleinsinger and Paul Tripp was recorded and lauded in trade
papers: *Happy Instruments*. This included *Pee Wee the Piccolo*.
I attended the recording of this "happy instrument."

The piccolo player gave the impression of appearing almost
as small as his piccolo. He resembled Danny Kaye, famed
dancer, actor, and master of fast talk. Like Kaye, his suit pants
were pleated at the top and tapered at the bottom. His thick,
wavy, slicked-back brown hair fell the same way upon his head
as Danny Kaye's red hair fell upon his. He had the same broad
forehead and pointed chin, a face shaped like a triangle, and
he moved with the agility and the quickness characteristic of
Kaye. His demeanor was jolly like the smiling Danny Kaye.
His fingers played upon his piccolo as though dancing upon
it with the same sprightliness seen in each jump, leap, and
bound of Kaye's dancing steps. His facial expressions accented
each move of a finger, and his torso leaped with every breath
taken. However, he was far smaller than the renowned entertainer and as I looked at this piccolo player, I thought of a
feather blowing into a silver reed. If the reed could blow back,

the feather would blow away. The words to the song reinforced my reveries about the shiny instrument's player.

> I'm Pee Wee the Piccolo. I whistle everywhere I go,
> Pee Wee the Piccolo, I whistle high and never low.
> Underneath the sky there's nothing quite so high
> As a tune that's played by I—that's me!
> Though I am so small, my tunes are very tall,
> So high they bump their heads against the sky.

The series included "Jojo the Banjo" with its plinkety plunks; "The Happy Clarinet," whose ticklishness causes her to sing "Do and re and mi, fa, so la ti-hee—ti-hee—ti-hee"; "The City Violin and the Country Fiddle," who point out their differences and praise each other's individual talents; "The Big Bass Fiddle," who sings, "When the others sing, 'High diddle, diddle,' The big bass fiddle goes, 'Low diddle, diddle,'"; and "Sliding Sam the Trombone Man," who warns: "Meet sliding Sam, a little man We call him Sam, the Trombone Man When his trombone he starts to play, Please watch the room—get out of his way!"

The *Masterworks* series continued with Eugene Ormandy, Andre Kostelanetz, Thomas Beecham, and Efrem Kurtz all adding their talents in the recording studio. George Kleinsinger joined forces with Bob Rolontz of *Billboard* to write "Tweeter and Woofer," a big seller that explained through the two characters of the Tweeter and the Woofer how speakers work. Wonder Books released a publication for children, *Kewtee Bear, Santa's Helper*, by Alan Reed. Hecky quickly responded to this book. Alan Reed narrated the story for Columbia, and its release coordinated with the sale of the Kewtee Bear toy and the resulting Kewtee Bear Clubs, which collected old toys from children, repaired them, and redistributed them to less fortunate children. The Honeydreamers also recorded "The Kewtee Bear Song," a big seller for Columbia.

Rosie was interviewed by *The Saturday Evening Post* and said that of all the recordings she'd made to date, the children's ones with Hecky Krasnow were her favorites. "These," she told her interviewer, "get the only honest approach given by the recording industry. The arrangements can be cute, but your diction has to be perfect. Kids have to understand every single word, because you're telling them a story and they insist on hearing it. Never sing down to children. If you do, they recognize it and can't stand it." Rosie recorded new songs and her previous hits continued to sell. A compilation album of favorites sung by Rosie came out on a 10-inch LP along with one of Gene Autry's biggest kid-disk hits.

. . . .

Jimmy Boyd, Josef and Miranda, Burl Ives, Tom Glazer, Paul Tripp, Arthur Godfrey, Lu Ann Simms, Dottie Evans, Sally and Lee Sweetland, Bob Hannon, Captain Kangaroo—all continued recording. The business was thriving. Christmas was coming and "Rudolph," now recorded by others of fame, again sold millions. "Rudolph" had become as much a part of the holiday as a Christmas tree, likewise, the beloved snowman, "Frosty."

Art Carney added to the joy of the 1955 holiday season with an unplanned piece. I had been in New York City for a dance lesson, for I'd started lessons at the Martha Graham School. After class, I would usually joined my father at the studio and go home with him. On this evening, Art was recording Moore's poem, "'Twas the Night before Christmas," like so many of the other artists had already done with success. The poem never failed to please no matter how many versions were heard.

When I arrived at the studio, the session was over, and the musicians providing the background music were virtually packed up except for the drummer. He started playing a boom-boom-dada rhythm. Carney pulled a flask from his pocket and took a sip. As the drummer played, Carney began to recite Moore's poem in between sips. The result was rap before its time. Everyone in the studio stopped what they were doing and started snapping fingers or tapping their feet. Carney began moving with hip-hop gestures long prior to hip-hop. He modulated his voice up and down in hilarious tones from high nasal to low near-growls.

My father was laughing as he watched and listened.

"Daddy, this is great. You should record it."

My father agreed. "Art, Art. I don't want to interrupt this improvisation, but get to the microphone right away. Keep it up on the drums too," my father instructed with urgency. Art slid to the mike with more humorous movements. My father quickly adjusted some levers on the board and recorded the improv-in-action. The ending of the poem grew more and more hilarious with Carney's incantations. When he finished the poem and the drummer gave an appropriate finale, everyone broke up in laughter. When we finally stopped laughing and listened to the take, my father said, "That's it. That is it. That IS it! This is definitely something new for Christmas."

Disc jockeys played it. The public loved it. Already it was decided that there would be an Easter follow-up of this drum and voice combo. Children would hear the story of "Flop, Mop, Cottontail, and Pete" told by Carney in rhyme with the rhythm of drums in the background. The man's spontaneity (perhaps enhanced by whatever had been in that flask) was sheer genius.

. . . .

Christmas brought another new hit for Columbia. Sid Tepper and Roy C. Bennett wrote a song about a boy who'd definitely not made it onto his mother and father's gift list for Christmas let alone Santa's: "I'm Gettin' Nuttin' for Christmas." In it the child confesses to various acts of misbehavior like "putting a tack on teacher's chair." Unfortunately for him, somebody snitches.

Comedian Stan Freberg recorded it as well as child star, Barry Gordon. Hecky knew Columbia had to compete with the fast-selling Gordon recording. As *The Daily Mirror* wrote on December 23, 1955, in an article by Sidney Fields,

> Nine-year-old Ricky Hugo Zahnd of Flatbush, was plucked out of the choir of the Little Church Around the Corner to record "I'm Gettin' Nuttin' For Christmas." There are seven different discs of the tune . . . but the two running neck and neck

for the Christmas record sweepstakes are MGM's by Barry Gordon, and Rick's for Columbia. . . .

Last August, Hecky Krasnow, Columbia's director of children's records, phoned the Little Church Around the Corner, and asked choir director Mr. Stuart Gardner for his best kid voice. Gardner suggested Ricky. . . .

Ricky was very nervous. . . . "But my mother was there, and Mr. Gardner," he says. "That was nice. But when we did the first one, 'Something Barked on Christmas Morning,' I had to do it eight times. And I had to do 'Nuttin' for Christmas' six times before I got it right."

He puts every penny of his choir money right into the bank. When he got paid $100 for recording "I'm Gettin' Nuttin' for Christmas" he hurried right into the bank. It's all to pay for college and he says it will come in handy when he's a big person and gets married and raises a family. Doesn't he ever buy anything he likes?

"Anytime I have to pay for anything I like," he answers, "I don't like it anymore."

(Zahnd grew up to be vice president of the New York Knicks and Rangers.)

When Ricky was a child, his father, a Columbia graduate and chemist, also played the piano. He took Ricky to a Yehudi Menuhin concert. This inspired Ricky to also want to learn to play the violin. Hecky, in an effort to put Ricky at ease, told him of his training under Leopold Auer.

"Mr. Auer was very strict, Ricky, but I loved my violin. I wanted to play it very well, so practicing was fun for me. Of course, I must confess I got a little nervous before each lesson, but that nervous feeling went away as soon as I'd begin to play." Perhaps these words made six and eight takes of the songs possible instead of 10 or more.

Karen and I participated in the success of the song as the two female singers in a quartet with two boys, George Werner and Angelo Roselli, also from the choir of the Little Church Around the Corner. We were given the name of The Blue Jeaners. We provided the backup for Ricky Zahnd on the A-side as well as the B-side, "Something Barked on Christmas Morning." The scenario went as follows:

Blue Jeaners: Hey, Ricky, whatcha gettin' for Christmas?
Ricky: I'm gettin' nuttin' for Christmas.
Blue Jeaners: Nuttin'?
Ricky: Mommy and Daddy are mad.
Blue Jeaners: What's a matter?
Ricky: I'm gettin' nuttin' for Christmas.
Blue Jeaners: Just nuttin'?
Ricky: Cause I ain't been nuttin' but bad.
Blue Jeaners: Whatcha do?

Ricky: I broke my bat on Johnny's head;
Blue Jeaners: Somebody snitched on me.
Ricky: I hid a frog in sister's bed;
Blue Jeaners: Somebody snitched on me.
Ricky: I spilled some ink on Mommy's rug;
I made Tommy eat a bug;
Bought some gum with a penny slug;
Blue Jeaners: Somebody snitched on me.

Chorus:
Ricky: I'm gettin' nuttin' for Christmas. (slide trombone—wa, wa)
Mommy and Daddy are mad (slide trombone—wa, wa)
Ricky: I'm gettin' nuttin' for Christmas (slide trombone—wa, wa)
Ricky: For I ain't been nuttin' but bad!

Ricky: I put a tack in my teacher's chair;
Blue Jeaners: Somebody snitched on me.
Ricky: I tied a knot in Susie's hair;
Blue Jeaners: Somebody snitched on me.
Ricky: I did a dance on Mommy's plants,
Climbed a tree and tore my pants,

Filled the sugar bowl with ants;
Blue Jeaners: Somebody snitched on me.

Chorus:
Blue Jeaners: He's gettin' nuttin' for Christmas.
Ricky: Yeah, nuttin'.
Blue Jeaners: His Mommy and Daddy are mad.
Ricky: Boy are they mad.
Blue Jeaners: He's gettin' nuttin' for Christmas,
Ricky: Nuttin'
Blue Jeaners: 'Cause he ain't been nuttin' but bad.

Ricky: I won't be seeing Santa Claus;
Blue Jeaners: Somebody snitched on me.
Ricky: He won't come visit me because
Blue Jeaners: Somebody snitched on me.
Ricky: Next year I'll be going straight;
Next year I'll be good, just wait;
I'd start now but it's too late;
Blue Jeaners: Somebody snitched on me.

All Together: So better be good whatever you do,
'Cause if you're bad, I'm warning you,
You'll get nuttin' for Christmas.
NUTTIN'!

The advent of television created another element through which songs were promoted. Hecky knew that if Ricky Zahnd and The Blue Jeaners sang "I'm Gettin' Nuttin' for Christmas" on the celebrated *Ed Sullivan Show*, the song would zoom to the top and compete with young Barry Gordon's fast-selling version. Sullivan's show was the crème de la crème of variety shows in spite of Mr. Sullivan's hunched shoulders and seldom-smiling, somber expression. Truly, his appearance seemed almost cadaver-like and may well have inspired the role played by Fred Gwynne in the 1960s as Herman Munster of *The Munsters*. Yet, he and his show were loved and viewed by millions weekly each Sunday night at 8:00 P.M. Each artist appearing on the program had to be of genuine professional caliber. For a song, a performance on the program was a sure pat on the back.

Hecky had contacted the producer and was told that it was not certain that there would be time for us to sing our brief song. The week leading up to the program we were on call. Perhaps we'd be on, perhaps not. My father rehearsed with Ricky, Karen, George, Angelo, and me. He coached us on not only the singing, but choreographed expressions and movements.

Late Sunday morning, my father, Karen, and I drove into New York City. We arrived at the CBS television studios and were led to a dressing room. Karen and I wore skirts to the theater as the era and our mothers demanded of "proper" young ladies. In a suitcase were our blue jeans, western-style blouses, and cowboy boots. Though the song we were to sing was not country-western, the name of our quartet, namely The Blue Jeaners, dictated the attire. The double-standard of dress for girls confused me, and I was thrilled that show biz permitted me to be comfortable. I detested skirts that necessitated wearing knee socks that slid down in my boots, a slip that created static electricity and slid upwards into a lump under the skirt, or nylon stockings held up by a garter belt that perpetually slid downwards, which put pressure on my bladder and caused me to have to pee frequently. "Wear a girdle," my mother insisted. "I will not," I insisted back. "At the Martha Graham School we dancers are told that we are our own girdles and to wear one would only weaken our muscles." This usually ended the tete-a-tete.

Ricky Zahnd and his mother arrived as did the two other Blue Jeaners, boys who had the right as males to wear their blue jeans to the theater. We were told by the stage manager, "If the time can be made, you will be on the show. The other artists have been booked many months in advance, but something can always come up at the last minute." We learned that acts like ours stand by in the wings for just such emergencies. We were not there long when it became apparent that controversy over a performer was afoot, and there was great tension regarding this mystery entertainer and tonight's program. A rising new rock star's manager insisted that, since his client was in town, he should be on the program. It appeared that the star in question was a young, handsome singer named Elvis Presley, whose gyrations and swooning audiences were not wanted by Ed Sullivan. We heard the talk in the hallways about the lack of enough security for such an appearance and major concern over the fact that Elvis fans might well be antagonized since they would not receive the advance notice necessary for them to stand in line early enough to get tickets to the show.

With the hubbub going on regarding this matter, Mr. Sullivan never swayed from his somber stance and serious manner of speaking. His resistance to the new and growing phenomenon of Elvis won out until nearly one year later when, on September 9, 1956, Sullivan could no longer resist the wave that Elvis had set in motion. Elvis the Pelvis, as he then had come to be called, made his first appearance on the show with strict orders to the cameramen not to get shots of him from anywhere but the waist up.

The hubbub the day we were there lasted for hours. We were bored in the dressing room and hungry too. One of the assistants saw to it that sandwiches were ordered and delivered for us. We were not permitted to leave the theater even for a breath of fresh, cold winter air. On standby we could be called for stage placement and rehearsal at any moment. My father insisted on a few more practice runs right there in the dressing room. At about 6:00 P.M., with only two hours until showtime, we were told it was a "go." Comedians Abbott and Costello, famous for their hilarity and skits, including the ingenious classic "Who's On First?" had cancelled their scheduled appearance at the last minute. Ushered to the stage, we ran through our introduction by Ed Sullivan, our entrance, placement, and rehearsed the song with the illustrious Ray Bloch Orchestra, another of the program's long-standing institutions.

The evening's program included famed singer Teresa Brewer singing "There'll Be Some Changes" and "A Good Man Is Hard to Find." Boxing champion Sugar Ray Robinson was to talk about his comeback. His manager Joe Glaser would also make an appearance. The Sugar Bowl Queen was another of the evening's enticements, as was Mimi Benzell, the opera star who would sing the song "Autumn Leaves" in French. The

Oberkirchen Choir from Germany would present their rendition of "God Rest Ye Merry Gentlemen" and a German Christmas Carol entitled "Deck the Halls." A famous trio of comic acrobats, The Three Markays, would dazzle the eyes of the audience with their acrobats, contortions, and amazing feats on the parallel bars. Little did we know that amidst all these famous acts, sitting in the audience viewing our antics and hearing our voices, would be George Meany, president of the AFL/CIO, and John S. Pillsbury, of the famed flour with which housewives across the nation baked, plus a host of several other dignitaries and U.S. servicemen.

All of us children felt nervous knowing that we were, indeed, to appear on this gala show. We got into costume. A makeup artist rouged our cheeks, put lipstick upon our lips, eyebrow pencil and shadow on our eyes, and then brushed all this over with powder.

My father used the pay phone in the dressing room and called my mother and Helen with the good news. He instructed them to call his parents and his brother Bob in Hartford. Then he called my twin aunts and his brother Al in California. Long-distance calls were extremely expensive. So, he called each relative collect and told the operator that he wanted to speak with "Mr. Eddie Sol Ivan," hoping the operator's suspicions would not be aroused. Our family, already familiar with signals like this, answered, "He's not in, but we expect him at 8 P.M." They all now knew to definitely watch the program and that we would be on it.

The bewitching hour of 8:00 P.M. EST arrived. Ten minutes prior to our number, we were once again ushered out of the dressing room and downstairs to take our place in the wings. My heart was pounding. I felt as though I was in a royal court being prepared to pay my respects to the king and queen. We moved forward in the lineup in the wings. Before we knew it we were told to go to the stage and stand at the tape markings we rehearsed behind earlier. The orchestra began to play. Ricky sang his opening lines. Our quartet responded with our song lines and choreographed movements. I felt like I was floating in timelessness with no forward or backward motion. When we finished the song it felt like we'd just begun. How was it we were already done? Our three minutes and 41 seconds flew by as though they'd never happened. We quickly bowed as instructed, turned, and walked off into the wings to loud, enthusiastic applause and the sound of Ed Sullivan's voice saying, "What talented kids. How adorable. A winning song if ever there was one!"

The anticipation of a whole week ended in those brief few moments of glory. The next day several congratulatory telegrams arrived at our house. Returning to school at Gorton Jr. and Sr. High the next morning, Karen and I had a near red carpet welcome. It seemed all of Yonkers had watched *The Ed Sullivan Show* that night.

The Columbia version of "I'm Gettin' Nuttin' for Christmas" rose to number 21 in the Top 40 charts for the year 1955 and graced Columbia with another major hit as it was played across the nation by disc jockeys every hour on the hour as part of the Top 40 countdown.

. . . .

At home, things were not so jolly. Helen refused to follow Jacques Lifshitz to Quebec where he'd accepted a job as a head doctor in a major hospital. He'd proposed and willingly accepted Karen and Jean, but Helen wished to stay in her own country and nearer to her family. She was now working as the receptionist for our dentist, Dr. Raymond House. The frustration of another love gone from her life and the burden of having to work every day while caring for her children unleashed her anger. Night after night, we'd hear her screaming at Karen and Jean. They'd often come downstairs, but the peace they'd find in our house could not obliterate the unhappiness and turmoil in their abode upstairs.

Steffi had entered Sarah Lawrence College in Bronxville, New York, in the fall of 1954. Meyer Kupferman and Henry Walsh, both professors at the college, encouraged my father to head the chamber music concert series in which quality chamber music groups presented concerts at Reisinger Auditorium four times a year. Through his participation in the series, Hecky met other professors. Soon, at our house, my parents hosted soirées that included mythologist Joseph Campbell, author of many books, including *The Hero with a Thousand Faces* and *The Power of Myth*; his wife, dancer Jean Erdman; lawyer and anthropologist Dr. Adda B. Bozeman; and philosopher Dr. Maurice Friedman, author of many books about Martin Buber, the Jewish philosopher whose work regarding faith as a life of dialogue between man and God influenced others, including the great Protestant thinkers Paul Tillich and Walter Nigg. This professorial group attended one of the Columbia parties, and Joseph Campbell and Josef Marais, with their abounding enthusiasm, held all guests rapt as they told and discussed myths from Africa.

However, one evening prior to one of these soirees, Helen's screaming upstairs so upset my mother that she told my father, "I can no longer bear to live under the same roof as your sister. With all the success you are having at Columbia and with all the parties we are hosting, I think it's time for us to go house hunting."

More yelling was heard from upstairs. The next day, my parents contacted a realtor. He suggested looking in Westchester County, particularly in areas like Scarsdale, Larchmont, and New Rochelle. These were popular with many at Columbia including Percy Faith and Bob Keeshan and his wife Jeanne. The suggested areas combined the peace of the suburbs with the sophisticated intelligence of a city. Soon, the realtor took us to see a house in Scarsdale. Though Scarsdale was somewhat of an elite suburb, the house was considered moderate in both price and size. We followed the directions the realtor had given and met him at the house.

The outside resembled a combination of a gingerbread house, a Swiss chalet, and an English lodge. Inside, several windows were shaped like the small turret windows of an old castle with three panes of glass at angles to one another. Each of these windows had cushioned seats. We sat upon one of these in the living room and looked out onto a quaint cobblestone walkway, which led from the gate at the sidewalk to the front door. A huge old oak tree stood to the right of the walkway. The floors in the house displayed the beautiful grains of the oak wood from which their planks were made. The rougher dark wood beams in the ceiling provided a warm and cozy feeling. The fireplace with its stone mantel reminded me of the fireplace at my grandparents' beach house in Saybrook. The house had a woody scent that added rusticity. In the small, pretty yard a colorful garden grew, filled with tulips, a forsythia bush, Chinese red maple tree, and two heavenly smelling lilac trees. I begged my parents to buy the house. I could tell they were as taken with it as I.

"Honey," my father said to my mother, "this place is us. I don't even think it is necessary to look at another house."

"Just think of the parties I could give here. Oh, it's not Mitch Miller's mansion, but it is at least twice or more the size of our present place, and at last we could live in a place of our own . . . without Helen."

"I'll miss Karen," I said, suddenly aware of the reality that moving would separate us from the only life I'd known, from someone who might as well have been my twin. "How will we rehearse? What will happen on weekends for sleepovers with her and on Christmas Eve?"

"Scarsdale is not far from Yonkers. We have cars. You can spend weekends together and rehearse then," my father answered. "As for Christmas, we'd have a guest room and den here for Helen, Karen, and Jean to stay, and three bathrooms instead of one." The one bathroom in our Yonkers dwelling had always been an issue as my father spent so much time in it against his will and because of his constant stomach battles with Crohn's. Add to that three females clamoring for mirror, makeup, and bath time.

"It might be good for you and Karen to be apart a little more," my mother commented. "You know, Judy, you can sing alone too. You do that frequently when you practice. Helen is always telling me how she wishes Karen were more outgoing like you."

Messages, often more silent than open, were conveyed to both Karen and me about what each of our mothers wished to see in their daughters and instead saw in the other's daughter. Steffi was the first Krasnow female to willingly be sent to college. Much was expected from her. Both Helen and my mother wanted Karen and me to model ourselves after Steffi education-wise. Because I was praised for my extroverted nature, Karen seemed a better candidate for intellectual pursuits as though being outgoing negated the ability to also be intellectual. My mother did not want to be absorbed in such a competition, but living in the same house with Helen had set certain patterns between them. "I think moving here would definitely be a breath of fresh air for all of us," she said with emphasis on "all of us."

I loved the house. My parents loved the house. They sat down with the realtor and talked financial details. They listened and said they would be in touch after mulling it over for a day or two. Three days later, after discussion, conflict, hope, then disappointment, my parents decided not to purchase the house.

"It will simply put us in the red in terms of the monthly mortgage payment and upkeep, honey," I heard my father say in the kitchen as I bent and stretched doing dance exercises in the living room.

"What if I got a job?" my mother suggested.

"A job? HUHney, who will take care of Judy?"

"Half the time she doesn't even come home until dinner," my mother responded. "She's old enough to travel into the city for dance lessons. She can come home and be alone until we get home."

"Honey, you are wonderful, smart, talented, but you haven't even taught piano lessons for years now. You don't type. You are over 35. Where can you get a job and what kind? And what about your heart? How could you work, run a house, give parties? No, honey, I don't think that's the solution. Both of our health issues make it too risky."

"I love the house," my mother sounded choked up.

"Honey," my father became defensive in tone, "believe me, you won't love the house when we can't pay the bills with ease, when even Alexanders' bargains are too costly as you want to buy Juddie and yourself some new clothes, and when we want to take a vacation and can't afford it."

Moments like this reminded my father that even though he had brought Columbia its biggest fortune to date with "Rudolph"—not to mention the many other hits and major projects he'd masterminded and produced that had put Columbia in the lead and big money in the children's record business—as only a company employee, he could not afford to risk the expenditures involved with this modest house in Scarsdale.

"You are right," my mother said. I could hear the sadness in her voice. I knew that she had just put on her smile. I knew she shook her head and pointed her chin upwards, forcing a cheery sound. "Honey, we have never lived above our means. We know how to save money. We can take trips with our children at vacation times. For heaven's sake, Steffi couldn't get a scholarship to college because your income is just over the borderline to qualify for one."

"Which reminds me, honey, that's the other payment we now have, namely, college loans." I smelled the odor of a match lighting a cigarette as my father spoke these words.

"Right. Think of it. We eat well, can buy sufficient clothing, and we've managed here in our crowded quarters all these years to give parties people enjoy. We'll continue. I just wish Helen would stop yelling so loud."

I sensed my mother wished for more, but once again, as she'd done all her life, she faced reality by defying it with her smile and always half-full glass.

Eventually, Helen did stop yelling. She and Ray House, the dentist, were having an affair. His wife was divorcing him as a result. It became obvious that he and Helen intended to eventually marry.

. . . .

Success at Columbia continued to escalate. Our family drove to Indiana, where my father met with Jack Watson of the Silver Burdett Publishing Company to discuss a major series of music books Burdett intended to publish. The Silver Burdett Publishing Company, known for their high quality textbooks for preschool through college, selected Columbia to publish a whole music series called *New Music Horizons*. Hecky suggested the innovative idea of having record albums accompany each volume as he firmly believed that listening and sight-reading went hand in hand. Watson, one of the authors of Burdett's basic music series, liked the idea. The beautifully illustrated books would be advertised with the following slogan: *From the bright-eyed beginnings of the child's musical experience through the magical teen-age years—the best in school music always means SILVER BURDETT COMPANY.*

The company financed our trip so Hecky and Jack Watson could discuss this matter in person and Hecky could get a firsthand look at all the company had to offer with future projects in mind. Since Lebanon, Indiana, where Silver Burdett was located, was not far from Bloomington, our family could visit the University of Indiana with Steffi. She'd been advised that the school had an outstanding writing department and was interested in possibly getting a master's in writing once she graduated from Sarah Lawrence.

My father had traded in our Nash Rambler for a 1955 slick-looking, four-door Desoto Fireflite in black and white. Our trip to Indiana proceeded in total comfort. The Desoto was the snazziest, smoothest-riding car we'd ever had. We stopped at historic sites along the route and in Indiana, the Hoosier State that claimed to be the birthplace of the likes of the flying Wright brothers, famed socialist presidential candidate Eugene Debs, rebel actor James Dean, environmentalist James Muir, bank robber John Dillinger, and John Chapman, better known as the legendary Johnny Appleseed, whose story, adapted by Henry Walsh and Hecky and recorded by Gene Autry, continued to sell in large numbers annually.

When we arrived in Lebanon, Indiana, Jack Watson took us out to dinner. He was a tall, sliver-haired man who looked happy and healthy. His Hoosier accent was warm and friendly. For the next several days, we would hear him say, "That's peachy keen, just peachy keen," about everything good and fun. At a barbeque at his home the second night of our visit, the steaks he broiled were "peachy keen." The squirrels climbing the trees were "peachy keen." The deal made with Columbia was "peachy keen." Each time he said "peachy keen," he expressed such enthusiasm that his naturally rosy cheeks grew redder, like some people's cheeks do when they laugh heartily.

Our visit enabled us to see the many beautifully laid out books published by Silver Burdett and the layout design and plans for the volumes for which Columbia would record the music. We left Lebanon with my father extremely pleased. The deal was huge for Columbia, and as a trained and caring musician, Hecky was immensely pleased to be an instrumental part of it.

Karen and I were hired to sing on the recordings of the Silver Burdett series, and since there were so many volumes, we had a lot of paid work. In addition to learning many new songs, we sang folk classics like "Shenandoah," "On Top of Old Smokey," and more. We recorded these with artists Dottie Evans, Tom Glazer, and Sally Sweetland at Columbia's 30th Street studio. In addition to the pleasure of recording and the practice we got in harmonizing with these talented singers, we could indulge in the delicious Italian hero sandwiches from the deli down the street, the epicurean delight I had first tasted while lunching with Jackie Robinson and Pee Wee Reese.

At Columbia, Goddard Lieberson received a letter from Charles E. Griffith, First Vice President and Music Editor of Burdett. Jack Watson had been in New York attending the recording sessions of the *Music for Living* series.

> Dr. Jack Watson, one of the authors of our basic music series, has just completed the last recording sessions covering MUSIC FOR LIVING. It has been an interesting experience both to him and to our Silver Burdett personnel who have assisted in working to the details, particularly because of the expert and kindly help secured from Mr. Hecky Krasnow.
>
> His taste, discrimination, and sensitive ear are exceptional and invaluable when producing children's records that are both learning aids for the classroom and entertaining and fascinating materials for young and old alike.
>
> It is a pleasure to express this appreciation of Hecky to you for his high professional attainments.

. . . .

Leo Israel and my father were busy writing for Captain Kangaroo, with song titles like "Five Little Engines, Six Little Taxis," "Riddle-a-Diddle," "More Riddle-a-Diddle," "Dance-Along Zoo," and "The Littlest Snowman," which was written under their pseudonyms of Leo Paris and Steve Mann, along with Charles Tazewell, the author and actor who had written the recently published book of the same title. Karen and I recorded backup on several of these pieces.

Money was to be made in publishing. Leo Israel, with Hecky's input and partnership, set up Reynard Publishing as a subsidiary of Sam Fox Publishing. Reynard published their compositions for Captain Kangaroo. In 1956, only a few months after the program aired, 30 songs were composed for the Captain.

CHAPTER 24

What Goes Up Must Come Down

. . . .

n Columbia's 30th Street studio, an orchestra and chorus assembled with a cast of actors including narrator Garry Moore. The popular and widely known Moore had co-hosted a 1940s radio show with comedian Jimmy Durante and presently hosted *The Garry Moore Show*, an afternoon variety show that aired skits and monologues, and touted guest performers like comedian Don Knotts and actor/comedian Jonathan Winters. Moore also hosted the game show *I've Got a Secret*. Joining Moore was Sandy Fussell, the dwarf actress who played the parts of young Mozart and Haydn on the *Introduction to the Masters* series.

Today's recording was of three tales from Rudyard Kipling's *Just So Stories*: "How the Elephant Got His Trunk," "How the Whale Got His Throat," and "How the Camel Got His Hump." Leo Israel and Hecky had collaborated to put these stories together with cleverly adapted words and an original score. Even Steffi took time off from her college work to come to this recording, for she loved the story about the elephant and had heard the well-crafted lyrics and wonderful music both at home and at the Israels'.

I had the privilege of being home on the evenings and weekends that my father sat at the Chickering composing the music. "Juddie," he'd call to me. "Come sit here and tell me what you think of this." I'd offer my occasional, "It should be a little faster," or "The melody there should go upwards, not down," but mostly I'd say, "Please, Daddy, play and sing that again." I loved the sound of the music to words like, "gray, green, greasy banks of the Limpopo River."

At the recording, I was utterly intrigued by Sandy Fussell. She completely brought the characters to life. As the little elephant's child, she pinched her nose to make the sound of an elephant who was having trouble breathing. Her facial expressions shaped the words and created a little elephant one could only love. Garry Moore, as he did on his programs, remained the relaxed, laid-back narrator but in no way lacked in drama. His intonations created or dispelled the tension of the story line.

The orchestra began with the mysterious music my father had written. Its mode and cadence immediately established curiosity as to what would unfold. The chorus joined in with the words,

> In the high and far off times, (men's voices)
> In the high and far off times, (women's voices echo)
> We elephants had no trunks (men)
> We elephants had no trunks (women)
> We only had noses, mere, smear noses (Chorus)
> With which to drink, and which to think
> As we wandered in the roses.
> We couldn't pick up things with them (Sandy Fussell)
> Or do many things with them. . . . (Chorus)

It posed a wonderful beginning. The session felt like a crowded, bustling concert hall teeming with talent. My father, working with an assistant engineer, had to keep sounds balanced with microphones for one track placed among the orchestra, and others on the second track, used by all the vocalists. It wouldn't be until 1958 that stereo recordings would be made and the innovative KLH speakers sold to play these records. This was, in effect, a live concert performance. The actors created total suspension of disbelief and one believed the guile of the crocodile, felt the anger of the cousins, uncles, aunts and parents of the little elephant upon seeing his stretched nose, and participated fully in the adventures of the stubborn, galumphing camel, and the frightened sailor and uncomfortable whale. The end result would still be heard monaurally, the spirit of the performers captured forever without anyone altering it afterwards through a mix of many tracks. This gala session held great hope in its finesse and the quality of the material being recorded. It felt like a crowning glory to the nearly seven years in which Hecky had brought Columbia out of the red and into the limelight with one successful project after another during the golden age of children's records. However, times were changing.

. . . .

In 1949, the sale of radios across the nation amounted to $415,200. In contrast, the sale of televisions brought in $34,300. In 1953, radios showed purchases amounting to $475,300 and televisions $431,800. By 1956, radio sales stood at $480,600. Televisions had soared to $896,900. The visual medium was fast taking over the listening medium, which had entertained decades of listeners since its invention. In 1950, the cumulative total of televisions in homes amounted to 9,734,872. In 1956, the number had climbed to 49,698,333.

In November of 1955, teacher and singer/musician Beatrice Landeck, author of several books, including *Songs to Grow On*, wrote an article that appeared in the *New York Times*. Television, still so new and not yet an ingrained, irrevocable part of the American consciousness, had hope of being offset if kept in balance with other forms of entertainment. Landeck opened her article with these words: "Parents, duly concerned about the excessive time children spend in viewing television might consider counterbalancing this kind of entertainment by providing a new stock of well-selected records. The pleasurable stimulation of good recordings is manifold: the child enjoys personally choosing a record from his own collection; he holds it in his hand; he sets it in motion, playing his favorites over and over at will. The freedom of choice and action affords pleasure and satisfaction."

Landeck wrote about the offerings from all the record companies engaged in the production of music for children. Focusing on those recordings that educate while entertaining on the subjects of music, musical instruments, and folk music (her specialty), she points out the *Masterworks* series; "Tubby the Tuba"; "Pan the Piper," which covers the history of instruments from their earliest beginnings; "Benny the Beaver"; and individual folk artists like Josef Marais and Miranda and Burl Ives.

In an attempt to make records desirable by selling them cheaply, Columbia along with Decca, Capitol, and Mercury alternately emphasized sales of 45-rpms, LPs, and 78-rpms. Columbia decided to eliminate the latter. Hecky felt that at the prices records were selling for—anywhere from 25¢ in the supermarket to 49¢ for an album to $1.24 by the Children's Record Guild and Young People's Records, that a 78-rpm 10-inch disk was simply not profitable at a price like 49¢. The trend was towards LP albums.

An article in *Billboard* emphasized that most of the major companies were not producing new projects but simply promoting the old ones at the lowest possible price that could still bring some profit. The article stated that "Capitol . . . has pulled in its reins somewhat in what it feels is a rapidly diminishing market." Capitol stated that the cultural and educational aspects of kid-disks had increased, but that releases such as their *Music Appreciation* and *Learning Is Fun* series currently were the only level at which children's music could be merchandised. Simon & Schuster found that their best market for children's records now lay in selling 25¢ releases in dime stores, candy shops, and newsstands.

Record companies were, in fact, closing down their children's departments and simply reselling already produced material. In some instances, these departments would become subsidiaries of other larger divisions within the companies. It seemed that only the Children's Record Guild and Young People's Records, both of which appealed to a select and more intellectual group of parents, continued to have high sales in 1956.

Hecky, fearing the writing on the wall, wrote a memo in May of 1956. In it he claimed that part of the sluggishness in the children's market was due to "negative reaction created in parents, dealers and others interested in children's records who began to get surfeited with a record diet . . . of 98 cent 'kiddie-pop,' and the 'Tin Pan Alley' approach to children's records which paid off well for a while." He stated that he fully understood the need to develop a competitive line of releases revolving around TV tie-ins like characters from Paul Terry's Terrytoons studio, Mighty Mouse, Daffy Duck, etc. He suggested using a name such as Gene Autry's and "covering hit pop tunes which appeal to youngsters." He noted that "packaging ideas are essential to such a market." He also emphasized that, though occasionally there will be hits like a "Davy Crockett" or an "I'm Gettin' Nuttin' for Christmas," this type of material cannot be relied upon to be the "backbone of our children's business."

The memo continued with specific suggestions recognizing the need for periodic crossover hits at holidays and records that reflect the changing children's pop culture due to television, but also the necessity to continue offering quality educational entertainment via records. There must be a focus not only on singles sold cheaply, but 10- and 12-inch LP albums like the *Just So Stories* and other fine literature for youths such as the Landmark Books, plus folk songs, singing games, further series about classical music, and the continuing of western adventures with Gene Autry. Hecky maintained that building up a new catalog to meet the demands of the changing times was an absolute necessity. He expressed the opinion that the catalog should include material for all tastes and also listed the still popular items such as *Children's Favorites* with Rosemary Clooney, Burl Ives, and Gene Autry; the *Rin Tin Tin* series; the humorous songs with Art Carney; the Captain Kangaroo material; and the Disney fare. He ended with,

> It goes without saying that the major changes in emphasis and basic A&R policy outlined here can only produce successful results if there is agreement with it and support of it on all levels. From the A&R point of view, I am convinced that it can produce nothing but worthwhile results. . . . The children's market has

had its fat days and its lean. With the children's population already tremendous and growing at a rate of over four million a year, there must be a reasonable part of its ready to absorb a healthy quantity of records specially designed for its enjoyment at its level. We have to offer it an attractive and irresistible product and let them know it's available. It has done it in the past. History can repeat itself, even with television.

Television was not the only new entry to the media. Records were selling well, but not in the children's departments. Television catered more divisively to different ages. Captain Kangaroo appealed to very young children, but not to their older siblings who had their westerns or *Leave It to Beaver* to watch. Parents had their programs. A broadcast like *The Ed Sullivan Show* could be safely viewed by the entire family and often was. In the early '50s, the pleasant, relaxing, feel-good songs reflecting the mood of post-World War II were the pop tunes of parents but were also heard by their children, for there was seldom, if ever, anything that could be considered offensive for children to hear. In addition to this, children of all ages had their own records to listen to. Now, the children's departments were losing a large number of past buyers—teenagers—as parents were losing their own children to a new pop culture whose seeds had suddenly sprouted. Through a new generation of DJs, one in particular named Alan Freed, a revolutionary kind of music hit the airwaves with vigor. It was called rock 'n' roll.

In 1952, in Cleveland, Alan Freed began playing black R&B songs. He moved his show to New York in 1954 and not only played recordings, but offered live performances, particularly with groups whose harmonies he enjoyed most. For a long time, due to segregation, white artists often recorded cover versions of black artists who, though they were gaining popularity, were not able to perform in many venues and were not played on the air. However, as, for example, Pat Boone's version of the song "Tutti Frutti" clearly demonstrated, these cover versions could not last long. Black artists and their own versions were bound to emerge. Not only did Alan Freed have the courage to play the real versions and invite the genuine artists to sing live on his program, but in the South, Sam

Phillips opened the Memphis Recording Service, the first studio where black musicians, along with anyone else who wished, could record. Later it was renamed Sun Studio. Recordings here launched artists of many musical genres including Ike Turner, B.B. King, James Cotton, Johnny Cash, Carl Perkins, and Jerry Lee Lewis. It was here, in 1953, that a young truck driver named Elvis Presley stopped by and recorded two songs: "My Happiness" and "That's When Your Heartache Begins."

A band in Chester, Pennsylvania, Bill Haley and The Comets, began to see some success with a sound that combined country with R&B. In 1954, they recorded a song called "Shake, Rattle and Roll," and another, "Rock Around the Clock." The songs saw moderate success until "Rock Around the Clock" was used as the theme song of a movie that turned into a major box office hit: *Blackboard Jungle.* For the first time, the movie exposed the public to the world of juvenile delinquency in city schools and, though relatively few teenagers were classified as delinquents, the content of the movie and its theme song gave teenagers a musical culture that they could call their own. The music certainly had more excitement and energy than the more sedate and romantic songs of their parents.

This was not the only hit changing the tone of the music scene. Two savvy Polish immigrants in Chicago, the Chess brothers, established Chess Records and signed up the best black blues performers for their label sensing the turning of the tides and recognizing the great talent among black artists. One of these was a fellow born in St. Louis, Missouri named Chuck Berry. In 1955, his hit song, "Maybellene," reached number one on the charts for rhythm and blues and number five for rock 'n' roll. In 1956, "Roll Over Beethoven," written by Berry, rang with a message loud and clear through electric guitar riffs, a pounding rock piano, and these words, "Roll over, Beethoven/And tell Tchaikovsky the news."

In January of 1956, Elvis Presley's "Heartbreak Hotel" was released. It sold 300,000 copies in the first week dwarfing, for example, the 250,000 copies sold over a few months of songs like "Suzie Snowflake," sung by Rosemary Clooney. Television now played an important role in the launching of superstars and their songs. Jackie Gleason's show aired

Elvis Presley six times between January and the end of March. April brought him to *The Milton Berle Show* where he sang "Heartbreak Hotel" and "Blue Suede Shoes." After signing a seven-year movie contract with Paramount Pictures, he reappeared in June on *The Milton Berle Show*, pelvis gyrating in the highly controversial performance of "Hound Dog," and "I Want You, I Need You, I Love You." July brought him to *The Steve Allen Show*. By September, Ed Sullivan, behind on the Elvis bandwagon, had to concede that eyes could not be closed to this new phenomenon of what, in the era, was considered a far too blatantly sexual—almost obscene—artist with a great voice who was ushering in an era of a totally new popular music. In an unprecedented contract, Sullivan signed a three-appearance deal for the then-unheard-of sum of $50,000. Women and girls screamed and swooned uncontrollably watching and listening to Elvis, now entrenched in their minds and hearts as "Elvis the Pelvis."

In 1956, I was approaching age 14 and was already out of junior high school, where I'd won the name "Pinko Krasnow" for a famous/infamous class discussion in which I dared to defy my Legionnaire social studies teacher by defending Paul Robeson and saying that I had indeed gone to one of his concerts. I continued openly espousing my desire for peace and equality even when Sputnik was launched in 1957. Now in high school, I had several new friends, many Jewish, who had moved into a newly built complex called Greystone. Actress Gloria Swanson, one of its backers, visited frequently and developed a friendship with Aunt Helen who now ran the rental offices. At Gorton High, I'd become buddies with Carol Sperling, who lived at Greystone.

Carol succumbed to total infatuation with Elvis. Visiting at her house, we did nothing—at her insistence—but listen to Elvis records on her blue-and-white Motorola phonograph. It was ten plays for "Blue Suede Shoes"; twenty consecutive plays of "Heartbreak Hotel"; tears, screams, and sighs for "I Want You, I Need You, I Love You"; and by the time she turned on "Hound Dog" and began gyrating her hips Elvis-style, I had politely excused myself, said goodbye, returned home, taken out my guitar, and sang "St. James Infirmary," or some other folk song. Elvis was forbidden to be heard in our house. It wasn't until I was in my 50s that I even realized he had a decent voice. Carol Sperling seldom visited our home. She couldn't live without Elvis that long.

Hecky not only viewed Elvis with disdain, he viewed what was happening in the field of music with fear and trepidation. Firstly, he sensed that his job was in jeopardy. The times were not only changing, but the tides of change were swelling to proportions that could drown out everything he believed in, had worked so hard to accomplish, and the kind of music and thoughtful, quality projects to which he'd so genuinely dedicated himself. To Hecky, Elvis became the symbol of all that was going astray, of an uncertain future whose musical—and moral—changes he could not embrace. This new music stood in total opposition to everything he'd known and knew: his training with Leopold Auer, study at Juilliard, playing with symphonic orchestras, and numerous enriching, educational productions for children. How could the great voices of Rosemary Clooney, Dinah Shore, Gene Autry, and Burl Ives give way to these new voices that represented nothing but fun, pleasure, loud volume, and rebellion against everything classy, tender, even meaningful? How could his Juddie—barely 14—and other youths with innocent and still supple minds (and bodies), bear witness to Elvis, his highly sexual pelvis, and music that would teach them nothing of beauty, masterful composition, and the refined emotions that result from these?

Hecky wasn't the only one swept up in change and questioning the future. The entire recording industry stood shaken up by the virtually overnight arrival of rock 'n' roll. Columbia alone held a superior position in the early '50s with stars like Rosemary Clooney, Frankie Laine, Gene Autry, and Doris Day. Mainstream pop music and country-western were thriving. But in 1956, these stars, their popularity and that of their music no longer mattered. Companies were out for the mega-money. Loyalty was nonexistent. By 1959, Rosemary Clooney would perform with rocker Fabian as her opener or not draw an audience. Elvis had arrived and rock 'n' roll was now the dominant force in the pop singles market.

Additionally, though Elvis was sold by Sun Records to RCA, a major company, many independent record labels were suddenly springing up all over the country. Whereas major record companies had begun eliminating singles on 78-rpm and 45-rpm in favor of 10-inch and 12-inch

LPs, these smaller companies were releasing rock 'n' roll 45-rpms fast and furiously. Payola went hand in hand with the onset of rock 'n' roll. Disc jockeys were rolling in the dough. Alan Freed made money by having his name added to songs as a co-composer in exchange for playing them on the air. Who could prove that his name was there without his having contributed one word or note? Payola, combined with the less costly and numerous 45-rpms of rock 'n' roll, quickly pushed the major companies into the backseat.

In the 1940s and early '50s, articles regarding marketing for children and children's records classified children, as did Hecky and Phil's book *A Guide to Children's Records*, as between the ages of three and sixteen. In the '40s and '50s, record companies including Columbia and Decca hired top-notch people skilled in the field to research teen interests and needs in order to specifically produce records for this age group. The companies wished to offer educational and uplifting material to young people. Through well-researched surveys, they learned what parents wanted their children to hear or not hear, and they listened and responded accordingly to these demands. Now the companies listened only to their desire for profit: Do unto others as will result in your getting rich.

Rock 'n' roll appealed to baser instincts with no educational or uplifting qualities. To quote Jon Guyot Smith, educator, music historian, and writer of many present-day CD inserts about Gene Autry, "By 1956, rock 'n' roll was being promoted as the music of 'kids,' and the darker side of the American teenager was being glorified throughout the mass media. Suddenly, for the first time, being a teenager was widely promoted as being synonymous with dwelling in paradise. Small children stopped dreaming about growing up to be adults, preferring to concentrate their hopes and dreams on the day they would be teenagers. Rock 'n' roll became the 'property' of youth, in general."

. . . .

The corporate world of Disney also played a role in the decline of children's records. Ironically, after increasing their sales and visibility through Hecky's efforts of having others record and further spread sale of their wares, Disney's entrance into the children's record field with its popular name and wealth—hence power—forced out the children's offerings of the major record companies. Disney proceeded to promote its own products. Stores like Sam Goody and other retail outlets, formerly stocked with a variety of children's fare from many record companies, now displayed only Disney albums leaving parents and their children at a loss to find the enriching and diverse material once so easy to spot and purchase.

. . . .

The memo sent by Hecky to Goddard Lieberson and others at Columbia was his last gasp on the sinking ship of the children's record market. Hecky and Leo Israel, through Reynard Publications, assured their part in royalties gleaned from their writing for Captain Kangaroo. This was a market that could be counted on. Rock 'n' roll did not include preschool children, and Keeshan's very young viewers were increasing in number, particularly as the population of the children known as "baby boomers" grew. *Billboard* wrote about Reynard, "Like the Kangaroo songs, material is being developed specifically for children's TV shows, utilizing the educational approach and with song-folio publications scheduled to follow each production. . . . Material will be offered as individual projects to attempt to stimulate the diskeries interest in children's disks, which has been declining steadily."

Columbia, still holding on and trusting Hecky as their captain, allowed him to proceed with several of the suggestions in the memo. Goddard Lieberson, who prided himself on Columbia's lead in the field of classical music and children's fare, was no more pleased with the turn of the tides than was Hecky. Hecky was to go ahead with the line of 12-inch LPs he'd successfully launched the past winter, namely the musical productions of the *Just So Stories,* a set of *French Children's Songs,* and several remastered versions of *Treasure Island* and *Robin Hood* narrated by Basil Rathbone. Also to be released would be albums with Errol Flynn narrating *Oliver Twist* and *The Three Musketeers.* Four western adventure stories were part of the package, as were Frankie Laine's recent recordings of a shortened version of Melville's *Moby Dick* and other adventures at sea. Captain Kangaroo songs and items would be part of the big marketing push along with a Columbia innovation, to be released in September, the Record-A-View gimmick, which combined a disk with a Viewmaster kit. Eight sets of these were to be released with artists including Rosemary Clooney, Art Carney, Eddie Bracken, Garry Moore, and the *Let's Take a Trip* cast. The Silver Burdett *Music for Living* series, containing 60 disks, would also be out by the end of the year.

The sale of recordings for children rose from 2,000,000 in 1941 to more than 30,000,000 by the early '50s. Some half-dozen new companies entered the children's record field in the first six months of 1947 alone. By 1954, songs like "Rock Around the Clock" held the big numbers with sales like 20,000,000, for just one song. (Of note, by the year 2000, 13,040 children's CDs had been sold versus 6,222,894 in the pop/rock genre.)

. . . .

In spite of big ads and a push in the trade papers in August, September sales of children's records reached an all-time low. My father grew increasingly upset. Though over the years he had suffered bouts with Crohn's and had to be hospitalized for treatments for a few days at a time, now, due to stress, his painful battle with the disease increased. My mother had been admonishing him frequently to calm down. "Your gut has been acting up almost daily, honey. Getting sick is not worth it. Life works out. We'll find a way through this. It's another chapter in the book of life. Now calm down."

"I just can't bring myself to believe what is happening. How can a whole nation care so little about its youth? The media should refine and elevate the musical tastes of young people. What you give them is what they get—and what they become. Money, money, money—it always comes before quality of human life. Between the growing obsession with television and the decline in the refinement of music, you will see for sure that in the future schools are going to have one major problem teaching kids to read."

"You are probably right," my mother agreed, "but the problem we must face is what *you* are going to do now."

"We have some savings, but where am I to go? Goddard talked to me about heading a rock 'n' roll department. He said the children's releases could come out of this new department. The sale of rock 'n' roll would balance the potential losses of the children's material, and, hopefully, with time, when parents realize the damage that has been done to their children, they will return to wanting quality material. Then we'll be in the position to get things rolling again—you know, that old swinging pendulum."

"What did you tell him?"

"I told him I'd be glad to help out in the classical music field. I think there are still enough people not swept up by rock 'n' roll to buy classical—that maybe we could release children's material from that department. For heaven's sake, even Mitch Miller won't get involved with rock 'n' roll because you can't without payola, the kind of payola that would have the Feds investigating and checking the Columbia books constantly. What is Goddard thinking? That Columbia can remain creative and pristine engaging in this new music?"

"Did he consider your request?"

"He said an outright, 'No!' He told me that he can handle the classical department as he has done successfully. He told me, 'In spite of your classical background and knowledge, Hecky, you aren't needed in the classical department. Like it or not—and I don't like it either—rock 'n' roll is the future.' *That's* what he told me!"

"So what will you do?"

"We have savings, but not much, and we can't afford to totally deplete our money in the bank. What if one of us gets sick? That is a very real possibility. Judy isn't far from college age. What will we do about her college education?"

"What about working for independent companies? Honey, a lot of independent producers are suddenly sprouting up and making good money. You can write for adults as well as children. Pop music hasn't gone out of the world completely. Its sales have dropped because now it's only considered music for adults. There are still plenty of adults. Rosie and Sinatra aren't going to just fade from the picture."

"I have it in mind to take Columbia or Johnny Marks to court to collect money I deserve for 'Rudolph.'"

"And what do you think you'll accomplish?"

"When a judge hears the full story, I think he will say, company employee or not, contract or not, this man deserves more than he's received. Now he has to search for new employment in a fast-changing world. Reward him for this accomplishment."

"I don't know. I don't like the idea of pursuing a lawsuit. You never know what bridges will be burned in doing so."

"HUHNEY, you never change—always worried about the other's side, fearing to antagonize. My career in the children's field may be ending, and you are thinking about burning bridges?"

A couple of weeks later, at the end of September 1956, my father came home and announced, "I am leaving Columbia. I don't have to hear it one more time to see the writing on the wall. Goddard asked me again to head the rock 'n' roll department and, under its umbrella, continue with children's music—and this, with a slight increase in salary and basically the same contract I have now, meaning Columbia owns everything, even if I write it. How many pseudonyms can one man have just to collect royalties? What if I produce a 'Rock Around the Clock'? Will it be another 'Rudolph,' another 'Frosty'—all for the company, all for the artist, none for me? It would be so easy to just say yes, to just stay put, to spread my wings and fly forward with Alan Freed. I wish I could. I wish I could close my mind and heart to all I believe in. But I can't! I don't understand rock 'n' roll. I don't have the heart—or the stomach—for it. What instincts could I follow to pick the songs when my heart and mind would be saying I don't want my own daughters to hear this? After the intelligence and refinement of Dinah Shore, Paul Tripp, Rosie, Gene, Josef and Miranda, even Carney, how could I work with the people recording this music? I don't want to be around their drugs and booze and wonder who's going to collapse in the studio, not show up at all, or become violent and smash the piano. I could not live with myself playing a part in the decline of teenagers, ethics, morals, and music."

That night, my father stayed up late. I heard the typewriter keys clicking away as he typed his letter of resignation. As I lay in bed, I stared at the ceiling and felt as though our lives were experiencing an earthquake. For years my father had been busy, happy, creative, and doing what he loved to do. Our home rang with the sounds of songs and stories in the making and with constant descriptions, told with excitement and satisfaction, of this recording and that, this project and that. Would my father still sit at the piano and call me to his side, "Juddie come hear this?" Would he come home each summer from L.A. with gifts for me, like the bizarre pogo cello with its all-inclusive percussion sounds and with Lulu Bird, the blue parakeet he bought for me at the farmer's market? Would celebrities still come to our house, and would we go to parties at theirs? Would Karen and I still record? Was my charmed childhood coming to an end?

Before rock 'n' roll hit the scene, I dreamed of Karen and me forever together, sharing microphones and stages. I saw the advantages we'd have getting heard and hired with all of my father's contacts. I felt like the child of a movie star with access to the Hollywood studios and an assured career if talent matched contact. In addition to singing with Karen, I wanted to be in Broadway musicals. My childhood to date was spent taking lessons in dance, drama, musical instruments, and, most recently (at the bidding of Jerry Silverman, my guitar and banjo teacher), voice lessons. What would happen now? Would I ever be in a recording studio again? I lay there detesting Elvis and this new music as much as my father did.

I finally fell into a fitful sleep to the sound of my father's voice as he momentarily stopped tapping the typewriter long enough to say to my mother, "HUHney. I will not change my mind. Even Tom Glazer has been complaining that he used to perform for audiences from age three on up through teenagers and their parents. Now his market has become only the two- to five-year-olds. Tom Glazer—can you believe it—a has-been for children over the age of five! Rock 'n' roll is robbing children of their childhood." The typewriter resumed clicking.

On October 8, 1956, Goddard Lieberson wrote to Hecky,

Naturally, we were all very sad at the sudden turn of affairs in the Children's Department and for your resignation of October 15. However, I know that it goes without saying that you understand that you have all our best wishes and enthusiastic good luck for your new venture in the music-publishing business. You will undoubtedly end up the richest man in the business next to the Aberbachs! I sincerely hope that will be the case.

Best wishes,

As always,

Goddard

To "The Organization" on October 10, announcing Hecky's resignation, Lieberson wrote, ". . . During the years Hecky has been with us, he made a very valuable contribution to the growth of Columbia Records. He established the Columbia Children's Catalog as the leader in its field, and was responsible for many hit records including one of the all-time best sellers, 'Rudolph The Red-Nosed Reindeer.'. . ."

Prior to these announcements, Hecky had sent personal letters telling of his resignation to Gene Autry, Rosemary Clooney, Burl Ives, and others with whom he'd worked so closely and for so long while also establishing cherished friendships. Gene Autry wrote,

Naturally, I am terribly sorry to see you leave Columbia. But after all, it might be a far better opportunity for you if you go on your own. I wish you all the luck and success in the world. If there is anything I can do, don't hesitate to call me.

Will be in touch with you the next time I'm in New York. Very best wishes and kindest personal regards to you and the family.

Most sincerely,

Gene

Prior to presenting Goddard Lieberson with his letter of resignation, my father had interviews with others in the music business. He and my mother discussed where he might best carry on the kind of work he was doing and where he could earn more money for his talent and effort. Music publishing seemed the area, for publishers, too, earned their fortunes through hit songs. As a publisher, he could still compose and earn royalties as a composer as well as from publishing what he wrote and the music others wrote. He'd be free to work as an independent producer, a new term that, thanks to rock 'n' roll, had sprung up in the business. The job he found was in joining the already established Sam Fox Publishing Company where Reynard, in which he and Leo Israel published their collaborations, was an affiliate. Here he would create material for both the educational and pop markets as well as handle record production. Reynard's plans included production of its own disks for the educational market and supplying material for the major labels.

Writing about his resignation from Columbia, the trade papers commented how "Krasnow was a long important figure in the field of children's records," and that he "produced several of the all-time best-selling children's records." They listed the songs he'd produced including "Rudolph," "Frosty," "Me and My Teddy Bear," "Little White Duck," and a long list of others. They spoke of the artists he hired to sing the songs mentioning Gene Autry, Rosemary Clooney, Burl Ives, Frankie Laine, Arthur Godfrey, Lu Ann Simms, and Dinah Shore. They spoke of the major disk series "conceived and executed by Krasnow": two tie-in Silver Burdett deals, the Introduction to the Masterworks, Masters, and Instruments series, and many more. They announced that he would now enter the music publishing field and concentrate on the development of educational and children's material on independent record production.

Captain Kangaroo's contract with Columbia still had another year to run. Hecky remained his recording producer and continued to compose, direct, and produce the recording sessions with the Captain in the Columbia studios. Karen and I continued our backup singing for the Captain. Likewise, the Silver Burdett series needed completion, and Hecky was in the studio to produce these recordings, still hiring Karen and me as the child singers. Things seemed relatively normal, except now, if we met my father at his office, we went to the Sam Fox Publishing Company, not the Columbia building.

Within three months of Hecky's leaving Columbia, the children's record department closed. Shortly after this, Gene Autry left Columbia along with many other artists, including Tony Bennett. Autry, who had for years been a successful Columbia artist in the country-western field and who had recorded Columbia's all-time biggest-selling single on the Columbia label, namely "Rudolph," was now viewed as an artist with a "lack of sales." Many other changes were taking place in the media. Even the low-budget films that were a staple for Autry were giving way to higher budget productions. Autry left CBS-TV and radio at the end of 1956. To quote Jon Guyot Smith, "Gene often said, he never quit show business . . . it quit him. He was a major star of low-budget films. By 1956, they ceased to exist. He sang western music. By 1956, it was virtually extinct. He made great records for children. By 1956, that market was devastated by rock 'n' roll. He continued to make personal appearances until 1961 and a final album in 1962, and then called it a day."

Hecky was not alone.

Royalty checks came in from songs Hecky had already written that were still played on television, radio, and in countries like France and Japan, songs like "Little Red Monkey" or holiday favorites like "Grandfather Kringle" or "Peter Cottontail." Fairly high sums arrived in the mail from the voluminous Captain Kangaroo material Leo Israel and Hecky had written and continued to create.

Hecky did go to court and sued Columbia and Johnny Marks for compensation for his role in the success of "Rudolph." The case was tricky, for under Hecky's contract with Columbia at the time, one could debate what could be construed as payola should he receive money for his role in the song. Just what might be construed as legitimate and what not? The presiding judge awarded the sum of $5,000 as a "parting bonus" for the fine work Hecky had accomplished at Columbia. This sum was far smaller than Hecky had hoped considering the huge amounts Columbia and Johnny Marks continued to earn each Christmas and would continue to receive in spite of rock 'n' roll.

However, the income Hecky now received was not paid every two weeks. Royalty checks came in quarterly from ASCAP. The sum for administrating the Reynard Catalog was minimal though regularly paid bimonthly. Composing and recording took time, and it was some months until a few tunes Hecky wrote were recorded and distributed. One, "Eighty-Eight Keys to Romance," was used by the Chanel No. 5

company for its perfume ad and brought in a fair sum as the commercial aired on television and radio. The financial ups and downs of such payments with a house and family to support and Steffi at college posed new problems for Hecky and Lillian.

A dear friend, Lillian Elkin, had taken a job working at the Mount Vernon Jewish Community Center. There she met a woman whose husband worked for the Manhattan Yellow Pages, run by the Reuben Donnelly Company. Reuben Donnelly sought a salesperson to go out in the field and acquire new accounts while maintaining already existing ones. The ad stated, "preferably a man, and, if a woman, she must be no older than 35." Lillian Elkin told my mother about the job.

My mother knew the record business was in great flux and that Hecky's dream of getting rich in publishing could take more time than he wished, if it came true at all. Lillian was fully aware that in a clearly defined position like the one he'd held at Columbia, Hecky's talents could soar. Within the children's field, he knew musically and creatively what would and wouldn't sell, from songs to record players to joint television/record deals. If he had any doubts, he could turn to the company's research department as he had done when working with Dinah Shore during their conflict over lullabies. With the support system Columbia provided as a big company, Hecky did not have to rely solely on his own business savvy (or lack thereof) to clinch business deals, and certainly not to market them. He could function relying primarily on his artistic savvy in which he excelled. However, now Hecky was in a very different situation, and Lillian didn't want to take any chances. Why not get a job before a possible setback? She had time on her hands with Steffi at college and me almost always at one lesson or another or playing with Karen and other friends.

Lillian applied for the Reuben Donnelly job. The ad had stated that Reuben Donnelly would train the person and that the candidates had to have people skills. Lillian certainly had those. As she put her resume together with the help of her confidante, Sherry Walsh, and her clever friend, Lillian Elkin, my mother began to see a whole new person in herself. She made it to the third and final interview where, perky as she looked, the man read each detail on her application and discovered that she was 47—an over-the-hill old lady in the year 1957!

"How dare you take up our time applying for this job? You are an old woman. You are 12 years over the age listed in the ad. The first rule in business is time equals money, and your interviews have cost Reuben Donnelly a lot of time, hence money. Goodbye!"

"Excuse me, sir. Had you not looked at my application, would you have thought that this petite, energetic, well-spoken woman sitting before you was over 35? Sir, it is my very maturity that makes me far better able to deal with people than a younger person. I have been around people of all sorts long enough to sense their idiosyncrasies and quirks, likes and dislikes, and much more. Hire me and I'll bet I can even get Cadillac to finally overcome its snobbishness and advertise with everyone else in the Yellow Pages."

Silence reigned as her interviewer stared at her. Then, "Sold American!" he answered. "No one has ever sat here and so convinced me that they were worthy of this job. Age or no, Mrs. Krasnow, you are hired!"

And thus, financial security entered our home again. Things changed. Hecky did not go into the office every day but often stayed home composing. He frequently picked Lillian up at the station, or else the two went into the city together, parked the car at the station, and drove home. My mother taught me how to make chicken and roast beef, and to broil steaks and lamb chops. Many a night, I was the family cook in between lessons and homework. Many a night, my father sat with my mother helping her with the layouts she had to prepare for her clients. He was meticulous on paper as his handwritten manuscripts displayed, resembling the work of a lithographer. My mother learned that her people skills made her a terrific salesperson. She made history by persuading Cadillac that not only the very wealthy, but others, too, might buy Cadillac cars if the company advertised where those other than the very well-to-do looked when desiring to make a purchase: namely, in the Yellow Pages. Cadillac decided to give it a try. Their sales increased tremendously. They remained a faithful client. At the end of 1957, Hecky and Lillian went sailing on a cruise to the Bahamas. My mother had come in as the top salesperson of the year. The cruise was her bonus.

CHAPTER 25

Gobbledegook

ecky and Leo Israel were in a heightened state of productivity. In addition to regularly creating material for Captain Kangaroo, they engaged in writing an album filled with zany characters, humorous words, and upbeat melodies to which one could get up and dance a polka, march, or square dance. Captain Kangaroo gave the tunes a lot of airplay. However, these absurd songs had broader appeal than simply for preschool youngsters.

The title song tells of a boy who finds a hole in the fence of his backyard. His parents tell him it was made by the Gobbledegook. The boy captures the Gobbledegook, who talks in language the same as his name. They become friends.

Sometimes when the moon is high
He hears him calling through the sky
He calls out high, he calls out low
Always in Gobbledegook, you know.

Another tune, "Ump Diddle, Diddle," is about a community band that can only play one tune: *Ump Diddle, Diddle, Diddle-Day*. The mayor and townspeople beg them to stop. The dogs bark, cows walk by and sing moo, sheep lend their baa, chickens their clucks, until all the town's creatures create a varied and endless song loved by townsfolk and mayor alike.

Another song, "The Laughing Giraffe," asks,

> Do, do, do you know what has happened at the zoo,
> Happened at the zoo, happened at the zoo?
> The giraffe is laughing, yes, what I say is true!
> Said the camel to the bison, "This is really quite surprising."
> Said the leopard to the llama, "He'll be quiet when he's calm-a."
> Said the zebra to the rabbit, "Looks like it's become a habit."
> Yes, the giraffe is laughing at the zoo.
> You laughed at him and now he laughs at you.

Hilarious laughter at the end makes it difficult not to burst into giggles too.

Amid Elvis, Bill Haley and The Comets, Chuck Berry, Little Richard, and others adding to the growing list of rock 'n' rollers, the *Gobbledegook* album rose to the top of the trade paper charts as a great buy for "kids of all ages and their parents and grandparents too." Perhaps part of its success lay in its singer: Stanley Holloway, fresh from playing Alfred P. Doolittle, father to Julie Andrews's Eliza in the smash Broadway musical *My Fair Lady*. With his clipped British accent making the inane words he sang sound pompous and important, the intended hilarity worked well. Hecky's royalties flowed in.

. . . .

A new record label, Colpix, was established in the late 1950s and was the first recording company for Columbia Pictures-Screen Gems. Colpix never quite defined its genre in the changing market and released records in a variety of areas from folk to jazz, classical to documentary, and, of course, rock and pop rock. Artists who recorded on Colpix included James Darren and the Marcels. The latter recorded one of the label's *Billboard* Hot 100 Singles, "Blue Moon." An artist costarring on *The Donna Reed Show*, Shelley Fabares, added another hit with "Johnny Angel" in the spring of 1962. In this year, Colpix also produced soundtracks for Hanna-Barbera cartoons, and later, under the name of

Colgems Records, would produce the smash hit group, The Monkees, who'd ride high for four years and then become extinct.

In 1958, Hecky began working with Colpix as an independent producer. In their publicity about new releases, Colpix wrote of Hecky, "To the producer of an LP album falls the responsibility of the final music selection, the engaging of an arranger and the general guidance of the technical and artistic elements that go to make up a best seller. Hecky Krasnow was the natural selection by reason of his background, temperament and skill."

Hecky's initial projects were *Two Pianos in Stereo* and an audio documentary, *Nautilus*. *Two Pianos* combined two goals: one, to be a pleasing listening experience that would bring a family or group of friends together in front of twin speakers time and again, and two, offer a demonstration of range, a variety of musical experiences, and a "perfect marriage of electronic and aesthetic values." As Roger Caras, author, television host, newscaster, and early animal rights activist wrote about the series, "In the era of music to dance to, music to drink to, music to eat to—here, certainly, is music to listen to—here are TWO PIANOS IN STEREO."

With its fine musicianship, this project appealed to Hecky's trained musical tastes. It included widely loved pieces such as "Pavanne," "Hawaiian War Chant," "Song of India," and "Malaguena."

Nautilus was an exciting documentary about the first atomic submarine. In addition to the information about this new invention, which transformed Jules Verne's futuristic fantasy novel *Twenty Thousand Leagues Under the Sea* into reality, the album included actual sounds of the Nautilus mission sailing under the North Pole.

With these two projects, and *Nautilus* receiving acclaim from many organizations and much publicity, earning the recording the title of "renowned documentary," it appeared that records of quality were succeeding in spite of rock 'n' roll.

· · · · · · · · · · ·

Hecky's fine reputation followed him in his new position as an independent producer and publisher. Apparently this reputation included

Karen's and mine as backup singers for celebrities and as performers for the UN family Christmas party, which had become an annual gig. Hecky received a call from a television program that had swept the nation in 1955 and was still airing in 1958. It was called *The $64,000 Question.* Contestants on the show chose a category, such as classical music, boxing, Abraham Lincoln, or WWI, from a category board the whole audience could see. If the contestants correctly answered questions in the chosen category, money earned for each correct answer doubled. The questions became progressively more difficult. If a contestant reached a sum of $4,000, that contestant would return each week and answer only one question. Those playing the game had the choice to quit at any time and take the money won to date. The decision was a difficult one, for until they reached a sum of $8,000, they were eliminated without winning anything if they missed an answer. If they reached the sum of $8,000 and then answered a question incorrectly, they could not continue, and did not go home with $8,000, but instead received a Cadillac. If they achieved the $8,000 level by answering all questions correctly, the contestants then stood in an isolation booth where they could hear absolutely nothing except the words of Hal March, the host of the program. Several of those contestants who reached the prized goal of $64,000 became overnight celebrities. Dr. Joyce Brothers, at age 27, was one of these. With a near-new doctorate and small private practice, her overnight celebrity status caused people to regard her as an expert. Her psychological advice was offered in newspaper columns and TV shows for the following 40 years.

The show spawned not only overnight celebrities, but also other quiz shows. The saying, "That's the $64,000 question," was added to American jargon, and some hilarious parodies brought great laughter to television viewers—for example, comedians Bob and Ray with their "That's the 64-cent question," and Ed Norton on *The Honeymooners* commenting that there are three times in a man's life when he wants to be alone, the third of these being "when he's in the isolation booth of *The $64,000 Question.*"

The program's producers, Steve Carlin and Joe Cates, wanted two bright, poised, and talented children to appear on the show together working as a team to answer the questions. They requested that Karen and I come for an interview. Hecky set up the appointment for us. Helen drove us into the city, and Hecky met us at the producers' offices. Carlin and Cates took us to a room for the interview, a room that looked and felt more like an interrogation room in a crime movie. As we entered, the odor of at least 50 years of stale tobacco seeped into my nose and I could taste it in my mouth. The walls were drab yellow with dark wood molding where the ceiling and walls met. A few black office chairs stood in random corners. A scratched and chipped desk rested near the room's one window opposite the entrance door and appeared to be virtually unused with not a pad or pen upon it. One brown, grainy wood table lay at the side of the room perpendicular to the desk and looked like it came from the courtroom set of a Perry Mason episode.

Carlin and Cates wore a brown suit and a gray one, respectively, and looked like Mafia. From the moment we entered the room I felt uncomfortable. I relaxed a little when they asked questions of Karen and me about our music, our childhood together, school, and hobbies. However, when the two men talked about the facts of the show itself and what would be expected of us, I felt ill at ease.

"What categories do the two of you like, and feel competent in?"

"Geometry," Karen answered.

"The history of America in folk songs," I answered, having recently completed a term paper for social studies on this topic.

"Hmmm," Mr. Carlin answered. "Audiences love kids who know their math and social studies. Just what do you know about geometry, Karen?"

"I know all about angles, lines, planes, circumferences, parallel lines, and calculations, you know, the stuff we learn in class."

"Do you know any of the history of geometry, about Euclid and the Hellenes of Ancient Greece?" Carlin continued.

"A little. Our teacher gave us some history of how the study of geometry began."

"And you, Judith—should I call you Judith or Judy? . . ."

"Judy is fine."

"Okay, Judy," now Mr. Cato spoke. "Could you, too, answer some questions about geometry?"

I was doing okay in the geometry class but knew after this school year, mathematics would not be included in my list of study choices. "I do know something about Ancient Greece and the Hellenes," I answered. "Could Karen answer the geometry questions and leave the history part to me?"

"We could arrange that. When you work as a team, an answer from one is as good as an answer from the other," Mr. Cato responded. "Judy, you say you know a lot about American history through the folk songs you sing. Can you give me an example? Though that is certainly not on the category board, Revlon, our sponsor, has deemed it okay for us to add new categories, even at the very last minute if one of our favored contestants wishes that category."

Red lights flashed for Hecky and Helen. Perhaps Messieurs Cato and Carlin didn't notice, but I could read my father and aunt's faces. My initial feelings of discomfort leapt forward to a nine on a scale from one to ten. Cato continued.

"Tell me what songs you know that reflect the history of the American Revolution?"

"'Revolutionary Tea,' 'Johnny Has Gone for a Soldier,' 'Yankee Doodle,' 'Paul Revere's Ride,' . . .'"

"You know many. That could be a category. And what about you, Karen?"

"Well, I sing with Judy. We both know the same songs."

"That should be the category—Folk Songs of the American Revolution. It makes sense. After all, your singing together is why we invited you to begin with." Both Carlin and Cato looked at copies of a resume that my father had prepared for them. Mr. Carlin spoke. "Hmmm, I see you two sing international songs. Perhaps we could focus on songs from countries around the world."

"We know many specific songs, but I'm not sure we could answer questions about ones we don't know," I told them. "What happens if we can't answer a question?"

"Don't worry," Mr. Cato replied. "Listen to what we are doing right here in this room." At the mention of "this room" my hairs stood on end. "We will decide the category here and now, today, right here in *this room*. You will know if we do international songs or folk songs from the American Revolution. We'll discuss the songs and any other questions that might possibly arise about them. You and Karen have good memories. You won't forget the titles and things we discuss here, and we will be writing all this down."

Something didn't feel right. When the contract was handed to Hecky and Helen at the end of the session, they chose to take it home, look over every detail, and mail it back. We would appear in approximately two months, so there was time to review the contract.

Mr. Carlin and Mr. Cato insisted, "I can't imagine why you wouldn't sign. Look at all the money these two girls can win—that's $32,000 each. They can go to college and each buy their own houses."

The contract was never signed. Helen and Hecky were now convinced that the show was rigged, if not overtly by supplying answers directly to contestants, then behind the scenes. If the meeting we'd had was any indication, there'd been many such meetings in which categories were concocted in accordance with the contestant's knowledge and fully discussed ahead of time, at least with those contestants the producers thought the audience would love: in the case of Karen and me, two young kids with talent who'd already sung with famous artists.

Our instincts served us well, for less than two months after this interview the scandals of television quiz shows came to light as contestants revealed true stories of their appearances. The biggest culprit was the program *Twenty-One* and runner-up, *Dotto*. *The $64,000 Question*, when investigated by the federal government, was not cited in particular for supplying answers to its contestants. However, Charles Revson, head of Revlon, the program's sponsor, was suspected of attempts to bump other quiz shows' contestants whom audiences might like too much and who would detract from *The $64,000 Question* as well as contestants on *The $64,000 Question* that the audience might not find as appealing as others. It was simple to do. Categories were changed, added, or subtracted at the last moment. Likewise, questions kept secure in a bank vault might be altered at the last minute. It also came to light that for contestants with appeal, pre-air screenings in which the category and questions were discussed at length were common practice. Quiz shows abruptly ended with President Eisenhower telling the nation that laws were to be passed preventing the public from ever being so duped and lied to again.

. . . .

In 1958, the name Harry Belafonte was well established and brought to mind calypso rhythms, folk songs, an extremely handsome singer from the West Indies, the "Banana Boat Song," and an outspoken artist for black America and peace. In spite of the McCarthy era and blacklisting, the Weavers with Pete Seeger, Ronnie Gilbert, Lee Hayes, and Fred Hellerman had made a comeback and performed to sellout audiences at venues like Carnegie Hall. Other groups such as the Gateway Singers and the Tarriers offered the listening public the opportunity to enjoy folk-oriented music. In Greenwich Village each Sunday, the famous arch in Washington Square Park drew crowds with guitars, mandolins, banjos, and tambourines to sing the songs of the people. In the Village, places like the Village Vanguard, Village Gate, Bitter End, Gerde's Folk City, and Café Wha? were venues for folk and jazz performers and hangouts for artists, poets, and musicians. Izzy Young's Folklore Center at 110 MacDougal Street, filled with records, books, and all sorts of instruments, served as a gathering place for those into the folk music scene. The beat generation was in full swing with poets like Allen Ginsberg reading to audiences in dimly lit cafes often set up in basements of buildings where the scent of marijuana wasn't as detectable as on the main floor with its open windows. Writers Jack Kerouac and William S. Burroughs gave vent to those with more curiosity and intellect than the rock 'n' roll culture provided, allowing this contingent of the population, in their own way, to ride the waves of change and rebel against the momentary peace and suburban dream following WWII. This counterculture had a large following, not only in Greenwich Village, but in cities like San Francisco, Chicago, Boston, and Seattle.

In 1958, inspired by the Weavers, Belafonte, The Gateway Singers, and the Tarriers, three young men from Palo Alto, California, Bob Shane, Nick Reynolds, and Dave Guard formed a singing group called The Kingston Trio. Their harmonies and upbeat sound brought the folk music counterculture into the mainstream once again as songs in 1950 like Mitch Miller's "Tzena" and the Weavers' "Goodnight Irene" had done before McCarthyism silenced them. The Kingston Trio's "Tom Dooley" resulted in a gold record as it told the story of a man who murdered his fiancée and was "bound to die." The song was based on an actual murder written as a poem by a local North Carolina poet, Thomas C. Land. The song brought accolades to the trio as they won the first Grammy Award for Best Country and Western Performance in 1959, and a year later, the first Grammy Award for Best Ethnic or Traditional Folk Recording for their album *The Kingston Trio at Large*. Along with rock 'n' roll, folk music—rebellious by its very definition ("songs of the people")— aired across the nation. The trio's hit ushered in the beginnings of a folk era in a time when the momentary peace following war rumbled with the beginnings of the civil rights movement and the era of flower children who would come to be known as the hippie generation.

Karen and I often hung out in the Village on weekends together or with friends. I'd carry my guitar and we'd go into cafes and sing a few songs for which we'd get free cappuccinos, a pastry, and tips. We hung out at Izzy Young's, where I purchased many folk music books and drooled over guitars and banjos for sale. For the past few summers we'd been going to Bucks Rock Work Camp. The camp was a non-traditional one where sports were offered. However, the emphasis was on activities in the arts. A camper could make up his or her own schedule rather than constantly being part of group activities. The choices included drama, dance, folk singing, orchestra, and chorus, as well as the opportunities to work in an actual print shop where all the steps that go into the production of the written word could be learned and practiced, and to work on an animal and vegetable farm, where campers got a taste of agriculture.

Steffi, who had just graduated from Sarah Lawrence and, come September, would spend a year in Israel through a scholarship she'd won with a group of select students from various states, worked as a counselor in the Girls House, the quarters for teenage girls. Among her campers was a 15-year-old girl named Erica who used to leave her room at midnight and dance to the moon. Talk around camp had it that she would either grow up insane or become highly successful in some artistic field. Eventually, the latter would be her fate as Erica Jong became a best-selling author.

It was the end of the summer season of 1958. The Bucks Rock annual festival took place in which campers in all the activities displayed their accomplishments of the summer. Karen and I performed as the two female folk singers in the Bucks Rock Folk Quartet. The two males, Barry Kornfeld and Paul Prestopino, would in later years play their banjos, guitars, mandolins, slide guitars, and dobros for the likes of Peter, Paul & Mary, The New Lost City Ramblers, Bob Dylan, and others. Barry would also teach songwriting and guitar at Paul Simon's music school in New York City.

My parents had come, as did most everyone's, to spend the weekend at the festival and to see the accomplishments of their children. Now they would hear the quartet. We sang songs like "Rock About My Saro Jane," "Kumbaya," and "Tom Dooley," which we'd been singing for years in folk circles before The Kingston Trio rendered their gold record version. The concert went well. When it was over, my father said he wanted to work with us when we all returned back to New York, and in the case of Paul, to New Jersey. He thought, with folk music on the horizon, that an audition with Colpix might land us an album, possibly a contract, and he would produce us.

Barry and Paul liked the idea, and once we were all home, we began rehearsals. My father wanted to combine the general folk music and Americana with some of the international material Karen and I sang. The name we selected for ourselves was The Golliards, a name given to wandering French poet minstrels of medieval times. I played rhythm guitar. Barry supplied lead guitar and also picked on the banjo. Paul, a master on five-string banjo and mandolin, played these. Karen played accent instruments. Helen and my father together coached us on gestures and dialogue. The audition date at Colpix was set for right before Christmas, and we had nearly eight more weeks to practice.

We were well prepared when the day arrived, but unfortunately, I was ill. Laryngitis ruled me now like a mean tyrant. No matter what I tried—

teas and honeys, throat sprays, silence, bed rest—my usually booming voice sounded like a train without wheels squealing along the tracks. "Can't you explain and change the audition date?" I croaked to my father.

"No, certainly not after it's been set up months in advance," he replied with a tinge of annoyance in his well-functioning voice. "Don't worry. In this business they understand such things. What they will look for is stage presence, appearance, quality professional instrumentation, and well-done harmonies. If your voice isn't heard, they will certainly hear Karen, Barry, and Paul's. A "yes" will depend most on whether they think the genre and material will sell."

Our audition took place in a cramped office, and the Colpix A&R man seemed hurried. I got the feeling he was doing this more as a favor to Hecky than to really listen to what we had to offer, as though he'd already made up his mind that folk music was not the future.

We apologized for my laryngitis and explained how we understood how very valuable his time was, hence would not have considered canceling. We sang four numbers, mostly with three voices. However, with our fine instrumentation, upbeat tunes, one slow ballad, and rehearsed gestures, we projected as though we were before the large audiences The Kingston Trio now performed for. In spite of my missing voice, we all knew we'd done well.

"I'll get back to you," Mr. A&R said, and he did.

Dear Hecky and The Golliards,
Thank you for the engaging performance on December 10. It is evident that the group has tremendous talent. However, at this time, it is my belief and that of others at Colpix that despite the unique success of The Kingston Trio, another folk music group would have a hard road ahead competing with the Kingston Trio phenomena, for that's what we feel it is—a one-shot fluke that took on. Please feel free to contact us again if this genre of music continues to spread and grow in the changing pop music world of this moment.

Yours Truly . . .

Needless to say, we were all very disappointed.

Karen's and my spirits were at least momentarily uplifted at the thought that come Christmas this year, we would jointly celebrate our Sweet 16 birthdays, Karen's having occurred in October and mine on December 8. We had both spent a summer at a place called Fellowship Farm in Milford, Pennsylvania, as part of the American Jewish Society for Service's camp. At Fellowship Farm, with students from countries around the world, we'd helped repair a barn. Here we made many friends, several of whom remained in the country as college students. They were coming from Pennsylvania to spend Christmas and celebrate our rite of passage. The party was wonderful. The two boys from Sierra Leone brought their drums and played magnificent African rhythms. We played folk dances from my large record collection, and in our small living room, danced Greek, Iranian, English, Israeli, Russian, and Arabic dances we'd learned at Fellowship Farm. I was happy to partner with Mohammed Latif, a magnificent folk dancer whose heart mutually fluttered with mine the entire summer we'd spent together, constrained only by the fact that he was betrothed to a woman in his native land of Iraq. Everyone slept over as, between our house and Helen's, there was plenty of room to camp in sleeping bags.

The next morning, we awoke to find swastikas with the words "Kike" and "Nigger Lovers" painted on our dining room and kitchen windows. The police were summoned, then Hecky, Lillian, and Helen led the discussions on prejudice, lack of understanding, and fear, and how all of us at this party were an example of how people can get along and must work together to do so. Apparently, though we'd solved much religious prejudice and friction several years ago by inviting our Christian friends to a Seder, which they loved, and Karen and I had agreed to attend a service at both the Protestant and Catholic churches to see what they were like, there were others whose actions were still prompted by fear, hate, and misinformation. This was the North, but if the Ku Klux Klan wasn't banned here, they wouldn't have had much trouble finding recruits to carry out their attacks.

The party ended. We said our goodbyes, and our foreign friends of rainbow colors sent letters of praise to our parents and us for a good time and for our open minds amidst the threats of closed ones.

My thoughts returned to The Golliards, and I hoped we'd have an opportunity to audition for Colpix again and include some folk songs about love and peace. Maybe some other record company would be interested, as Hecky continued to make new contacts with more independent labels forming.

. . . .

My hopes had an unexpected enemy who launched a surprise attack. After the party, Helen got the notion that Karen should become the academic that Helen always wanted to be. Perhaps it was the revelation that Karen had suggested geometry as a category in *The $64,000 Question* interview. Perhaps it was the refusal at Colpix. Whatever her motive, virtually overnight, all the things Helen had always told me she loved about me—my outgoing personality, my organizational abilities, my enthusiasm, my warmth, my talent—somehow transformed for her into negative traits. Angrily she let my mother and father know in no uncertain terms that, "Judy is a deterrent to Karen." To me she gave the message, "You overshadow Karen with your aggressiveness," the term she now applied to *outgoing*. *Organizational abilities* became, "Because you are taller and larger in general, people think you are the boss." *Enthusiasm* was now described as the "total inability to differentiate between reality and fantasy." *Warmth* transformed to, "You exacerbate Karen's shy nature with your talkativeness." *Talent* now classified as, "People think you have the talent in the duo because you play the guitar." I was completely baffled, hurt, angry, and depressed.

"HUHNEY, we've got to move!" My mother felt desperate. "I won't let your sister destroy our daughter," she said emphatically to my father. But she knew moving was an impossibility at the moment. Steffi had written from Israel that she missed Gerry terribly and thought she might marry him upon coming home. Lillian felt almost without doubt, and certainly with great hope, that there would be a wedding to finance when Steffi returned and this with my college years soon coming up.

The situation felt like Helen's divorce from Phil, only this time, she couldn't give Hecky an ultimatum of "it's either me or your daughter." Hecky had been like a father to Karen all those years. He felt like he was losing a daughter. We now lived estranged in our three-family house, talking only when absolutely necessary. I'd walked to school with Karen nearly every day of our Yonkers's lives. Now no longer allowed to be my friend or spend any time with me, we'd walk on opposite sides of the street all the way up the long hills leading to Gorton High. There were no more sleepovers, no more rehearsals, and no more performances together. I threw myself more heavily into dance and traveled each day, except for Sunday, into Manhattan to study at the Graham School and the New Dance Group. For many months, I could not take my guitar out of its case.

Fortunately, my father continued to involve me in his work, whether it was as he sat at the piano composing, when he needed a backup singer for a Captain Kangaroo recording, or when he auditioned a new artist.

CHAPTER 26

A Singer Named Nina and a Trio Named Chad Mitchell

n 1958, word of a singer named Nina Simone spread across the nation as DJs followed the lead of a Philadelphia DJ named Sid Marx and aired Simone's version of the song "I Loves You Porgy." She'd recorded it for Bethlehem Records, ignorant of her contract, dreaming that an album would make her rich and famous overnight, leaving her without a care in the world. Bethlehem didn't follow up, and she wondered why they'd made the album to begin with. Sid Marx's airing of "Porgy" launched her into popular stardom she never dreamed of.

Born Eunice Waymon in Tyron, North Carolina, she was the sixth child in a family of seven. Her talent at the piano became evident when she was four years old. With the help of a family friend and her music teacher, the Eunice Waymon Fund was established so that she could continue piano studies. Ultimately, she went to Juilliard.

She changed her name to Nina (meaning "little one," which a Latino friend had called her) and Simone after French actress Simone Signoret. The name change seemed appropriate when she held her first performance gig in a dingy but musically inclined bar called the Midtown Bar and Grill on Pacific Avenue in Atlantic City.

Trained as a classical pianist, Nina never gave much thought to her voice and the sounds it might produce. When the proprietor of the Midtown Bar and Grill said she'd either sing while she played or leave, she tapped upon her heretofore unknown talent. Thus, she began a career that would leave a legacy of music and song that would earn her the name of the "High Priestess of Soul" and a reputation as an artist who combined classical music, jazz, folk, and protest into her own unique category that could only be called "Nina Simone." By the time of her death on April 21, 2003, she had earned an honorary doctorate in music and humanities as well as numerous other awards in various different countries. Dubbed a diva, in her death she is followed by the reputation as one of the last true griots to sing her songs and tell lasting stories through them.

When 1959 rolled around, Nina Simone's rendition of "Porgy" caused Joyce Selznick, cousin to film producer David O. Selznick, to want Simone to sign up for the Colpix Label for which Selznick was the Eastern talent scout. Simone was performing frequently at Art D'Lugoff's Village Gate. Colpix called upon Hecky to attend one of her performances and see what he thought. He, my mother, and I went to the Village on a Saturday night to hear this singer whose sultry voice and piano playing had people calling her the "Queen of the Village."

We were seated in the roomy but intimate place, which smelled of alcohol and tobacco that had seeped into every inch of wood, metal, and leather. We ordered drinks and snacks and waited with the rest of the audience for the program to begin. The lights finally dimmed and the blue and gold spotlights shone on the piano. A white ray of light guided Nina Simone to the small platform stage. She was tall and thin with short wavy hair framing her face. Her eyes struck me as the largest eyes I'd ever seen. The sparkles on her long, straight cocktail dress reflected the spotlight and the rays of light bounced onto her cheeks, illuminating her eyes, made even larger by thick eyeliner. She looked like an Egyptian princess painted upon papyrus. A mysterious darkness surrounded her, magnified by those huge eyes, which seemed to hold a secret of some deep, undefined sorrow.

She briefly introduced herself, then sat at the piano and began to play. Her fingers were quickly warmed up and the sounds made by them filled the air with electricity. When she opened her mouth and sang, a rich, slightly husky sound poured out. It sent shivers up and down my spine. She deftly went from one song and piano interlude to another, the rich sound always there, the huskiness giving way to a smoother sound, highs, lows, loud and soft, as though her soul were talking through the music with each and every nuance of emotion her words expressed. When she sang "Porgy," I saw a tear roll down my father's cheek. At the end of the program, the audience applauded madly, and Nina Simone returned for four encores.

Afterwards, we went to her dressing room. The energy from her performance still electrified her, and she was gracious and excited to discuss the possibility of a contract with Colpix. Hecky said he fully intended to insist they sign her on and praised her obvious knowledge and facility as a classical player. "Your music is fascinating, Miss Simone. The way you blend the sound of Bach with improvisation, jazz riffs, even the folk-style songs you sang is totally intriguing. You keep the audience on their toes not knowing what sounds they will hear next."

"I just play as it comes to me. The music tells me what to do, prompted by the emotion it inspires."

Hecky, Lillian, and Nina Simone got into a conversation about Juilliard, and Hecky told of his childhood as a violin prodigy. All three shared their appreciation of various composers.

"Bach has always been my favorite," Nina commented. "Johann Sebastian finds his way into my fingers when I least expect him to. All those fugues make great jazz points and counterpoints."

"Bach is my favorite too," I now found something that Nina Simone and I definitely shared in common. "Practicing Bach for me is never practicing. It always feels like a walk in the woods seeing more and more interesting things with each step of the way."

"What an interesting way of looking at Bach, Judy. But that is what playing jazz feels like. Thanks for such a good description."

The evening ended with Hecky telling Nina Simone that if she and Colpix agreed, he would be most interested in producing her first album. "I like you, Mr. Krasnow—Hecky—what an interesting name. How did you come by that?"

My father told of his childhood mischief and the name it resulted in.

"I think we'd work well together, Hecky," Nina smiled and shook his hand.

The deal came through, and Nina Simone was signed to Colpix. Hecky produced the album entitled, *The Amazing Nina Simone*. Nina commented, "If I had to be called something it should have been a folk singer because there was more folk and blues than jazz in my playing."

Hecky chose both jazz and folk material that, having heard Nina, he thought she would enjoy. Together, they decided the final selections. They joined forces in writing some adaptations. Hecky suggested Bob Mersey for the arranger. He'd known him from Columbia where Mersey was staff arranger and composer. He served this role for CBS-TV too. Nina agreed. The album included the songs "Blue Prelude," "Children Go Where I Send You," "Tomorrow (We Will Meet Once More)"— written by Hecky and my guitar teacher Jerry Silverman—"Stompin' at the Savoy," "It Might As Well Be Spring," "You've Been Gone Too Long," "That's Him Over There," "Chilly Winds Don't Blow," "Theme from 'Middle of the Night,'" "Can't Get Out of This Mood," "Willow Weep for Me," and "Solitaire."

. . . .

Hecky had expanded his publishing realm, adding Kradar Music with collaborator Joe Darion. The two had written some songs at Columbia and Hecky continued to compose music for Joe's clever lyrics. They were presently creating several prospective projects. Hecky also established his own company, Unicorn, the name inspired by a beautiful movie our family had seen, *A Kid for Two Farthings*. Perhaps the name would bring him luck as he still aimed to write, produce, and/or publish a big hit that would make him his millions. In this company, his joint works with Nina Simone were published. As they worked together, Nina Simone, like Rosie, felt Hecky was someone she could trust implicitly.

One night while performing in New York at Basin Street East, Nina met a man named Andy Stroud. He'd told her that he was a bank teller, but it turned out that he was a cop, a detective sergeant in New York's 26th Precinct. He'd been married three times. Apparently, he knew what women liked, at least during the courtship phase. Nina received flowers and expensive jewels. She'd heard from various people that Andy Stroud was not the kind of man one messed around with. Rumor had it that he'd once thrown a suspected criminal off of a rooftop in Harlem. Whenever this was mentioned, no one who knew Andy laughed or joked about the rumor.

Regarding her career, Nina longed for peace, safety, and routine. Often she became exhausted on tours and contrasted these with days, if possible, weeks of mindless rest. Nina admitted she desired someone who could protect her. She felt no one would dare do anything to her with Andy around. After all, he carried a gun. So, when he asked her to marry him, she said yes.

When she took Andy to meet her family, her father didn't take to him, feeling uncomfortable that the man had been married three times. He reminded Nina of this fact and warned her not to marry him. She tossed his wariness off to the fact that her father doted upon her. Andy and she remained engaged. During a trip to Philadelphia for a concert, Nina became extremely ill, fainted, and awoke in a hospital, where doctors told her she had either non-paralytic polio or spinal meningitis. Andy was there at her side. Since they had not been able to properly celebrate their engagement due to her illness, back in New York after she'd recovered, they went dancing in Harlem at a small club. Andy was not a big drinker, but on this night he began drinking rum and continued to do so, getting quieter as the evening wore on.

When they were leaving the club, a patron recognized Nina, and, as had happened many times to her before, slipped a note into her pocket. Andy observed this. It prompted an evening of battering. While hailing a taxi, he hit Nina. He hit her in the taxi, when they got out of it, again as they walked towards her building, in the lobby, in the elevator all the way up to the twentieth floor, and down the hallway. By the time they entered her apartment, she was bleeding. He pointed a gun at her head as he forced her to take out the stack of letters he knew she had from her Tyron, North Carolina childhood sweetheart. He grabbed the letters from her and tied her to a chair with her hands behind her back. He burned the letters as he proceeded to scream at her, accusing her of having all sorts of affairs. This abusive behavior continued for five hours. Then he took her off the chair and into the bedroom with her hands still tied behind her back. He forcibly had sex with her then passed out. Nina twisted the cord off of her hands and ran out.

It was still dark when our telephone rang. Frightened that something had happened to his mother, or Steffi in Israel, my father ran to the telephone. My mother jumped out of bed running after him. I followed.

"Calm down, Nina. . . . Take a deep breath. I can't understand what you are saying. . . . What? He beat you? . . . You can barely see? Both eyes are swollen? I think you should go to a hospital. . . . Okay, Okay. I'll come and get you. Where are you? . . . Wait—Honey, can you write this down? . . . The corner of 103rd . . . yes, yes, my car is a black-and-white Desoto. Are you safe where you are? A diner around the corner—okay, give me about one hour."

"What's going on, honey? Where are you going?"

"That was Nina Simone. Her boyfriend has beaten her to a pulp. She's afraid to call anyone he might know—he might track her down. She said I'm the only one she feels safe with."

"How very awful; how could anyone do that? But, honey, will you be safe in Manhattan at night—and after midnight too?"

"What can I do? I can't just leave her outside injured and frightened."

"I know. Let me come with you."

"No, honey, I don't think that's wise. If I had to defend myself plus two women, it would be impossible."

"I can help. I can keep an eye out for anyone trying to follow us while you concentrate on driving." I think my father wanted company. He'd never had to pick up a beaten woman in the middle of the night.

"Good point. Okay, hurry, we have to go. Juddie, you can help. Get out the linens and put them on the daybed in the dining room."

"Okay, Dad." I was baffled. Who would beat his girlfriend? The battered wife syndrome was still hidden under the carpet, not discussed out in the open, barely known about at all by the public.

I made up the daybed, put out some towels at the foot of it, and climbed back into bed unable to fall asleep. My parents returned when the sun was coming up. When I saw Nina I had to do everything in my power to stop staring. This intriguing woman, whose huge Egyptian-like eyes I'd gazed upon at the Village Gate, now looked like a human with a mangled eggplant for a head. My father led her to the couch. Her cheeks were swollen and her lips were split with scabs already forming over the wounds. She held one of my father's handkerchiefs to her bottom lip. The white hankie was red with blood. My mother bent down and removed Nina's shoes. She laid a towel over the pillow and helped her to lie down.

"Ouch!" Nina cried. Her face wounds slurred her speech as she said, "I fink I 'ight 'ave a boken 'ib."

"Nina," my father said, "you have to see a doctor."

"Hecky, 'ey're all de same. 'E'y'le tell de nespape.' Andy can't kno' 'ere I am. He'd neve' 'uspect you. I met 'im afte' the albu' wi' you."

"We have to take you to the Yonkers hospital in the morning. You are badly beaten and we can't take a chance. No one will recognize you the way you look now. In the meantime, Lillian will get you an ice pack."

My mother was preparing one at the moment. My parents sat with her until I left for school. Then all three went to the hospital. I was sworn to secrecy, but I was so tired in school that day that I didn't *want* to talk, a rarity for me. My father had informed Helen of what happened and told her to tell no one, and to not dare to mention it to Gloria Swanson. Helen kept mum.

Fortunately, Nina suffered no breaks in her jaw. Her nose was swollen, but not broken—a fear of every singer, for nose repair and jaw repair can alter, even if ever-so-slightly, the sound of one's voice. She did have a hairline fracture in a rib. The hospital swore to secrecy. For two weeks, Nina Simone slept on our daybed. My mother went into the city to see clients with whom she had appointments, made no further ones, and came home early each day to nurse Nina back to health with lots of chicken soup, and more importantly, the kind of mothering that was so much a part of her. Nina welcomed the mother-like care and commented that she'd wished her mother had given her the same. Hecky arranged his schedule so he could be home to administer medicine until Nina could open her eyes to see. I skipped a few dance classes and came right home from school to help out too, making sandwiches and cups of tea. My father added some whiskey to the tea at night at Nina's request.

When the swelling went down around Nina's eyes, and her face began to look like a face again, she sat upon the daybed and talked. We heard about her sister Lucille, her mother the preacher, her invalid brother, and, of course, her piano teacher "Miz Mazzy." I found her stories utterly intriguing and I couldn't help but study every expression and gesture she made. That same sorrow I'd seen in her eyes at the Village Gate surrounded her now and made the shade of her skin seem even darker.

One day she got off the daybed and walked to the piano. She sat down and ran her fingers over the keys creating beautiful rhythms and sounds. The darkness lifted like the dawn greeting the sun when she played her music. Her whole being seemed to glow. Soon it felt like she was gone and only her music sat on the chair at the piano in the living room. She strummed the keys and began to sing "Black Is the Color of My True Love's Hair." I shivered and felt like a spirit from another realm had entered our house. *I Put a Spell on You* would later be an apt title for her autobiography.

The day came when she was well enough to go home, and my parents drove her to her apartment, took her in, and made sure she was safe. Fearing that, as a detective, Andy would track down where she'd been, she didn't want to leave any clues. "Please don't call here. If I need you, I'll call from a pay phone," she told my father.

When she saw Andy again, he had no recollection of what he'd done to her. He visited two psychiatrists. Since he'd never shown signs of brutality towards Nina prior to this incident, the doctors each commented that the rum he'd drunk that night triggered a "freak accident." One doctor openly advised Nina not to marry him. The other said it was up to her and believed the violence would most likely not happen again provided he stayed away from too much rum. For various reasons, she did marry him and, to anyone's knowledge, was never beaten again. They had a daughter, Lisa. Andy became Nina's manager for the many years of their marriage until she ultimately walked out on him, as he continually refused to take into account her needs regarding touring time and resting time and several other matters in her burgeoning career. She never told anyone, not even her closest friends, who her protector had been for those two weeks after the beating. It was a well-kept secret should she ever need such refuge again.

．．．．．．．．．．．．

Hecky was doing well with his producing and publishing. Then Crohn's reared its ugly head in a surprise attack and Hecky was hospitalized at Monte Fiore Hospital in the Bronx. My mother did not enjoy driving, particularly at night in a big city and after a day of carrying her briefcase up and down subway stairs and in and out of taxis. She was now competing with herself, for she'd come in as top salesperson in 1958 again, and she and my father had sailed upon another cruise. I had my junior license and was only allowed to drive at night accompanied by an adult, but this did not include driving in any of New York City's boroughs. "I trust you as a driver far more than myself," my mother confessed. "I'll sit by your side, but you are the chauffeur to the hospital at night, legal or not." I navigated my way through city lights, under elevator trains, alongside buses, and into the hospital parking lot.

Fortunately for Hecky, the doctors decided that surgery was not necessary, at least not yet. The section of intestine under siege was not yet dead and decaying. Intravenous cortisone would most likely relieve the inflammation. Hecky had to stay in the hospital for a minimum of five days on this treatment plus a bland, but frequently administered diet to arrest the involuntary anorexia creeping up upon him. On the third night of his hospital stay, my mother and I arrived for our visit just as a Code Blue signaled. Attendants, nurses, and doctors ran down the hall into the next ward of beds, leaving the section my father was in empty. When we walked into his room, he looked like a man drowning. He could barely breathe. He mumbled to us that he'd been ringing for several minutes for a nurse and to quickly get help, that he had severe pains in his chest. There wasn't a nurse to be found. My mother pushed the button to the double doors leading to the next ward. As soon as they began to open, a guard yelled, "OUT! No one is allowed in now."

"But my husband has been ringing for a nurse. He has an emergency. He can't breathe. He has pains in his chest!" The guard simply closed the doors.

My mother ran back to my father. He pointed to his I.V. Apparently, right before the Code Blue, a nurse had put a full bag of the cortisone mixture on its stand to flow into his arm. The mechanism that allows for it to drip at timed intervals had snapped open and all the cortisone emptied into his body at once. When we were finally able to get help, which wasn't until some 20 minutes later, we learned that the Code Blue had been a heart attack and the patient had died.

"That's awful," my mother said to two nurses who had now returned to their post. My father lay in bed looking like a balloon blown up. "I am so sorry, but what kind of a hospital leaves all other patients unattended to for one patient? At least one of you should have remained behind. Look at my husband!"

Another Code—Red, Yellow—rang, this one for Hecky. When they were finished with the many procedures they had to do to attempt to reverse the damage from eight ounces of Cortisone infiltrating his body in one fell swoop, we learned that the mitro-valve in his perfectly healthy heart had suffered damage. "You can live life as though nothing is wrong with your heart," the doctor told him. "Most likely, you won't notice any difference until you are in your 70s."

At home, there was talk of a lawsuit. It never happened. It is hard to prove one's life is changed when the change won't occur until the future. Furthermore, other than the attempt to get some money for "Rudolph" when Hecky left Columbia, my parents were not the suing type. They simply thanked their lucky stars and the God of their hearts that he was alive and came out as unscathed as he did.

Steffi's return from Israel helped his recovery. She was filled with interesting stories from this newly formed land. Grandpa Harry had died in 1954, during the height of Hecky's Columbia career, proud to see his son doing so well. Grandma Sarah, now a widow, visited to hear the tales of Steffi's journey. Steffi had fulfilled two of Sarah's dreams: graduating from college and going to Israel. Now, a third was about to come true: Steffi and Gerry's wedding date was set for December 26, 1959.

. . . .

In the world of music, The Kingston Trio's success continued. Word spread throughout the Greenwich Village folk scene about a popular trio of two men and a woman who simply called themselves by their names: Peter, Paul & Mary. A young Jewish fellow from Duluth, Minnesota, Bob Zimmerman, who called himself Bob Dylan and modeled himself after his mentor, Woody Guthrie, was also stirring up interest. The Limelighters and Tarriers were making headway, and across the nation coffeehouses offering live folk music sprang up. Hecky believed there was a future in folk groups. He pursued finding one to produce.

In Spokane, Washington, three young members of Gonzaga University's glee club, William Chad Mitchell, Mike Kobluk, and Mike Pugh, formed a trio and sang in local cafes in the area. Heard by a Roman Catholic priest, Reinard W. Beaver, who loved folk music, Beaver encouraged them to come to New York with him in the summer of 1959. There he would take some courses at historic Fort Slocum in Long Island. All of them could live in the bachelor officers' quarters. He had faith that The Chad Mitchell Trio, as they called themselves, were talented enough to compete with other groups in the burgeoning folk-music scene and promised to help them get bookings. They accepted.

At first they sang in clubs around the fort and wondered if the trip wasn't simply a folly. Father Beaver continued his inquiries and contacted Colpix Records. Colpix asked Hecky to set up an audition. Father Beaver suggested they meet in an Italian restaurant where he knew one of the owners rather than in a studio. He preferred the friendly atmosphere. The restaurant had a downstairs kept closed until the busy dinner hours. Here they could play, and after the audition, the boys, Hecky, if he wished, and the Father could enjoy their excellent food. My father agreed to the time and place, curious about these three youngsters come to New

York City all the way from the state of Washington at the urging of a priest. My father asked me to join him as a "second set of ears."

We entered the restaurant located across the street from a Catholic church in the 40s off Eighth Avenue. It looked like every Italian restaurant in films. The tablecloths were the standard bright red and white checkered ones. The waiters were dressed in white shirts, black pants, black ties and patent leather shoes. The scent of garlic, tomato sauce, and wine warmed my nose and kick-started my stomach into talking. My father introduced himself, then me. The host called the boss, true to the Italian scene, one Mr. Giovanni, who greeted us joyously, shaking my father's hand heartily and repeatedly as he said, "This is so wonderful of you, Mr. Krasnow. Father Beaver has told me about the boys and how talented they are. The Father loves music. He knows a good sound when he hears one. I am sure your time today will not be wasted. And who is this lovely-looking young lady with you, may I ask?" He looked at me with a smile.

"Please meet Judy, my daughter. She is a folk singer herself, and I value her opinion highly."

"Ah, the bambina takes after the papa! Welcome, welcome." Turning to Hecky, he continued, "Father Beaver called a short while ago. He was a little bit confused as to which connections to make coming from Grand Central Station. He will be here with the boys shortly. Let me take you downstairs."

It was a very sunny day and the sun shone on the stairs, which wound downwards next to the restaurant's large front window. The downstairs room was radiant with sunlight and warmed by it. Mr. Giovanni called up the stairs to a waiter named Bobby who promptly came down. "Bobby, meet Mr. Krasnow and his daughter Judy. Please remove the chairs from the top of the tables, make the room comfortable, and bring them whatever they want—water, wine—whatever." We heard a voice from the top of the stairs, "Mr. Giovanni, Father Beaver is here."

"Send him and the boys down, please."

The first thing I noticed walking down the stairs were a pair of long legs bedecked in black. Following the legs was a body and a red-hued, pleasant face capped by gray hair. Following him were three handsome, somewhat ruddy-looking men with fresh, wholesome appearances carrying instruments in their cases.

"Father Beaver," Mr. Giovanni shook his hand as he had my father's, "Father Beaver it is so good to see you. How are you? How are you?"

"Fine. Well. And you, Johnny, how about you?"

"Well, things are going well, Father. Have you met Mr. Krasnow yet?"

"Thank you so much for coming to hear the boys today," Father Beaver shook Hecky's hand. "Let me introduce them. This is Chad Mitchell from Spokane, Mike Kobluk all the way from Trail, British Columbia, in Canada, and Mike Pugh from Pasco. Wait until you hear their voices."

"I am eager to do so, but first let me introduce my daughter Judy. She has been playing and singing since she was eight. She serves as my 'alter-ears.'" My father chuckled, pleased with this twist on "alter-ego." I shook hands with all of them.

"Well, I am sure you want to get started," Mr. Giovanni said. "Is there anything you need before I go upstairs and back to my work?"

"Could we have a bottle of red wine, Chianti?" Father Beaver requested.

"Of course, Father. It's on the house. Bobby, go get a bottle of our finest Chianti and some glasses."

"Not necessary for me," my father said, "I'd like some ginger ale." He was being super cautious after his latest bout with Crohn's. He cleared his throat. "Well, take out your instruments, young men, and we will get this audition rolling."

Bobby brought the wine. Father Beaver sniffed the little bit Bobby had poured into the glass and nodded. Bobby filled the rather large wine glass and Father Beaver drank the contents in three gulps. Bobby, standing there ready to serve, promptly filled it again. Father Beaver downed three such glasses before the trio even opened their mouths to sing. "Wait until you hear them, Mr. Krasnow," Father Beaver repeated. I think my father wondered as he saw the priest down another full glass of wine if Father Beaver had ever heard them sober or if, through a wine haze, he imagined they were good.

They were now ready and began with a dialogue as though starting a performance. In the first song their voices and harmonies sounded crisp and fresh. They were pleasant to look at and adept on their instruments. Their repertoire was eclectic, some pop and some Kingston Trio, and one choral song they'd put into a folk-style arrangement. I liked them but sensed they didn't quite know what they wanted to sing. My father looked poker-faced.

In the meantime, Father Beaver had kept Bobby very busy running up and down the stairs and was on the second round from a third bottle of wine. His face was now red as a beet. My many Catholic friends talked about sin and sinning, and I thought drink was included in the carnal sins they spoke of. I watched Father Beaver and found myself distracted from the music as I contemplated whether he drank bottles of wine and then confessed to some other priest.

After five songs, my father left his poker face behind and broke into a warm grin. "Nice, very, very nice. You definitely have possibilities. Your voices are terrific. You play your instruments well and perform with feeling. I sense your weakness is that you don't know quite in which direction you want to go. The folk songs you sang were the best and folk music is the direction you should take."

"We agree," Chad Mitchell answered. "At least in our end of the country, the folk trend is growing, and from what we've heard and read, certainly in Greenwich Village that's the trend."

Speech a bit slurred, Father Beaver piped in, "I was in Boston, too, and that's the way things are going. It seems music for the public is taking two paths: rock and folk."

"It does, indeed," my father agreed. "Not quite a year ago, I had Colpix audition another folk group called The Golliards. Judy was one of the quartet. Colpix didn't feel folk music would go much beyond The Kingston Trio. In a few short months, things have changed. That's why I am here today."

My heart sank as I heard these words. Ironically, Paul Prestopino, who had also been one of The Golliards, would become a musician for The Chad Mitchell Trio.

"Well, Mr. Krasnow," Father Beaver said with a smile, "do you intend to sign them up?"

"My next step is persuading Colpix. I know where to reach you. I'll get on this right away. Hopefully, before you return to Washington in a couple of weeks, we'll have a deal."

"Come on, Juddie," my father said. "Time to go. Goodbye, Chad, Mike, and Mike. I'm sure we'll be seeing each other again in the very near future. I look forward to working with you."

We all shook hands. My father and I went up the stairs and out into the late, sunny afternoon. "So, what did you think, Juddie?"

"Just what you seemed to think, Dad. That they are really good. They have a lot of energy, and that comes across. I just don't think they've thought too much about being famous, I mean about what they will sing to become famous or when they are, but they are definitely professional and appealing."

"So you agree that their repertoire will need honing."

"Yes, Dad, I agree. Hey, Dad, how can a priest drink? Isn't that a sin?"

"Juddie, there are a lot of priests who drink. Wine, which is part of many religious rituals, like at our Seders, is not a sin. It's just sad when someone has to drink so much. But he seems a nice enough man. He certainly is dedicated to the trio and is doing them and a potential listening public a favor through his efforts."

. . . .

Colpix wanted The Chad Mitchell Trio and assigned Hecky as their producer. Hecky had done some work with a man named Milt Okun. Milt was a folk singer himself. He'd been a junior-high music teacher, played piano, sung with various groups around Greenwich Village, and had played guitar and written the arrangements for many folk albums with the Stinson, Riverside, and Warwick labels as well as played piano for some RCA productions. Presently, he was singing and playing with the Belafonte Folk Singers. Hecky hired him as the arranger for the Chad Mitchell album. The two men worked well together, became friends, and our families visited. Milt lived in an apartment in the Village in Chelsea. The rooms were very small. The bookshelves were carved into the walls and, like our home, were filled with interesting literature, history, and many folk music anthologies. Three steps led down into the tiny living room where holding a guitar seemed to take up almost all of the space. Rosemary, Milt's wife, was a dancer. I enjoyed her company and our talks about modern dance. Milt's stepdaughter Jenny and I played guitar together and swapped songs.

For the trio's album, Hecky selected a variety of upbeat and slower songs, all folk songs with a good story or square dance flair or piece of history. Protest songs had not yet become part of the kind of folk songs aired on major radio stations, and like other companies, Colpix would have vetoed them. Hecky and Milt collaborated on writing or adapting a few of the songs. The title of the album would be *The Chad Mitchell Trio Arrives.* On the album were "Tina," "Chevaliers," "Walkin' on the Green Grass," "Sweet Mary Jo," "Pretty Saro," "Sally Ann," "Up on the Mountain," "Paddy," "I Do Adore Her," "Paddy West," "Gallows Tree," and "Hey Nanine."

The album sold well, though it produced no major hits like "Tom Dooley." The trio needed a manager, for to sell an album, live performances would be necessary. Father Beaver gladly handed them over to Bertha Case, the manager Hecky suggested. Bertha Case, a literary agent who handled the written works of the Bertolt Brecht Estate, opted to become a manager of up-and-coming entertainers. Nina Simone had recently hired her in this capacity.

Harry Belafonte knew Nina Simone and Bertha Case. He was friends with the dynamic folk singer Odetta, whose powerful and haunting voice was heard in folk circles throughout the country. She, like Nina Simone, was a regular at the Village Gate along with Belafonte and Africa's "Mother of Music," Miriam Makeba, who, banned in her homeland of South Africa, was making her name known throughout the U.S. with Belafonte's help.

New York City intended to tear down historic Carnegie Hall, and people were outraged. Harry Belafonte organized a concert both to protest its demolition and to raise funds to fight against its demise. He invited The Chad Mitchell Trio to participate. My father, mother, and

I were at the concert. My mother fluttered around with the same ecstasy she'd exhibited when she was to meet Gene Kelly. She liked charismatic, handsome men with breathy, but good voices. A party would follow the concert. She was to meet Mr. Belafonte! Little did she know then that she would give a party which he would attend, arriving at our quaint home in a limousine with all the neighbors gaping, some looking out their windows and some standing in their yards. Again, warmth, good food, political views, and lively conversation would make a memorable evening in spite of elbow-to-elbow folding chairs.

The concert was extraordinary. The dedication of its performers reflected in the tremendous energy that charged the air and the robust applause the audience gave to each song.

Miriam Makeba thoroughly engaged the audience with her "Click Song," demonstrating this unique sound made in her spoken language. The over-250-pound Odetta simply stood and opened her mouth. The sounds that came out were gripping.

My father was extremely pleased as the audience cheered for The Chad Mitchell Trio. They had, indeed, "arrived." The concert, without doubt, would promote the sale of their album and make them part of the upper crust of the present popular folk music performers by virtue of their talent and by association with the likes of Odetta, Belafonte, and Makeba.

Right after the first album, it was necessary to plan for the second album. The trio had found their genre: folk songs. The second album could play with more than a selection of just straight, Carl Sandburg, *American Songbag*-style folk songs. Humor and mild social commentary would add spice. The trio liked Hecky. Chad Mitchell later said of him, "Without the alliance of Hecky who obviously had a background in folk music, his choice of songs and his engaging Milt Okun as arranger, we would never have made it."

Colpix, however, had a different idea for the trio's second album. The head of A&R, Stuart Phillips, wanted gimmicky songs more in keeping with rock, even if done in folk-style. Phillips would go on to produce one-shot wonder songs like James Darren's "Goodbye Cruel World" and Shelley Fabares's "Johnny Angel." His innovations in establishing the creative role of the producer in rock 'n' roll led to hits by groups like the

Marcels. Their song, "Blue Moon" rocketed to number one on pop and R&B charts in America and reached the Top 10 in more than 20 countries worldwide after Phillips suggested that they steal the intro of the Cadillacs' song "Zoom" for their version of "Blue Moon."

The Chad Mitchell Trio had found their genre and wanted to stick with it. They trusted Hecky's choices in material and felt that these were in keeping with the music that honestly reflected them and the reason they'd formed their trio to begin with. Colpix wouldn't bend, and despite the trio's plea to have Hecky produce their second album, Colpix remained firm regarding Stuart Phillips. The trio refused to work with Phillips and managed to break their contract with Colpix. Harry Belafonte became interested in the group after hearing them in the Carnegie Hall concert and several times at the Blue Angel, where they played in between sets of his and Odetta's. He offered to sign them to Belafonte Enterprises, his management agency. Here, Bob Ballard was their assigned producer. Milt Okun remained as their arranger.

The trio underwent a personnel change as Mike Pugh left the group to return to college. Out of over 150 singers, a young fellow named Joe Frazier (not the heavyweight champion) was selected as Pugh's replacement. Satire songs were becoming popular. Along with their conventional folk songs, the trio recorded the satirical song by Michael Brown, "The John Birch Society." The Society, founded by conservative Robert Welch, smacked of McCarthyism, believed education was solely up to parents and government had no role in it, and was against the fluoridation of water. The lyrics of the song reflected the organizations founding principles.

> Well you've heard about the agents that we've already named
> Well MPA has agents that are flauntedly unashamed
> We're after Rosie Clooney, we've gotten Pinkie Lee
> And the day we get Red Skelton won't that be a victory
>
> Oh we're the John Birch Society, the John Birch Society
> Norman Vincent Peale may think he's kidding us along
> But the John Birch Society knows he spilled the beans
> He keeps on preaching brotherhood, but we know what he means

The song touched something in a public who'd suffered the rule of McCarthyism so recently. It enhanced the trio's reputation as a group who could perform more controversial material than other groups. This gave them a niche of their own and they went on to record songs like "Rum by Gum" about the temperance and prohibition movements, and "Lizzie Borden," a satire about the infamous yet celebrated axe murderess. The trio went through further changes. Chad Mitchell himself left the trio in 1965 to embark on a solo singing career. A young man named John Denver replaced him. Frazier left and David Boise took his place.

The swan song of the group's rise to fame was a song called "Blowin' in the Wind," passed out on the streets of New York City on sheets called broadsides. It was written by the young folk singer making waves at the time, Bob Dylan. Producer Bob Ballard refused to let the trio record the song claiming that "no song with the word 'death' in it makes it." Milt Okun was also working with another group gaining popularity in the Village, Peter, Paul & Mary. They recorded the song for the Warner Brothers label. It soared to the top of the charts, sweeping the nation with its message and ushering in the folk era in full, controversial protest songs included. The Chad Mitchell Trio left Belafonte Enterprises over this song.

Milt Okun thought John Denver had possibilities with his Irish tenor voice and his talent for writing excellent lyrics and haunting melodies. He encouraged him to record a solo album and became his arranger and producer. Okun's publishing company, Cherry Lane Music, published many of Peter, Paul & Mary's songs as well as those of John Denver. Milt Okun went on to make a fortune as an arranger and publisher as the folk era rose to its heights.

Hecky, on the other hand, found the talented Chad Mitchell Trio, gave them their direction, produced their first album that got them started on a successful career. Once again, like Moses leading the Israelites to their promised land but not being able to go there himself, Hecky had launched a highly successful act but did not make the megabucks or receive the recognition brought about by this success. His coffer remained the same. Perhaps Nina Simone and The Chad Mitchell Trio could be said to represent the "Rudolph" of his new life as an independent producer and publisher.

· · · · · · · · · · · ·

CHAPTER 27

A Wedding Song, Lullaby at the Zoo, a Fiddle Again

· · · · · · · · · · · ·

In December of 1959, Steffi married Gerry Schamess in a wonderful wedding where our Great Tante Becky, Lillian's aunt, at age 70, danced the *kazatzki*. She would live to be 103 and die in a hospital bed singing Yiddish songs at the top of her lungs before falling back upon her pillow dead with a broad, happy smile upon her face.

In the fall of 1960, I entered Sarah Lawrence College. I intended to major in modern dance. My parents finally moved to their own place, selling their share of the Yonkers house to Helen, who was now married to the dentist, Raymond House.

Hecky and Lillian moved to the newly built condominiums along the Hudson River and near Lincoln Center, where they frequently enjoyed concerts. Their new place was even smaller than our Yonkers home, but they still entertained their array of interesting friends from the music world, Sarah Lawrence, and the many other doctors, professors, artists, and one-time leftists they had socialized with all of their lives. In Lincoln Towers, they acquired more friends.

Hecky wrote several musical pieces recorded by different musicians including a composition called "Swinging Ghosts," which received a lot of airplay and served as background music for commercials and television programs. It became popular in Europe too. Pop music still aired on radio stations that catered to the generations who claimed it as their music. Hecky's compositions fell into this category and many could also be improvised as jazz pieces.

Not wishing the *Now We Know* series with its wonderful science songs to vegetate in Columbia's stacks, Hecky, along with writers Hy Zaret and Lou Singer, revived the series under the name of *Ballads for the Age of Science*. They added some new songs and singer Dorothy Collins of *Your Hit Parade* fame, a television show viewed by millions weekly. An educational record company, Motivational Records, put the series out in a box of six 12-inch LP albums, beautifully designed and packaged with lyric sheets for all of the songs. The series sold as well as it had before under its former title and was purchased not only by schools and other educational institutions, but by parents for their children to listen to at home.

. . . .

Hecky and Joe Darion now collaborated on many projects. In addition to writing some pieces together for jazz pianist Mal Waldron, their joint company, Kradar Music, published many pieces composed by Waldron. These included "Vibrations, Themes 1, 2, & 3," "Quiet Temple," "All My Life," and "Call to Arms." Waldron had been the regular pianist for the Charles Mingus Jazz Composers Workshop from 1954 to 1957. Between 1957 and 1959 he played piano for the legendary singer, Billie Holiday. His other credits included house pianist for Prestige Records, where he recorded with Jackie McLean, John Coltrane, Eric Dolphy, and others. In 1960 he began playing with drummer Max Roach and singer Abbey Lincoln. He also had his own groups and played extensively at the Five Spot, a jazz haven where many of his albums were recorded live. In 1965, he settled in Europe, living in Munich, and became a major influence in European jazz. Even after his death in Brussels, Belgium, in 2002, his works continue to be bought and heard, including those published by Kradar.

The nation was promoting safe driving. Hecky and Joe wrote a group of songs called *Songs with a Safety Kick*. They presented them to the National Safety Council hoping to get backing, which would help in getting the interest of a record company to record and promote them. To various dance rhythms, the songs reminded people to think before driving and while on the road. The "Keep Your Hands on the Wheel Cha Cha," talked about distractions.

The National Safety Council responded with, "We like your 'Songs With A Safety Kick.' Among the many weapons used in the organized war on accidents, there's always room for some good 'fighting" songs. . . . You have NSC's official permission to say that your recording project is "in cooperation with" or "in support of" the National Safety Council. . . . Here's an offer: . . . We'll be glad when the time is right to get out a letter to stations helping to inform them of the availability of the recorded safety songs."

The songs were recorded, aired, and, hopefully, saved some lives.

. . . .

In spite of rock 'n' roll, schools still demanded educational, enriching projects. Hecky and Joe spent many months researching an educational project called *Sing a Song of America*. It would be recorded and put out in book form with suggestions in the back for school staging. It included narration, solo voices, two-part harmony, and a chorus. The production began with a prologue with voices singing "What made America . . . Who made America . . . the country it is today? . . . Did it have millions of people? Factories? Railroads? A Constitution? . . ." The narration continues with Columbus sailing to the New World thinking he'd found India. A song follows, "He thought he'd come to India, India, India/ But what he really found was America/ What a mistake to make. . . ."

All these projects resulted in royalties, yet the time spent researching and writing was unpaid time. My mother's job brought in the basic income, but how long she could trudge up and down subway stairs and traipse around Manhattan remained to be seen. She had undergone a transformation living under her own roof without having to see Helen each day. They remained in touch, of course: Helen was still Hecky's sister, after all, but my mother was now free to pursue her own life. Her social life with my father could be conducted independently of always having to involve Helen.

My mother had undergone other changes. She was a woman working in the business world and dressed herself in smart outfits. She carried herself with confidence knowing that she'd made history as the first and only woman over 40 to be hired by a major company, and she was tickled pink that she was noted as Reuben Donnelly's top salesperson in Manhattan for every year since landing the job. She and my father had gone on another cruise, this time to the Mediterranean.

After Hecky had left Columbia—the job he'd loved and the security it offered—he spoke with me each time I befriended another musician, particularly a male one, usually encountered at the arch in Washington Square Park where most of my Sundays were spent. "Juddie, the world changes fast these days. Music is not a field to go into and expect to earn a consistent and livable salary. Don't marry a musician. Marry someone who can support you and your children."

I succumbed to his warnings. A senior in high school, I went on a blind date arranged by a dear friend, Susan Warshall. We double-dated with her boyfriend, a Harvard student and roommate of Daniel Markewich, the latter of whom was a budding lawyer from a family of prominent lawyers. He was the son of Arthur Markewich, a renowned justice on the New York State Supreme Court known for his objectivity and fairness. Daniel's grandfather, Samuel, was a leading labor union lawyer who worked with, among others, David Dubinsky and whose firm represented the International Ladies Garment Workers Union. This family's political leanings and connections sounded like Daniel and I might well be a good match; and he was graduating Harvard and going to law school at Columbia University. Daniel was handsome and eccentric, which I mistook for offbeat, hence more like the artists I knew than the lawyers I didn't know. Within one year, we were engaged.

I should have heeded the sign the night of our blind date when he insisted that I must be a communist because I admired Pete Seeger, who "obviously is one of the biggest commies around. His singing incites people to riot." Daniel was so eccentric that I couldn't quite tell if he was serious or kidding. He enjoyed playing devil's advocate. He let me know he was intrigued by my modern dancing, beatnik attire, and long, un-fettered hair, which, later, he required me to pin up in order to meet his mother. Whoops!—another sign.

I entered Sarah Lawrence College. While there, Bessie Schoenberg, head of the dance department, wanted me to audition for a children's performance troupe called The Merry-Go-Rounders. The group sought a talented performer who could dance, sing, and play the guitar. My father warned, "You are engaged, Judy. How do you think you will go on tour as the troupe does and still be a wife? What will happen when you have children?"

This message contradicted everything I'd been raised to do. I sensed that my father was expressing his own fears and doubts. My closeness to my father all these years made it difficult for me to separate myself from him, and that included his anxiety. I was on the cusp of the era of the women's liberation movement and an awareness of "Reviving Ophelia"; but poor Ophelia was still not of the generation of Ophelias that hope-fully could be revived. I succumbed to practicality and left the dance department to train as an elementary school teacher at the suggestion of my mother-in-law to be, May Markewich.

As the engagement progressed, my father grew worried about some events that occurred with Daniel and the manner in which he spoke to me at times. Perhaps he was also thinking what his own life might have been like without a musician as his wife, but a lawyer or doctor instead. After his admonishments for me not to marry a musician, he now changed his tune. Like Nina Simone's father with her and Andy Stroud, Hecky tried hard to dissuade me from marrying Daniel in spite of the financial security a lawyer might offer. The tides of fate pulled Daniel and me together in spite of my father's continuous warnings. On June 17, 1962, we married at the end of my sophomore year at college (which I would continue) and right after Daniel's graduation from Harvard with him about to start Columbia Law School. My engagement and marriage in-spired further collaboration between Hecky and Joe Darion.

The *World-Telegram* printed an article on July 13, 1961, in Women's Editor Claire Wallace's column: "Father of the Bride: Something in Dad's Eye Day Daughter Marries." Its author was Morton Grove III.

The premise of the article was that mothers, though they may weep at their daughters' weddings, are happy with the thought that they are not really losing a daughter, but they are gaining a son—ah, another child to dote over. Fathers, however, though they may not shed tears at the wedding for shame of showing such emotion, are not happy. They are not gaining a son, but losing a daughter—to a younger man, at that! "This is terribly hard on papa who resents all boys. . . . He criticizes the boys who call to see his pet and take her out. He doesn't like their clothes, or their cars or their manners or their haircuts. . . . He hates them all, whatever he may say. And finally he suffers that cruel stroke of irony: he pays for the wedding. Why can't something be done to change things for papa?"

Inspired by this article, Hecky and Joe wrote a song whose lyrics and melody synchronized perfectly in waltz time to bring tears to the eyes of all those attending weddings. It expressed what every loving and doting father feels as he walks down the aisle handing his daughter to her husband-to-be. I think in my father's case, his misgivings about the man I was marrying in spite of his and his family's outward credentials caused the ultimate twist in the lyrics:

Oh Papa, please stand beside me in my moment of joy and trial.
Oh Papa, please hold and guide me in that long, lonely walk
    down the aisle.
I go to the arms of another, who will take me and make me his
    bride,
But wherever I go, in my heart I will know, you will always be
    there by my side.

Papa, when I was younger, in your arms I could always rest,
But now I'm a child no longer, and the bird has to fly from the
    nest.
Oh Papa the organ is playing, so please whisper a prayer up
    above,
And help me to smile as I walk down the aisle to the warm,
    waiting arms of my love.

The song was played and sung at my wedding, and there was not a dry eye among the guests. Even Grandma Sarah, who had suffered several strokes by the time of the wedding, was alert enough to understand the song's message and cried. She would die that December, but not before losing the ability to speak in any language besides her old native tongue of Russian, which she hadn't spoken in years. She would speak in Russian to Daniel, who had studied the language, and send him downstairs at the beach house to tell me not to forget to give him a glass of milk with his cake.

Had it been 1952 instead of 1962, there is no doubt that Hecky would have had a hit song with "Oh Papa, Please Stand Beside Me." Sung by Rosie, it would have melted every father's heart across the nation. Unfortunately, it was 1962, and sentimentality of this kind did not make it over the airwaves, and Rosemary Clooney was no longer a frequently heard voice on groovy radio shows. The year's top hits included "The Loco-motion" with Little Eva, "Big Girls Don't Cry," sung by the Four Seasons, "Surfin'" by the Beach Boys, and "Twistin' the Night Away," by Sam Cooke who was riding high on the new dance, The Twist. Even the dancing reflected a new era where couples twisted and gyrated on the floor, not holding their partner in an upright, romantic position.

The record companies weren't interested. Hecky and Joe returned to Captain Kangaroo. The baby boomer generation were now becoming parents and giving birth to a long-term following for the Captain. Hecky and Joe created *Little Red Train to the Zoo*. Children were asked to close their eyes and imagine that the chairs they sat upon were seats on a train taking them to the zoo on a musical journey to see and learn about the animals. By the end of the train ride, they are tired. Returning home, they fall asleep to "The Lullaby of the Zoo," where they hear how different animals actually sleep.

RCA said they would record *The Little Red Train to the Zoo*, but they kept the project on the back burner. In the meantime, Hecky and Joe sent a demo recording of the album to Bob Keeshan. Keeshan played it frequently and singled out the song, "The Lullaby of the Zoo." The response was overwhelming. Thousands of letters poured into CBS from all over the country asking where the entire album, and certainly this song from it, could be purchased. This song *was* a hit, but a hit with a major record company letting it sit on that back burner, for the children's market simply did not take precedence any more.

RCA's procrastination regarding *Little Red Train to the Zoo* was viewed by Hecky as simply another sign of the times. Even thousands of letters couldn't get them to put the song on the front burner. Record companies simply were not interested in children's material, and individual publishers, producers, and composers could not compete with corporate Disney, who had the power, money, name, and distribution to glut the market with their offerings as though this was all that children should be exposed to or needed. Lillian, always the cockeyed optimist, stepped in having proved what a terrific salesperson she was. I visited my parents' apartment during one of her sales pitches.

I had never heard my parents fight. They had bickered and their "HUHNEES" had reflected some sort of disagreement, but they'd never actually yelled, stormed out of rooms, or slammed doors. On this day, I walked in expecting to sing a few new songs Hecky had written while he played piano and recorded them on his new, compact, lightweight Wollensac tape recorder: his amazing new toy—imagine being able to record at home. It was a sunny spring day and the light shone in from their balcony with a view of the Hudson River. The sun was so golden and bright it appeared that the pineapple plants on the tea cart were actually growing before my eyes. My mother had an extremely green thumb and was proud that she discovered in order for pineapple plants to grow, a male and female plant had to be placed side by side. The scent of cinnamon blended with the smell of eggs and challah bread. She'd made her scrumptious French toast.

I walked in to see my mother's face grim, that vein in her neck pumping. My father did not come out to greet me. "Are you okay, Mom?"

She swung her head back, put her chin up, a forced smile on, and said, "Of course. Why shouldn't I be?"

"Where's Dad?"

"Your father is acting like a child today."

I'd stepped into the lion's den.

My father stormed out of his room and yelled, "I heard that, Huh-Neeey! I'm the reasonable one here, the one who can look the bull in the eye and know it's mad."

"Well, go take your bull by its damned horns and let it spear you!" My mother had actually cursed. This was bad.

"Why must you be such a nosy-body? Mind your own business and stay out of mine." My father slammed a folded newspaper against the wall.

"But your business is my business and mine is yours. What each of us does concerns and affects the other. When have we ever not shared, not discussed, not helped each other?" My mother's voice had a yodel sound to it when she raised it. "Look, HONEY, be reasonable. *You* are the artist. *I* know how to sell. For God's sake, let me take those letters about 'Lullaby of the Zoo' now taking up the top of your whole damned desk and go with them to other record companies. Somebody has got to have sense. It's all in the presentation. The hell with RCA! You don't need them."

"Can't you see this is the way it is? The big companies don't want to waste their time on a children's album, popular or not."

"Wrong! RCA is dragging its feet. You haven't even tried another company."

"I don't want my wife selling my work. How would that make me look?"

"Oh, so that's what's behind this. Who cares? Isn't Nina Simone's husband her manager? And aren't there others whose spouses are their agents, producers—you name it? So, let me sell *your* wares. You're the artist. I'm the salesman!"

"I will not have my wife involved in my business. It isn't right."

"Oh, for God's sake, HUHney, you sound like your father."

"Well, what's wrong with that? I loved my father."

"Of course, so did I. But times have changed. I don't have to stoop to pick up money you throw to me like Sarah had to do. Together we discuss how to spend *our* money. You want to see success. You obviously have a successful product in *Little Red Train to the Zoo*. If you were at Columbia, their marketing department would be selling it. You don't have that now. Let me use my knowledge of marketing to help you achieve the success your creativity deserves."

"This discussion is over. NO! My work should stand on its own. RCA isn't interested—it's their loss. I shouldn't have to send somebody to convince them of the value of a project they are closing their eyes to while sitting on their hands. That's it. Lullaby to the 'Lullaby of the Zoo.'"

My father went back into his room and closed the door loudly. My mother sat down. She didn't try to smile. She would never let on to the depth of her feeling in the moment. It wasn't her way. Smile and it will go away. She did speak, however. "I'm so worried about your dad. He's had such a bout between his Crohn's and that gall bladder operation. Can you imagine the stupidity of those doctors sending him to a psychiatrist for his pain when it was his gall bladder? He's depressed. I think he's become addicted to the codeine they gave him for the Crohn's pain. He's taken it far too long and it just drains him of his sparkle, of his energy. He tries not to take it and gets even more depressed. He barks at me every day. I don't know what to do."

"Speak to the doctor. Codeine keeps one in a stupor. If he's in a codeine dream world and has no energy, he can't pursue his work actively. Then he feels like he's not accomplishing anything. It's a vicious cycle. Mom, talk to his doctor."

My mother did just that. So did my father. He had to go off codeine. He'd become addicted. It took nearly a year, but he freed himself from the drug. His sweetness, sparkle, and delightful chuckle returned. However, *Little Red Train to the Zoo* remained on RCA's back burner. Even off codeine, my father seemed unable to escape his upbringing and the influence of his father regarding a wife playing a direct role in his business. He couldn't come to grips with my mother serving as his marketing agent. Joe Darion didn't have the time to market it. He was working on the libretto for a musical version of a non-musical teleplay called *Man of La Mancha* written by Dale Wasserman for CBS's Dupont Show of the Month.

. . . .

November 22, 1963, arrived with the news of President John F. Kennedy's assassination. I sat in class on this snowy November day waiting for my writing teacher, poet Jane Cooper, to arrive. She came in late, crying, and announced the dreadful news. Class was dismissed, and I returned home to Dan's and my little apartment on Riverside Drive and 116th Street, a Columbia-owned building to house married graduate students. Sorrow and shock hung in the air so thick it can never be forgotten when recalled. A high school student, Barbara Jones, wrote a poem in remembrance of Kennedy, and Hecky was asked to compose music for it. The song was called "Special Delivery from Heaven."

> Sorry I had to leave right away. I look down and smile at you every day.
> Little Patrick asks to say "Hi," I love you. I'm happy, so please don't cry.
> And Caroline I'd like to say, how proud Daddy was of you that day
> When you stood like a lady and watched me go by, and doing as Mommy did,
> you tried not to cry.
> Little John, now you're the big man, so take care of Mommy the best you can.
> You were just like a soldier—that salute was so brave.
> Thanks for the flag that you placed on my grave.
> And Jackie, there was no time for goodbyes,
> But I'm sure you could read the "farewell" in my eyes.
> Watch over our children and love them for me. I'll treasure your love through eternity.
> So please carry on as you did before 'til all of us meet on Heaven's bright shore.
> Remember, I love you, remember I care. I'll always be with you though
> you don't see me there.

The song aired on radio stations, including rock stations, all over the nation, around the world, and, of course, on television. It was written with the agreement that the proceeds would go to charitable causes. Millions did.

. . . .

In the summer of 1964, the family gathered at the Saybrook beach house for a reunion. Helen and Ray were about to buy out the shares of the other five Krasnow children. Harry and Sarah had left the house to all six children, but the twins and Al were living in California, we were in New York, and the cousins were spreading all over the country as we went to college, got married, and started families of our own. During this reunion, a short trial run of the musical version of *Man of La Mancha* was playing at the Goodspeed Opera House in East Haddam, Connecticut. Joe and Helen Darion had become good friends of the Krasnows and had often visited in Saybrook. They had served as babysitters for Dan's and my English rabbits when we took a belated honeymoon trip by train across the country, ending up in San Francisco. In her 90s, Helen Darion laughingly recalled how they'd kept the rabbits next to their radiator lest they catch a chill and how they'd feed them pellets, which promptly came out the other end. She had suggested to Joe that they simply scoop up what came out the back end and put it back in the dish at the front end since it barely looked any different than the food right from the package. Now, with the rabbits safely adopted by a farm, Dan and I joined the Krasnow family to go to the Goodspeed Opera House to see the preview of Joe's new show for which he'd written the lyrics and Mitch Leigh, the music. The producers did not know if such an esoteric musical could ever make it onto Broadway, but that is where they wanted it to go. The previews would give them some answers and, most importantly, the necessary financial backing if people felt it had possibility.

Joe and Helen were fluttering around excitedly greeting people. Everyone was curious about this show having seen the award-winning television play. The buzz became silence as the lights went out and the curtain rose. The story of imprisoned Miguel de Cervantes unfolded as he enacted the tale of Don Quixote de la Mancha and set out to find adventures with his "squire," Sancho Panza. The encounters, real and imagined, and the presence of the Spanish Inquisition, chivalry, brutality, rape, love lost and found and lost again, created an emotional, thought-provoking theater experience. One song in particular brought moving applause. Its title was "The Impossible Dream." It touched more than Cervantes or Don Quixote's hearts. At the Goodspeed Opera House it was a highlight of the program. No one knew then that once the show did make Broadway, was polished and honed and sung by its final all-star cast, that this song would become a super hit and find its way into the hall of fame of classics.

Hecky certainly didn't know. When the show was over, the pitch was made for contributors. Hecky's brother Al said, "Hecky, you should contribute $2,000. What have you got to lose? If the show goes that money could double, triple, quadruple, or more. If it doesn't, so chalk it up to giving it a try and losing $2,000. That's not much."

"Maybe it's not much for you, Al. You own two Cadillacs and have a trust fund in the bank for your wife and kids."

"Spend money, make money. That's my motto. Maybe that's why I turned Pa's business into a million-dollar one."

"You were lucky he left you a thriving business to begin with." Al had given my father and mother advice on investing in stocks for utility and new appliance companies. To date, they had lost a few thousand over these investments. If Al was telling him to invest tonight, a red warning light said, "Don't."

Brother Bob advised, "I personally enjoyed the show. I don't know if people will clamor to see it on Broadway. It's a bit way out there. But, my motto is since you don't know, if you take a chance and you're right, you'll be happy. If you take a chance and you lose, you'll call yourself stupid. Toss a coin if you can't make up your mind."

Hecky had liked what he saw. After all, wasn't "Rudolph" way out there at the time he believed in it and no one else had? Could this musical be like that? Hecky had just about made up his mind to invest that $2,000. It just might pay off. At this moment, Joe Darion came by.

"Well, what did you think?"

Hecky and his family all gave their responses to the evening which we'd all found intriguing if a somewhat offbeat as a musical. Everything else was changing. Why not musicals too? Then Joe took Hecky aside.

"If I were you, Hecky, I'd save your $2,000. I think we'll make it to Broadway, but end up off Broadway or simply traveling as a road show fairly soon. I still think as a musical it's too intellectual for a general public. I love it, but don't waste your money thinking it will pay back big."

Hecky didn't follow his own gut instinct that night, that this musical in its own way was another "Rudolph." If Joe Darion himself advised against investing, who better would know than the lyricist? Hecky didn't invest.

Not following his gut instinct, Hecky lost out where a lot of other investors gained sizeable fortunes. *Man of La Mancha* became the biggest musical hit of the decade. In 1966, Joe Darion won a Tony Award for his lyrics and for the song, "The Impossible Dream."

. . . .

In 1964, Rosemary Clooney's personal manager, Walter J. Murphy, sent a letter to Mo Ostin, general manager of Reprise Records. Rosemary had contacted Hecky wishing to record children's records with him again.

> Many thanks for taking the time to chat with me the other day regarding the possibility of Rosemary's doing some children's records with her old friend and associate, Hecky Krasnow.
>
> As you suggested, I asked Hecky to prepare an outline. He has done this and you will find it enclosed along with bio notes on him and his partner, Joe Darion. A pressing of "Lullaby At The Zoo," which he refers to in the outline, also is enclosed.
>
> As I mentioned to you, Rosemary and Hecky were a successful combination in the children's field when both were at Columbia. We estimate that she sold about 2,000,000 records. Rosemary would like very much to reenter this market.
>
> Rosemary joins me in sending warmest regards.

The deal never went through. Quality children's material, other than that which Captain Kangaroo used targeting a very particular and young age group, would not have a revival until the advent of NET's *Sesame Street* in November of 1969; and then, NET becoming PBS, would market *Sesame Street*, creating another corporate monopoly of almost Disney magnitude in the sale of music, records, cassette tapes, and later CDs and other products from clothing and books to toys, movies, and home videos with the advent of video players. Competition would see a few individuals rise to fame like singer/songwriter Raffi, who sold millions of cassettes and later CDs and filled concert halls with happy children singing along. But the variety and assortment of offerings stimulated by multiple competitive companies in the golden age of children's records was a thing of the past.

. . . .

The times were definitely "a-changing." Daniel, our two young boys, Joshua and Noah, (our third son, Sam, growing within), went to Central Park at 125th Street in Harlem, a place where white people usually never went. This time, we joined Martin Luther King, Jr., in a march for civil rights. We were early and found ourselves on the front of the line. I held hands with Coretta Scott King, just one step away from her husband. Thousands of us marched through Central Park with our banners and songs for integration and against the Vietnam War. I'd gone from beatnik attire to that of flower child, promoted love not war, and joined the Riverside Democrats of Upper Manhattan where parents came, shedding tears as they spoke of sending their sons off to Canada rather than "knee deep in the muddy" of Vietnam.

Hecky turned on the radio and heard the hits of the day: "The Ballad of the Green Berets," by Sgt. Barry Sadler; "Summer in the City," by The Lovin' Spoonful; "Good Vibrations," by the Beach Boys; "California Dreamin'," by The Mamas and the Papas; "Somebody to Love," by Jefferson Airplane; and "Yellow Submarine" and "All You Need Is Love," by The Beatles. The times had changed, and it was time for him to return to his violin.

Through the chamber music circles in which he'd continued to play throughout the years, he was offered a position playing second violin with the Orlando Symphony in Florida. He and my mother rented a small apartment in Orlando. She would visit for weekends twice a month, for her income at the Manhattan Yellow Pages was the steady sustenance for them at this point, though Hecky continued to receive royalties for his many compositions, his Captain Kangaroo works, and through his publishing companies. He would now also earn a modest salary from the orchestra during their performance season.

Daniel, the boys—Sam had now been born and was 18 months old—and I visited my parents in Orlando during one Christmas holiday. Dan, raised in New York City, had never learned to drive, so that was left to me. En route, in Georgia, we were pursued at night by a pickup truck with rifles hanging in the window. Word had gotten out at one of our motels that Jews from New York were in town. Jews from New York meant supporters of the civil rights movement. We were not welcome in the South. On a dark country road, tailgated and with the pickup's horn blowing constantly, we swerved and curved and prayed we'd get to our motel before our pursuers were able to do whatever might have been in their minds. We were relieved to see the flashing neon sign of a Howard Johnson Motel.

When we arrived in Orlando, we discovered that Hecky and Lillian's apartment complex was lined with banana trees minus bananas. "Take care of the kids," Dan said to my parents. "Judy and I have to pick something up. We'll be back soon."

Dan told me to wait in the car as we pulled up to a fruit stand where he purchased baskets full of bananas. We returned to the apartment complex where he promptly disappeared. He returned to the apartment. About one hour later, after the apartment dwellers, predominantly older retirees, had eaten their lunch and emerged from their naps, we heard quite a commotion. Up and down the walkway that led from one apartment building to another, people were marveling that the banana trees were fecund with ripe bananas. They were quite surprised to find how easy they were to pick. The laughter began when someone finally figured out it was a joke. A few complaints also followed. My parents did not return to this complex once the season was over.

After one season in Orlando, Hecky was offered a position with the Miami Symphony Orchestra and also as a violin instructor at the University of Miami. He accepted. Lillian had earned her bonus cruises and other gifts at Reuben Donnelly, always coming in as their top salesperson each of the 14 years. In one more year, she could retire with a decent pension. This was not to be. For the past year, her heart, already ticking 20 years beyond what doctors had predicted in her youth, began to fail. She was not receiving enough oxygen, as the hole in her aorta had widened with use and age. Those subway stairs and taxis were no longer negotiable.

At this time, Dr. Michael DeBakey was performing innovative open heart surgery and training others at Baylor College of Medicine. He had devised an operation to repair torn aortas. Two of his disciples were on the staff of Mercy Hospital in Miami where Lillian went for tests. They advised that she could no longer continue such strenuous work, and that her only choice for survival was an operation or she might not live out the year. Rueben Donnelly gave her a parting bonus, but their policy was firm: work for fifteen years and get a pension; work for fourteen years, and you don't.

Told she had a 50-50 chance of survival, my mother held a party at the hospital two nights prior to her operation. By then, she and Hecky had made many new friends, including a prominent radiologist at Jackson Memorial Hospital and the University of Miami School of Medicine, Dr. Henry Lerner. Dr. Lerner's son was a rising acclaimed pianist for whom Aaron Copland had personally written a score. Hecky and Lillian had left the world of the record business and now attended parties with the likes of Copland and Leonard Bernstein.

Steffi and I came to Miami for my mother's operation. The hospital allowed my mother to hire a caterer and use the lounge to hold the celebration she wished. My mother, as she had done throughout all the Columbia parties, was the hostess with the mostess and charmed everyone as though nothing was amiss. She said, as she done so many years ago, "I'll show them." And she did. However, prior to the days of screening blood for disease, the seven transfusions her open-heart surgery required left her with hepatitis C. She showed no signs of the disease for several years, and her heart beat strongly and in regular beats. One night at the opera as silence filled the auditorium right before the orchestra burst into the overture, a man sitting next to Lillian said, "Madam, would you mind turning off your watch or putting it in your purse. The ticking is quite loud." My mother turned to him and said, "I wish I could oblige you, sir, but that isn't my watch, it's my heart. I have a fake aorta, and the tick is the little ball bouncing back and forth. Dr. DeBakey, you know."

. . . .

Steffi had two sons, and I now had my family of Josh, Noah, Sam, and Sarah, named of course after Hecky's mother. Hecky and Lillian were loving grandparents. Hecky sang songs and played games with his grandchildren with the same relish he had written and produced songs for children across the nation. He took them on adventurous "joy rides" where the children would tell him turn right or left, or go straight and they would end up someplace unexpected, then find an ice cream parlor and have sundaes before finding their way home again. He kept in touch with Gene Autry, who, having left the world of show biz, was now owner of the Los Angeles Angels. Autry sent various baseball paraphernalia to Josh, my eldest son and an avid baseball enthusiast. Josh got to go to a party with Hecky and meet Arthur Fiedler of the Boston Pops when Hecky had played First Violin in a concert given by Fiedler and the Miami Symphony.

One day, during a Christmas visit, we all sat on the damp benches at the Miami Seaquarium inhaling the salty air and lingering smell of raw fish while waiting for the wondrous whale, Lolita, to put on her show and hopefully soak us as she heaved herself into the air from the deep pool, then crashed back into the water. The loudspeakers emitted a continuous medley of holiday songs: Gene Autry singing "Rudolph," "Frosty," and "Here Comes Santa Claus," followed by Burl Ives singing, "Grandfather Kringle," Rosemary Clooney with "Suzy Snowflake," Rosie and Gene singing "'Twas the Night Before Christmas," and Ricky Zahnd and The Blue Jeaners singing "I'm Gettin' Nuttin' for Christmas." Hecky's grandchildren often inquired, "What did you do when you were a man, Papa—we mean a *young* man—you know, before you had us around?"

There on the bench at the Seaquarium, he told them. "Do you want to know what I did when I was young and not yet your grandpa? Did you hear all those songs? That's what your grandpa did."

Epilogue

. . . .

Hecky spent the following year organizing his many contracts, publishing information, lists of titles of the songs he'd written and their publishers, and his collection of the records he'd produced. I was now living in Miami, and he showed me everything and in which file each item was located. It seemed he was reviewing his life.

"Look at all I have done, Juddie. I just wish I had something to leave to you and Steffi, I mean an estate like Johnny Marks has, or the money of Gene Autry. I wish I had money to leave to charity, but I don't. There's some money in the bank and this condominium, always a little home, smaller than everyone I worked with."

"But always a home filled with love, Dad—love, music, laughter, honesty, working for good causes, unique collectibles, books, good food, and nice, intelligent people and conversations."

"But you can't live on those."

"Dad, we have."

. . . .

At age 73, Hecky's damaged mitro-valve needed replacement. During his hospital stay, he contracted a staphylococcus infection. At 74, after treatment for the infection, which lingered, he was due to go home the next day. He never left the hospital. A clot caused by the infection formed in the pig's valve that had replaced his own heart valve. The pig's valve was resistant to the medication and the clot traveled to his brain. He died one week later on April 23, 1984.

Lillian, who until now had held her hepatitis at bay and functioned with a fake aorta totally healthfully, succumbed to grief. According to her hepatologist, the liver is the source of grief. Without Hecky to love, feed, and care for, she could not contain this grief. Her liver deteriorated rapidly. She passed away on August 24, 1986.

Hecky and Lillian lie in the King David Cemetery in Miami with a bronze plaque over their graves that says, "Together Forever." By the time of their deaths, "Rudolph, the Red-Nosed Reindeer" had sold multi-millions of records, tapes, CDs, videos, toys, and books. It had been recorded by artists too numerous to name including Elvis Presley, Elton John, Ringo Starr, Queen, Sting, 2 Live Crew, and Dolly Parton.

· · · · · · · · · · · ·

At Christmastime in 1998, I walked down a quaint, winding street in Kyoto, Japan, gazing at the charming architecture, storefronts, mailboxes, and all the other things that dazzle the eyes of a tourist in a new and exotic land. I passed what appeared to be a school. Children as beautiful as any I'd ever seen, who looked like painted dolls with rosy cheeks, dark eyes, and black shiny hair, walked out two by two, hand in hand. I continued on as they walked down the street behind me. Their happy laughter turned into singing that rang like crystal clear chimes in the cool winter air. The melody was unmistakable. In Japanese, they sang "Rudolph, the Red-Nosed Reindeer." My heart swooped right down to my toes, and my hairs stood on end. On that Kyoto street, I stopped and lifted my arms upward towards the sky, bending my head back to look into whatever realm my father now inhabited.

"Do you hear that, Daddy? Do you hear that? Fifty years later, Daddy—here in Japan, Daddy, do you hear that?"

Index